GREAT BATTLES
OF THE
BRITISH
ARMY

AS COMMEMORATED IN
THE SANDHURST COMPANIES

This book is dedicated to
the Gentlemen Cadets and Officer Cadets
of all generations
who were trained in the essentials of the Profession of Arms
at

THE ROYAL MILITARY ACADEMY WOOLWICH
(1741 to 1939)
THE ROYAL MILITARY CADET COLLEGE GREAT MARLOW
(1802 to 1812)
THE ROYAL MILITARY COLLEGE SANDHURST
(1812 to 1939)
No. 161 (INFANTRY) OCTU and No. 101/100 (RAC)
OCTU (1939 to 1945)
and
THE ROYAL MILITARY ACADEMY SANDHURST
(1947 to the Present Day)

with the inspirational mottoes

*'SUA TELA TONENTE'** and *'VIRES ACQUIRIT EUNDO'***
(RMA Woolwich, 1741–1939)   (RMC Sandhurst, 1812–1939)

and thereafter

'SERVE TO LEAD'
(RMA Sandhurst, 1947 to the present day)

'Only be thou strong and very courageous. As I was with
your fathers, so will I be with you.'
(Joshua ch.x. v.25)

*To the warrior his weapons
**He gains strength as he goes along

GREAT BATTLES OF THE BRITISH ARMY

AS COMMEMORATED IN THE SANDHURST COMPANIES

FOREWORD BY HIS ROYAL HIGHNESS
FIELD MARSHAL THE DUKE OF EDINBURGH
KG, KT

EDITOR-IN-CHIEF DAVID G. CHANDLER

ARMS AND
ARMOUR

Arms and Armour Press
A Cassell Imprint
Villiers House, 41-47 Strand, London WC2N 5JE.

Distributed in Australia by Capricorn Link (Australia) Pty. Ltd, P.O. Box 665,
Lane Cove, New South Wales 2066.

British Library Cataloguing in Publication Data
Great battles of the British Army, as commemorated
in the Sandhurst companies.
1. Battles, history
I. Chandler, David 1934–
355.409
ISBN 1-85409-022-4

The illustration on the jacket of the Blenheim Quit-Rent banners is reproduced
by gracious permission of Her Majesty the Queen.

Maps and orders of battle by Keith Chaffer, RMA Sandhurst; line drawings by
Malcolm McGregor.

Designed and edited by DAG Publications Ltd. Designed by David Gibbons;
edited by Michael Boxall; layout by David Gibbons; typeset by Typesetters
(Birmingham) Ltd, Warley, West Midlands; monochrome camerawork by M&E
Reproductions, North Fambridge, Essex; printed and bound in Italy by Olivetto.

The opinions expressed in this volume are those of the authors and do not
necessarily reflect the policy and views, official or otherwise, of the Royal Military
Academy Sandhurst or of the Ministry of Defence.

CONTENTS

The training of leaders for war has a history as long as warfare itself. In many societies, military skills were the basis of the education of all gentlemen. By the 18th century, the power and even the survival of nations had come to depend on highly organised armies and navies. Repeated threats of invasion, maintaining the balance of power in Europe, the need to protect an expanding commercial empire and rapidly developing technology, provided ample motive for the British to take military matters very seriously. The foundation of the Royal Military Academy Woolwich in 1741 is a reflection of just how concerned the government of the day had become about national security and British influence on international affairs.

This book is a timely tribute to all those who have taught and studied at Woolwich and Sandhurst over the last 250 years and I hope it will be an encouragement to all who begin their careers at the Royal Military Academy Sandhurst. The battles, which have given their names to the Companies at the RMAS are all, in their way, examples of the best of British military leadership. Circumstances may have changed and military technology may have become much more sophisticated, but the qualities of leadership and the ability to inspire confidence and loyalty are just as vital as ever.

1989

PREFACE

The Sandhurst Company battles! What an imaginative approach, and one that is so typical of that great military historian David Chandler, who has done so much for War Studies at the Royal Military Academy Sandhurst.

Sandhurst has no battle honours. However, its sons have taken part in all the battles described in this book with the exception of Blenheim and Dettingen, and so, in a way, the great battles described here perform that role for the Academy. Another memorial that also serves to remind us of the sacrifices that have been made by the officers of the British Army, is the series of beautiful tablets in the Royal Memorial Chapel at the Academy on which the names of 3,274 former Gentlemen Cadets who died between 1914 and 1919, are recorded – and that is in just one, albeit a major, war. In both cases – battle honours and memorial tablets – the purpose is to remind us of great deeds and to commemorate those who gave their lives for their country, and this book simply and most effectively gives such a reminder.

It is good, too, that this book is published to commemorate the 250th anniversary of the foundation of The Royal Military Academy, Woolwich. The 'Shop', as it was called, was established in 1741 to provide specialist training for the technical arms of the day – the Gunners and the Sappers. The others – cavalry and infantry – could learn their trade 'at the cannon's mouth' until the Royal Military College Sandhurst came into being in 1812, to produce trained officers for the non-technical arms.

Today, change and development continue, though not as dramatically as in 1947 when the two establishments amalgamated and the Royal Military Academy Sandhurst was born. The move, of course, reflected the need for a common training at the start of a young officer's career and the main part of that training then as now, concerned leadership. Leadership is clearly brought out in this book. The need for the Army to produce leaders with the qualities of pride – not arrogance – in themselves, their regiment and in their professional skills; integrity – honesty and high moral standards and values; knowledge and the desire to keep up to date with professional developments; a sense of humour; a caring attitude towards the soldiers one leads, which, in its widest sense includes caring for their training and their development as much as for their welfare and administration; and finally courage, both moral and physical, without which no great leader can survive. The need remains and can be met to some extent by studying books such as this.

Of course, in these pages, reference is made to those regiments of the former Empire, many of whom today are represented at Sandhurst by overseas cadets. What a wonderful contribution they have made over the years and continue to make to the Academy today; long may they add a special richness to our courses.

I would also like to pay tribute to the often unsung Academic Staff at the Academy – another group who add a special flavour to life at Sandhurst. Many of them have contributed to this book and indeed they all contribute towards the teaching of the academic side of our profession – the study of war, defence and international affairs, and communication. Woe betide those who under-rate this aspect of the profession of arms. All officers and officer cadets should be grateful for the excellent Academic Staff we have today who play such an active part in the life of the Academy.

I believe too that this book will appeal to many former cadets who look back with great affection on their days in this, their *alma mater*. I am sure many value their time here and continue to take pride in the fact that they, too, have marched through the portals of The Grand Entrance, in a company bearing the name of one of the great battles covered in this book – one of the Sandhurst battle honours.

Major-General Peter W. Graham, CBE
Commandant, the Royal Military Academy,
Sandhurst

ACKNOWLEDGMENTS

The Editor-in-Chief wishes, first and foremost, to express his gratitude to His Royal Highness the Duke of Edinburgh, KG, KT, for graciously agreeing to provide the *Foreword*. He also wishes to thank General Sir William Jackson, GBE, KCB, MC for writing the *Epilogue* at very short notice, and Major-General Peter Graham, CBE, for providing the *Preface*, and (with Major-General Sir Simon Cooper, his immediate predecessor as Commandant at Sandhurst) for affording much encouragement and support over the past few years while this book was being prepared.

He also wishes to thank his seventeen fellow-authors in the volume – busy men all – for contributing their interesting studies of the sixteen battles whose names are, or have been, commemorated by the RMA Sandhurst Cadet Companies since 1947, and which form the basis of our volume together with the first two *Appendixes*. In particular he records his gratitude to General Sir Martin Farndale for agreeing to write the *Amiens, 1918* chapter after deteriorating health (leading indeed to his regretted death) compelled Major-General B. P. Hughes, a fine product of 'the Shop', to withdraw from the project; and similarly to his friend, Lieutenant-Colonel Charles Grant, for stepping in to write *The Marne, 1914* following the sad passing in September 1988 of Brigadier Peter Young, DSO, MC, the Editor-in-Chief's predecessor-but-one and friend of many years' standing. He would also thank Mrs. Jill Day-Lewis for agreeing to the inclusion (in edited form) of a piece written by the late Antony Brett-James, MA, FRHistS, on *Burma, 1942–45*. He was a veteran of Slim's 'Forgotten Army', serving in the Royal Signals attached to the Fifth Indian Division; later, following appointment to the Sandhurst faculty in 1961, he was for many years a Company Tutor in Burma Company, and for a decade the Editor's immediate predecessor as Head of the (then) Department of War Studies and International Affairs at Sandhurst. It was also particularly kind of another old friend, Professor Don Schurman, sometime Head of the History Department at the Royal Military College Kingston, and Dr Jeffrey Grey of the Department of History at the University of New South Wales and Australian Defence Force Academy (formerly, in part, RMC Duntroon), Sandhurst's sister regular officer training establishments in Canada and Australia respectively, to accept invitations to join the team.

Considerable debts of gratitude are owed to Andrew Orgill, Senior Librarian, and the staff of the RMAS Central Library, for finding books, 'ancient and modern' and both articles and the sources of certain quotations relevant to preparing this volume. Thanks are also due to Philip Annis of the Royal Artillery Institution (housed in the Old Royal Military Academy Woolwich) for help in acquiring information relevant to the 'Shop' for the Appendixes (not least in securing the valued recollections of Lieutenant-Colonel (Retd.) W. M. D. Turner, late RA – another of the dwindling band of officers trained at the 'Shop' before 1939); and also to his friend, Dr Tony Heathcote, Curator of the Sandhurst Collection, who, besides contributing the first appendix, has afforded much valuable information and provided useful leads on many related subjects (not least about what took place at Sandhurst between 1939 and 1945).

Special thanks go to Mr Keith Chaffer of the Methods/Reprographics Department at the RMAS, for drawing the maps and diagrams from rough designs (and for researching not a few of them), all in his spare time during evenings and week-ends; he is also to be commended for his excellent work on the series of Company Ante-Room Battle Displays that is gradually approaching completion around the Academy, and which provided the first spark of an idea that led to this book commemorating the 250th Anniversary of the Foundation of the Royal Military Academy Woolwich in 1741. Several of these presentations were designed by respected friends and former colleagues, including Eric Morris (the writer of

9

Salerno, 1943 below), Lieutenant-Commander A. G. Thomas, MBE (who helped with no less than three), and Dr Paddy Griffith, as well as by esteemed members still serving including Drs Christopher Duffy and Duncan Anderson.

Sterling (and very patient) professional services in respect of typing or word-processing several of the Appendices have been uncomplainingly provided in their own time by the hard-worked, stalwart and cheery ladies of the Department of War Studies Office – Mrs Maureen Stanyard and Mrs Chris MacLennan – and the Editor warmly thanks them both.

Last, but by no means least, the Editor-in-Chief thanks his wife, Gillian, and their sons, for putting up with such veritable mountains of files and papers all over the house at 'Hindford' during the last few years, and for philosophically helping an occasionally rather distraught husband/father to hunt down the odd stray reference, file or book gone temporarily 'AWOL' (or 'absent without leave').

And of course, a great deal is owed to Roderick Dymott of *Arms and Armour Press*, part of *Cassell*, and the members of his publishing team, not least David Gibbons of DAG, for safely steering this book past sundry rocks and whirlpools during the more than usually intricate preparation and production processes to what it is hoped everybody will agree is a very satisfactory conclusion.

LIST OF CONTRIBUTORS

(in alphabetical order)

The late ANTONY BRETT-JAMES, MA(Cantab), FRHistS, was Head of the Department of War Studies and International Affairs at RMA Sandhurst (1969–79). Educated at Mill Hill School, the Sorbonne and Sidney Sussex College, Cambridge, he came to Sandhurst in 1961 following war service with the Royal Signals in the Middle East and Burma and a period post-war in publishing. The author of twelve books, two of them on Burma – *Report my Signals* (1948) and (with Lieutenant-General Sir Geoffrey Evans) *Imphal* (1962) – many of the rest on aspects of the Napoleonic period, most notably his biography of *General Graham, Lord Lynedoch* (1959). Shortly after his retirement he became seriously ill, and died, aged 63, in March 1984. His last book, published posthumously, was *Conversations with Montgomery* (1984) reflecting the help he provided the Field Marshal in writing his *History of Warfare* (1968).

Field Marshal LORD CARVER, after education at Winchester and Sandhurst, joined the Royal Tank Corps in 1935, and was serving with 1st Royal Tank Regiment in Egypt in 1939. He was GSO1 of 7th Armoured Division (the 'Desert Rats') at El Alamein. Thereafter he commanded 1st Royal Tank Regiment in North Africa, Italy and Normandy, where he took command of 4 Armoured Brigade, remaining in command until after the end of the war. After it, he held many important staff appointments and commanded 6 Infantry Brigade, 3rd Division, Far East Land Forces, Far East Command and Southern Command (in the United Kingdom) before becoming Chief of the General Staff and then Chief of the Defence Staff. From 1977 to 1978 he was Designate British Resident and Commissioner for Rhodesia. He has published twelve books, including studies of *Tobruk* (1964) and *Alamein* (1962), *The War Lords* (1976) as Editor; a biography, *Harding of Petherton, Field-Marshal* (1978), and a volume of memoirs. He lives in Hampshire.

DAVID G. CHANDLER, MA(Oxon), Cert(Edn), FRHistS, FRGS, was educated at Marlborough and Keble College, Oxford. After service on secondment to the RWAFF in Nigeria, he joined the Sandhurst faculty in 1960, becoming Head of the Department of War Studies in 1980. For nineteen years he headed the British Commission for Military History, and is now its President of Honour, and is also an International Vice-President of the CIHM (since 1975). He is a Trustee of the Royal Tower Armouries, a Council member of both the SAHR and Army Records Society, and has held two chairs as Visiting Professor in the USA (1960 and 1988). He is the author of twenty books, many specializing in the Marlburian and Napoleonic eras, including *The Campaigns of Napoleon* (1966); *The Art of War in the Age of Marlborough* (1975); *Napoleon's Marshals* (1987) (Editor); *Battles and Battlescenes of World War Two* (1989); *Austerlitz – 1805* (1990). He lives in Surrey.

General SIR MARTIN FARNDALE, KCB, was educated at Yorebridge Grammar School and RMA Sandhurst. He joined the Royal Artillery in 1948, and spent most of his Regimental Service with 1st Regiment Royal Horse Artillery, which he commanded from 1969 to 1971. He subsequently commanded 7 Armoured Brigade, 2nd Armoured Division, I (British) Corps (1983–5) and Northern Army Group (1985–7). He has also served as Director of Public Relations and Director of Military Operations. From 1980 to 1988 he was Colonel Commandant of the Army Air Corps, and is now Master Gunner, St James's Park. He has published two volumes of *The History of the Royal Regiment of Artillery*: 1. *The Western Front 1914–18* (1987); and 2. *The Forgotten Front and the Home Base* (1988). He lives in Sussex.

General SIR ANTHONY FARRAR-HOCKLEY, GBE, KCB, DSO, MC, BLitt(Oxon), was educated at Exeter School. He joined the Regular Army in 1941, was commissioned in 1942 and served with the Gloucestershire and Parachute Regiments during the Second World War and several subsequent campaigns, including Korea and the Radfan. He has held numerous staff appointments, commanded 16 Para Brigade (1966–8), 4th Armoured Division (1971–3), and was Commander-in-Chief, Allied Forces Northern Europe (1979–82). A former Defence Fellow at Oxford, he is currently Cabinet Office historian for the Korean War. His nine published books include *Edge of the Sword* (1954); *The Somme* (1964); *Defeat of an Army* (1968); *'Goughie'* (1975); and *Opening Rounds* (1988). He lives in Oxfordshire.

General SIR DAVID FRASER, GCB, OBE, Vice Lord Lieutenant for Hampshire, was educated at Eton and Christ Church, Oxford. He joined the Grenadier Guards in 1940, and was commissioned in 1941. He served with the 2nd Battalion in north-west Europe. He commanded the 1st Battalion in 1960, 19 Infantry Brigade (1964–5), and 4th Division (1969–71). He was later Assistant Chief of the Defence Staff, Vice Chief of the General Staff, British Military Representative to NATO, and Commandant, Royal College of Defence Studies. Since retirement in 1980, he has published one biography, *Alanbrooke* (1982), one book of military history, *And We Shall Shock them* (1988), and six novels, including the *Treason in Arms* series (1985–7), spanning both world wars. He lives in Hampshire.

Lieutenant-Colonel CHARLES STUART GRANT was born in 1948. He was commissioned from Sandhurst into the Queen's Own Highlanders (Seaforth and Camerons) in 1968, and has served in the Middle East, Germany and Northern Ireland. He returned to Sandhurst to command Marne Company (1985–7). A keen war-gamer and military historian, he has written books on both subjects. His recent publications are *From Pike to Shot, 1685 to 1720* (1988), and *Wargaming in History – Waterloo* (1990).

Dr JEFFREY GREY is a graduate of the Australian National University and of the University of New South Wales, and is a lecturer in the Department of History, University College, Australian Defence Force Academy (formerly RMC Duntroon), an integral part of UNSW. He is to date the author of two published works: *The Commonwealth Armies and the Korean War* (1988) and *A Military History of Australia* (1990). He is currently engaged upon a volume of the Australian Official History dealing with his country's

involvement in the Confrontation with Indonesia during the 1960s. He lives in Canberra.

General SIR JOHN WINTHROP HACKETT, GCB, DSO*, MC, DL, BLitt, MA(Oxon), LLD. Educated at Geelong Grammar School and New College, Oxford, he was commissioned into the 8th Hussars in 1931. After active service in Palestine (1938–9), he served in the Middle East (1939–43) and at Arnhem (1944) as commander of 4 Parachute Brigade, where he received his third wound. Post-war service included command of 20 Armoured Brigade (1954), 7th Armoured Division (1956), appointment as Commandant of RMCS Shrivenham (1958) and GOC-in-C Northern Ireland (1961). He then became Deputy Chief of the General Staff (1964), C-in-C BAOR and Commander Northern Army Group (1966). After leaving the Army he became Principal of King's College London (1968–75), receiving many scholarly distinctions. His many publications include *The Profession of Arms* (the Lees Knowles Lectures of 1962 republished in 1983); *I was a Stranger* (1977 and 1988); *The Third World War* (with others) (1978); and its sequel . . . *The Untold Story* (1983); and most recently, as editor, *Warfare in the Ancient World* (1989). He lives in Gloucestershire.

Dr T. A. (Tony) HEATHCOTE, TD, MA (London) was educated at Cheshunt Grammar School and the University of London, where he took his degrees at the School of Oriental and African Studies of that university. From 1963 he worked at the National Army Museum, Chelsea for seven years. He is presently Curator of the Sandhurst Collection at the Royal Military Academy, Sandhurst – a post he has held since 1970 – responsible for the many paintings and artefacts throughout most of the Academy. He is the author of two published books: *The British Indian Army* (1973), and *The Afghan Wars* (1980), and also wrote the short *Guide to RMA Sandhurst*. He held the rank of Major in the Territorial Army before transferring to the Royal Auxiliary Air Force in 1989. He lives in Surrey.

Dr RICHARD HOLMES, OBE, TD, MA(Cantab), was educated at Cambridge, Northern Illinois and Reading Universities – receiving his doctorate from the last-named. He taught in the Department of War Studies for eighteen years (1969–88), serving latterly as its Deputy Head. In 1986 he received special leave of absence to command the 2nd Battalion, the Wessex Regiment, at Reading. He now divides his time between writing and acting as Consultant Historian at the Staff College, Camberley, where he shares in the instruction of the Higher Command and Staff Courses. He has written several television documentaries, including part of the BBC *Soldiers* series, and programmes on the Fall of France in 1940 and the Eisenhower–Montgomery relationship. He has also written a dozen books including (with Brigadier Peter Young) *The English Civil War* (1974); *The Little Field Marshal: A Biography of Sir John French* (1981); *Firing Line* (1985); and co-authored *Soldiers* (also 1985). He lives in Hampshire.

General SIR WILLIAM JACKSON, GBE, KCB, MC, was educated at Shrewsbury, RMA Woolwich (where he won the King's Medal in 1937), and King's College Cambridge. He was commissioned into the Royal Engineers in 1937, and saw active service in Norway, Tunisia, Sicily, Italy and the Far East (1939–45). After the war he instructed at the Staff College and then as a Company Commander at RMA Sandhurst (1951–3). After holding senior MOD staff appointments, he became GOC Northern Command (1970–2), became QMG (1972–6) and was ADC (General) to Her Majesty the Queen (1974–6). He served two periods as a Cabinet Office military historian, and from 1968 to 1982 held the appointment of Commander-in-Chief and Governor of Gibraltar. He is the author of eleven books, including *Attack in the West* (1953); the *Battle for Italy* (1967) and *. . . for Rome* (1969); *Alexander of Tunis as Military Commander* (1971); *The North African Campaign* (1975); edited the *Official History of the Mediterranean and Middle East*, vol. VI (Pt. One in 1984 and Pt. Two in 1987); and *The Rock of the Gibraltarians* (1988). He is at present co-authoring a work with Field Marshal Lord Bramall. He lives in Wiltshire.

ERIC MORRIS, BA (Lampeter), MA (Leics.), JP, is a consultant political analyst and author. Educated at the Universities of Wales and Leicester, he taught at Liverpool University before joining the academic faculty at RMA Sandhurst in 1970. He became Deputy-Head of the (then) Department of War Studies and International Affairs in 1980, before moving into industry in 1984 to work as a political analyst. He is the author of a number of books including *Corregidor – the End of the Line* (1982);

Salerno (1983); and more recently a two-volume series on *British Special Forces* (1986 and 1989). He lives in South Glamorganshire, and in 1989 was admitted to the Bench as a Justice of the Peace.

MICHAEL J. ORR, MA(Oxon), was educated at Balliol College, Oxford, where he read modern history. He joined the Department of War Studies in 1969. He studied Russian at the University of Surrey, 1978–9, and became a Senior Lecturer in the Soviet Studies Research Centre, Camberley in 1984. He has written numerous articles on twentieth-century warfare and the Soviet armed forces, and in 1972 published a study of *Dettingen, 1743*. He was a Consultant Editor to *The Times Atlas of the Second World War*. He lives in Surrey.

Dr JOHN PIMLOTT, BA(Leics.) was educated at Brigg Grammar School and Leicester University, where he took his doctorate. He was appointed to the academic faculty at RMA Sandhurst in 1973. Since 1987 he has been Deputy Head of the Department of War Studies. He has written a considerable number of books on military topics, including *Vietnam, the History and the Tactics* (1982); *Middle East Conflicts* (1983); and *Guerrilla Warfare* (1985); co-authored (with Doctor Ian Beckett) *Armed Forces and Modern Counter-Insurgency* (also 1985); and contributed to others, including *Napoleon's Marshals* (1987); *The Roots of Counter-Insurgency*; and *Warfare in the Twentieth Century* (both published in 1988). He lives in Surrey.

Major (retd.) R. d'A ('Buck') RYAN, MA(Cantab), MSc(Econ) (Wales), was commissioned from Sandhurst in 1950 into the Royal Artillery. He qualified p.s.c. at the Staff College, Camberley, in 1960, and retired from the Army in 1967. He then took his degree in modern history at St. Catharine's College, Cambridge, and subsequently undertook postgraduate studies at Aberystwyth as a Senior Research Fellow. He later became a Principal in the Ministry of Agriculture and Fisheries, Home Civil Service (1971–3), before transferring to the Sandhurst Academic Faculty in 1973. Until recently he carried out special responsibilities in the Department of War Studies for JCSC4 (the correspondence courses required as preparation for the Captain-to-Major promotion examination). He has for many years been a part-time tutor in modern history for the Open University. He was for many years an officer in the Territorial Army, and is now a Warning Officer in Civil Defence. He lives in Hampshire.

Professor DONALD M. SCHURMAN, PhD, is a Canadian who served in the RCAF (1942–5), and flew in 6 Group, Bomber Command. He is a graduate of Acadia and Cambridge Universities. He taught history at Queen's University, Kingston, Ontario, and at the Royal Military College of Canada, where he was, latterly, Head of the History Department. Widely travelled, he has held appointments at the National University of Singapore, lectured at several Scandinavian Universities, and he has held Research and Visiting Fellowships at Sidney Sussex College, Cambridge. He has published two books on naval writers: *The Education of a Navy* (1965) and *The Life of Sir Julian Corbett* (1982), and was an editor of the first two volumes of *The Complete Letters of Benjamin*

Disraeli (1982). He is at present completing a work on the Anglican Church in Eastern Ontario. He is Emeritus Professor at RMC, and lives in Ontario.

Dr JOHN SWEETMAN, MA, FRHistS, attended Portsmouth Grammar School and Brasenose College, Oxford, where he read modern history. He later gained his PhD at King's College London. In 1969 he joined the RMA Sandhurst academic faculty as a Senior Lecturer in the Department of War Studies and International Affairs and is now Head of the Department of Defence and International Affairs. He is the author of numerous books and articles, including *War and Administration in the Crimea* (1984); *Operation 'Chastise' – the Dambusters Raid* (1982); and edited and contributed to *Sword and Mace – Civil-Military Relations in Britain* (1986). His latest book is *Balaclava, 1854* (1990). He lives in Camberley.

▼ Sovereign's Parade, RMA Sandhurst. Her Majesty the Queen takes only one parade every decade – but is represented by a member of the Royal Family once a year. There are currently three Sovereign's Parades a year.

EDITOR-IN-CHIEF'S NOTE

At the outset I wish to make a few points concerning the planning and execution of this book for the convenience of our readers. The length of the chapters that follow average out at about 3,000 words apiece, but a few are longer, and a few more slightly shorter. Obviously, to achieve a reasonably uniform treatment of a selection of battles that cover a period of almost three hundred years certain problems have had to be addressed. How could a one-day battle such as Blenheim (1704), or a half-day engagement such as Inkerman (1854), be treated in a broadly similar way to great offensives lasting five months such as the Somme (1916), or even a whole campaign, virtually a war in itself, such as Burma (1942–5)? The answer is that it simply was not possible.

As a result there will be found below a considerable variety in methods of treatment, in many ways making for livelier reading, but these have been kept within certain prescribed parameters. All contributors were asked to be sure to make their battle, or its most important period, the focal point of their chapters (save in the case of Burma, which it was decided from the outset would need to take the form of an overall account of the whole campaign). Authors were asked to say a little about the rival commanders-in-chief in each case, and about the forces they commanded. As this is a book to commemorate the 250th Anniversary of the foundation of RMA, Woolwich, they were also requested to be sure to include gunner, sapper and signalling aspects (without going into excessive detail) when applicable to their subjects. The need to set a particular battle within its strategic setting – its causes and its aftermath – was also stressed. For the rest, authors were invited to choose their own approaches. Our team (details of which will be found above in the List of Contributors) contains fairly formidable military as well as academic expertise. The fifteen contributors with military experience of one sort or another in the widest sense of that term (regular, short service, national service, territorial or other reserve) comprise one sapper, four gunners (including one who has become an auxiliary airman and another turned civil defender), one (late, alas) sometime signaller, two members of the armoured corps (one a cavalryman turned paratrooper and one a 'tankie'), and five infantrymen (including one para and one who served with the US National Guard), with one Canadian airman and, last of all, one army educator bringing up the rear (or possibly taking the lead insofar as this particular project is concerned: 'everything comes to him who waits'!). By broad calculation this amounts to a total shared military service of at least 450 years (please note we carefully say 'at least', for field marshals never fully retire but go on half-pay) – longer *in toto* by a century-and-a-half, it may be noted, than the historical period covered by this volume. In academic terms we include eight Doctorates of Philosophy (or twelve if Honorary awards are included), and between us have published well over 100 books on many diverse aspects of Military History and War Studies. All contributors have been members of military academies or service colleges, eight of us in the Department of War Studies or its immediate predecessors at the Royal Military Academy, Sandhurst.

Each chapter includes two maps and as many diagrams giving orders of battle. In each case, one map in colour relates to the battle itself in almost all instances; that in monochrome to the campaign area. There are two exceptions. As the chapter on *Alamein* covers both battles (July and October–November 1942), there are two coloured battle maps in this single case, one devoted to each engagement, and no campaign map. In the case of *Burma*, which is essentially a campaign rather than a battle study (as will be explained in the General Introduction), the colour map has been devoted to the campaign area (with an inset showing the defensive battle of Kohima/Imphal in slightly more detail), while the monochrome map relates to the great offensive battle of Meiktila–Mandalay.

As the subjects treated go back to the early eighteenth century, it was felt that modern NATO symbols would not be wholly appropriate for the depiction of troop positions, formation names, etc., and accordingly with the aid of our cartographer, Mr. Keith Chaffer, we developed conventions of our own for use all the way through the book from *Blenheim, 1704* to *Burma, 1942–5*. Single-edged boxes around names invariably relate to 'friendly' military forces; double-edged boxes to our various opponents over the centuries. Most other symbols are self-explanatory, but where thought desirable a small explanatory key has been included on the map or diagrams concerned. We are well aware of the deficiencies of 'bold arrows on a map' as accurate indications of combat detail, but as we could not have more maps in each chapter we have done what we can to indicate major thrust lines as clearly as possible. The Editor-in-Chief is grateful to his fellow-contributors for checking the galley proofs and art work for their respective chapters, and to Keith Chaffer for making the necessary changes to the latter. The same applies to the orbats giving the outline structure of the main armies involved in the various battles. These have in most cases been kept as simple as possible, and we apologise for any *lacunae* or inaccuracies that may have crept in despite our best endeavours.

As it is clearly impossible to say everything that is necessary in between 2,500 and 3,500 words, each contributor has supplied a list of suggested books for further reading, with a word or two of comment upon each for the guidance of any reader who may wish to delve more deeply. Similarly, the attention of readers wishing to learn more about the Royal Military Academy, Woolwich (1741–1939), the Royal Military College, Sandhurst (1812–1939) or the Royal Military Academy, Sandhurst (1947 to the present), is directed to the Select Bibliography towards the end of the volume, following the Appendixes.

Each chapter also contains a number of colour and black-and-white pictures, portraits and battle-scenes, both paintings and photographs. Every attempt has been made to provide appropriate acknowledgments – but in certain cases it has not proved possible to trace original copyright holders. In these cases we beg the owners' indulgence.

David Chandler, Editor-in-Chief

GENERAL INTRODUCTION

by David Chandler, Editor-in-Chief

'The next greatest misfortune to losing a battle is to gain such a victory as this,' the Duke of Wellington stated with good reason on the late evening of 18 June 1815. It is proper to recall at the outset of this commemorative volume the appalling cost in terms of human lives and suffering that almost every battle represents to victor and vanquished alike. Later that night, as he wrote his Waterloo Despatch in the upstairs room of the posting-inn at Waterloo, with his friend and senior aide-de-camp, Colonel Sir Alexander Gordon, dying of wounds in the room next door, the Duke declared to Lord Fitzroy-Somerset, himself a serious casualty of the day's ten hours' severe fighting: 'I have never fought such a battle, and I trust I shall never fight such another' – and so, mercifully for him, it was indeed to prove. A day or so later he burst into tears in Brussels when acquaintances pressed around the hero of the hour. 'Oh!' the Duke exclaimed, 'Do not congratulate me. I have lost all my friends.' And indeed that was the case. Many of his personal staff had become casualties, only a few had escaped death or some degree of physical harm, Wellington himself being one of their charmed number. And, as Sir David Fraser reveals below in his fine chapter on *Waterloo*, this was the merest tip of the iceberg: at least one man in seven in the Allied Army had become a casualty before nightfall ended the fighting.

It is indeed a saddening – but also an inspiring – matter, as the Commandant has written in the *Preface*, to visit the Memorial Chapel here at Sandhurst, and there to study the many memorials to the fallen. The large majority relate to the First World War, but a side-chapel reminds us of those officers who died in many earlier campaigns fought by the British Army over many parts of the globe – Afghanistan, the Sudan and South Africa amongst them – during the nineteenth century. Rolls of Honour bring the grim but glorious record up to date, commemorating those many regular officers who died between 1939 and 1945, and in more recent years in Malaya, Kenya and

Cyprus, at Suez in 1956, in Aden and Oman, and during the South Atlantic Campaign of 1982; and, of course, over the last twenty years in Northern Ireland – all the way down to the present day. Sacrifice has always accompanied both triumph and defeat in war. The impression of sacrifice and gallantry is strong. As General Sir John Hackett described one aspect of an officer's duty in the thought-provoking 'Profession of Arms' film of the Canadian television series on *War* (1986), an officer does not so much set out to slay, but 'rather offers himself to be slain'. Clearly, some concepts of mediaeval chivalry continue to inspire modern officers at all levels of seniority.

'But what good came of it at last?', asked little Peterkin of Old Kaspar in Robert Southey's poem, *After Blenheim*. The wise old man replied, 'Why, that I cannot tell,' – but there have been many conflicting opinions expressed since, not least by military historians. Do the horrors inescapable from warfare ever justify its use? The plain answer has, unfortunately, to be 'yes'. There are certain eventualities that are worse than war itself – enslavement of peoples, racial hatred leading to genocide or enslavement, and wholly perverted political systems, amongst them. Of course force of arms should only be indulged in as the very last resort when all other possibilities of resolving the crisis or issue at stake by peaceful means – negotiation, international pressure, economic sanctions – have been exhausted, as in 1991's Gulf conflict.

This has not always been the case. No nation has a wholly blameless record in this respect. How can I, as (it is to be hoped) a reasonably objective British historian, attempt to claim that Great Britain has invariably fought only in 'just wars' (that difficult concept capable of almost infinite definition)? Not when we come to look at such struggles as the 'Opium Wars' of 1839–42, when the British government declared war on China in order to force the acceptance of British trade in, among other items, narcotics (which the Chinese emperors and their mandarins had in their wisdom banned from their realm). One outcome of this 'successful' if not exactly 'just' war was, interestingly enough, the cession of Hong Kong to the British Crown by the Treaty of Nanking – setting in train another historical process that has now almost come full circle. The modern equivalent of such an act as the First Opium War would be, perhaps, for the United States to intervene in Panama to enforce the importation of cocaine on behalf of the 'drug barons' of Bolivia and Peru, taking the Panama Canal into perpetual ownership as its price. Such a concept is pure fantasy, of course, but stranger things have happened in the long course of human history. Clearly, then, no war is justified if it ends by creating more permanent misery or greater problems and wrongs than it originally set out to redress.

For this book I have been fortunate to recruit a group of noted military historians – many of them serving or retired soldiers of great distinction; with published books or articles to their credit. Our task has been to re-describe the celebrated major engagements fought over three centuries by the British Army (alongside, in almost all cases, allies of many nations in numerous, often-shifting, combinations), which for one reason or another were chosen in 1947 or subsequently to provide the proud titles of the Officer-Cadet Companies at Sandhurst.

The book is being published at this particular time in order to commemorate the 250th anniversary of the foundation of the Royal Military Academy Woolwich by a Royal Warrant signed by King George II on 30 April 1741. King George, as Michael Orr reminds us in *Dettingen, 1743* below, was the last King of England to serve in battle as monarch, and so it is fitting that it was he who should have acted upon the advice of his ministers to set up an institution in south-east London for the purpose of instructing '. . . inexperienced people belonging to the Military Branch of this office [the Board of Ordnance] in the several parts of Mathematics necessary to qualify them for the service of the Artillery, and the business of Engineers; and that there is a convenient room at Woolwich Warren, which may be fitted up for that purpose' – as Tony Heathcote recalls in Appendix A devoted to *The Sandhurst Companies* towards the end of the volume. The total expenditure for this undertaking, it may be somewhat wryly noted, was not to exceed £500 per annum. So began the tradition of formal education and instruction of young officers – at first for only the 'technical arms' of the day, the gunners and sappers.

Up to that time, aspirants to His or Her Majesty's commission as officer in the Land Forces had been expected to pick up the essentials of their profession 'at the cannon's mouth', in some cases by attaching themselves as supernumeraries to the staffs of the 'Great Commanders' of the day. Thus the young John Churchill, later First Duke of Marlborough and victor of *Blenheim, 1704*, learnt the rudiments of what the Bard of Avon dubbed 'the bless'd trade' from the great French general, Marshal Turenne. Gunners and engineers – such as Jacob Richards – were on occasion sent by the Board of Ordnance (which did in fact provide officer training of a sort under the Master-Gunner for the technical arms long before the RMAW was instituted for the purpose) to 'observe' foreign wars, many of them being fought by Austria against the Turk. Most young men in other parts of the army, rather less fortunate than the favoured few, simply reported for duty to the Adjutants of their appointed Regiments wearing their brand-new 'regimentals' (uniforms) as ensigns or cornets, and at home or abroad jumped in at the deep end of the profession of arms.

Alas, in too many contemporary accounts of the seventeenth and eighteenth centuries a young man's worth was too often mainly judged by his peers and superiors according to the money in his pocket (many promotions, it will be remembered, until as recently as 1871 had to be bought after the necessary vacancy had occurred and the right recommendations secured). Further 'desirable' qualifications included a good head for liquor (many an officer was expected to be at least a daily 'five bottle of claret' man), backed by a reputation as a gambler and a womanizer, and, last but by no means least if he was to survive at all, by a fair ability at wielding the short-sword. Little regard was paid to any tendency towards paying undue attention to books and studies, or to such boring matters as drill and tactics. They were rough old times, to be sure, but somehow the Army, in fact, muddled through thanks to a vital leavening of truly professional officers in every regiment.

Nevertheless, from the last day of April 1741 formal British officer training had been born, perhaps none too soon, albeit only for gunners and engineers. At Sandhurst memories of our artillery predecessors are constantly brought to mind by the fine array of Ordnance displayed around the grounds, which 'Buck' Ryan fully describes in Appendix B.

It is not our purpose to provide a history of R.M.A. Woolwich (see the Select Bibliography, for sources), but rather to commemorate its foundation – although the pages on '*The Sandhurst Companies*' include a brief description of the RMA Sandhurst's antecedents. Sandhurst, of course (which *The Economist* described in January 1990 as today '. . . the world's best-known military academy'), came into full operational existence in 1812 to train the 'Junior Department' as the Royal Military College Sandhurst. Before this there had been temporary sojourns at High Wycombe and Great Marlow over the decade following the signature by George III of another Royal Warrant dated 24 June 1801, which set up in principle both a 'Senior' (staff-officer training) and a 'Junior' (Gentleman-Cadet) educational and instructional institution. This came about after much lobbying by a group of influential soldiers and politicians (William Pitt the Younger prominent among them) which also included Colonel John Gaspard Le Marchant (a Channel-Islander by birth). He was to become Sandhurst's first Lieutenant-Governor, who soon thereafter, following his recall to active service, was to be killed breaking a French formation at the head of the heavy cavalry at *Salamanca, 1812* (see p. 57 below). This influential group felt strongly that the British Army also badly needed formally and identically instructed young cavalry and infantry officers, as well as more competent staff, in order to meet successfully the considerable military challenge posed since 1793 by the French Revolutionary and then, from 1799, Consular and Napoleonic armies.

As readers of the first Appendix will appreciate, the training of regular officers for the British Army (and for many overseas countries – some 74 in all have been represented here since 1947) has seen considerable evolution over the years, and doubtless will continue to do so. This constitutes probably 'our greatest challenge' in peacetime as General Sir William Jackson points out in his *Epilogue*. Perhaps 'revolution' would be the more apt word. For in many ways policies concerning length of courses, their military content, and the importance to be accorded academic preparation of future young officers (or not, as the case may be: unfortunately the MOD authorities of the late twentieth century have not invariably shown themselves notably enlightened in this respect in their ceaseless quest for the right (often the most economical) solution). Naturally, changing times and social attitudes, and the eternal demands for financial cutbacks and rationalizations, call for continual rethinking and (when truly necessary) restructuring. But a major upheaval on an average of every five years since 1960 has been, it can be argued (without being unduly critical or pessimistic) a trifle excessive.

To be effective, education requires an essential basis of continuity, and over recent years the academic side of Sandhurst has been particularly hard-hit by the processes of 'fine-tuning', or to be more accurate and frank, radical surgery. No less than three of the five original departments have been closed down: Languages in 1972, Mathematics in 1974 and Military Technology disappearing in 1986; and later the two original survivors — Defence and International Affairs, and War Studies, together with our relatively new (founded in 1986) sister-Department of Communications appeared to face the prospect of privatization before the end of 1991. But the challenges of change have always had to be balanced against the benefits of continuity. To function properly, and even to survive, any great effective institution must be dynamic and accept the process of change. In this regard nobody could fault Sandhurst at the present time, and even now particularly in the dramatically changing east European circumstances (and the effects on the British Army likely to follow), it would be rash and unrealistic to expect a period of stability. But as a worldly-wise Roman commander, Gaius Petronius Arbiter, allegedly wrote in about AD 65: 'We trained hard — but it seemed that every time we were beginning to form into teams, we would be reorganized. I was to learn later in life that we tend to meet any new situation by reorganizing — and a wonderful method it can be for creating the illusion of progress.' The modern situation is not so very different.

Returning to the eighteenth and nineteenth centuries, it is distinctively doubtful whether all of the products of first Woolwich (and later Sandhurst) were truly credits to the profession of arms. Bullying was rife (has not MacDonald Fraser missed a trick by not writing *Flashman at Sandhurst* — it would surely be the ideal transition between that notorious anti-hero's sojourn at Dr Arnold's Rugby School and his world-famous (and equally fictional) martial and amorous exploits of later years). Some early Woolwich cadets were, to quote one of their early mentors, '. . . scabby sheep, whom neither lenity will improve, nor confinement in a dark room and being fed on bread and water'. Absenteeism was rife, and many a muster-roll entry ends with the plaintive remark: 'I know not where they are,' or, 'A very idle fellow.' There were plenty of brushes with local shipyard workers ending in not a few bloody noses (given and received, it would appear, in roughly equal proportions).

Early Sandhurst also had its occasional little problems. An early Governor, Sir George Scovell, GCB (see Appendix E) spent many a dark night with his servants attempting to apprehend Gentleman-Cadets indulging in unofficial night exercises in raiding the College Farm rabbit-warrens, which he considered to be his exclusive preserves and they regarded as a legitimate means of supplementing their diet. Indeed complaints over food constituted a recurring grievance, culminating in at least two mutinies, the most famous of which (in 1862) was deemed so serious that no less a personage than the Royal Commander-in-Chief, the Duke of Cambridge, had to be called down from the Horse Guards to persuade the recalcitrant cadets to abandon the redoubt known as 'Fort Royal' (today the kennels of the RMAS guard-dogs). They had been holding this strategic position for three days against all comers with well-aimed volleys of hard-as-stone bread rolls which, as well as ammunition, provided one of the major complaints at issue. In due course they agreed to return to their duty to Queen Victoria, and marched out. But the food promptly improved in quality.

Almost annually there were riots associated with the Blackwater and Bagshot Fairs, and Sandhurst had (and some darkly aver still has) a 'Black Hole' under the steps of Old Building, which in the last century was rarely uninhabited by the most reprehensible miscreants. However, the Royal Military College's Gentlemen-Cadets never quite plumbed the depths of their earliest Greenwich predecessors when it came to the matter of misbehaviour on ceremonial parades. On one occasion in June 1744 the Royal Regiment of Artillery was to be reviewed by His Royal Highness William Augustus, Duke of Cumberland, destined in the following year to become the loser of Fontenoy and in 1746 to earn after Culloden a double nickname: 'Sweet William' (after the flower so named in his honour by his admirers), and 'Stinking Billy' (a Highland name for a species of ragwort) by those who did not appreciate 'Butcher Cumberland's' ensuing 'Pacification of the Highlands'. At the ceremonial review in 1744, His Royal Highness was observed to note with disfavour a disorderly mob, without officers or uniforms, milling about at the right of the line (traditionally the place of greatest honour). They proved to be, alas, not the media representatives of the day, but the Gentleman-Cadets of the Royal Artillery.

Matters improved somewhat in 1745 when — perhaps as a direct result — there was the formal creation of a Cadet Company of between 20 and 48 cadets (the number varied widely over the years), with a regular establishment of serving officers and a full curriculum. But that same year the Lieutenant-Governor still found it necessary to patrol the corridors of the infant Academy in an attempt to check the merciless ragging inflicted on the hapless civilian professors. One wonders how, rather later, Professor Michael Faraday ever managed to find the inspiration to discover electro-magnetism in 1831. A stream of disciplinary edicts poured forth from the 'Shop's' headquarters forbidding, under pain of severe penalties, such practices as 'smouching' ('liberating' other people's property), or '. . . shutting their desks with violence'.

Since the merging of 'the Shop' and 'the Royal Military College' into a single body in 1947 it is to be noted that some equivalent high-spirited pranks are not wholly unknown down to the present day. Certain Adjutant's Rehearsals in preparation for Sovereign's Parades have been disrupted by monstrous, compressed-air filled, rubber octopuses appearing over Grand Entrance. 'Bunny' and 'Kissogram' girlies clad much as Mother Nature intended have also been known to be smuggled on to parade. But this has by now become something of an accepted and even hallowed tradition — and one Academy Adjutant was gallant enough to dismount on a particularly cold morning rehearsal, to sheathe his sword and to offer his cloak to a scantily-clad (and distinctly blue) 'bimbo' who had been smuggled on to the 'sacred turf' by the Senior Division. So the Officer-Cadets of the Royal Military Academy Sandhurst still have their little jokes (and long may these continue), although modern young men and women are perhaps today generally rather more serious-minded than were their predecessors of even thirty years ago.

A select few of all intakes and periods have earned well-deserved honours while at Woolwich or Sandhurst, and the names of all known recipients of the various Swords of Honour, and of all Queen's and King's Medallists will be found on pages 273–81. The recipients of the Overseas Cane since its institution in 1973 (Sandhurst is proud to recall that many future leaders of their countries and armies — including King Hussein of Jordan, Sultan Hassan of Brunei, Sultan Qaboos bin Said of Oman and the earlier President of Pakistan, Ayub Khan, to name but four

— have trained to become officers here and have passed up the steps of Grand Entrance), and winners of the WRAC Sash since 1984, are listed at Appendices J and K respectively. Many of these chosen representatives of their various generations have gone on to achieve great things in many different spheres — not least during campaigns and on battlefields, but in many other areas of national life as well, as typified by Sandhurst's greatest son, Sir Winston Churchill — but whether Prize Winners or not, every young man and woman that pass out of Sandhurst has been inspired by its motto: 'Serve to Lead'.

Any institution relies heavily on the calibre of its staff. At Appendix E will be found the names of the Governors and Commandants who have given the lead. The longest serving (but not necessarily the most distinguished) at Sandhurst was Wellington's former code-breaker in the Peninsular War and Waterloo Campaign, Sir George Scovell (whose portrait is to be found in 'Topper's Bar' in Old College, and whose medals are on display in the Central Library), who was either Governor or Lieutenant-Governor for all of 27 years without a break (March 1829 to April 1856), progressing from Colonel to full General in the process. The 1947 and 1990 senior members of the RMA Sandhurst staff — military and civilian — are listed in the final Appendix; all named — and many more — have played their parts in whatever degree.

This volume contains short accounts of sixteen important battles in the history of the British Army since the advent of the age of gunpowder. Not all can be accounted victories in the full sense of the term. Who, apart from an unscrupulous Propaganda Ministry, could call the opening of the *Somme, 1916* — graphically described below by Sir Anthony Farrar-Hockley — and its four-month sequel, or its 1918 Second Battle, a 'military victory' in the usually accepted sense? Who could really term any one of the Three Battles of *Ypres* — least of all the last, so movingly analysed by Professor Donald Schurman — a 'triumph'? *Salerno, 1943*, as Eric Morris reminds us, was a near-run thing indeed, particularly in its later stages. And even *Arnhem, 1944*, so vividly recalled by a participant, General Sir John Hackett (at the time a Brigadier), which Field Marshal Montgomery described as '90 per cent successful', was hailed by Dr Goebbels as a major German strategic victory in the West, for once with some justification. Its outcome certainly delayed the Allied crossing of the Rhine, and thus into the Ruhr, heartland of German war industry,

for more than six months. But it has always been the idiosyncratic British habit to glory in our gallant martial failures as well as in our outright victories — such as *El Alamein, 1942* which Field Marshal Lord Carver — again a participant — so cogently dissects in his chapter below, or hard-won *Normandy, 1944*, Richard Holmes's evocatively written subject.

But seen as triumphs of individual human courage, moral as well as physical, over fear of death, wounds and the unexpected, any battle of any period is commemorable. And that, of course, is the main point of this volume. We aim to commemorate the valour of the sons of Woolwich and Sandhurst, of the men they led, the Allies they fought alongside, including the Canadians at *Third Ypres* and the Australians and New Zealanders who made such a contribution to Allenby's triumph at *Third Gaza, 1917* (as Dr Jeffrey Grey so cogently reminds us), or the Americans throughout the Italian and north-west European campaigns. Nor should we fail to acknowledge the courage and skill of the opponents they fought. For who, as individuals, were ever braver than the French grenadiers who formed the last square of the Old Guard at Waterloo, than the German Gunner of Flésquières at Cambrai, or than the Japanese attackers at *Kohima-Imphal, 1944* and defenders of *Mandalay-Meiktila, 1945*? Of course certain other attributes in certain opponents were less commendable, and rightly so regarded and recorded, but 'courage unto death' cannot be justly written-down by some such diminutive adjective as 'senseless', 'unthinking' or 'fanatical', except, perhaps, in the heat of the moment or during the immediate aftermath. Our purpose, then, is not to score points of any kind over adversaries long departed, or over issues long dead, but simply to salute the British Soldier and his allied comrades-in-arms of all periods. *Inkerman, 1854* is a classic example of 'a soldiers' battle', as John Sweetman reminds us, but our troops owed not a little to our French allies in the Crimean War. Our object, therefore, is neither to stir up sad memories of 'old, unhappy, far-off things, and battles long ago', nor to indulge in a feast of jingoistic national self-adulation; but, quite simply, to adapt the words of Virgil, *'arma virumque canemus'* ('we sing of man and of arms').

How the names of the original dozen Sandhurst Companies came to be chosen has not, to my knowledge, been recorded. Doubtless the award of a Battle-Honour to considerable numbers of individual units of the British Army had some bearing; the *éclat* of certain battles on the popular consciousness, particularly of the young, was no doubt also taken into account. The original Old College quartet of *Blenheim, Dettingen, Waterloo* and *Inkerman* would be hard to better, reflecting, as they do, our country's first emergence to martial pre-eminence in modern times, a special royal connection, our most popular commander-in-chief ever (at least in retrospect), and 'the soldiers' battle' respectively. The former New College list of *Marne, Ypres, Somme* and *Gaza*, similarly commemorate in turn 'the battle that saved the world' (in former Gentleman-Cadet Winston Churchill's trenchant phrase) — so concisely described for us by Lieutenant-Colonel Charles Grant; the agonies we shared with what was left of 'gallant little Belgium'; the worst casualty list ever sustained by the British Army in a single day's fighting; and the first large victory in Palestine. These were four important British battles in the First World War to be sure, but in almost all of them we shared the heat of the day with Commonwealth and Empire comrades, not to forget our ally since the *entente cordiale* of 1905, our former great centuries-old opponent – France. Today the first three names are allotted to Victory College companies; the fourth (Gaza) is 'resting' (like *Inkerman*) in suspended animation.

Here may I mention how pleased I was to be afforded the assistance of two well-known historians representing Sandhurst's two oldest sister-Royal Military Colleges — in Canada and Australia respectively. The Royal Military College Kingston, and the Royal Military College Duntroon (now the Australian Defence Force Academy, a constituent part of the University of New South Wales) may, perhaps, on the whole reflect more closely in organizational terms the United States Military Academy, West Point. Both officer-training institutions, for example, have a standard four-year course leading to a degree as well as a commission. But both to this day still award a Queen's Commission to their young men and women, and 'blood is thicker than water'.

However, in allocating the First World War subjects to appropriate authors I faced one 'command decision', for naturally we wished to give our Canadian and Australian colleagues subjects particularly appropriate in terms of their countries' participation alongside the British armies of 1914–18. The *Third Battle of Gaza* of late 1917 presented no problem where Dr. Jeffrey Grey was concerned: the Desert Cavalry Corps which played so prominent a role in Allenby's notable victory (and repeated the task the

next year at Meggido) contained numerous Australian and New Zealand mounted units, and therefore it was a very appropriate subject. *Ypres, 1917,* however, was a different matter. The fact that the Company name was always placed next after *Marne* in all RMAS documentation infers that in chronological terms it must refer to either the First Battle of 1914 (at the end of the 'Race to the Sea') or the Second Battle of 1915 (memorable for the first large-scale use of poison gas in modern war), and *Somme, 1916* was, thereafter, next in line. And yet there was no denying that the great Canadian contribution to the struggle came in the Third Battle of mid-1917, often also known as Passchendaele — one of the most bravely fought, most expensive, and ultimately least-successful in terms of ground gained, of the great Western Front offensives of what used to be called 'The Great War'. Accordingly I decided to make Third Ypres the focal point of Professor Don Schurman's notable contribution (with due reference to the earlier two battles to be sure), and to place the *Ypres* chapter next after General Farrar-Hockley's excellent account of the Somme. The Ypres Company Crest gives us no clue — being the coat of arms of the City of Ypres — so I trust my decision will prove acceptable. But the original intention may well have been to stress the sacrifice of regular officers and men in late 1914.

The original Victory College list (in pre-graduate course days, but now allocated to New College) related to notable battles of the Second World War, comprising *Alamein, Normandy, Rhine* and *Burma*. The first three are unexceptionable. The great desert double battle that proved the major turning-point in the whole war in the Middle East, and the last truly 'British, Commonwealth and Empire' victory (there were, of course, also Free French, Greek and Jewish formations present) before we found ourselves sharing every major endeavour in North Africa and northwest Europe with our American allies, was thus an obvious choice for selection as a Company Name, and who better to contribute the subject here than Field Marshal Lord Carver who held an important staff appointment in 7th Armoured Division during October and November 1942?

The events surrounding the vast amphibious invasion of north-west Europe on D-Day, and the subsequent hard battles of the 'build-up' in, and of the 'break-out' from, *Normandy, 1944,* was an equally obvious choice for a Company Name. And Dr Richard Holmes, with his keen professional interest in the British Territorial Army as well as his qualifications and experience as a former Sandhurst military historian, was an obvious author to invite. The same may also be claimed for *Rhine, 1945*. The great river constituted the final major physical (and psychological) barrier separating the Allies from the Ruhr and the interior of Germany. Dr John Pimlott, besides possessing a nigh-encyclopaedic knowledge of the north-west European Campaign, had also assisted the Editor-in-Chief a few years back in setting up and running an annual summer battlefield tour to Remagen for the Officer-Cadets and Graduate Students taking part in their final pre-commissioning major exercise in the Eiffel; and also played a part, again with the Editor, in advising the Services' Sound and Vision Corporation in the making of the short documentary film, *'The Bridge at Remagen'* — which examines how a small American force captured intact a large Rhine bridge on 8 March 1945 — and how this chance opportunity (the major crossings were to come three weeks later) was exploited by SACEUR and the American First Army with commendable speed and flexibility. The only British force present was a barrage-balloon unit.

The final original Company Name, however, was the 'exception that proved the rule'. *Burma*, by any computation, is most definitely the name of a complete campaign, and not that of a single battle. It would have been unthinkable to leave out commemoration of Bill Slim's 'Forgotten Fourteenth Army' altogether, and one can hazard a guess that the reason why 'Kohima-Imphal' or 'Mandalay-Meiktila' was not selected for a Company title lay in the fact that they were double-barrelled names, and hence rather clumsy titles for administrative purposes. Perhaps it would have been unfair to have named just a 'Kohima' or 'Meiktila' company to represent the rest (although it was decided to have a simple 'Waterloo' rather than a more accurately titled 'Waterloo-Wavre' as a Company title: no doubt the inclusion of the Prussian connection was thought inappropriate in the immediate post-War period). In deciding to include an edited version of an excellent overall description written in 1964 by the late Antony Brett-James, I felt that it was quite proper to salute his memory in this fashion, and to accord rather more space to this final, chronologically speaking, Company Name.

The history of Sandhurst since 1947 has not been uneventful in institutional terms as already mentioned. Some Company names have been added, transferred between Colleges, or placed on the retired list, for reasons of reorganization and economy. The shortest-lived, *Salamanca, 1812*, was chosen for Victory College (recently designated for the Graduate Student Courses) in 1972, and disappeared only twelve years later, although Wellington's first great Peninsular offensive victory made a neat twin with his greatest defensive battle — *Waterloo, 1815*. As for *Amiens, 1918* and *Salerno, 1943*, these (together with *Arnhem, 1944*) had been the Cadet Company names employed at Mons Officer Cadet School, Aldershot. With Mons OCS's closure in 1972, these titles were transferred to Sandhurst. For a time, during a transitional period, New College bore the name of Mons College. Sir Martin Farndale, soldier-historian of the Royal Artillery in the First World War, was a good choice for the chapter devoted to *Amiens, 1918*, the last great British battle on the Western Front in which the artillery played a determinant role, causing 'the Black Day of the German Army' on 8 August, which led to the victory that at last came with the Armistice at 1100 hours on 11 November 1918.

As for *Salerno, 1943* — the reasons for its selection would seem to reflect the need to represent the Italian theatre of war. The actual Salerno landings near Naples were more dramatic politically than militarily — as they were immediately preceded by news of the Italian government's capitulation to the Allies. They led to grim fighting, however, as the Germans took over the defence of Italy against the British and American forces with exemplary efficiency. In Eric Morris we have another former Sandhurst lecturer who had already written a book in 1982 on this interesting and still fairly contentious subject.

This brings me to one of the basic factors that led to the production of this commemorative volume. It was at the suggestion of a Company Commander of Salerno Company, Major (now Brigadier) Jack Deverell, LI, that an illustrative display was devised by Eric Morris to portray the events of the 1943 amphibious landing graphically and comprehensively, combining artefacts and documents alongside maps and diagrams, for permanent installation in Salerno Company Lines, then situated in the Redoubt at Sandhurst. This was opened after a Company Dinner-night on the 40th anniversary of the landings, held on 9 September 1983, and was attended by three veterans of the subsequent battle, Major-General (retd.) David Appleby (who in 1943 had been a Captain on a Brigade Staff), Lieutenant-Colonel (retd.) 'Mad Jack'

Churchill of the Commandos, and Mr. Lew Hemmings (in 1943 a Lieutenant in the RNVR).

'From tiny acorns mighty oak-trees grow', and from the Salerno Company initiative developed the proposal that all Cadet Company Anterooms or Lines should be provided with similar permanent displays relevant to their particular names. At worst, a single framed map and brief caption had been all that provided Officer-Cadets with basic information about their Company affiliation. At best, a few portraits and contemporary relics — often unexplained — decorated the walls. To ameliorate this disappointing situation, a programme has now been proceeding for a number of years, and to date Blenheim, Waterloo, Inkerman, Marne, Amiens, Normandy and Burma Companies have received their displays in addition to Salerno. From this it was only a small step to envisage a book of broad appeal covering the whole subject, however incompletely (each battle, after all, provides enough material for a volume of its own). It is hoped this Academy-wide project will reach completion by 1994. However, as a realist after some 31 years of experience at RMAS, I would not be surprised if the MOD were to decide to set up a new committee in 1995 to consider renaming some or all the Sandhurst Companies with more modern, 'relevant', names: 'Imjin Company', 'Suez Company', 'Goose Green Company' and 'Gulf Company' amongst them. However, despite this potentially dire prospect, the approach of the 250th anniversary of the foundation of the first 'Military Academy' was a sufficient spur to start the processes leading to this volume.

Even with the coverage of sixteen subjects I am aware that the project is not complete in every respect. For several years during the 1950s and 1960s, for example, there was an Anzio Company giving special education to young men with inadequate academic entry qualifications for Sandhurst. This function (although not the name) was eventually moved to the Army School of Education at Beaconsfield, where it still operates as the Sandhurst Wing. Then there was the establishment in the early 1970s of Rowallan Company, named after Lord Rowallan of Scouting and Outward Bound Courses fame. This is a pre-Sandhurst training course for young people deemed by the Regular Commissions' Board at Westbury to be insufficiently confident and mature for entry to RMAS, but promising enough to merit places on a special three-months' course of mainly character-building outdoor activities to bring them up to the required standards. This has proved successful, and brought out and strengthened much latent talent. But the Company does not lend itself to our present purpose as its name recalls an individual, not a battle.

Since 1984 the RMAS has also been the home of the WRAC College. The ladies, too, brought Company titles with them — Richmond and Edinburgh — named after the town and city that were the sites of the first ATS Officer Cadet Training Units in the Second World War. Again, as in the case of Rowallan Company, these do not lend themselves to our particular purpose in the present volume.

If there is any truth in the saying that 'a nation gets the government it deserves', it may also be argued that a country also receives the army — and the type of young officer — that it merits. A high state of morale is a vital requirement for martial achievement. One ingredient of morale is a sense of inheritance of high standards from the near or more distant past. The impressive lists of winners of Victoria and George Crosses (see Appendixes C and D) displayed in letters of gold upon boards in the Central Library remind us of Woolwich's and Sandhurst's most valorous sons. It is our hope that this book will be read and enjoyed by soldiers of all generations, regiments and corps, whether from home or abroad, who have trained at either Woolwich (now, alas, a dwindling band) or at Sandhurst. And also by the wide sections of the general public that find pleasure in reading of past deeds of individual or collective martial valour. For, as Thomas Hardy wrote in *The Dynasts* in 1904–8, 'War makes for rattling good history, but peace only for poor reading.' True or false, the past certainly merits careful study if repetitions of old errors are to be avoided and guarded against. That is something that each successive generation of military staff and academic faculty must take serious care to ensure if they are to deserve the gracious words written about them by His Royal Highness the Duke of Edinburgh.

And so let this Introduction close with those inspiring words from the *Apocrypha*: 'Let us now praise famous men, and our fathers that begat us.' (Ecclesiasticus, xliv, v.1). Should the trumpets sound again, summoning the young to unavoidable battle, (as in the Middle East in 1991), we trust (and also feel confident) that they will again respond, as did their predecessors on so many earlier occasions, drawing strength and inspiration from the examples of earlier generations.

BLENHEIM COMPANY CREST
RMA SANDHURST

THE BATTLE OF BLENHEIM, 1704

by David Chandler

"'It was the English," Kaspar cried,
"Who put the French to rout;
But what they fought each other for
I could not well make out.
But everybody said," quoth he,
"That 'twas a famous victory."'

(Robert Southey, *After Blenheim*)

Robert Southey's poem is an early example of anti-war sentiment. It would have been surprising if 'Old Kaspar', whose '. . . father lived at Blenheim then', had displayed any grasp of the issues at stake that sunlit Sunday of 13 August 1704, when John Churchill, First Duke of Marlborough, and Prince Eugène of Savoy decisively defeated the combined forces of Marshals Camille d'Houston, Duke of Tallard and Ferdinand, Count Marsin, and their ally, Maximilian Emmanuel of Wittelsbach, Elector of Bavaria. But had the outcome been reversed, the power of Louis XIV would have become paramount, and the Second Grand Alliance – formed by England, the United Provinces (today Holland) and Austria in 1701 (subsequently joined by Portugal and Sardinia in 1703) to contain the 'Sun King's' ambitions over the Spanish inheritance – would have crashed in ruins.

Crisis on the Danube

Early in 1704 it had seemed that nothing could save the Allied cause as the forces of France and Spain prepared to converge on Vienna. The Austrian capital

◄ Marlborough in the years of his prime. He was considered one of the handsomest Englishmen of his day, and added a finely tuned mind to his other accomplishments as soldier, statesman, politician and family-man. (Detail from the *Höchstädt* tapestry by de Vos, after L. de Hondt.)

was already threatened by a serious Hungarian rising, and only the Margrave of Baden's 35,000 and Count Styrum's 10,000 imperial troops in the Lines of Stolhoffen and near Höchstädt respectively guarded western approaches. Elsewhere Marshal Villeroi was pinning the Anglo-Dutch forces in the Netherlands and the Duke of Vendôme was preparing yet another onslaught against Austria over the Alps from Savoy. The major threat to Vienna, however, was posed by the Elector of Bavaria and Marshal Marsin, whose troops were already poised around Ulm, only awaiting Tallard's arrival from Strasbourg through the Black Forest to launch an offensive with more than 71,000 men.

Despite the urgent entreaties of Austrian ambassadors during the preceding winter, the crises of southern Europe seemed comfortably remote to English and Dutch politicians. Only Marlborough and a few trusted friends realized the full implications of the developing situation on the Danube. 'For this campaign I see so very ill a prospect', he wrote on 20 February, 'that I am extremely out of heart.'

At almost 54, the Duke was widely regarded as a statesman of merit and a soldier of competence. In his

▶ The Allied army's mobility in 1704 was in no small part due to the light, two-horsed, two-wheeled wagons that Marlborough (as Master-General of the Ordnance, then responsible for military transport) insisted on being used. (The *Wynendael* (1708) tapestry by de Vos, after L. de Hondt).

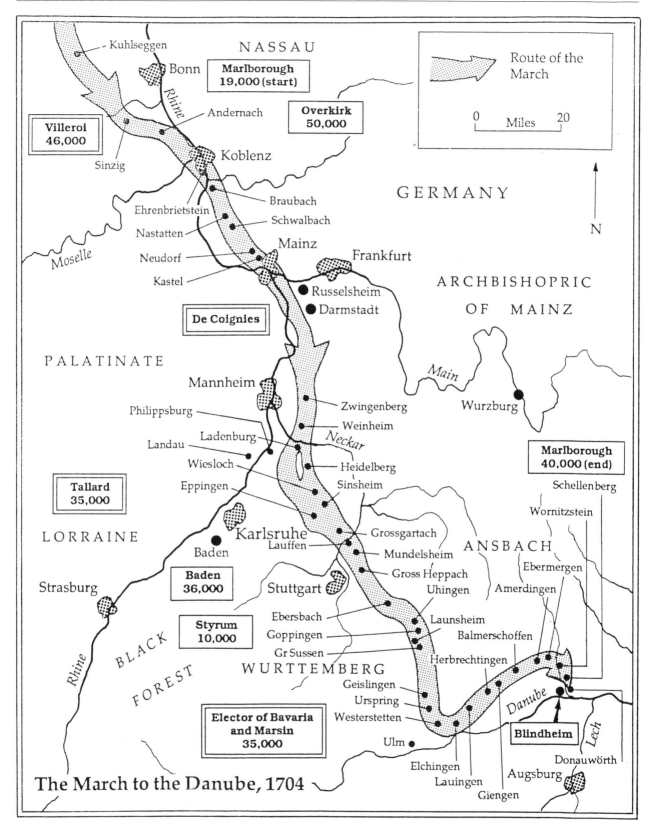

Kuhlseggen

NASSAU

Bonn

Marlborough 19,000 (start)

Andernach

Overkirk 50,000

Rhine

Villeroi 46,000

Sinzig

Koblenz

GERMANY

N

Braubach

Ehrenbrietstein

Schwalbach

Nastatten

Mainz

Frankfurt

Moselle

Neudorf

Kastel

Russelsheim

Darmstadt

ARCHBISHOPRIC

OF MAINZ

De Coignies

PALATINATE

Mannheim

Zwingenberg

Philippsburg

Weinheim

Ladenburg

Main

Wurzburg

Landau

Neckar

Wiesloch

Heidelberg

Marlborough 40,000 (end)

Eppingen

Sinsheim

Schellenberg

Tallard 35,000

Wornitzstein

LORRAINE

Karlsruhe

Grossgartach

Lauffen

ANSBACH

Baden

Mundelsheim

Ebermergen

Baden 36,000

Gross Heppach

Amerdingen

Strasburg

Stuttgart

Uhingen

BLACK

Ebersbach

Launsheim

Styrum 10,000

Goppingen

Balmerschoffen

FOREST

Gr Sussen

Herbrechtingen

Rhine

WURTTEMBERG

Geislingen

Danube

Elector of Bavaria and Marsin 35,000

Urspring

Westerstetten

Blindheim

Lech

Ulm

Donauwörth

Augsburg

Elchingen

Lauingen

Giengen

The March to the Danube, 1704

Route of the March

0 Miles 20

earlier career he had seen service on both land and sea, and as a young man had learnt his martial trade under the great French Marshal Turenne. King William III had used him to negotiate the Second Grand Alliance, and under his successor, Queen Anne, the fortunes of the Marlboroughs, husband and wife (long-established favourites of the new monarch), had seemingly reached their zenith. As Captain-General of the Anglo-Dutch forces, Marlborough had then fought two generally satisfactory if undramatic campaigns in the Netherlands region in 1702 and 1703, earning his dukedom thereby. The events of 1704, however, would earn him 'Great Captain' status.

A Famous March

Realizing the gravity of the situation facing Vienna, Marlborough secretly began to prepare the transfer of part of his Netherlands army to the Danube valley. He intended to remove Bavaria from the war with Austrian aid before Tallard could move his main army to Ulm. Such a project was fraught with immense political and military dangers. The Dutch – obsessed with their own security – would veto the scheme should they get wind of it; the Danish and German allies were already showing an unwillingness to participate. The stresses of a 250-mile march across Europe, much of the route dominated by French troops west of the Rhine with no friendly troops to cover Marlborough's advance from Mainz until he approached Philippsburg, appeared insupportable – especially as the survivors of such a dangerous flank-march could expect to fight a desperate battle after reaching the Danube theatre.

But Marlborough was the man for the task. By use of consummate bluff and comprehensive logistical planning, he proceeded to fool friend and foe alike. Leaving Bedburg on 20 May with 21,000 men, he announced he intended to campaign on the Moselle – as most expected he would. But crossing the Rhine at Koblenz (where he absorbed 5,000 unwilling Hanoverians, and then passing Mainz on 31 May (picking up 14,000 more Danish and German reinforcements), he confused both his opponents and allies. After Koblenz the Moselle bluff was patently over, but the army was now beyond recall, '. . . over the hills and far away', and a new apparent threat – to Louis XIV's prize acquisition, Strasburg, had replaced the earlier bluff. While the French marshals urgently sought fresh instructions from Versailles, Marl-

▲ John, Baron Cutts of Gowran (1661–1707). Nicknamed 'the Salamander' for his many times in the heat of the fray, Lord Cutts commanded the Allied left wing at Blenheim. (Attributed to G. Kneller)

borough carried through the most dangerous, uncovered, section of his march. The weather was appallingly wet, turning the crude roads into quagmires, but he required his men to cover only 10 to 12 miles a day, with a full rest-day after every four marches, and carefully laid out camping sites and supplies in advance of his 'scarlet caterpillar'. Fresh shoes and saddlery awaited the army at Heidelberg. No detail had been overlooked; each day's march was so conducted as to allow the men to rest during the main daylight hours. 'Surely never was such a march carried out with more regularity', wrote one participant, Captain Robert Parker, 'and with less fatigue to man and horse.'

With new lines of communication now running up the River Main, into friendly territory, Marlborough was no longer dependent upon the exposed Rhine. Assured by the Austrians that heavy guns would be provided, the Duke brought only his lighter pieces with him, and further to expedite the march he had equipped the army with light two-wheeled carts.

▲ Prince Eugène of Savoy – François-Eugène de Savoie-Carignan (1663–1736). Of Franco-Italian origins, by 1697 he had become an outstanding soldier in the service of Austria. In 1704 there began a special relationship with his older 'Twin-Captain', Marlborough. He would share in the credit for winning three of Marlborough's quatrain of great battles. (Painting by J. van Schuppen)

for Tallard, Marlborough took the less-reliable Baden with him, and suddenly seized Donauwörth and its bridges by a bloody *coup-de-main* against the Schellenberg Heights late in the afternoon of 2 July, for a price of 10,000 casualties. In an act of calculated ferocity, the Allies burnt between 300 and 400 defenceless Bavarian villages over a three-week period – but to no avail. The Elector would still neither fight nor negotiate – realizing that from early July Tallard was at last on the move to his aid. At length, shadowed by Eugène with a token force, a triumphant Tallard joined the Elector at Augsburg on 5 August for the loss of 5,000 stragglers and sick. But with a joint 73,000 Franco-Bavarians under command, Tallard believed the game was his. Passing the Danube by way of Lauingen, he turned east and leisurely proceeded towards Donauwörth, intent upon trapping the Allied army south of the river. Reacting to Eugène's urgent summons, Marlborough detached Baden with 20,000 men to besiege Ingoldstädt to the east while the remainder forced-marched via Rain and Merxheim to join the Prince near Munster. The scene was almost set for a major confrontation with the unsuspecting Tallard. A forward reconnaissance of the French encampment near Blindheim from Merxheim spire on the 12th convinced Marlborough and Eugène to risk all, to win or lose all by a surprise attack next morning following an approach march covered by darkness and the habitual river mist.

The Battle of Blenheim

Tallard never expected an attack. Fed with disinformation by Allied 'deserters' sent into his camp the previous day, he believed the Allies were heading for Nördlingen to protect their communications, as he wrote to Versailles as late as 7.30 a.m. on the 13th. It was only when his outposts fell back before the Allied columns, setting fire to the villages and mills as they came, that he realized he had been fooled. The French and Bavarian trumpets at last sounded the general alarm and by 8.30 p.m. they were clear of their camps and drawn up for battle. To anchor his right wing, in Blindheim village, Tallard placed nine battalions under the Marquis de Clérambault within the barricades and ready-loopholed farm walls, with a formation of dismounted dragoons linking him to the Danube's bank, and with eighteen more battalions – the army reserve – behind the village. Between Blindheim and Oberglau Tallard placed 64 squadrons

Supplies were bought in advance for gold, so there were few shortages, although prices rose rapidly. Thus, after a first conference at Gross Heppach on 13 June with 50-year-old Prince Louis of Baden and the 41-year-old Prince Eugène of Savoy (whose services Marlborough had secretly solicited the previous winter), the now 40,000-strong Allied Army linked up with the Habsburg forces at Launsheim on the 28th. Only 900 stragglers had fallen out from first to last, and Europe applauded a major military feat. The French had been out-thought, out-marched and out-manoeuvred.

But it remained to drive Bavaria out of the war before Tallard could reinforce the Elector. Now fate intervened. Austrian promises of field and heavy guns proved illusory; in consequence the foe could not be attacked at Ulm or Lauingen, where defended bridges spanned the broad Danube. Leaving Eugène to watch

of cavalry, supported by nine recently raised battalions, on a low ridge some 600 yards west of the Nebel. Oberglau itself was garrisoned by fourteen battalions under General de Blainville. Further north stood Marshal Marsin's cavalry (67 squadrons), and to hold his slightly refused left wing sixteen Bavarian battalions were placed in and around Lutzingen. To the north stretched a succession of wooded hills. Everything beyond Oberglau was under command of the Elector of Bavaria and Marsin. All in all it was a strong position, and with 56,000 men present to Marlborough's 52,000, and with 90 cannon deployed (to the Allies' 66) Tallard had reason for some confidence in the day's outcome.

He calculated, however, without taking Marlborough fully into account. Even worse, Tallard spent the whole morning in idleness, merely bombarding what he could see of Marlborough's left wing and centre to the east of the Nebel, where the regiments were ordered to lie down in the cornfields to minimize the effects of the French shot while Morning Service was said and rations issued. This was a time of some anxiety for Milord Duke, for Prince Eugène's columns had been badly delayed in the hilly country on the

▶ English grenadiers struggle through the Nebel stream and marshes during the battle of Blenheim. Each regiment of foot included one company of handpicked grenadiers who often served as storm-troops, using small axes as well as muskets, bayonets, swords and rudimentary grenades as weapons. (Painting by Louis Laguerre)

right, and could not be in position until after midday. Tallard could have used this period to launch an attack in overwhelming strength – catching the Allied army in two unconnected parts – but instead he preferred to hold his ground in inaction, thus surrendering the tactical initiative to his opponents. Marlborough used the long lull to bridge the Nebel and its marshes at several points with straw and timber.

At last, at 12.30 p.m., news arrived that Eugène was in position facing Lutzingen. At this stage the Allied army was disposed as follows. Nearest to the Danube stood twenty battalions (including most of the English formations) and fourteen squadrons under Lord Cutts. Facing the passive French centre General Charles Churchill (Marlborough's brother) drew up seventeen battalions in the front line, then two lines of cavalry totalling 72 squadrons, and in rear of all eleven more battalions. The Prince of Holstein-Beck faced Oberglau village with ten German battalions, while on the Allied right, Prince Eugène deployed his 92 squadrons and eighteen battalions of foot. The cannon were sited at intervals along the line.

Marlborough had long decided upon his plan of battle. While Prince Eugène kept the Franco-Bavarian left wing in play, Marlborough intended to break through Tallard's centre, having first captured or at least contained the village-fortresses of Blindheim and Oberglau so as to secure the flanks of his centre's advance. The passage of the Nebel would be far from easy, but the Duke had faith in the courage of his men and the fullest trust in his younger co-commander, Eugène. Neither was to be misplaced.

Shortly before 1 p.m., Marlbrough ordered Cutts to attack Blenheim. The advance was made in disci-plined silence, but the French positions proved strong. Two brigade attacks in turn were repelled (Lord Rowe was numbered among the killed), but Clérambault was so impressed with the ferocity of the British and Hanoverian attacks that he drew first seven and then the remaining eleven battalions of Tallard's reserve infantry into the village without informing his chief. So densely were they packed into Blindheim that many could not use their muskets. All this was clear to Marlborough's trained spyglass. Lord Cutts was about to launch a third assault when he was ordered to desist, and instead to hem in the village's overblown garrison by fire action alone with his fifteen remaining battalions. And this he proceeded to do – a good example of economy of force. Marlborough could feel that his left flank was now secure.

While these attacks were in progress, a celebrated cavalry engagement had been taking place just to the north of Blindheim. In support of their garrison spurred forward nine splendidly accoutred squadrons of the élite *Gendarmerie*. To meet them came Colonel Palmes at the head of only five scratch English squadrons. Under the eyes of both commanders-in-chief, Palmes proceeded to give the *Gendarmerie* a severe drubbing. This small setback preyed on Tallard's mind for the rest of the day, and formed the first tale of woe in his eventual report to Louis XIV.

While Eugène faced up to Lutzingen on the right, Marlborough next turned his attention to Oberglau. Holstein-Beck's first attack was driven back with severe loss by the 'Wild Geese' (Irish Catholic exiles in the French service). But the Duke was at hand to order up aid, including Colonel Blood who somehow manhandled eight cannon over the Nebel and its marshes to provide close fire-support. Thus by 3 p.m., Oberglau in its turn was safely contained and neutral-ized.

The flanks of his centre secured by these moves, Marlborough now ordered his brother to advance in his four lines of formations. Barely half were over the Nebel when their right came under heavy attack by part of Marsin's horsemen, who bypassed Oberglau to strike Churchill's flank. In dismay the Allies gave ground. To meet the crisis, Marlborough sent off a desperate message to Eugène, requesting his aid. Although deeply committed to battle himself, the Prince without hesitation sent over his last remaining cavalry – Brigadier-General Fugger's cuirassiers. These heavy horsemen crashed into the flank of Marsin's near-triumphant rallying cavalry in their

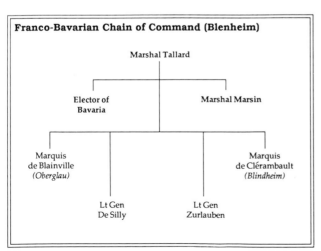

Franco-Bavarian Chain of Command (Blenheim)

Marshal Tallard

Elector of Bavaria   Marshal Marsin

Marquis de Blainville (*Oberglau*)   Marquis de Clérambault (*Blindheim*)

Lt Gen De Silly   Lt Gen Zurlauben

turn, and soon the Allied situation had been stabilized and conceded ground regained.

The time had come to launch the decisive attack against Tallard's centre. Forward rode the front line of Allied squadrons; but just as they were breasting the slope they received a down-hill countercharge led by the *Gendarmerie* under Count Zurlauben. The impact was terrible, and the Allied squadrons found themselves bundled back towards the Nebel marshes in complete disorder. Again the possibility of defeat stared the Allies in the face. But Marlborough had devised the four-deep centre to meet just such an eventuality. To the aid of the scattered horsemen marched the cool second line of infantry, including the brigade of Lord Orkney. 'I marched with my battalions to sustain the Horse, and found them repulsed, crying out for Foot, being pressed by the *Gendarmerie*. I went to the head of several squadrons and got 'em to rally on my right and left, and brought up four pieces of cannon, and then charged.' The French

▲ Derby's Regiment (later the 16th Foot, the Bedfordshire and Hertfordshire Regiment, today 3 Royal Anglian) marching to attack the village of Blindheim early in the action as part of Cutts's left wing. (Watercolour by R. Simkins)

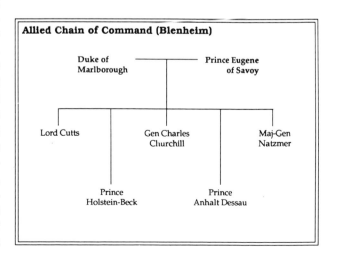

Allied Chain of Command (Blenheim)

```
        Duke of ————————————————— Prince Eugene
      Marlborough                    of Savoy
           │
    ┌──────┼──────────────────────┐
  Lord Cutts      Gen Charles      Maj-Gen
                   Churchill        Natzmer
       │               │
     Prince          Prince
  Holstein-Beck   Anhalt Dessau
```

cavalry recoiled in their turn. It was 4 p.m.. And now Marlborough had massed 80 squadrons and 23 battalions over the Nebel facing just 60 blown and disordered French squadrons supported by only nine battalions of foot. This grand tactical formula of concentration of force at the critical point and time gave the Allied command a considerable advantage. Tallard's centre was effectively doomed.

And so it proved. As Danish troops worked their way through the wooded hills to outflank distant Lutzingen, and Prince Eugène led a second (ultimately fruitless) frontal attack against the Elector's and Marsin's superior numbers, Marlborough ordered his cavalry to attack. The serried ranks of horsemen advanced uphill at a fast trot, and after a fierce struggle the French resistance cracked, and their cavalry turned and fled, some towards Höchstädt, others towards the Danube, where many drowned attempting to swim the river. The nine battalions fought and died where they stood – but of no avail to their comrades.

Marshal Tallard – whose son had been killed at his side earlier in the battle – made an attempt to reach his troops in Blindheim, but was intercepted, taken prisoner and escorted to Marlborough, who courteously put his coach at his disconsolate adversary's disposal. Away to the north, the Elector and Marsin adjudged the day lost, and proceeded to extricate their wing from Eugène's exhausted troops and retreated west.

Dusk was beginning to fall as the Allied left and centre closed in upon Blindheim village from all sides. Within its barricades stood some 21 battalions of virtually unused French infantry, far fresher and more numerous than the exhausted Allies who now penned them in. The battle might even now have had a different postscript but for certain circumstances. The Blenheim garrison at this crisis found themselves leaderless, for Clérambault had ridden into the Danube and drowned there. But the massed French infantry might still have fought their way out through the attenuated Allied lines. However, Churchill and Orkney found an answer to the problem. Setting fire to the thatch roofs on a group of cottages to the west of Blindheim, and then damping it down with water from the Danube, had the effect of sending dense clouds of smoke rolling down to blind and discomfort the French in Blindheim. The firing of the cottages, recalled Orkney, '. . . we could easily perceive annoyed them very much, and seeing two brigades appear as if

they intended to push their way out through our troops, who were very fatigued, it came into my head to beat a parley, which they accepted of and immediately their brigadier de Nouville capitulat [sic] with me to be prisoner at descretione [sic] and lay down their arms'. Within an hour, 11,000 dazed and bewildered French infantry – many from the cream of Louis XIV's regiments – had been disarmed.

The Strategic Situation Reversed

'I have no time to say more,' wrote a weary Marlborough in pencil on the back of a tavern bill in a message to his wife, 'but to beg that you will give my duty to the Queen, and let her know her army has had a glorious victory. Monsieur Tallard and two other generals are in my coach, and I am following the rest. The bearer, my Aide-de-Camp Colonel Parke, will give her an account of what has passed. I shall do it in a day or two by another more at large.' The message reached Anne at Windsor on 21 August, and its bearer was rewarded with a miniature of the Queen and a thousand guineas in gold.

▲ A charge of heavy cavalry, or cuirassiers, probably at Malplaquet (1709), Marlborough's final and most dearly bought field success. Huge cavalry attacks – delivered at a fast trot – clinched two of his major victories, the first being Blenheim.

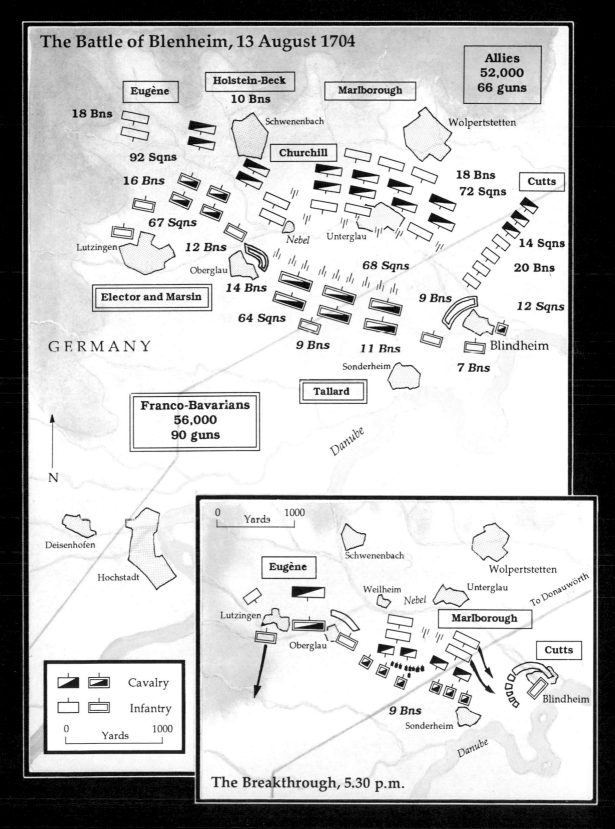

The Battle of Blenheim, 1704

The Battle of Blenheim, 13 August 1704

Allies
52,000
66 guns

Eugène

Holstein-Beck
10 Bns

Marlborough

18 Bns

Schwenenbach

Wolpertstetten

92 Sqns

Churchill

16 Bns

18 Bns
72 Sqns

Cutts

67 Sqns

Nebel

Unterglau

14 Sqns

Lutzingen

12 Bns

20 Bns

Oberglau

68 Sqns

9 Bns

12 Sqns

Elector and Marsin

14 Bns

Blindheim

64 Sqns

GERMANY

9 Bns

11 Bns

7 Bns

Sonderheim

Franco-Bavarians
56,000
90 guns

Tallard

Danube

N

Deisenhofen

Hochstadt

0   Yards   1000

Eugène

Schwenenbach

Wolpertstetten

Weilheim   Nebel   Unterglau

To Donauwörth

Marlborough

Lutzingen

Oberglau

Cutts

Blindheim

9 Bns

Sonderheim

Danube

Cavalry

Infantry

0   Yards   1000

The Breakthrough, 5.30 p.m.

The fruits of victory were impressive. For the loss of 12,500 casualties the Allies had inflicted (stragglers included) more than 40,000 on their foes, including 14,000 captives, and taken 60 cannon, 34 cavalry standards and 128 colours (many destined to decorate St. Paul's Cathedral). To this day the quit-rent for Blenheim Palace, built for the victor at the nation's expense, takes the form of a miniature copy of the *Maison du Roi*'s captured *fleur-de-lys* banner presented by the present duke to his sovereign on each anniversary of the battle. All the French and Bavarian baggage and camps were also booty of war. As an aghast Louis XIV wryly remarked when news of the disaster reached him, he '. . . had never heard of an army being taken before'. The strategic situation was reversed by the great battle besides the Danube. The threat to Vienna and the Alliance was abruptly removed; Ingolstädt duly fell to the Margrave of Baden (infuriated to find himself cheated of a share in the climacteric battle), followed by Ulm and Augsburg, and by the end of the year Allied troops would be west of the Rhine on French territory, besieging and capturing Landau on the approaches to Strasburg. Marlborough had emerged as a Great Captain.

Not since Agincourt in 1415 had British martial prestige been raised to a higher point. Richard Pope of the 7th Dragoon Guards enthused that '"Blenheim" [as it was instantly dubbed by the illiterate rank and file] . . . was the greatest and most glorious action that has happened in several ages'. Valour, trust and mutual co-operation, between officer and man, between Englishman, Dane and Austrian, and above all between Marlborough and Prince Eugène, lay at the heart of the victory. 'Without vanity,' concluded Orkney, 'I think we all did our pairts.' And such has been the verdict of posterity. As Marshal Tallard reviewed the victorious Allied army at Marlborough's side two days after the battle, he remarked sadly: 'I hope your Grace is aware that you have had the honour to defeat the best troops in the world?' To which the urbane Marlborough returned the perfect, polished reply that said it all: 'Your Lordship, I presume, excepts those who have had the honour to beat them?'

BIBLIOGRAPHY

Atkinson, C. T. *Marlborough and the Rise of the British Army*, London, 1921. In many ways the best overall coverage of its subject in a single volume.

Chandler, D. G. *Marlborough as Military Commander*, London, 1973 (reissued, Tunbridge Wells, 1990). A modern account incorporating recent research.

Chandler, D. G. *The Art of War in the Age of Marlborough*, London, 1975 (reissued, Tunbridge Wells, 1991). A useful analysis of the military organization, equipment and employment of armies in the early eighteenth century.

Churchill, W. S. *Marlborough – His Life and Times*, 2 vols. edn., London, 1947. Still the standard biography, although rather biased in its subject's favour. It contains a remarkable account and analysis of the campaign and battle of 1704.

Henderson, N. *Prince Eugène of Savoy*, London, 1964. A good biography of Marlborough's 'Twin Captain'.

Green, D. *Blenheim*, London, 1974. A useful description of the events of 1704, including modern photographs.

Hattendorf, J. B. *England in the War of the Spanish Succession*, New York, 1987. A masterly examination of English grand strategy throughout the war.

Verney, P. *The Battle of Blenheim*, London, 1976. A good, general account although it misidentifies the Deane Journal as that of a Captain Hunter.

Note: Much is also to be gained by reading the published memoirs of the following contemporaries and participants: Lieutenant-Colonel John Blackader; Private Sentinel John Marshall Deane; Sergeant John Milner; Brigadier-General Lord Orkney; and Captain Robert Parker. For the Franco-Bavarian view see Comte d'Arco and the Comte de Mérode-Westerloo. The reader should not be daunted by Murray's *The Marlborough Despatches*, 5 vols., London, 1845, which clearly show the range of duties – political and diplomatic as well as military that pursued the Duke in full campaign as well as out.

▲ In 1964, the South Wales Borderers (today the Royal Regiment of Wales) remarched the route of their ancestors (Marlborough himself held the colonelcy of what was later the 24th Foot from 1702 to 1704) and laid a wreath at the modern memorial.

DETTINGEN COMPANY CREST
RMA SANDHURST

THE BATTLE OF DETTINGEN, 1743

by Michael Orr

'Do ye see yon loons on yon grey hill?
Well, if ya dinna kill them, they'll kill you!'

(Sir Andrew Agnew to Campbell's Regiment)

The village of Dettingen lies some thirty kilometres south-west of Frankfurt; of major British battlefields only Blenheim lies deeper in the heart of Europe. Looking at the map it is hard not to wonder what a British army was doing there. The battle of Dettingen was fought between a French Army and an allied British, Hanoverian and Austrian army; at a time when these nations were not at war with one another. Why then were they fighting?

An Austrian Family Quarrel

The short answer is that they supported the claims of rival Habsburg princesses to inherit the Austrian Empire. The Emperor Leopold I had two sons, Joseph I, who ruled from 1705 to 1711, and Charles VI who was emperor from 1711 to 1740. Neither emperor had a son and Leopold had intended that Joseph's daughters should take precedence over Charles's. But by the famous Pragmatic Sanction of 1713 Charles had changed the order of succession in favour of his daughter, Maria Theresa. Charles had obtained the agreement of the major powers to this change but at the cost of involving Austria in two unsuccessful wars. Thus he weakened his army and impoverished the country while drawing attention to the vulnerability of the Austrian Empire.

The first predator to strike was the King of Prussia. Frederick II had succeeded his father in May 1740. Whereas the old king had been instinctively loyal to the emperor, his son had his eye to the main chance. In December 1740 he invaded Silesia and by the spring had defeated the Austrian army at Mollwitz. The Electors of Saxony and Bavaria put forward the claims of their wives, Joseph's daughters, and were supported by French troops.

England was inclined to support Maria Theresa, fearing French gains in the Austrian Netherlands. As Elector of Hanover, King George II had no wish to see his Prussian nephew increase his power in northern Germany. Parliament voted subsidies to Maria Theresa and George began to organize an army in Hanover. But when Prussia and France moved armies to the eastern and western borders of Hanover George had to agree to remain neutral for a year.

Although isolated, Maria Theresa launched successful counter-attacks against the French, Bavarian and Saxon forces. During the winter of 1741 and the summer of 1742 an Austrian army entered Bavaria

and blockaded the Franco-Bavarian army in Bohemia at Prague. Frederick was happy to make peace in return for much of Silesia, and Saxony also dropped out of the reckoning. With his year's neutrality ended, George was able to persuade Parliament to send English troops to join Hanoverian and Hessian contingents in the Netherlands. This force was known as the 'Pragmatic Army' and were officially only 'auxiliaries' of Maria Theresa, just as the French were only 'auxiliaries' of the Elector of Bavaria.

There followed an autumn of inaction in the Netherlands. The move of the French army in Westphalia southwards to secure Bavaria and support their forces in Bohemia exposed the French border. The commander-in-chief of the Pragmatic Army was Field Marshal the Earl of Stair. Stair had been a gallant if headstrong brigadier-general under Marlborough, and a most successful ambassador to France. He was now nearly 70 but still energetic. Stair put forward various plans for an invasion of France but none of

◄ **His Most Christian Majesty Louis XV (1715–74), whose army was defeated at Dettingen. His reign would see many set-backs, including the loss of New France (Canada), Bengal (India) and several 'sugar islands' in the West Indies.**

◄ **Unlike his father, King George II of the Royal House of Hanover did at least speak English. He had served as a prince under Marlborough, and is supposed to have worn his old red-coat at Dettingen. He was the last king of England to command in battle.**

▶ **French cavalryman, *c.* 1744. The *Maison du Roi* was the crack cavalry of the French monarchy, and comprised several regiments. The type represented here is a Horse Grenadier. (Engraving by de Ferhrt after C. Eisen)**

them met George's favour. The army settled into a not-uncomfortable existence in winter quarters. Many officers returned to England on leave and no doubt discipline suffered. A general order in December noted that, 'Lord Stair receiving daily complaints of disorders committed by drunken soldiers and particularly those of the foot guards, recommends it to the commanding officers to endeavour to suppress that scandalous practice so prejudicial to the Service and to the men's health.'

In Marlborough's Footsteps

During the winter plans were laid for the campaign of 1743. The centre of gravity was to be on the Rhine. The Austrians wanted to bring the Pragmatic Army to threaten the French retreat from Prague. King

▲ A British Royal Dragoon of the mid-eighteenth century. He carries a shortened musket (or carbine) as well as a sword and a pair of pistols, and wears two broad cross-belts. Thomas Brown of the Third Dragoons would have been equipped in this fashion.

George was not willing to go so far, but he did order Stair to concentrate in Juliers and then to join the Austrian army under General Ahrenburg on the line of the River Lahn which meets the Rhine near Koblenz. The severe winter delayed the march; by the end of April the bulk of the army was on the Lahn, though the cavalry was still lagging behind for lack of forage. George then authorized an advance to Mainz, where the River Main meets the Rhine, in order to ensure the election of his own candidate as Archbishop of the city.

Meanwhile the French had spent the winter raising a new army under Marshal de Noailles in Alsace. De Noailles was to observe the Pragmatic Army and cover communications with Bavaria. By the end of May he had crossed the Rhine at Worms and concentrated between the Rivers Main and Neckar. He was not seeking a battle with the Allies, but hoped to out-manoeuvre them and deny them supplies until they were forced to withdraw.

Stair as usual favoured aggressive action. He pushed a bridgehead across the Main west of Frankfurt and wanted to advance up the Rhine valley. He was prevented from doing so and when de Noailles declined to attack his bridgehead he withdrew it. If the army was to stay between Frankfurt and Mainz it needed a secure line of supply. The Rhine was closed by the French, leaving only the Main to bring supplies down from Franconia. Logistic necessity drove Stair to try to secure this line. However Ahrenburg distrusted Stair and refused to support him. The army reached Aschaffenburg in mid-June, but the French had already occupied the western bank of the river, so cutting off supplies from up river.

King George II joined the army at Aschaffenburg on 19 June, finding it on short rations and with its senior commanders squabbling among themselves. The French army was also going hungry and steady trickles of deserters passed from each side to the other, in the mistaken belief that they would find a square meal. George delayed until 26 June before giving the order to retire on Hanau, where he expected to meet reinforcements. But de Noailles had anticipated the move and ordered pontoon bridges to be built at Seligenstadt. By 24 June French troops were east of the Main, cutting the Allies' line of retreat.

In ignorance of the true position, the Pragmatic Army spent the daylight hours of 26 June in covert preparations for their retreat. No move was allowed before dark although units were camped in a very

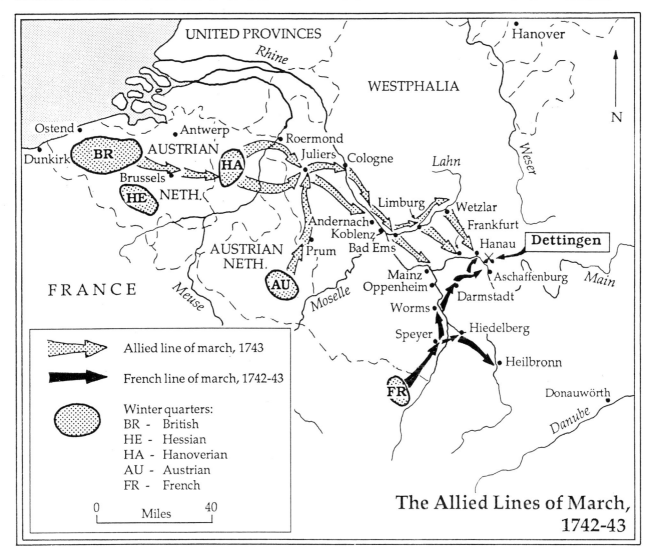

The Allied Lines of March, 1742-43

Legend:

Allied line of march, 1743

French line of march, 1742-43

Winter quarters:
BR - British
HE - Hessian
HA - Hanoverian
AU - Austrian
FR - French

0 — Miles — 40

different order from that in which they were to march. A strong rearguard was to be created from the English Guards, the Hanoverian élite Luneburg battalions and the Hanoverian cavalry because the main French threat was thought to come from the south. The retreat northwards was to be led by the bulk of the cavalry, followed by the infantry and the baggage train. The march was to be in two columns, but only one bridge was available over the Steinbach at Kleinostheim. Anyone who has ever taken part in a military night move can imagine the result. Confusion, curses and chaos abounded. Dawn found the Pragmatic Army in something like the correct order of march, but no nearer its destination. By an hour after midnight de Noailles knew of the confusion in the Allied camp and, having seen for himself that the

Allies were on the move, ordered more troops across the Main at Seligenstadt and Aschaffenburg.

The Day of Battle

De Noailles claimed that he had the Allies in a mousetrap and by 8 a.m. George must have begun to think so too. Across his army's line of retreat lay a strong French force. The enemy were well placed on a hill and their front protected by two boggy streams, the Forchbach and the Häggraben. The only dry crossing was a bridge in the village of Dettingen on the banks of the Main. The rear of his army was threatened by the French advancing through Aschaffenburg. On the opposite bank of the Main reinforcements could be seen hurrying to join the two blocking

◄ First Guards, *c.* 1745. The print shows two officers (left), a Grenadier (centre) and a 'private sentinel' (sometimes known in other units as a 'hatman'). (Print by Clayton)

forces. As they passed they revealed batteries of artillery which opened fire into the flanks of the Allied column. Only in the east was the enemy missing and on this side, within a couple of miles of the river, lay the Spessart Hills, completely impassable to formed bodies of troops.

There was little that George could do except fight his way out. He ordered his artillery to engage the French batteries west of the Main, though to little effect. The body of the army moved off at right angles to the road and deployed into a makeshift line of battle. Two lines of cavalry squadrons covered the deployment. Four Hanoverian battalions formed the right of the line; nine Austrian regiments took the centre and twelve British battalions stood on the left. The Foot Guards were allotted the task of defending the baggage train. At about midday the deployment was complete and the infantry battalions passed through the lines of cavalry to begin the grim task of clearing the ridge ahead. Sir Andrew Agnew, who commanded Campbell's Regiment (Royal Scots Fusiliers), is said to have briefed his men succinctly: 'Do ye see yon loons on yon grey hill? Well, if ye dinna kill them, they'll kill you.'

But the whole complexion of the battle was beginning to change. The French brigades north of Dettingen were commanded by de Noailles's nephew, the Duc de Grammont. De Noailles sent him an order to occupy the village of Dettingen, but de Grammont

thought he could do better than that. He began to march his entire corps through the village, determined to attack rather than be attacked. De Noailles, who had crossed to the eastern bank to hasten his reserves, could only watch as his nephew's folly destroyed his skilful plans. It was now the French line of battle which was disordered by passing through the village or the marshes to the east. It was impossible for the French to reform south of Dettingen for lack of space and they were forced into a series of disjointed attacks. We can establish some sort of sequence of these attacks but the reality was exceptionally confused, as assaults merged into one another.

As the two battle lines approached one another the inexperienced English troops began to open fire. The range was too great to be effective and one eye-witness said it was '. . . like a Feu de Joie, it was neither directed by officers nor regulated by platoons, except among some few Austrians'. The sudden crash of muskets frightened King George's horse which took off with its enraged master and was only halted some way to the rear. Tradition says that George's ride was halted by soldiers of the Cheshire Regiment, underneath an oak tree and that the regiment was later granted the right to wear oak leaves in their hats in commemoration, but there is no reference to the regiment's presence in contemporary orders of battle.

The first French attack was led by the *Gardes Françaises* themselves, but was not pressed home in

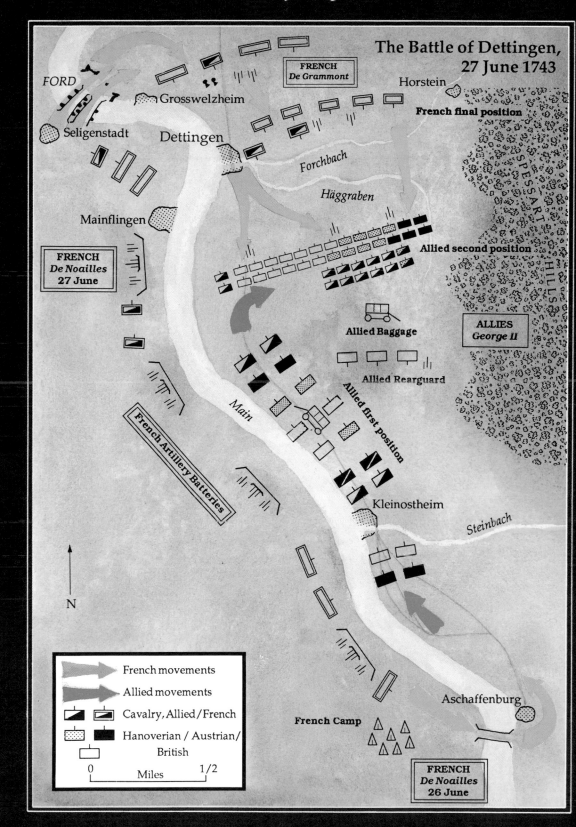

The Battle of Dettingen,
27 June 1743

FORD

Grosswelzheim

FRENCH
De Grammont

Horstein

French final position

Seligenstadt

Dettingen

Forchbach

Häggraben

SPESSART HILLS

Allied second position

Mainflingen

FRENCH
De Noailles
27 June

Allied Baggage

ALLIES
George II

Allied Rearguard

Main

Allied first position

French Artillery Batteries

Kleinostheim

Steinbach

N

French movements

Allied movements

Cavalry, Allied / French

Hanoverian / Austrian /
British

0   Miles   1/2

Aschaffenburg

French Camp

FRENCH
De Noailles
26 June

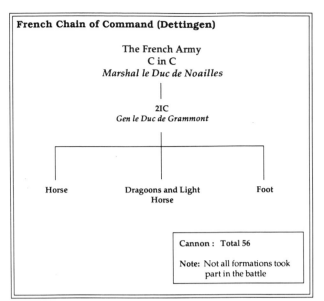

French Chain of Command (Dettingen)

The French Army
C in C
Marshal le Duc de Noailles

2IC
Gen le Duc de Grammont

Horse   Dragoons and Light Horse   Foot

Cannon : Total 56

Note: Not all formations took part in the battle

the face of steady Austrian fire in the centre. As the French foot guards fell back the household cavalry, the *Maison du Roi*, seized their chance to charge. In a solid mass, eight to ten ranks deep, they struck at the Allied left. Here there was a gap of a few hundred yards between the river and the infantry which was at first covered only by two squadrons of Bland's Dragoons (3rd Hussars). Bland's met the challenge heroically, cutting their way through the French cavalry. When one of the Third Dragoons' guidons was captured, Trooper Thomas Brown recovered it, although he received three bullets through his hat and seven sword wounds in the process.

▼ British infantry in close action, Dettingen. Amid the smoke of battle George II mistook one unit for 'the Buffs' (the 3rd of Foot). Apprised of his error, he promptly dubbed the regiment (in fact the 31st of Foot) 'the Young Buffs'.

Bland's could not stop the *Maison du Roi* completely, however, and the *Gendarmes* and the *Chevaux-Légers* struck some of the English infantry as they endeavoured to form square. The fighting was confused but Campbell's, Huske's (Duke of Cornwall's Light Infantry) and Sowle's (Devonshire Regiment) men stood their ground. The impetuosity of the *Maison du Roi* left their own flank open. General Clayton sent forward Honeywood's and Ligonier's Horse (1st King's Dragoon Guards and 7th Dragoon Guards). They made the mistake of trusting to their pistols rather than charging home with the sword, and by galloping too fast lost formation. As they recoiled Honeywood's troops crashed into the Blues who were

▼ George II launches the British cavalry forward in a charge at Dettingen.

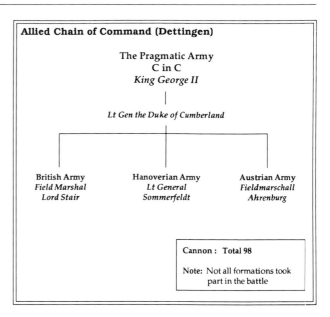

Allied Chain of Command (Dettingen)

The Pragmatic Army
C in C
King George II

|
Lt Gen the Duke of Cumberland

British Army	Hanoverian Army	Austrian Army
Field Marshal	*Lt General*	*Fieldmarschall*
Lord Stair	*Sommerfeldt*	*Ahrenburg*

Cannon : Total 98

Note: Not all formations took part in the battle

moving up in support. The Blues wheeled back and forced their way through their own infantry.

Eye-witness accounts of the battle are confused about the order of subsequent events. The French infantry had returned to the attack but a confused cavalry fight still continued on the left. At one stage the *Mousquetaires Noirs* swerved across the battlefield to the right flank, possibly in the hope of capturing the king. They were met and shattered by English and Austrian dragoons. Eventually weight of numbers began to tell on the *Maison du Roi* and they gave ground under flanking fire from the English infantry and frontal attacks from the Allied cavalry.

Meanwhile the French infantry were making little progress against the Allies. Unable to deploy their full strength because of the cramped battlefield, the French continued to attack as their brigades came up. Forced back, they would rally and return to the assault

with some fresh force, only to be halted and driven back again.

The volume of fire and the steadfastness of the Allied infantry, backed by some skilful work from the Hanoverian artillery on the right flank, eventually gave the Pragmatic Army the upper hand in the fire fight. De Noailles later told the French king that, 'The oldest officers have never seen such a heavy and continuous fire, which unfortunately is completely unknown among Your Majesty's troops.' However, many Allied officers were not so impressed by their musketry. James Wolfe who, at the age of sixteen, was adjutant of Duroure's (the Suffolk Regiment), wrote that, '. . . the Major and I . . . were employed in begging and ordering the men not to fire at too great a distance, but to keep it until the enemy should come near us; but to little purpose. The whole fired when they thought they could reach them, which had like

◀ Cornet Richardson of Ligonier's Horse (later the 7th Dragoon Guards and today the 4th/7th Royal Dragoon Guards) defending his regimental standard at the battle on 27 June 1743. (Painting by Harry Payne)

▶ Private Thomas Brown of the 3rd King's Own Regiment of Dragoons recapturing the regimental guidon from the French during the battle. (A painting attributed to Richard Ansdell)

to have ruined us. We did very little execution by it.' Another officer recorded that, 'They were under no command by way of Hyde Park firing, but the whole three ranks made a running fire of their own accord, . . . The French fired in the same manner, I mean like a running fire without waiting for words of command and Lord Stair did often say he had seen many a battle, and never saw the infantry engage in any other manner.'

English officers may have been conscious of the failure to observe the Drill Books, but the French were more aware that their enemy continued to stand and fire. In the contest of wills the French impressions were decisive. Pursued by Allied cheers they began to pull back through Dettingen although no more orders were given for the retreat than for the original attack. Although Stair urged a vigorous pursuit, the Allied soldiers had been on their feet for nearly 24 hours and

the plan was simply not practicable. The French were shepherded across their bridges by some long-range artillery fire but once the Pragmatic Army had passed the Dettingen bottleneck it bivouaced where it was, although tents and bedding had been left behind at the start of the day. Almost immediately it began to rain. On the battlefield marauders began to strip the dead and wounded of their valuables.

Next day the Pragmatic Army continued its withdrawal to Hanau, leaving 400 of the most seriously wounded to the care of the French. Total Allied casualties were about two and a half thousand, with French losses being nearly twice as high. Although 12,000 reinforcements joined them at Hanau, the Allies still had no overwhelming superiority over the French. Morale and discipline in the French army were weak and an aggressive strategy might have brought great gains. Two months passed in haggling

◄ Contemporary print of the Battle of Dettingen, seen from the south. To the left is the River Main, and the two French pontoon bridges linking Seligenstadt to Grosswelzheim. Less accurately, Aschaffenburg is depicted in the foreground – in fact two miles distant – and Dettingen is placed beyond the bridges.

about a joint campaign with an Austrian army under Prince Charles of Lorraine from the upper Rhine. Operations petered out with a weak thrust across the Rhine at Oppenheim at the end of August which had reached Speyer by 27 September. On 11 October the Pragmatic Army began to move back into winter quarters which were once again located in the Netherlands.

So, despite the wild celebrations with which London greeted the news of victory at Dettingen, the summer campaign of 1743 actually achieved very little. 'A lot of noise about very little and a lot of men killed uselessly,' was Frederick the Great's harsh verdict. France eventually declared war on England and Hanover in March 1744 and in May invaded the Netherlands, provoking four years of stalemated campaigning in the 'cockpit of Europe'. But if Dettingen had little positive impact on the outcome of the War of the Austrian Succession, the battle may well have influenced the fate of the British throne. If de Noailles's plan had succeeded as it deserved George would have been forced into a capitulation. The war was not popular in England and defeat would almost certainly have been followed by the fall of the government. A new administration would probably have been forced to negotiate withdrawal from the continent. Would the humiliated George then have been able to resist the pressure of a Jacobite Rebellion? As it was, the 1745 Rising was crushed at Culloden by battle-hardened troops from Flanders, including six battalions that had fought at Dettingen,

and commanded by another Dettingen veteran, the Duke of Cumberland.

Between the glories of Marlborough's campaigns and Pitt's colonial victories in the Seven Years War, the events of the War of The Austrian Succession tend to be forgotten. If the battle of Dettingen is remembered today it is usually as the last occasion on which an English king commanded his troops in battle. But it would be wrong to take a purely negative view of the victory. After thirty years of peace and neglect it was no mean professional achievement to have defeated an army thought to be the best in Europe. The credit for victory belongs to the junior officers and their men who kept their nerve and saved the day, despite the failures of their generals.

BIBLIOGRAPHY

Bolitho, H. *The Galloping Third*, London, 1963. Contains an interesting account of a cavalry regiment (the 3rd Dragoon Guards, now part of the Royal Scots Dragoon Guards).

Graham, J. M. *The Annals and Correspondence of the Earls of Stair*, London, 1875. Useful documentation on political and higher command aspects.

Orr, M. J. *Dettingen 1743*, London, 1972. The only relatively modern overall account – concise and interesting.

Pajol, Comte de. *Les Guerres sous Louis XV*, Paris, 1884. The French view.

Robinson, R. E. R. *The Bloody Eleventh*, Exeter, 1988, vol. 1. Another regimental history (of, today, the Devon and Dorsetshire Regiment) with a careful and detailed account of the battle of Dettingen.

Skrine, F. H. *Fontenoy and the War of Austrian Succession*, London, 1906. A masterly work, if now rather dated.

SALAMANCA COMPANY CREST
RMA SANDHURST

THE BATTLE OF SALAMANCA, 1812

by David Chandler

'The battle almost raises Lord Wellington to the level of the Duke of Marlborough . . . At Salamanca he has shown himself a great and able master of manoeuvre.'

(General Foy, French divisional commander at Salamanca)

By April 1812 the capture of the frontier fortresses of Ciudad Rodrigo and Badajoz (controlling the Spanish exits of the two main corridors linking Portugal to Spain) at last permitted Wellington to plan a major offensive deep into French-held territory. The Peninsular War was already well into its fifth year. Since August 1808 British troops had been committed to the aid of Spanish and Portuguese resistance to French occupation, but only when Napoleon transferred substantial forces to prepare for the invasion of Russia did a real opportunity for initiating the reconquest of Spain itself materialize.

Liberation for Spain

The possession of the two major invasion routes permitted Wellington to select his line of advance and at the same time confuse French military intelligence as to his true intentions. There were five French armies still in Spain – totalling some 230,000 men – while the Earl could call upon a notional field army of 75,000 Anglo-Portuguese and Spanish regulars and perhaps as many more in garrisons, supported by an uncertain number of partisans and guerrillas. Large numbers of King Joseph Bonaparte's formations were fully occupied in countering the disruptive activities of the latter and in neutralizing what was left of the Spanish regular armies, so the initiative rested with the Allies.

When he launched his major offensive in mid-June 1812, Arthur Wellesley was aged 43. The third son of an aristocratic Anglo-Irish family, his abilities as a commander and military administrator – built upon experience in Flanders, India and more recently Portugal – were approaching their highest development. Following the fall of Badajoz in April he could choose between two courses of action. He could either strike through the southern corridor against Marshal Soult's *Armée du Sud* to raise the blockade of Cadiz and liberate Andalusia, or advance through Ciudad Rodrigo along the northern invasion route to strike Marshal Marmont's so-called *Armée de Portugal*. On balance, the latter course held more apparent advantages. Although Marmont might receive aid from French armies to his north and east, Allied possession of Alcantara bridge on the Tagus effectively isolated him from Soult; further, any thrust towards Burgos on the key Madrid to Bayonne highway was likely to lead to a major battle –

▲ French *voltigeurs* (literally 'leapers') who were supposed to be capable of keeping up with trotting cavalry. All the line and *tirailleur* formations contained one company of these highly mobile skirmishers. (Engraving by Villain)

Wellington's main desire. Moreover such an advance into Leon and Castile could be supported logistically along both the Tagus and Douro, and might catch his opponent before the harvest. Marmont was therefore designated the major target.

It would be desirable to distract the remaining four main French armies. To keep Soult occupied, General Hill with 18,000 men would support and supply the guerrilla Ballasteros from Cadiz. To distract General Cafarelli's *Armée du Nord*, the guerrillas Porlier and Longa would disrupt Galicia, aided by a Royal Navy squadron carrying an amphibious force. Similarly, Marshal Suchet's *Armée de l'Est* would be tied down in Catalonia by 17,000 troops transported from Minorca and Sicily. To confuse and weaken Marmont prior to his receiving Wellington's major blow, a mixed force of Spanish regulars and Portuguese militia was to attack Astorga and Toro. Covered by these secondary operations, Wellington would mass

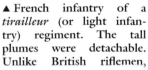

▲ French infantry of a *tirailleur* (or light infantry) regiment. The tall plumes were detachable. Unlike British riflemen, *tirailleurs* were armed with the smoothbore Charleville muskets. (Engraving by Lacostaine after de Maris)

▲ French line infantryman – the archetypical *fantassin* or *grognard* ('grumbler'), who formed the basis of every Napoleonic army. In battle they invariably proved formidable. (Engraving by Villain)

28,000 British, 17,000 Portuguese and 3,000 Spanish regular troops about Ciudad Rodrigo ready to march on Burgos. Along the route lay the ancient regional capital and university city of Salamanca. By late May all stood ready, and on 13 June the advance began.

The French were taken completely by surprise. As Marmont strove to concentrate his forces behind the River Tormes, Wellington marched into Salamanca on the 17th. Three forts held out – and were promptly besieged by General Clinton's 6th Division (the last fort fell on 27 June). Meanwhile Wellington moved north to the San Christóbal hills ready to intercept the French if they attempted to save their garrisons.

Marmont made no such attempt. Aged 38, Auguste Frédéric Louis Viesse de Marmont was the youngest Napoleonic Marshal and a gunner like his master; and although in 1814 his conduct would earn him obloquy, at this time he was a favourite of Napoleon's. He had earned his baton at Znaim in 1809, and had earlier made his mark at Marengo, Ulm and Ragusa, taking his ducal title from the last-named. In 1812 he was regarded as a well-read and experienced, zealous commander. He held his opponents in low regard, and was popular with his men.

Instead of falling for Wellington's lure, throughout late June and early July Marmont conducted a skilled campaign of manoeuvre, which can only be described as masterly. The two armies marched and counter-marched, each seeking an advantage over the other, but beyond minor skirmishing little transpired. At times the armies moved within musket shot of each other, but with the passage of time it became clear that the less-encumbered French could out-march the British by a few miles a day – reinforcing Marmont's scorn for his opponent. Some of Wellington's officers grumbled to London of the hot and dusty marches, and their commander was anxiously aware that Marshal Jourdan was preparing to reinforce his

▲ Marshal of the Empire Auguste Frédéric Louis Viesse de Marmont (1774–1852) was a favourite of Napoleon, and he was a fellow gunner by training. Appointed to take over the Army of Portugal from a burnt-out Massena in April 1811, Marmont soon evinced scorn for Wellington. This did not save him from a heavy defeat on 22 July 1812, and a serious wound. (T. Johnson after Guérin)

▲ *'Le roi Joseph'* – Napoleon's elder brother, Joseph Bonaparte (1768–1844). In 1808 he most unwillingly exchanged the crown of Sicily for that of Spain, at his dominating *fratello*'s insistence – and lived to regret it. Although Salamanca's outcome did not doom his kingdom in 1812, Vitoria the next year most certainly did. As well as his country he lost his treasure – including a personal gift from Napoleon, the Emperor's silver chamber-pot. (Portrait by Gérard)

colleague with 14,000 men from Madrid. Unless he could induce Marmont to attack him in a position of the British choosing, 'the Peer' realized that he would soon have to retreat back into Portugal, which would be virtually to acknowledge defeat.

'From a check to a view . . .'

Late on 18 July the Allies were back at the River Tormes with nothing to show for three weeks of exhausting marching. Marmont was close behind them, and on the 21st crossed the Tormes further east at Huerta – causing Wellington to pass the same river with most of his army to take up a position south-east of Salamanca facing east. The same day he detached General d'España with a force of Spaniards to occupy the bridge at distant Alba de Tormes. As the French deployed through Calvarrasa de Abajo only a narrow stream divided the dust-choked armies. For nine hours the rival artillery batteries growled at one another, and eventually a sharp fight broke out for possession of the ridge near the small chapel of Nuestra Señora de la Pena close to Calvarrasa de Arriba. The French had made some ground when a violent thunderstorm and torrential rain ended the struggle during the evening. Examining the situation, Wellington ordered the military hospitals and convoys to leave Salamanca early the next morning and head west for Ciudad Rodrigo.

Dawn on the 22nd found the Anglo-Portuguese army 'soaked, aching and sullen' hidden among the valleys and re-entrants near Arapiles village. The French had fared rather better, having found some shelter in the cork forests covering much of the plain. In terms of overall manpower there was little to choose between the rival armies. Wellington had six infantry divisions (each comprising two British brigades and one Portuguese save for the all-British 7th and Light Divisions), two independent Portuguese brigades, a small Spanish division, five cavalry brigades and 60 guns – totalling 48,500 men, three-quarters of them infantry. Marmont's *Armée de Portugal* consisted of eight infantry divisions, two small cavalry divisions (one heavy and one light), and 78 guns – a matter of some 50,000 men including 3,400 cavalry. The armies were facing each other amidst rolling wooded countryside in an area 81 square miles in extent contained within a broad bend of the Tormes. Three divisions of the Allies, facing east over the Albagete brook, were in sight of the French; but the rest of Wellington's army – save for the 3rd Division and d'Urban's cavalry which were

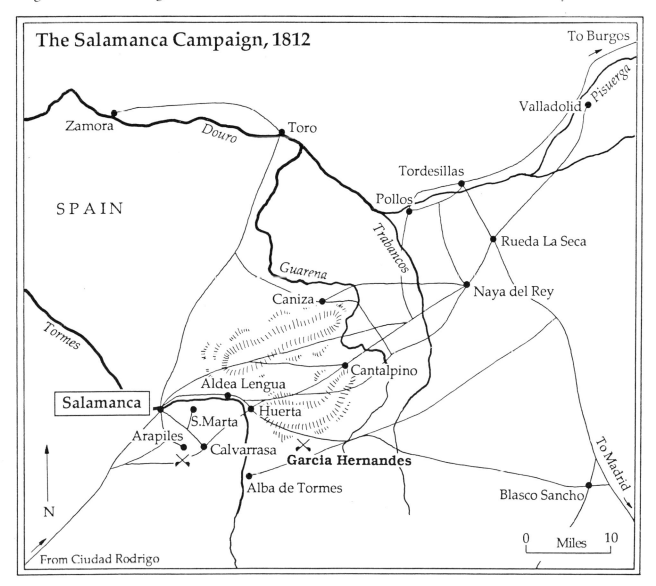

The Salamanca Campaign, 1812

To Burgos

Zamora

Douro

Toro

Pisuerga

Valladolid

Tordesillas

Pollos

SPAIN

Trabancos

Rueda La Seca

Guarena

Naya del Rey

Caniza

Cantalpino

Aldea Lengua

Salamanca

Huerta

S.Marta

Garcia Hernandes

Arapiles

Calvarrasa

Alba de Tormes

Tormes

To Madrid

Blasco Sancho

N

0   Miles   10

From Ciudad Rodrigo

▲ Soldier of the Grenadier Company of the 3rd (or Scots) Foot Guards. Note the pack and blanket-roll on the ground. (Print by Martinet)

▲ Officer of the 95th Rifles. Officers usually wore dark green breeches and black boots, but grey overalls were an alternative. (Print after P. W. Reynolds from a portrait of Captain E. Kent)

still beyond the Tormes near Carbajasa – was out of sight amidst broken ground four miles south-east of Salamanca. On Wellington's right rose two distinct features – the Lesser and Greater Arapiles (also known as Point 901 and Obelisk Hill) some 600 yards apart. Behind the army two roads ran westwards towards Portugal – to which Wellington still expected to have to retreat.

As for the French, they stood in two large columns: the northern comprising three divisions with Curto's light cavalry on the open flank, the southern four divisions strong, with the eighth division linking the two, and Boyer's heavy dragoons farther to the west. By 8 a.m. the French had driven the King's German

Legion from Nuestra Señora Chapel and, observing their every move, Wellington deduced that Marmont intended to move round his southern flank. So, to protect his right flank, at 10.30 a.m. he called up the 1st and 4th Divisions to Arapiles village facing south, and summoned Pakenham's distant 3rd Division and d'Urban's horsemen to march from the Tormes to Aldea Tejada three miles south of Salamanca. An attempt by Portuguese *caçadores* to occupy Obelisk Hill was forestalled by Bonet's Division, and Marmont proceeded to deploy his guns along the height. The French commander was already convinced by what little he could see (including the retiring Allied convoys moving west in the far

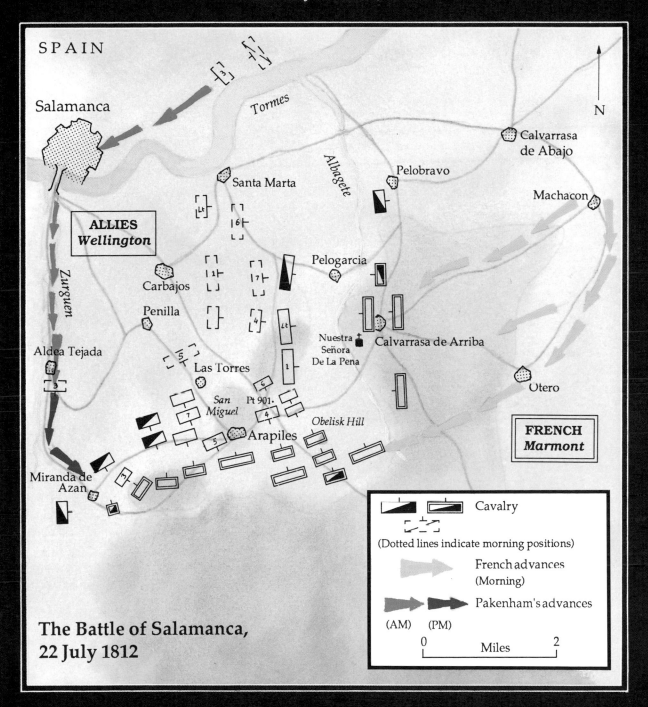

The Battle of Salamanca, 22 July 1812

SPAIN

Salamanca

Tormes

Calvarrasa de Abajo

Santa Marta

Albagete

Pelobravo

Machacon

ALLIES
Wellington

Zurguen

Carbajos

Pelogarcia

Penilla

Aldea Tejada

Nuestra Señora De La Pena

Calvarrasa de Arriba

Las Torres

Utero

San Miguel

Pt 901.

Obelisk Hill

Arapiles

FRENCH
Marmont

Miranda de Azan

Cavalry

(Dotted lines indicate morning positions)

French advances
(Morning)

Pakenham's advances

(AM) (PM)

0   Miles   2

distance) that he was facing only an Allied rearguard, and that Wellington was already in full retreat. The repulse of a probe towards Arapiles village at midday served to confirm his view. So the cocksure Marshal determined that he would head his opponents off, confident of his ability to out-march his foes. Consequently orders were sent to Generals Thomières and Maucune to step out and move parallel to the supposed Allied line of retreat, followed by the rest of the French army in a long column of divisions. Unbeknown to the Marshal, he was making a fatal error.

'By God – that will do!'

As Wellington sat eating luncheon outside a house at Las Torres at about 2 p.m., an aide galloped up with news that '. . . the French are extending to the left.' 'The Devil they are!' exclaimed the Earl who, still grasping his lunch, at once rode to the summit of Point 901. As 30 French guns roared into action on Obelisk Hill, he realized that a great opportunity was unexpectedly materializing. 'Mon cher Alava,' he remarked to the accompanying Spanish officer, 'Marmont est perdu!' – flinging away, tradition would have it, a chicken bone over his shoulder as he spoke. His telescope had revealed that the French line of march was already becoming strung out and dispersed, inviting defeat in detail. A few scribbled orders and a number of aides-de-camp were tearing away downhill to alert the divisional commanders. If Pakenham's 3rd Division could move from Aldea Tejada to intercept Thomières' division there would

be time to defeat him as a mile-wide gap already separated his formation from the following Maucune. Behind that commander came the divisions of Brennier and Clausel – but then there was a second mile-wide gap between Marmont's centre and the four remaining French divisions (those of Bonet, Sarrut, Ferry and Foy) bringing up the rear. With his calculating eye Wellington realized that he might be able to deploy 40,000 men against the French advance guard and centre (totalling 23,000 men) before Marmont could bring up his rear. But timing would be of the very essence, together with skilled co-ordination of effort. Accordingly Wellington rode downhill to brief his generals. By 3 p.m. he had seen General Leith, whose 5th Division, with Le Marchant (recently arrived in the Peninsula from serving as Lieutenant-Governor at the newly opened Royal Military College, Sandhurst) commanding heavy cavalry on his right, and 7th Division, Bradford's Portuguese, the Spaniards and Anson's cavalry in support, was to attack Maucune. To their left Cole's 4th Division was tasked to hold Point 901 come what might, supported by 6th Division, in readiness to attack Bonet's troops to the west of the Arapiles features, while Pack's Portuguese Brigade was to storm Obelisk Hill when the time was ripe. Meanwhile the left of Wellington's position would continue to be held by the 1st and Light Divisions, with Beck's cavalry on their extreme flank – some 10,000 Allies facing nearly 24,000 Frenchmen – but Wellington calculated that the intended fate of their comrades further forward would banish any thought of attack.

All depended on achieving initial surprise – and to

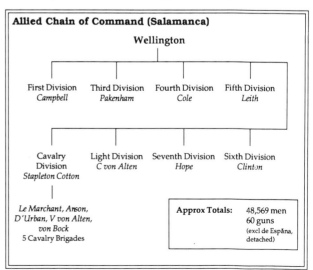

French Chain of Command (Salamanca)

Marmont

First Division	Second Division	Third Division	Fourth Division
Foy	*Clausel*	*Ferry*	*Sarrut*

	Seventh Division	Sixth Division	Fifth Division
	Thomières	*Brennier*	*Maucune*

Eighth Division	Cavalry Division		
Bonet	*Boyer, Curto*		
	2 Cavalry Brigades		

Approx Totals: 49,999 men / 78 guns

Allied Chain of Command (Salamanca)

Wellington

First Division	Third Division	Fourth Division	Fifth Division
Campbell	*Pakenham*	*Cole*	*Leith*

Cavalry Division	Light Division	Seventh Division	Sixth Division
Stapleton Cotton	*C von Alten*	*Hope*	*Clinton*

Le Marchant, Anson, D'Urban, V von Alten, von Bock
5 Cavalry Brigades

Approx Totals: 48,569 men / 60 guns (excl de España, detached)

ensure that Pakenham understood his critical role exactly Wellington rode over to Aldea Tejada to meet his brother-in-law. 'Attack the French on their heights and drive all before you,' was the order. 'Give me your hand and I will do it,' replied Sir Edward. Wellington then returned to Point 901 and resumed his study of the French advance. It was 3.45 p.m.

'From a view to a kill . . .'

For an hour there was little change. The French column tramped on west, as Pakenham – out of their sight – moved into position near Miranda de Azan. Then, at 4.45 p.m., the leading troops of 3rd Division came suddenly into sight. Wheeling left into two lines of scarlet battalions, Pakenham bore down on Thomières' astounded men. Curto's cavalry tried to attack Pakenham's right, but were repulsed by fire and then charged by Alten's dragoons frontally as d'Urban's cavalry enveloped their rear. Pakenham's attack gathered momentum and the French 7th Division first crumbled then scattered before the shock, their commander among the killed.

The same moment that Pakenham attacked, Wellington launched Leith's division from concealment. Maucune, in turn, was caught unsuspecting. As the French hesitated, Le Marchant and Anson came charging down. At the head of 1,000 horsemen, Le Marchant smashed into half-formed French squares and scattered them in ruin. Maucune's men joined the rout – and so did part of Brennier's command next in line – but Le Marchant lay dead. Nevertheless one-quarter of Marmont's army had been routed beyond repair in forty minutes. The Marshal had become aware of developments as Pakenham appeared. Calling for his horse, he was shouting orders to his staff when a British shell exploded by his steed, seriously wounding his arm and side. General Jean Bonet succeeded to the command – only to be struck down in his turn. It was twenty vital minutes before the French army was back under full operational control under General Bertrand Clausel.

Yet all was not decided. The new French commander – the third in half an hour – was a tough professional, and quickly sized up the situation. It was high time for a telling counterstroke against the Allied centre to be prepared. Brennier's and Sarrut's 6th and 4th Divisions were placed under Maucune with cavalry in support and ordered to await Clausel's order. The rout could still be turned into victory.

▲ British heavy cavalry trooper. Note that, unlike the French equivalent, a cuirass is no longer worn. (Painting by Harry Payne)

Meanwhile, at 5 p.m., Cole's 4th Division had advanced with Pack's Portuguese to its left. Parts of Bonet's Division were scattered, and several guns captured. Less fortunately, a gap developed between Cole and Pack, and when the Portuguese tried to storm steep Obelisk Hill they were charged by several more of Bonet's battalions and flung back. Raked by cannon fire from Obelisk Hill and attacked in flank, the 4th Division was brought to an uncertain halt, Lowry Cole being among the wounded, as it encountered steady formations of the French second line. Clausel's moment had come. At 6 p.m. he ordered an all-out attack.

By the plan Brennier, backed by Ferry, was to check the reorganizing Allied 3rd and 5th Divisions; Sarrut was to protect the French batteries; and

◀ British cavalry charge at Salamanca. Brigadier-General Gaspard Le Marchant was killed while scattering a French formation caught in the act of forming square. (Engraving by Terry and Pound)

Clausel's own troops, with Bonet's and Boyer's cavalry, were to charge the tired 4th Division between Arapiles village and Point 901. The French columns swept forward. For Wellington the moment of crisis had come: his entire centre stood in peril of defeat.

The impact was horrendous. The 4th Division and part of the 6th to its rear were shattered – and the entire Allied centre reeled back. To exploit this Boyer's heavy dragoons came thundering forward, their sabres rising and falling remorselessly. For several minutes that seemed like hours the outcome of the engagement hung in the balance. Fortunately for the Allies, however, Wellington had positioned Clinton's 6th Division in rear of the 4th ready to meet just such a

crisis. The men of the 6th fought back magnificently. Boyer's dragoons found themselves funnelled between Allied batteries on either flank but pressed on, decimated, only to be halted by a cool British square near Las Torres. They turned and retired – and the French chance of victory had passed.

Without a pause Clinton began a remorseless advance. Marshal Beresford brought up Portuguese battalions from 5th Division (which had by now got the measure of Brennier), drew them up in line near Arapiles, and opened a withering fire into the flank of Clausel's division. Soon two French divisions were shredding away to the rear, seeking the safety of the cork forests, accompanied by many of Brennier's men.

Now only three French divisions remained unrouted – but this measure of success had only been achieved at heavy Allied cost. The 6th Division alone had lost a third of its strength in the space of just five minutes at the grim climax of Clausel's bold – but ultimately doomed – advance.

Clausel's bold throw to win or lose all had failed him. As dusk deepened the Allied attempt to capitalize their now undeniable victory was thrown into considerable confusion as Wellington launched forward the Light and 1st Divisions of his practically intact left wing. The 1st Division, instead of passing east of Obelisk Hill as ordered, ended by storming the feature – only to find that it had been abandoned. In the gathering gloom, General Foy's intact division fought a masterly rearguard action, keeping both the 1st and Light Divisions at bay and thus aiding the flight of his compatriots. Farther south, Ferry's division, commanded by Maucune, also distinguished itself astride the road to Alba de Tormes, holding off both the British 6th Division and the Fusilier Brigade of the 4th. Thus for vital minutes the impetus of the Allied advance died away; and it was only when Pakenham's 3rd Division turned Ferry's flank that this French force abandoned its ridge position, and fell back, parallel to Foy. At 9.30 p.m. all was over.

The Allies had lost 5,200 casualties, more than 3,000 of them British, in the space of five hours' fighting. French losses were at least 14,000 men, including 7,000 prisoners and 20 cannon captured. The *Armée de Portugal*'s loss could well have been far graver, had not Wellington miscalculated its line of retreat. Believing (erroneously) that the bridge at Alba de Tormes was safely in d'España's hand, the Earl directed the pursuit towards Huerta. In fact the Spaniards sent to Alba de Tormes on the 21st had decided to abandon their positions – and in consequence the battered remnant of the French army was able to pass the river there. But nemesis was at their heels, and next day the cavalry of the King's German Legion caught Foy's Division on a hillside near Garçia Hernandes, and actually broke a formed French square before being beaten back by heavy fire. Foy continued his retreat, and soon after broke contact with the enemy. Wellington halted the pursuit on the 25th at Flores de Avila, and afforded his weary men some overdue rest.

The strategic aftermath of Salamanca held both triumph and tragedy for the Allies. On 12 August, Wellington rode into a cheering Madrid – a political triumph, but one that gave the French a chance to recover. Soult marched hard north-east, and the *Armée de Portugal* reorganized its shattered formations so that when Wellington advanced to besiege the key position on the Royal Road at Burgos (19 September), he soon found himself at the focal point of four converging French armies. As a result he had to begin a hard retreat for Portugal in late October, abandoning most of his gains which would have to be rewon in 1813.

Despite this set-back, the overall achievements of 1812 were considerable. The Hispano-Portuguese frontier area had once and for all been cleared of the French, and Soult had been induced to abandon Andalusia in the south of the Peninsula. The centre and north had still to be fought for, but great heart had been given to the guerrillas, and before 1813 was out the French would have been driven back into the Pyrenees. For the British Army, Salamanca was probably its greatest victory since Blenheim. As for Wellington, his abilities as a great battle commander in the offensive role had been demonstrated and proved. As a generous foe, General Maximilien Foy, writing several years later, conceded: '. . . the battle almost raised the Duke of Wellington to the level of the Duke of Marlborough. Hitherto we had been aware of his prudence, his eye for choosing a position and his skill in utilizing it. At Salamanca he has shown himself a great and able master of manoeuvre. He kept his dispositions concealed for almost the whole day; he waited until we were committed to our movement before he developed his own. He fought in the oblique order – it was a little after the style of Frederick the Great.' The events of 22 July 1812 will be long recalled.

BIBLIOGRAPHY

Bryant, A. *The Age of Elegance*, London, 1950. An excellent overall treatment of Salamanca within its period setting.

Christophe, R. *Le maréchal Marmont, duc de Raguse*, Paris, 1968. A good biography of the French commander at Salamanca.

Cornwell, B. *Sharpe's Sword*, London, 1980. Although a novel, this treatment has a sure sense of period British Army atmosphere.

Glover, M. *Wellington's Peninsular Victories*, London, 1963.

The section devoted to Salamanca is valuable.

Oman, C. *History of the Peninsular War*, vol. 5, Oxford, 1914. Still, after 75 years, the most important single work on the period and battle.

Young, P. and Lawford, J. *Wellington's Masterpiece – Salamanca 1812*, London, 1976. A most thorough and engagingly written account of campaign and battle.

Ward, S. G. P. *Wellington*, OUP, 1963. Still the best short military study of the Duke.

WATERLOO COMPANY CREST
RMA SANDHURST

THE BATTLE OF WATERLOO, 1815

by Sir David Fraser

*'I never gave myself so much trouble as I did that day to place
the troops. I went and chose the ground for every corps myself,
and placed them.'*

(Wellington in conversation with G. W. Chad)

In March 1815 the world supposed that Europe had heard the last of Napoleon Bonaparte, Emperor of the French and victor of battles from Scandinavia to Egypt, from the Russian steppe to the soil of France itself. Turned before Moscow, savaged at Leipzig, his armies driven from the Peninsula, Napoleon had been forced back to his exhausted and depleted homeland by a formidable Alliance of Powers, including Russia, Austria, Prussia and Britain; had abdicated, enabling the Bourbon Royal family to resume the throne; and had been exiled in petty dignity to the island of Elba. The victorious nations had assembled in Congress in Vienna to dispute and determine the map of Europe.

The Landing of the Eagle

Then the thunderclap burst. On 1 March, slipping past a naval patrol, Napoleon had landed with 800 men near Antibes in the South of France and instantly began his march to the north. In Vienna and in Paris the response was instant and fearful – the 'Corsican Bandit' must be seized, his insurrection crushed. Marshal Ney, Duc d'Elchingen, Prince de la Moskowa, now serving the Bourbons, was sent south with troops to apprehend the invader and promised to bring him back 'in an iron cage'. Instead, as Ney's soldiers, muskets levelled, met their old chief in a village near Grenoble, Napoleon threw open his overcoat to display his stars, to remind those facing him of what he and they had once endured and achieved together. 'Soldiers of the 5th Regiment, would you shoot your Emperor?' The magic was irresistible to them – and to Ney. Napoleon moved north in triumph, old soldiers of every rank flocking to join him. He entered Paris on 20 March. Once again he was master of France.

To his enemies, French or foreign, this was the return of a nightmare, of a ghost supposed laid. A comprehensive plan was agreed. There would be a convergent offensive – from the east the armies of Austria and Russia would assemble and advance towards the Rhine, while in the north the Prussians under Marshal Blücher, Prince of Wahlstadt, would join hands in the Low Countries with a British–Netherlands Army (within the British part of the force were a number of brigades of the King's German Legion and from Hanover – approximately equal to the British brigades in numbers) under the command of Field Marshal the Duke of Wellington, hero of a

▲ Arthur Wellesley, Duke of Wellington, KG (1769–1852). The same age as Napoleon, Wellington had learnt much of his profession in India and earned his reputation in the Iberian Peninsula. His career reached its culmination in June 1815, the only time he faced the French Emperor. (Portrait by William Robinson)

long and brilliant campaign against the French in the Peninsula. Until the Allies were ready to synchronize an offensive movement their strategy would be defensive. The initiative lay with Napoleon.

Not least of Napoleon's achievements was the speed with which he reconstituted the Army of the North. To overturn a regime, re-establish the Imperial system and produce an Army ready to take the field against a great alliance of Powers – to do all this and take the offensive in eleven weeks showed the daemonic energy of that extraordinary man. His strategy was simple. France must, as quickly as possible, move against one of her enemies before the weight of the other could be brought to bear. Geography and time dictated that the first move must be to the north, against the combination of Blücher and Wellington. By 14 June Napoleon was ready to cross the northern frontiers of France and open the campaign. In the small hours of 15 June, at about 3 a.m., he crossed the Sambre.

Humbugged, by God!

Across the frontiers, in what is now Belgium, Blücher's Army of four Army Corps, totalling 120,000 men, was quartered in the area of the Meuse and Sambre valleys, extending as far east as Liège and as far west as Charleroi on the main road running north to Brussels. Wellington's nine divisions and some special detachments – in sum about 90,000 – were quartered in an area south and west of Brussels, bounded roughly by Brussels, Genappe, Mons and Oudenarde. Armies had to disperse to live and concentrate to fight; and the point of concentration depended essentially on Napoleon's moves.

Napoleon had several choices of thrust line. The Army of the North totalled some 125,000 – outnumbered by his enemies if combined but a match for each independently. It was thought likely – even certain – that French operational policy would be directed towards preventing Blücher and Wellington uniting, towards defeating each separately; and this might imply a move towards the boundary between the Prussians and their Allies, to drive them apart rather than towards each other. On the other hand Napoleon could threaten Wellington's communications with England through Ostend, by moving on Tournai or on Mons; while any manoeuvre well to the east could menace Blücher's lifeline to the Meuse, the Rhine and Germany. Defensive plans and possible concentration areas had to cover these eventualities; and time and space would necessitate very accurate deduction and very rapid action when French moves made sufficiently plain Napoleon's intentions. Wellington had always placed high importance on Intelligence and analysed it with perceptive brilliance. His agents were active in France, his outposts forewarned. He and Blücher were well-informed on French strength and dispositions. Nevertheless both knew how disastrous it might be to react prematurely, to respond excessively to a feint.

▲ Marshal Michel Ney, Prince of the Moscowa, Duke of Elchingen and 'Bravest of the Brave' (1769–1815). Only restored to Napoleon's favour on the eve of the campaign, he was nevertheless given command of the French left wing and – despite a poor showing at Quatre Bras – made battle commander at Waterloo itself – with well-known results. (Portrait by Gérard)

In the event Wellington miscalculated. In mid-June signs of French activity had quickened, but the French main thrust line was still obscure and when, during the evening of 15 June, Wellington received in Brussels the latest news of Napoleon's moves he realized that he had lost precious time. For Napoleon had decided to march straight up the Brussels road through Charleroi, striking the Prussians at the westernmost point of their area; to smash Blücher while holding Wellington off and to turn on him with

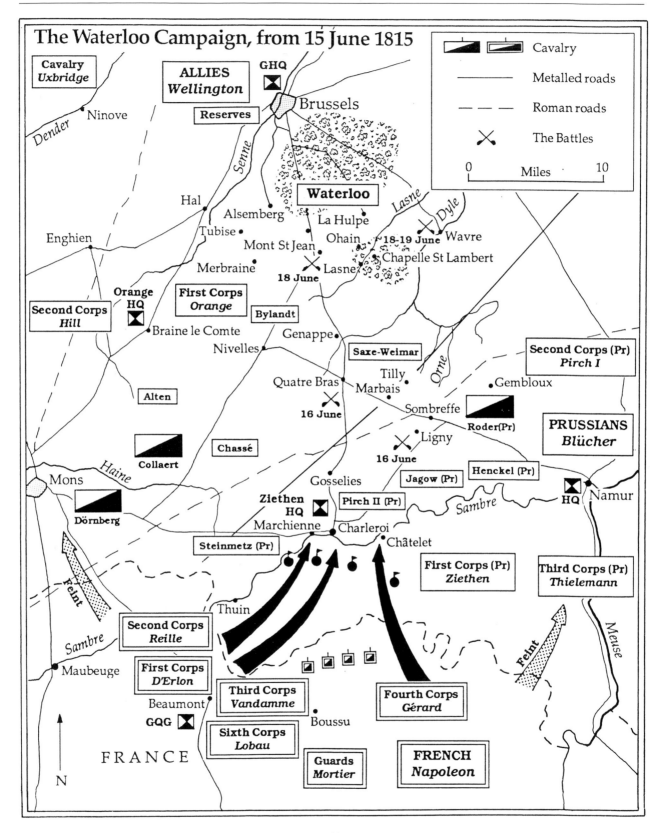

The Waterloo Campaign, from 15 June 1815

Cavalry

Metalled roads

Roman roads

The Battles

0   Miles   10

Cavalry *Uxbridge*

ALLIES *Wellington*

GHQ

Brussels

Reserves

Dender

Ninove

Senne

Hal

Alsemberg

Waterloo

La Hulpe

Ohain

Lasne

18-19 June

Wavre

Dyle

Mont St Jean

Chapelle St Lambert

Tubise

Merbraine

Lasne

18 June

Enghien

Orange HQ

First Corps *Orange*

Second Corps *Hill*

Bylandt

Braine le Comte

Genappe

Orne

Second Corps (Pr) *Pirch I*

Nivelles

Alten

Quatre Bras

Tilly

Marbais

Gembloux

16 June

Sombreffe

PRUSSIANS *Blücher*

Chassé

Collaert

Ligny

Roder (Pr)

Mons

Haine

16 June

Gosselies

Jagow (Pr)

Henckel (Pr)

HQ

Namur

Dörnberg

Ziethen HQ

Pirch II (Pr)

Marchienne

Charleroi

Châtelet

Sambre

Steinmetz (Pr)

First Corps (Pr) *Ziethen*

Third Corps (Pr) *Thielemann*

Meuse

Feint

Thuin

Second Corps *Reille*

Sambre

First Corps *D'Erlon*

Maubeuge

Beaumont

Feint

GQG

Third Corps *Vandamme*

Boussu

Fourth Corps *Gérard*

Sixth Corps *Lobau*

F R A N C E

N

Guards *Mortier*

FRENCH *Napoleon*

his united force thereafter. It was direct, it was rapid, it was envisaged as driving an all-conquering Army of the North like a wedge between the Allies. 'Bonaparte has humbugged me, by God!' Wellington exclaimed. 'He has gained twenty-four hours' march on me!' Until then Wellington, for some anxious hours, had continued to believe that Napoleon might still be aiming farther west, towards Mons at least. Now, however, there was already action in the central sector. A Prussian Corps had already been attacked. Wellington's troops began forced marches towards the crossroads of Quatre Bras, where the lateral communication eastward towards Blücher crossed the Charleroi–Brussels road.

The Prussians, meanwhile, were deploying south of the village of Ligny, eight miles east of Quatre Bras, and here Napoleon attacked them on 16 June, intending to defeat them decisively before turning in force on Wellington. The upshot was different. At Ligny the Prussians fought an action terrible with casualties – Blücher himself, aged seventy-three, was ridden over by three charges of French cavalry – but they inflicted serious loss on the French, and although they withdrew northward towards Wavre they were fit to fight another day. Napoleon believed – wishing to believe – that Blücher had been beaten so soundly he could do nothing but retreat to the Meuse and the Rhine; but it was not so.

At Quatre Bras a fierce encounter battle was fought, Allied regiments marching more than twenty miles in the June heat and then fed into the battle like sticks on a fading fire. Wellington was everywhere, as always – driving, inspiring, patching up sudden holes in his improvised front, directing reinforcements into the woods and fields and farms around the crossroads. Napoleon's object at Quatre Bras was to prevent any Allied move towards Blücher, in which he succeeded; but it was also to hold Wellington to the ground by fighting, in order to smash him from south and east later, and in this he failed. Wellington was determined to hold Quatre Bras until the outcome of the fight at Ligny was clear; but when the Prussian withdrawal became known to him the Duke was equally determined to withdraw. Brussels must be covered. Contact with the Prussians must be maintained. On 17 June Wellington marched his exhausted battalions, covered by cavalry, northward up the Brussels road and deployed them, as night and rain fell, on a long, curving ridge south of Mont St Jean, twelve miles west of Wavre. The French followed up – a Corps was detached to watch Blücher in order, as Napoleon assumed was required, to shepherd him eastward and away from Wellington – and by nightfall on the 17th the Army of the North, now 72,000 strong, was deployed on the next ridge south of Wellington, with the village of Plancenoit on the deep right flank, the farm of La Belle Alliance marking the centre.

A few miles away Wellington rode to the next considerable village north of Mont St Jean, where he spent the night: Waterloo. Blücher had assured him that if he fought next day the Prussians would do their utmost to join him; and Blücher, at Wavre, was only twelve miles away.

Hougoumont

Wellington detached a substantial force – about 18,000 men – at Tubize, some five miles west of his main position, and has been much criticized for so doing. He was still concerned that Napoleon might seek to march round his right, and this force – unengaged throughout the day – gave him some insurance. On the main position, a crescent-shaped, two-mile ridge, he deployed the Army in a line of divisions – some 68,000 men in all. Most Divisions were formed of a mix of British and Hanoverian or King's German Legion brigades, although there were three 'Dutch–Belgian' divisions with no British troops. The cavalry were organized in brigades and placed at points behind the main line, ready to counter-attack.

On Wellington's left the ground fell away into a broken valley, containing the farms of Papelotte and La Haye. The Allied centre was marked by a crossroads where the Ohain road – roughly parallel to the front – intersected the Charleroi–Brussels road, with the farm of La Haye Sainte just over one hundred yards south of the intersection. And on Wellington's right the ridge, and thus the front line, curved southward towards the enemy. Forward of this right-hand sector, and in lower ground, lay the small château, garden, woods and farm buildings of Hougoumont.

In front of his line on the ridge Wellington garrisoned, strongly, La Haye Sainte and Hougoumont. The defenders of these places could, by their fire, break up enemy attacks on the main position: they had the effect of constricting the enemy's front of attack in Wellington's right half of line – the distance between the inner flanks of the two garrisons

◀ Lieutenant-General Sir Thomas Picton (1758–1815). He was one of Wellington's most trusted lieutenants in the Peninsular War, and commanded the veteran 5th Division in 1815. He wore civilian dress from the Duchess of Richmond's ball onwards, was gravely wounded at Quatre Bras, but concealed the fact, and was finally killed by a French musket ball through the front of his top hat shortly before 2 p.m. on 18 June. (After a portrait by Dawes)

▶ Much fighting centred around the Château de Hougoumont to the fore of the Allied right wing. The battle began — and ended — here. One crisis was averted when Driver Brewer (or Brewster) of the Royal Wagon Train drove an ammunition cart into the courtyard as the Guards' supply ran low in mid-afternoon. (Painting by Charles Stadden)

was only about eight hundred yards: and in the case of Hougoumont could force any outflanking move round Wellington's right further away, thus adding to warning.

The battle of Waterloo, fought on Sunday 18 June, can be divided into five main acts, but the first act – the attack on Hougoumont – lasted throughout the day and thus overlaid the others. Hougoumont, with its orchard, was defended by the light companies of the two brigades of Foot Guards forming the British 1st Division, and by a battalion of Nassauers. At about 11.30 a.m. a great mass of French infantry, led by Prince Jérôme Bonaparte (Napoleon's youngest brother, previously the King of Westphalia), swarmed down from the heights west of La Belle Alliance, came through the woods and attempted to carry the orchard, gardens and buildings. Napoleon's estimate of Hougoumont's significance corresponded to Wellington's.

Then and throughout the day the French attacks were driven off. At one point French infantry broke into the courtyard itself, to be ousted in desperate

close-quarter fighting. At another point the British Guards were forced back through the orchard and a French gun was brought up to blast them at point-blank range. And at another point the château was set on fire and the defenders had to deal simultaneously with the French and the flames. Hougoumont, throughout the day, had no respite but it was never taken. Reinforced by more companies from 1st Division it held to the last; and because it held, Wellington's right flank was firm.

D'Erlon's attack

Napoleon was an artilleryman. He believed in the concentrated power of artillery and before the two greatest assaults of Waterloo – Lieutenant-General Drouet, Comte d'Erlon's infantry and Ney's cavalry – the French artillery were massed to form a 'grand battery', and poured the heaviest fire into the defenders' ranks that any of them could remember. Before d'Erlon's attack the French guns – about eighty, on the next ridge to Wellington's and east of

▶ Hougoumont today — what is left of the same gateway depicted in the last picture, seen from the French side. The main château building, burnt down during the battle, stood in the centre. Only the chapel survived the conflagration — and is today a Brigade of Guards Memorial.

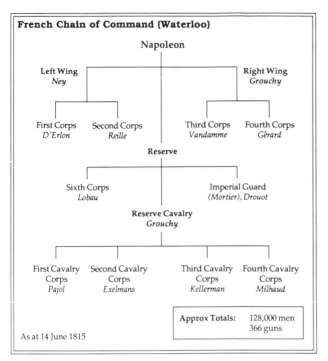

French Chain of Command (Waterloo)

Napoleon

Left Wing — *Ney*
Right Wing — *Grouchy*

First Corps — *D'Erlon*
Second Corps — *Reille*
Third Corps — *Vandamme*
Fourth Corps — *Gérard*

Reserve

Sixth Corps — *Lobau*
Imperial Guard (Mortier), *Drouot*

Reserve Cavalry — *Grouchy*

First Cavalry Corps — *Pajol*
Second Cavalry Corps — *Exelmans*
Third Cavalry Corps — *Kellerman*
Fourth Cavalry Corps — *Milhaud*

Approx Totals: 128,000 men / 366 guns

As at 14 June 1815

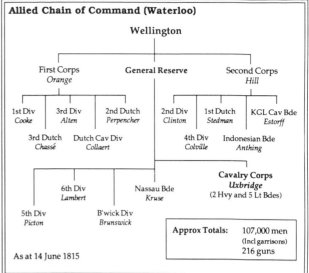

Allied Chain of Command (Waterloo)

Wellington

First Corps — *Orange*
General Reserve
Second Corps — *Hill*

1st Div *Cooke*
3rd Div *Alten*
2nd Dutch *Perpencher*
2nd Div *Clinton*
1st Dutch *Stedman*
KGL Cav Bde *Estorff*

3rd Dutch *Chassé*
Dutch Cav Div *Collaert*
4th Div *Colville*
Indonesian Bde *Anthing*

6th Div *Lambert*
Nassau Bde *Kruse*
Cavalry Corps *Uxbridge* (2 Hvy and 5 Lt Bdes)

5th Div *Picton*
B'wick Div *Brunswick*

Approx Totals: 107,000 men (Incl garrisons) / 216 guns

As at 14 June 1815

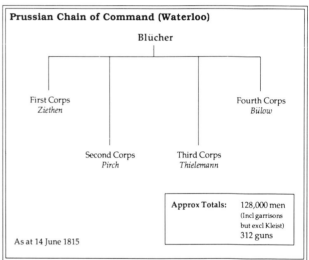

Prussian Chain of Command (Waterloo)

Blücher

First Corps — *Ziethen*
Fourth Corps — *Bülow*

Second Corps — *Pirch*
Third Corps — *Thielemann*

Approx Totals: 128,000 men (Incl garrisons but excl Kleist) / 312 guns

As at 14 June 1815

the Charleroi road – started at about midday. The range from Wellington's line was 600 yards.

Immediately east of the Ohain crossroads Wellington's front was held by Lieutenant-General Sir Thomas Picton's 5th Division. At about 1,30 p.m. Picton's men saw the four French divisions of d'Erlon's Corps advancing up the slope. These divisions came on in line, the right-hand division directed towards Papelotte, the left division towards the area of La Haye Sainte and the crossroads, while between those two, two more – sixteen battalions – marched towards the 5th Division. The formation of the French divisions slightly differed from one another, but the impression to the defenders was the same – a solid mass of infantry, depth roughly equivalent to frontage, an irresistible phalanx, drums beating the 'pas de charge'.

Picton, a rough-tongued, fierce and formidable eccentric of great experience, disliked his division's position and had said so. When the guns opened he drew his battalions back to get some shelter from the convexity of the ground, for in that sector was no friendly, protective reverse slope. Now the guns were silent and the ground shook with the tread of d'Erlon's divisions, marching up the steep gradient beyond the Ohain road.

Now it was the turn of the British Artillery to pour a shattering fire into the heads of d'Erlon's columns.

But they came on, and as they breasted the ridge the British infantry opened fire at extremely close range into the advancing French. Soon the French divisions were a mass of wounded, struggling men, trampling and tripping over dead comrades, unable to advance, pressed by those behind and unable to retreat. At that moment Picton, with a shout of 'Charge, Charge! Hurrah!' (he was shot and killed a moment later), sent his nearest battalions forward with the bayonet into the checked French columns before them and the action rippled down the Division's line. At that moment, too, Lord Uxbridge (Lieutenant-General the Earl of Uxbridge, commander of Wellington's cavalry and effectively his second in command) ordered the two heavy cavalry brigades behind

▶ During the first mid-afternoon cavalry charges, some French cuirassiers fell into a sunken road near the Mont St. Jean crossroads. This event was over-stressed by Victor Hugo to explain away the French failure. (Painting by V. Checa)

▼ French heavy cavalry attacking the British guns of Captain A. C. Mercer's Troop. (Painting by J. S. Seccombe)

Wellington's centre – the Household Brigade (commanded by Major-General Lord Edward Somerset) west of the Brussels road, the Union Brigade (commanded by Major-General Sir William Ponsonby) east of it – to charge; to turn a check into a rout.

The charge of the Household Brigade, west of the Brussels road and La Haye Sainte, was a controlled and effective operation which threw out of the way the French cuirassiers advancing in support of d'Erlon's left and crashed into the left and rear of the left-hand French division. The Union Brigade had to charge through the fighting ranks of Picton's division, inevitably losing formation; and took the hedge which ran along the Ohain road, in many cases jumping it as if in the hunting field. They then rode down the slope into the crowded and panic-stricken French

columns by now in full flight, cutting down all before them.

Such a charge was impossible to control. The enthusiasm of the British cavalry took them farther than Wellington or Uxbridge desired. They reached the French guns but Napoleon – not an enemy with whom to take chances – counter-attacked with reserve cavalry and few of the Union Brigade returned. Nevertheless d'Erlon's attack had been completely defeated. Allied casualties were heavy but the line was intact. It was 3 p.m.

The British Square

Throughout the day the Allied line was subjected to harassing fire from French artillery, just as the French main attacks were themselves bombarded with maximum artillery fire from the Allied guns as they developed. The casualties on both sides from cannon fire at Waterloo were immense. The Allied line was also incessantly plagued by the fire of French sharpshooters who worked their way forward to snipe at Wellington's line from as close a range as they could manage.

But the next main act began shortly before 4 p.m. when Wellington's troops in the centre and right saw an astonishing sight. An immense mass of cavalry (in all some forty squadrons, about 4,000 horse, took

▲ The 7th Hussars in the dramatic charge against the French cavalry. (Painting by Henry Martens)

part, although not necessarily all in the first charge) were moving forward from the French line. Largely unsupported by infantry, this was an attempt to smash the Allied line by sheer weight of charging horseflesh and determined men.

To receive cavalry, infantry battalions would form square from line – a well-rehearsed and rapid drill movement. At Waterloo these squares (so-called, although sometimes rectangles would be formed; the size of a square naturally varied with the surviving strength of a battalion – at Waterloo the average was probably a 'face' of about twenty-five yards) were disposed checker-wise on the reverse slope. The French cavalry, suffering greatly from the Allied guns on the ridge, came on at a trot or slow canter, breasted the ridge and only then saw the squares – forming, as they did, human fortresses with gaps between them of distance varying from one to two hundred yards. The cavalry were only vulnerable to infantry when approaching the face of a square, but that vulnerability was great. Disciplined volleys cut down huge numbers, the muskets often aimed at horses' legs to bring down the wretched animal and thereafter pick off the trooper at leisure.

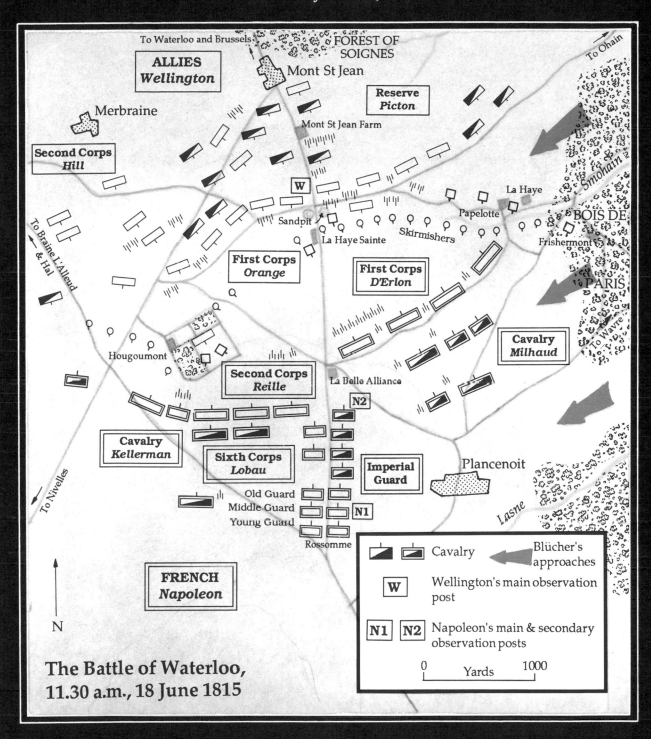

The Battle of Waterloo, 11.30 a.m., 18 June 1815

▲ Blücher at the head of the Prussian 'Death's Head' Dragoons at Waterloo. The arrival of eventually three corps of Prussians during the afternoon of 18 June on Napoleon's right flank and Wellington's left was of critical importance to the outcome. (Painting by an unknown artist)

Although they could ride about the Allied rear areas almost unmolested, the French object was to smash Wellington's right-centre and in this Ney's cavalry conspicuously and gallantly failed. Not one square was broken. Nor were the squares all, for when the French withdrew and reformed and charged up the ridge again – and again and again at ever-decreasing speed over the heavy, trampled ground – they were again blasted by Wellington's artillery, guns manned to the last possible moment, gunners removing a gun-wheel and bowling it like a hoop to the shelter of the nearest square, gun immobilized and then rapidly restored to effectiveness when the enemy next withdrew. This was by Wellington's direct order – for which he has, by some, been criticized.

In the final charges the horses were incapable of more than a walk. By 5.30 p.m. the attempt was over.

La Haye Sainte

Like Hougoumont, La Haye Sainte had been held throughout the day, a breakwater to the waves of the French attack. Like Hougoumont it had been the scene of savage and incessant fighting, garrisoned by King's German Legion troops from Lieutenant-General Sir Charles Alten's 3rd Division, deployed west of the Ohain Crossroads, on Picton's right and on the left of 1st Division. At six o'clock the place was crammed with wounded and dying, ammunition was low and fire had caught hold; and at that time the French made a last and massive effort against the farm, with infantry swarming into the attack on both sides, supported by artillery brought up to fire at point-blank range. This was the fourth act of Waterloo.

Eventually, with the defenders' ammunition used up, with the King's German Legion reduced to defence by bayonet and rifle butt, La Haye Sainte fell. Of some 400 troops defending it at the start of the day only about forty were still effective. Two more battalions of the King's German Legion, sent down from the ridge by an unwise order of the Prince of Orange, in nominal command at this point of the front, were cut to pieces by French cavalry. And immediately thereafter French *tirailleurs* in huge numbers worked forward against Wellington's centre and right, until driven back by the volley firing of British and German battalions in line. The Allied centre was now alarmingly weak.

Wellington personally led every spare battalion he could make available to the threatened point and moved two cavalry brigades from the left flank to behind the centre as well as such guns as he could find, but the French had gained a lodgement at the lip of the ridge. At the same time a mass of French light infantry from D'Erlon's right-hand division swarmed into the attack round the valley farms which anchored Wellington's left. It was the moment of crisis in the day of Waterloo.

Wellington's glass was often lifted towards the east. Soon after the start of the battle he had spied in the far distance the leading Prussian columns. Blücher's men were exhausted after Ligny and the forced marches which followed, but the valiant old Hussar drove them on towards Napoleon's right flank, faithful to his word to Wellington. The Prussians, inevitably, could only be committed to battle piece-meal and vulnerable unless they were to wait an unacceptable time in order to effect a concentration. Piecemeal, therefore, they had moved into Plancenoit shortly before 5 p.m., in divisional strength, only to be counter-attacked successfully by several battalions of Napoleon's reserve, the Imperial Guard. But when Wellington's crisis came soon after 6 p.m., Blücher's troops were attacking again not only at Plancenoit but further north, against French infantry fighting round La Haye and Papelotte. Napoleon's enemies had now virtually achieved what he had been determined to prevent – a concentration on the battlefield.

La Garde recule!

There seemed, to Napoleon, one last chance to smash the Allied army before the full effect of the Prussians could be felt. Blücher's main body was still on the march rather than arrayed in a full battle line. Wellington's centre seemed vulnerable, perhaps beaten. And now the Emperor launched his final reserve – seven battalions of the Imperial Guard, fresh and uncommitted until that moment. Marching up the muddy slope towards the crest between Hougoumont and the Ohain crossroads they were intended to administer the *coup de grâce* to an army which must, Napoleon calculated, be near collapse from the intensity of the fighting and the presumed immensity of the casualties – an accurate presumption, for out of about 68,000 men Wellington lost 10,000 at Waterloo.

For reasons still in dispute the battalions of the Guard deviated somewhat from their intended central thrust line and made their main effort further to their left, striking Wellington's line at the points held by the 1st Division (commanded by Lieutenant-General Sir George Cooke; only one brigade of two battalions was complete on the main position, the other brigade having been committed almost completely by now to the defence of Hougoumont) and Major-General Sir Colin Halkett's brigade (now only one-third of its original strength) on the right of the 3rd Division. As they advanced the British artillery on the ridge took toll, but the Imperial Guard periodically halted, closed ranks, and came on in perfect order once again.

The French veterans reached the ridge before they saw their enemies. Then, at very short range, British infantry in line stood up on the reverse slope and poured a deadly volley, and another and another, into the French columns. The Imperial Guard reeled back.

Then, charged frontally by the British Guards, they turned and reformed at a little distance down the slope; and the British withdrew amid some confusion. The scene was then re-enacted, the French advancing again, driven back again and charged again. This time there was no French attempt to reform. Out from the right of the 1st Division had marched Major-General Adam's 3rd Brigade. This was the only British brigade in Lieutenant-General Sir Henry Clinton's 2nd Division behind Wellington's right, around Merbe Braine. A battalion of Adam's brigade now formed to its left, and, facing the left flank of the Imperial Guard, poured a deadly enfilade fire into Napoleon's last reserve. Caught in convergent fire from left and front the Imperial Guard broke. For the first time in all the Napoleonic Wars the cry ran through the Grand Army, '*La Garde recule!*'

Soon afterwards the exhausted Allied troops on the ridge saw their commander-in-chief, somewhere near the centre, sitting his charger 'Copenhagen' and raising his hat high in the air. This was the signal for a general advance and the Duke galloped along the line, waving the troops forward at last. At La Belle Alliance he met Blücher. Napoleon's Army was in full flight. The two commanders agreed immediate plans. Then Wellington rode back to his headquarters in the village of Waterloo.

An end of the War

'The battle is mine,' Wellington observed as early as 4.20 p.m., 'and if the Prussians arrive soon there will be an end of the War.' The words, uttered in the midst of Ney's cavalry charges, were as prophetic as they were confident. The Allies, with periodic skirmishes and sieges but without a major battle, marched forward into France. On 4 July Paris surrendered. Napoleon had abdicated at the end of June and Louis XVIII entered his capital once again on 8 July. The Napoleonic Wars were over. Waterloo had decided their outcome.

Wellington rated Waterloo among his three best battles. It was not his greatest in terms of tactical enterprise or originality – he, himself, reckoned that distinction lay with Assaye; others might award it to Salamanca. But Waterloo was the closing scene of a stupendous drama which had lasted twenty years; in the Duke's own words it '. . . did more than any other battle I know towards the true object of all battles – the peace of the world'. And Waterloo was the scene of Wellington's only encounter with Napoleon in the field. For both it was the last battle.

Waterloo will always be indissolubly linked with the name of its victor. It was a savage battle of attrition, a 'slogging match' with terrible casualties, and it made immense demands on the courage and stamina of the men who fought it; and on none more than Wellington himself. Exposed throughout the day as much as any man of whatever rank in the Allied Army he commanded: riding instantly again and again to the point of decision; observing, assessing, acting; calming the doubtful by the stern imperturbability of his presence; reacting with speed and assurance when crisis threatened; on that unforgettable Sunday Wellington mastered events from first to last, unshaken when sudden danger presented itself, unelated when it passed. Only when the casualty lists came in that evening did the composure of that great man break down, and he wept. At Waterloo Wellington demonstrated, up to and beyond the hour of victory, personal command in battle at its most sublime.

▲ A fanciful portrayal of Blücher's famous meeting with Wellington near La Belle Alliance farm on the later evening of Waterloo. The 73-year-old veteran's summation — *'Quelle affaire!'* ('What a do!') — 'about the only words of French he knew,' according to the Duke, was fair comment.

BIBLIOGRAPHY

Becke, A. F. *Napoleon and Waterloo*, London, 1914. Captain Becke, a Gunner, wrote his two-volume study in 1914. It is a first-class – indeed probably the best – minute-by-minute account of Waterloo and includes useful appendixes with documents. Becke, a great admirer of Napoleon, supplies a stimulating alternative to the praise of Wellington and criticism of Napoleon which, in English, dominate Waterloo history.

Booth, J. *Battle of Waterloo* ('By a near observer'), London, 1817. This two-volume account and anthology of contemporary accounts went through several editions.

Chalfont, Lord (ed.) *Battle of Three Armies*, London, 1979. The battle is described by different authors, phase by phase, from the different national military viewpoints.

Chandler, D. G. *Waterloo – the Hundred Days*, London, 1980. A recent account which develops the campaign from the French viewpoint and pays special attention to the aftermath of Waterloo.

Keegan, J. *The Face of Battle*, London, 1976. An admirable modern reconstruction of what actually happened to the individual soldier and of what it may have felt like to be him, at various stages of the battle.

Longford, E. *Wellington – The Years of the Sword*, London, 1969. The first volume of Lady Longford's biography of Wellington, including a vivid narrative of the battle, with individual anecdotes and pen-portraits.

Weller, J. *Wellington at Waterloo*, London, 1967. A shrewd, balanced assessment, and an excellent compendium of statistics and useful data.

Note: In addition to the above, any student of Waterloo is recommended to investigate the many admirable accounts by participants – Gronow, Mercer, Wheeler, et. al., as well as Wellington's *Despatch* (*Despatches*, vol. XII).

INKERMAN COMPANY CREST
RMA SANDHURST

THE BATTLE OF INKERMAN, 1854

by John Sweetman

'I have just been over the ground on which the Battle of Inkerman was fought. Many relics of that day remain . . . above all some hundreds of roundshot and shells unburst lay about in all directions. The graves of our brave men who fell that day are also to be seen, their heads marked by pyramids of the deadly missiles by which so many fell.'

(An anonymous soldier cited in the *Illustrated London News*)

On 14 September 1854, almost six months after the British declaration of war against Russia in support of Turkey, the first of 50,000 British, French and Turkish troops landed at Calamita Bay near Eupatoria on the west coast of the Crimean peninsula, 30 miles north of their military objective, Sebastopol. Within hours rain and high winds lashed the unfortunate men before tents could be beached, and four days elapsed before the unopposed landing was completed.

Grim War

At length, with high hopes and flamboyantly led by marching bands, on 19 September the Allies began to move south. By now, however, fierce heat had replaced the driving rain and soon 'clusters of wild-eyed stragglers, strewing blankets, greatcoats, shakos, even ration bags in their wake, [were] tumbling along after the main body'. Not quite so impressive.

That afternoon, enemy formations were sighted though not engaged; but next day a major battle developed on the banks of the River Alma. Under heavy fire British regiments bravely forded the stream and attacked uphill to carry two dominating redoubts on the Russian right, as French gunners similarly crossed the Alma to enfilade the left. By later afternoon, the road to Sebastopol lay open.

The invaders were too exhausted to pursue the broken foe at once; and three days passed before the advance resumed. Then, rather than assault its northern suburbs and cross Sebastopol Bay under the muzzles of enemy guns, the Allied commanders chose to march round the naval port and invest it from uplands to the south. By 27 September this manoeuvre had been executed, with the British holding Balaclava, the French Kamiesch and Kazatch, for supply ports. In theory, with naval domination of the Black Sea, the Allies could now effectively besiege Sebastopol. However, at no time would they have

▲ Field Marshal Fitzroy James Henry Somerset, Baron Raglan (1788–1855), commanded the British forces in the Crimea. He had lost an arm at Waterloo, and served Wellington long and faithfully as an ADC, staff officer, and at the Horse Guards. He died in post before Sebastopol fell. (Engraving by W. J. Edwards)

▲ General François Certain Canrobert (1809–95), later Marshal of France, was a favourite commander of Prince Louis-Napoleon. After Marshal St. Arnaud's death in September 1854, he took command of the French forces in the Crimea, but resigned in the following year. (Engraving by J. Edwards)

enough men completely to surround the city. Direct pressure could only be applied from the southern uplands.

There, lack of heavy artillery doomed to failure a bombardment on 17 October aimed at pounding the garrison into submission. Meanwhile, Russian soldiers and sailors in Sebastopol laboured frantically to strengthen the defences. Ships were sunk across the harbour entrance to bar entry, as 30,000 men

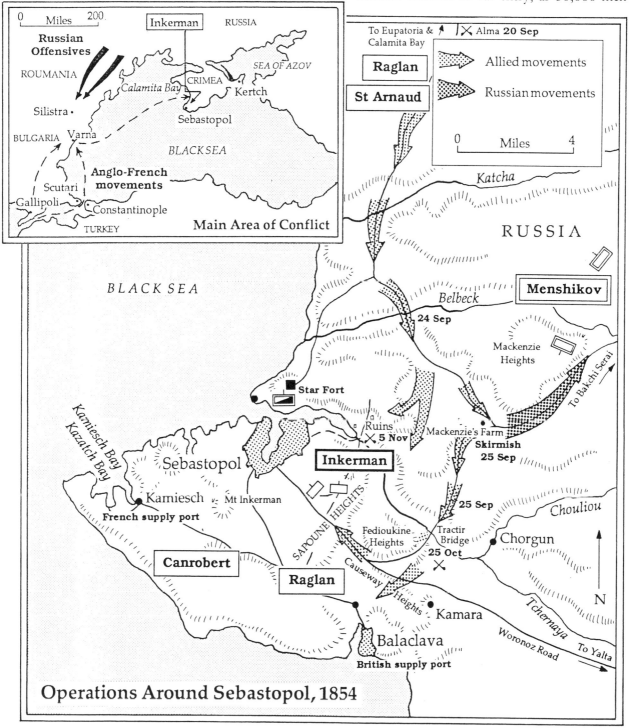

Main Area of Conflict

Operations Around Sebastopol, 1854

▲ General Prince Mikhail Gorchakov (1793–1861), Tsarist force commander at Inkerman and later commander-in-chief of the Russian army in the Crimea. (Engraving by D. J. Pound)

exposed weakness on the right of the Allied siege lines.

At the outbreak of war, Gunner Whitehead had written: 'Grim War does summon me hence/And I deem it my duty to fight.' On 5 November 1854, grimness and duty would be the lot of many a soldier on Mount Inkerman.

Mount Inkerman

Immediately south of Sebastopol, high ground rose gradually but unevenly south-eastwards to culminate in a line of cliffs 700 feet high and seven miles long, which ran roughly parallel to the River Tchernaya and overlooked the Plain of Balaclava. This extensive, triangular plateau was punctuated by prominent knolls, gullies and deep ravines. At its north-eastern extremity, between Careenage Ravine and the cliffs, lay a north–south ridge some 1½ miles long and 1,200 yards wide. Known to the Russians as Cossack Mountain, the British called it 'Mount Inkerman'. Here the probe of 6,500 Russian 'muffin caps' with four field guns had been rebuffed on 26 October.

Two gullies (the Miriakov and Wellway) branched eastwards from the Careenage Ravine, and three other small ravines (Georgievski, Volovia and Quarry) also gave access to the ridge. Roughly in the centre of 'Mount Inkerman', some 2,000 yards south–east of Sebastopol, stood Shell Hill. Six hundred feet above sea level, it spawned two shoulders – East and West Gut. Beyond, 400 yards from the southern end of Quarry Ravine, 30 feet higher than Shell Hill and 1,200 yards from it, stood an L-shaped feature (Home Ridge) destined to be the focal point of the forthcoming battle.

Although part of the British line, there were few defence works in the vicinity of Mount Inkerman. Failure to clear brushwood, loose rocks and stunted trees (up to ten feet high), which hampered movement and cramped artillery fields of fire, suggested that the Allies saw no threat to the position after Russian failure in the Little Inkerman encounter.

Just beyond Fore Ridge, the north-eastern extension of Home Ridge, was the empty Sandbag Battery, a 9-feet-tall defence work with embrasures cut for two guns to engage the enemy eastwards across the Tchernaya, but no *banquette* for men with small arms resisting an attack from elsewhere. In front of Home Ridge, where the old post road emerged from the Quarry Ravine on to the plateau, stood a 4-feet-high wall of heaped stones known as The Barrier. On

marched away inland to form a separate, menacing field army on the Allied right flank. It was this body which attempted a *coup de main* against Balaclava on 25 October, prompting Sir Colin Campbell's gallant and successful action with the 93rd Regiment ('the thin, red streak') and the charges of the Heavy and Light Brigades – collectively known as the Battle of Balaclava. The following day, 6,500 Russians sallied forth from Sebastopol to probe defences on the Heights. They were repulsed.

But the omens were not good. The 65,000 Allied troops totalled only half the combined strength of the Russian garrison and field forces, for which further men and supplies continued to arrive via the Perekop Peninsula in the north and the Sea of Azov in the east. The Battle of Little Inkerman on 26 October had also

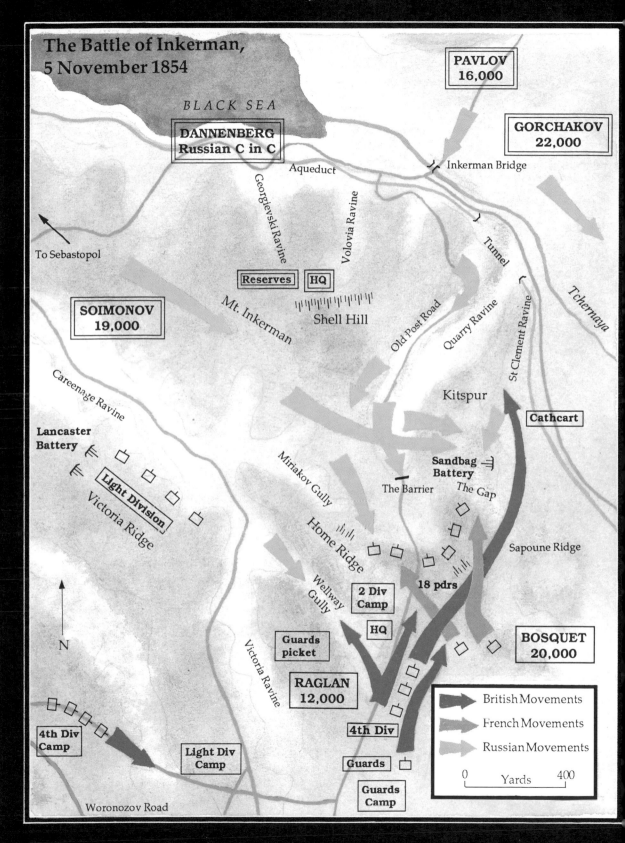

The Battle of Inkerman,
5 November 1854

BLACK SEA

PAVLOV
16,000

GORCHAKOV
22,000

DANNENBERG
Russian C in C

Aqueduct

Inkerman Bridge

Georgievski Ravine

Volovia Ravine

Tunnel

To Sebastopol

Reserves   HQ

Old Post Road

Quarry Ravine

St Clement Ravine

Tchernaya

SOIMONOV
19,000

Mt. Inkerman

Shell Hill

Careenage Ravine

Kitspur

Cathcart

Lancaster
Battery

Light Division

Miriakov Gully

Sandbag
Battery

The Barrier   The Gap

Victoria Ridge

Home Ridge

Sapoune Ridge

18 pdrs

Wellway
Gully

2 Div
Camp

HQ

BOSQUET
20,000

Guards
picket

Victoria Ravine

RAGLAN
12,000

4th Div
Camp

British Movements

French Movements

4th Div

Russian Movements

Light Div
Camp

Guards

0   Yards   400

Guards
Camp

Woronozov Road

N

Home Ridge itself another loose-stone rampart only two feet high ('Herbert's Folly') offered meagre protection to field gunners.

Two rudimentary stone walls and an abandoned battery in partial disrepair represented the sum total of defence works forward on the British right. Otherwise, the men must seek natural cover with the broken nature of the ground encouraging dispersal. So it would prove on the day.

Battle Line-up: the Allies

The Allied siege lines on the uplands south of Sebastopol were semi-circular, with the French on the left, the British on the right. However, whereas the French were within 150 yards of the outer defences, due to the rocky terrain British troops were still more than a mile away. Crucially, too, on the British right the Russians controlled a wide stretch of land from the shores of Sebastopol Bay to Shell Hill, along which reinforcements and supplies could pass freely into Sebastopol.

The British 2nd Division, commanded by Lieutenant-General J. L. Pennefather in the absence of General de Lacy Evans, deployed some 3,000 troops either in camp south of Home Ridge or thrown forward in pickets. A mile to its rear stood 1st Division camp, containing only the Guards Brigade and one troop of field artillery, though a detached picket had been stationed forward overlooking the Wellway and Careenage Ravine. West of the Guards' camp, divided from it by the Careenage Ravine and 1½ miles from the 2nd Division, were two brigades of the Light Division on Victoria Ridge. Even farther west, cut off by more ravines, were the 4th Division (2½ miles from Pennefather) and 3rd Division (too far away for intervention). The broken nature of the ground and distances involved would make reinforcement of the right difficult, to say the least; and Lord Raglan's Headquarters lay four miles behind 2nd Division, close to the siege-gun park.

Battle Line-up: the Russians

The enemy had almost 120,000 men in and around Sebastopol; and Prince Menshikov (the commander-in-chief) planned to use fresh troops of his IV Corps to exploit the weakness on the Allied right. From the Mackenzie Heights, east of the Tchernaya, 16,000 men and 96 guns under Lieutenant-General Pavlov

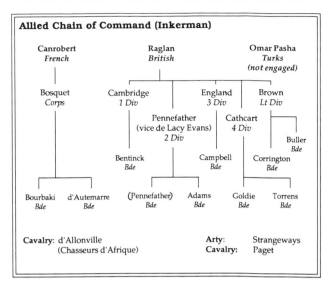

Allied Chain of Command (Inkerman)

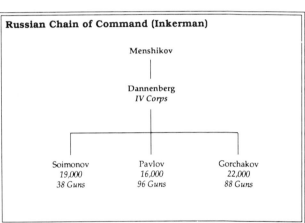

Russian Chain of Command (Inkerman)

would cross the estuary bridge and advance up ravines to the heights, as Lieutenant-General Soimonov with 19,000 men and 38 guns left Sebastopol to cross the Careenage Ravine and scale the plateau. Under the corps commander, General Dannenberg, the combined force would then sweep through the 2nd Division and the troops beyond to outflank the siege lines and cut them off from Balaclava.

To discourage the French on the Allied left from intervening, demonstrations were planned from Sebastopol. And, on the Plain of Balaclava, General Gorchakov would use his 22,000 men and 88 guns, based on Chorgun, to occupy the British near Balaclava and the French overlooking them. A total of 57,000 Russian troops with 222 guns, attacking in a half-moon from Sebastopol to Balaclava, were thus ordered by Menshikov to 'seize and occupy the heights'.

The Bear Stirs

Heavy rain on 4 November persisted well into the night. At dawn on Sunday 5 November, thick mist and light drizzle still cloaked Mount Inkerman, concealing the movement of Dannenberg's IV Corps, as each side of the Tchernaya the Russian Bear stirred.

Just after 2 a.m., Soimonov emerged from Sebastopol, crossed the mouth of the Careenage Ravine and, preceded by skirmishers, led his seven regiments with their artillery support on to the ridge. At 6 a.m. the Russians were engaged by outlying pickets and, shortly afterwards, Soimonov brought twenty-two 12pdr guns into action on Shell Hill and West Gut. Expecting the British to withdraw south of Home Ridge, as they had done on 26 October, he counted on this artillery to devastate the 2nd Division as it retired.

Advance to Contact

In fact, Pennefather did not retreat. He reinforced his pickets. On the right, 41st Regiment closed on Sandbag Battery, a mixed force of 49th and 30th advanced in the centre, on the left others from 49th and 47th made for the Miriakov Gully. As they edged into the mist, not knowing the strength of the enemy before them, twelve 9pdr field guns around Home Ridge fired over their heads into the gloom. Thus, apart from 95th Regiment, the 2nd Division had moved out of its camp before the main weight of Russian shells fell on it. Quite independently of Pennefather, Brigadier-General Codrington, on Victoria Ridge, had alerted Sir George Brown, Light Division commander, who in turn told Captain Ewart, the Headquarters staff officer, at that moment carrying out morning rounds, to warn Raglan.

At 6.45 a.m. Pennefather's probe towards the Miriakov came under fire and eagerly responded to Major Grant's exhortation to 'give 'em a volley and charge'. Sheer numbers made them slowly yield ground, though their stubborn resistance allowed 2nd Division time to regroup. Reaching Home Ridge at 7 a.m., but leaving Pennefather in charge of the battle, Raglan ordered up two long-barrelled 18pdrs from the siege park. Unfortunately, that message went initially to the nearby field gun commander and took time to reach its proper destination.

More immediate help was arriving, though. Men of 88th Regiment and Captain Townsend's 6-gun

▲ General Pierre Joseph François Bosquet (1810–61) commanded the French 2nd Division in the Crimea, part of which fought at Inkerman. In 1856 he was created a Marshal of France. (Engraving by T. W. Houghte)

▲ George William Frederick Charles, Duke of Cambridge (1819–1904). A grandson of King George III (and cousin of Queen Victoria), he commanded the 1st Division. He was later Commander-in-Chief of the British Army for 39 years. (Engraving by T. W. Hunt)

battery went into action on the left. Three of the guns were pushed forward towards the Miriakov Gully to find themselves engulfed by a mass of enemy infantry. With neither horses nor limbers, the gunners fought grimly with rammers, sponges and fists. In vain. The guns were overrun. Then, fatally, the Russians hesitated. As they did so, Pennefather ordered the 88th, in brushwood to their front, to 'give the Russians the bayonet or be driven into the sea'. They must – and did – stand firm.

That Russian hesitation allowed Brigadier-General Buller with 300 men of the 77th critically to intervene, as another column emerged from the Wellway gully threatening to outflank the entire Home Ridge position. Breasting a rise, Buller peered in disbelief at a grey mass just fifteen yards away. His ADC, Lieutenant the Hon Henry Clifford, did not falter. Crying 'In God's name, fix bayonets and charge!' he dashed into the fray. When his pistol failed, Clifford wielded his sword to kill one man and sever the arm of a second. The ferocity of the British attack drove the enemy back down the Wellway; and the Russians did not try that route again.

After being pushed back, Grant's men were still tenaciously holding on south of the Miriakov, supported on their left by the 47th under Major Fordyce. Now, after advancing from the Wellway, on their right Buller brought up the 77th. Tersely ordering the Regiment to 'Charge them!', he saw 77th drive back the Russians 'with fire and steel' headlong towards Shell Hill.

Meanwhile, to the rear and alerted by firing, General Bosquet ordered two French battalions with artillery support to move up. Riding ahead, he met Brown and Sir George Cathcart, commanding 4th Division, who politely assured him that the British could adequately cope with the situation. The French were not needed.

This did not seem unreasonable. For, despite the enemy's overwhelming superiority in men and artillery, with eighteen guns in action around Home Ridge, by 8 a.m. Soimonov's attack had clearly failed. He himself was dead and his beaten columns were back on Shell Hill. In the murky conditions, scattered groups of British troops had made good use of available cover. As Clifford later wrote: 'No order could be given owing to the fog. All we could do was to charge them when they came in sight.'

The Second Wave

The fight, though, was by no means over. Pavlov had not yet even reached the battlefield. His 11th Infantry Division had left camp on the Mackenzie Heights at 2.30 a.m., but did not cross the Tchernaya estuary until 7 a.m. By then it was light and fighting had already started on the ridge. Moving west along the Sapper Road, Pavlov divided his men into three groups. Each force began to climb separately through parallel ravines towards the plateau at about 8 a.m. Troops using the old post road in the Quarry Ravine were fired on by the British right, but debouching on to the ridge quickly overran the Sandbag Battery. The Russians held it for only a short time, before the 41st successfully counter-attacked – a pattern that would be repeated several times during the long, hard day to come. No wonder, on seeing bodies piled around it later, Bosquet graphically observed: *'Quel abattoir'*.

Need for the British to support the Sandbag area brought three 9pdrs on to Fore Ridge; and the Duke of Cambridge deployed 1,200 Grenadier and Scots Fusilier Guards also forward on the right. As these reserves arrived, enemy assaults were launched from the Quarry and St Clement Ravines.

Despite continuing poor visibility, the frequency and strength of the Russian assaults underlined the overall enemy might; and Cambridge became thoroughly alarmed at lack of cover for the 'Gap' of 700 yards between Sandbag Battery and The Barrier. He rode back desperately seeking assistance, only to find two French regiments near Home Ridge refusing to move without specific orders.

◄ **Top: The 55th (Westmoreland) Regiment during the battle. (Painting by Orlando Norris)**

◄ **Left: A famous combat was that of Sergeant Major Andrew Henry of the Royal Artillery who defended his** gun against two Russian infantrymen – an action that won him the VC. He was the sole survivor of his overrun detachment, suffered twelve bayonet wounds and was rescued in a counterattack. (Painting by Chevalier Desanger)

In a Mess

Meanwhile, three more batteries of 9pdrs arrived – making 36 guns in all – and Cathcart had brought up reinforcements from 4th Division. In response to his query about deployment, Pennefather replied that they were needed 'everywhere'. So the first arrivals were dispersed piecemeal. When another 400 ap-

◄ Inkerman was very much a 'soldiers' battle' with much close fighting. Here British infantry engage a Russian attack in hand-to-hand combat. (Painting after A. Dubruy)

◄ British Guards in close action. The murderous nature of the fighting is well depicted.

peared under Brigadier-General Torrens, Cathcart determined to keep them under his own command. He ignored Raglan's order to fill the Gap, whose vulnerability so worried Cambridge. Instead Cathcart plunged his men down the slope below Sandbag Battery towards the Tchernaya, aiming to attack the Russian left flank. Unfortunately, almost simultaneously, a strong Russian force emerged from the Quarry Ravine to capture ground above him and to his left rear. He was now in an impossible position. With studied understatement, he remarked: 'I fear we are in a mess.' Within minutes he had been killed; and the remnant of his force scattered into small groups seeking safety.

As they did so, Cambridge and the Guards were all but cut off at Sandbag Battery. They, too, had to fight their way out. A determined charge led by Assistant Surgeon Wolseley helped to clear the way for the Colours, but the Duke and his staff reached safety unaware of the fate of the main body. Calmly Colonel Herbert assured him: 'The Guards, sir, will be sure to turn up.' And just as the right seemed in grave danger, at 8.30 a.m. two French infantry battalions, four companies of chasseurs and twelve guns under General Bourbaki at last advanced to its support.

However, Dannenberg (exercising battlefield command) still had 9,000 reserves of Pavlov's division plus the 7,000 already committed, besides his massive

▲ **The British Guards Brigade of the 1st Division repel a Russian up-hill attack. (Print by J. J. Crow)**

artillery concentration around Shell Hill. He now made his main attack on Home Ridge – rightly seen as the key to the whole battlefield; 6,000 men advanced through thick brushwood to capture three guns on the left of the British line, in the centre to sweep through The Barrier and cross Home Ridge. With victory apparently within their grasp, yet again the Russians hesitated – fatally, especially as the Russian gunners were savagely hitting the British. One shell exploded in the entrails of Colonel Somerset's horse, spattering those around with blood and flesh. As a round shot tore off Brigadier-General Strangway's leg, he murmured: 'Will somebody be kind enough to lift me off my horse?' Two hours later, he died.

For the British the moment of maximum danger had passed, as more troops came into the line. Brown led a counter-attack; the French, who had fled before the renewed Russian advance, rallied; and thirty determined men of the 55th pierced the enemy right wing. Reinforcing the troops driven back from The Barrier, with canister and grape fired overhead by British gunners, the whole centre surged forward.

The Barrier was recaptured, as the French came under fire in the Sandbag area and Russian artillery continued to bombard Home Ridge. At 9.30 a.m. the two 18pdr siege guns finally arrived and were deployed at the junction of Home and Fore Ridges. Supported by twelve French guns, they quickly found the range of Shell Hill. But the Sandbag Battery, to which the Coldstreams had also been sent, remained the centre of fierce fighting. In mid-morning, however, Bosquet brought up more French reserves and at 11 a.m. the Russians were ejected from the position for the last time. Guarded mainly by the French, the right flank was now secure.

In the centre, at midday the Russians began to draw back from The Barrier, leaving heaps of dead 'as thick as sheaves in a cornfield'. As they did so, Raglan decided that the enemy must not be permitted to entrench on Shell Hill. Supported by fifty British and French guns, troops directed by Lord West attacked the West Gut outflanking the whole Russian position, causing them to limber up their guns and retire.

Acknowledging that the day was lost, at 1 p.m. Dannenberg ordered a general retreat behind a covering force. By 3 p.m. the enemy had vacated Shell Hill, as the French moved up to occupy East Gut. British troops pursued the fleeing Russians down the Carenage Ravine, and only a determined infantry counter-attack saved Russian guns on Sapper Road.

On Mount Inkerman, Sandbag Battery, The Barrier and Home Ridge had been secured. During the morning, forays from Sebastopol against the Allied left had been repulsed, though they had prevented French reinforcement from that quarter. In the east, Gorchakov's manoeuvres had quickly been seen as the mere demonstration that they were. Leaving only a token screen to face him, Bosquet and Cambridge had sent invaluable troops to Pennefather's aid. Thus had the Battle of Inkerman been won.

A Terrible Sight

Three days after the battle, with countless dead still unburied, the stench remained 'pretty awful'. Nor was the fate of the wounded pleasant. Pennefather noted: 'They are all about my tent, lying day and night on the wet ground, starving and dying and screaming in agony.' Surveying the scene of carnage, Captain Temple Godman observed: 'The field of battle is a terrible sight.'

On 11 November, a newly arrived officer found the British 'in deep gloom': 635 (including 43 officers) had been killed, 1,938 wounded, while the French had suffered 1,743 casualties (25 officers and 150 men killed). On the enemy side, an artillery officer reported 'a general depression everywhere'. Not surprising, perhaps. Of 35,000 Russians sent against Mount Inkerman, 11,959 became casualties (4,400 dead, including six generals). Down on the Plain, Gorchakov incurred just fifteen casualties.

Reasons Why

Colonel Men'kov complained bitterly that 'nearly all our regimental and battalion commanders and senior officers' had been 'lost . . . And all for nothing!'

The Russian plan of attack was, in truth, far too complicated and in practice badly executed. Dannenberg's IV Corps reached the area only on 4 November, was totally unfamiliar with the ground and carried out no preliminary reconnaissance. Lack of co-ordination next day meant that Soimonov and Pavlov attacked separately, and tactical formations acted in isolation. One British survivor held that, if the different advances up the ravines had been simultaneous, 'we should have been swamped'. The Russians' overwhelming strength in manpower was never properly exerted, and much of IV Corps' artillery stayed uncommitted on the Sapper Road.

Achievement of 'The Soldiers' Battle'

Undoubtedly, these Russian shortcomings were important. But, at root, positive Allied action not enemy weakness secured victory. The enemy artillery was far less effective than the British, especially after the two 18pdrs came on to Home Ridge. The Minié musket, too, proved its worth: 'files upon files [of Russians] . . . laid down in heaps' bore silent witness to that. Discipline and regimental spirit in the face of repeated mass assaults claimed the day. The ebb and flow around the Sandbag Battery alone underlined these qualities.

Success on Mount Inkerman prevented the Russians from outflanking the entire Allied position before Sebastopol and severing lines of communication with Balaclava. Small wonder that, in defeat, the Russians 'marched listlessly and unhappily'. On Mackenzie Heights 'yesterday there had been chatter, noise and mirth. Today there was melancholy and emptiness'. Pennefather exlaimed: 'I tell you, we gave 'em a hell of a towelling!'

To do so, '. . . colonels of regiments led on small parties and fought like subalterns, captains like privates. Once engaged, every man was his own general'. Thus, the Battle of Inkerman has gone down in History as 'The Soldiers' Battle'.

BIBLIOGRAPHY

Blake, ffrench R.L.V. *The Crimean War*, London, 1971. This tackles the battle by dividing the action into seven periods and putting Allied and Russian activity in chronological order side by side. A useful survey.

Hibbert, C. *The Destruction of Lord Raglan*, London, 1961. One very readable chapter of 30 pages, which makes good use of eye-witness comments. Not so detailed as Kinglake or Pemberton.

Kinglake, A. W. *The Invasion of the Crimea*, vol. V, London, 1875. A lengthy and extremely detailed account of the battle by a civilian observer at the front, who made later use of other sources. Concentrating on individuals and small actions, it has numerous maps and is comprehensive.

Pemberton, W. B. *Battles of the Crimean War*, London, 1962. Contains a 50-page chapter on Inkerman with one small, but clear, map. Quite detailed, it draws heavily on Kinglake and other contemporary sources.

MacMunn, G. *The Crimea in Perspective*, London, 1935. This includes a straightforward description of the battle in a 26-page chapter with a single map. A useful account without detail.

Seaton, A. *The Crimean War: A Russian Chronicle*, London, 1977. Uses Russian sources and is first-class on the battle from the Russian viewpoint. The shortcomings in planning and execution of the attack are analysed in a 25-page chapter.

THE BATTLE OF THE MARNE, 1914

by Charles Grant

'A small but highly trained force striking "out of the blue" at a vital spot can produce a strategic effect out of all proportion to its slight numbers.'

(B. H. Liddell Hart)

When the British Expeditionary Force (BEF) crossed to the northern side of the River Marne on 9 September 1914 they brought to an end the German dream of decisive and early victory in north-west Europe. It is difficult to imagine how a force of 100,000 men could so fundamentally influence a war which involved, at the outset, more than three million men on the Western Front alone. In order to understand the place of the Battle of the Marne in the events of the First World War it is necessary to understand how the BEF came to be where it was on that day in September 1914.

The Preliminaries of War

Few would question that the First World War was inevitable. The causes of the war have themselves been the subject of much study. Stated in the simplest terms it can be said that the roots of the war lay in the humiliating defeat which Germany inflicted upon France in 1870–1. The inevitability of the war lay in the complex series of alliances built up during the late nineteenth and early twentieth centuries. On one hand the Triple Alliance of Germany, Austria-Hungary and Turkey was countered on the other by *La Triple Alliance*. The latter did what the wise Chancellor Bismark had sought to avoid, it brought together Russia, France and Great Britain. This delicate web of alliances inextricably linked all the major powers so that any conflict involving one was almost certain to drag all of them into war. The catalyst for the war was the assassination of Archduke Franz Ferdinand, heir to the Austrian Empire, at Sarajevo on 28 June 1914. The nature of the alliances was such, however, that almost any event could have provided the *casus belli*.

Opposing Strategies

The basis of the plan for the German attack, which began on 4 August 1914 when the Second Army marched in to Belgium, had its roots in the previous century. Count Alfred von Schlieffen, the Chief of the Great General Staff, had evolved a strategy which would provide a concentration of force rapidly to defeat the enemy on one front before turning to the other. This plan required a massive concentration of force on the right wing of the German army facing France. Schlieffen originally intended to use sixteen corps and five divisions of cavalry to sweep through

Belgium and around Paris achieving decisive victory in six weeks. The mass of the German army could then switch to the eastern front and defeat the Russians. Schlieffen's successor, General Helmuth von Moltke, inherited the plan in 1906, but lacked the breadth of vision and understanding to implement it. Von Moltke was the nephew of the elder Moltke, who had masterminded the wars against Austria and France in the second half of the previous century and was the creator of the Great General Staff. From 1906 von Moltke gradually eroded the basis of the plan so that by 1914 Schlieffen's proposed superiority of eight to one on the right flank had been diluted to three to one. The advantages of German superiority had been dissipated across the front. Von Moltke had also abandoned Schlieffen's intention to invade through Holland in favour of attempting to reach agreement with Belgium. Finally, von Moltke either chose to overlook or ignored British participation.

▲ General Helmuth Johann Ludwig von Moltke (1848–1916), Chief of the German Great General Staff in 1914, was the mere shadow of his famous uncle. After the Marne he suffered a breakdown and was replaced by von Falkenhayn.

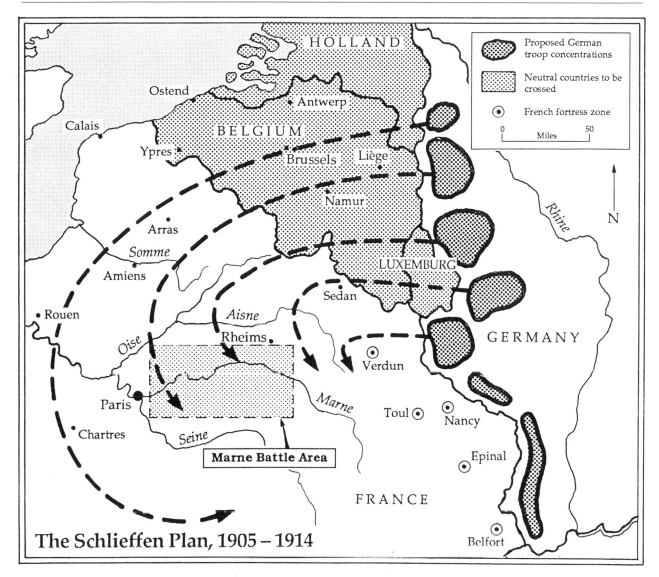

The Schlieffen Plan, 1905 – 1914

Legend:
- Proposed German troop concentrations
- Neutral countries to be crossed
- French fortress zone

Miles 0 — 50

Marne Battle Area

In contrast to the German plan, the French Plan XVII had evolved through a wide-ranging series of philosophical arguments from passive defence through defensive offence to the theory of *'offensive à outrance'*. (The latter tactic advocated the subordination of all other considerations to that of the offensive.) In 1911 General Joseph Joffre replaced General Michel as Commander-in-Chief. Joffre reappraised the then existing Plan XVI and Michel's proposals and produced Variation Number One. This accepted the offensive doctrine, shifted the mass of the army farther north and forward, and confirmed Russia's agreement to act swiftly and before complete mobilization in time of war. This plan was further modified in 1912 and became plan XVII in 1913. In outline, Plan XVII opted to fight a defensive action until the thirteenth day of mobilization and then to conduct a general offensive with the two right wing armies attacking Lorraine, a central army attacking towards Metz and the armies of the left counter-attacking into Belgium or towards Metz depending on the German attack. The army reserve would be left of centre and the BEF would take up position on the left of the army.

The Armies

The German Army of 1914 was overall the best trained and equipped in Europe. Of its eight field armies, seven (totalling more than 1,600,000 men)

▲ General Joseph Jacques Césaire, 'Papa' Joffre (1852–1931). Although his war Plan XVII was badly flawed, he kept cool during the great German offensive based upon the (much revised) 'Schlieffen Plan' in 1914, and masterminded the victory of the Marne and the subsequent 'Race to the Sea'. He was superseded in 1916 after Verdun and the Somme by General Nivelle, being created a Marshal of France in compensation.

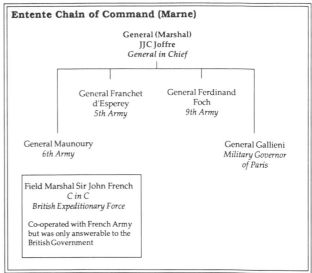

Entente Chain of Command (Marne)

General (Marshal)
JJC Joffre
General in Chief

General Franchet d'Esperey
5th Army

General Ferdinand Foch
9th Army

General Maunoury
6th Army

General Gallieni
Military Governor of Paris

Field Marshal Sir John French
C in C
British Expeditionary Force

Co-operated with French Army but was only answerable to the British Government

faced the west. Each army consisted of two or more infantry corps each of 44,000. An active corps consisted of two infantry divisions with supporting arms. Its reserve counterpart lacked both artillery and aircraft, but was integrated with the active corps in the same army – something the Allies had not foreseen. Two infantry and one artillery brigade made up the mass of the 17,500 men in a German active infantry division. In addition to the 22 active and 14 reserve infantry corps, the Germans had ten cavalry divisions making up four cavalry corps. One such division of 7,000 men consisted of three cavalry and three *Jaeger* brigades. The German equipment was first class. At divisional level the artillery were 77mm guns and

105mm howitzers; at corps level there were 105mm and 150mm howitzers. At army level there were 210mm and 420mm mortars. The infantry were equipped with 1898 Mauser, clip-fed, bolt-action rifles and the 1908 water-cooled Maxim machine-gun.

The French Army numbered 1,650,000 divided into five field armies, 25 reserve divisions and corps artillery. There were 21 active infantry corps each of 40,000 men. Each infantry division was 15,000 strong. The reserve divisions were not integrated into the field armies. The French 75mm gun was an excellent weapon, well ahead of its contemporaries. The infantry were armed with the 1886 Lebel rifle and dressed in a manner better suited to the previous century. The French cavalry in steel breastplate and helmet were no better.

The BEF landed in France and had arrived in their concentration area around Maubeuge on 20 August. The Commander-in-Chief, Field Marshal Sir John French, had agreed that it would be ready to advance on 21 August. The presence of the force was still unknown to German Intelligence. The BEF totalled 100,000 men of whom many were reservists quickly called up to bring battalions up to strength. It consisted initially of two corps each of two divisions; I Corps commanded by Lieutenant-General Sir Douglas Haig and II Corps commanded by General Sir Horace Smith-Dorrien. They were joined by Major-General W. P. Pulteney's III Corps on 29 August, just in time for the counter-offensive. There was also a cavalry division of 14,000 men divided into five brigades. The British khaki-clad infantry were armed with the Lee Enfield bolt-action rifle and were well-schooled in accurate individual fire.

The Battle of the Frontiers

From the start the German invasion of Belgium did not go according to plan. Liège, which the Germans anticipated falling by *coup de main*, did not fall until 16 August. The French, unaware of the German strength or intent, launched their planned offensive all along the front on 14 August. Fierce fighting ensued, but by the 20th any French illusions, and with them Plan XVII, were shattered. At Mornange and Sarrenbourg on the French right, the French First and Second Armies were defeated. On 21 August the French Third and Fourth Armies in the centre were in retreat and on the 23rd Lanrezac ordered the army of the left to retreat. The BEF had started to meet elements of von Kluck's First Army on 22 August. On the 23rd the Battle of Mons was fought. The withdrawal of the French Fifth Army on the 24th made the position at Mons untenable and the BEF also withdrew. So ended the Battle of the Frontiers.

The Retreat

The Allied armies began their retreat. On the night of 25 August Joffre issued General Instruction Number 2. This required a slow retreat of the French left pivoting on Verdun while a new army would form on the left with Maunoury's army of Lorraine transferred to that flank. The French had begun to shift their weight to the left.

By 25 August reports coming into Supreme Headquarters (*Oberste Heeresleitung* or OHL), convinced von Moltke that the necessary 'decisive victory' had been achieved. Before he could transfer VI corps to the Eastern Front, however, the French counter-attacked. Von Moltke therefore took II Corps for Prussia from his right. In less than a month the German right had been reduced from seventeen to twelve corps. On the 26th Smith-Dorrien's II Corps of the BEF made a stand at Le Cateau. The importance of this brave stand was that as they retreated on the 27th, von Kluck believed that he had destroyed the BEF, a belief which would radically influence his further actions.

As General Maunoury took command of the still forming French Sixth Army on the 27th, the German Great General Staff issued the General Directive to continue the offensive along the whole front. At this point von Kluck's army was removed from von Bülow's control. Von Kluck now dismissed the BEF from his mind and believed the key objective was to find the flank of the French army now falling back to the south and south-west. The attempt to exploit this view began the start of the gradual separation of the German First and Second Armies which the Allies would eventually exploit. On 29 August the French Fifth Army counter-attacked and engaged von Bülow's army at Guise-St Quentin to permit the BEF to withdraw cleanly. As the French line elsewhere struggled to hold, Maunoury's army was still detraining in Paris.

▲ **Field Marshal Sir John French (1852–1925), Commander-in-Chief of the British Expeditionary Force in 1914–15. A cavalry hero in the Boer War, he had less success in later** years as CIGS. In France and Flanders his main achievment was the saving of the First Battle of Ypres. His Earldom reflected this success.

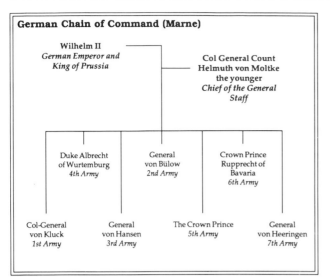

German Chain of Command (Marne)

Wilhelm II
*German Emperor and
King of Prussia*

Col General Count
Helmuth von Moltke
the younger
*Chief of the General
Staff*

Duke Albrecht of Wurtemburg *4th Army*	General von Bülow *2nd Army*	Crown Prince Rupprecht of Bavaria *6th Army*

Col-General von Kluck *1st Army*	General von Hansen *3rd Army*	The Crown Prince *5th Army*	General von Heeringen *7th Army*

John French to support a plan for a counter-offensive. It was not until 4 September that Joffre, now convinced of the weakness in the German front and his own ability to launch a successful counter-attack, went firm on his plan, which was to move forward to a suitable line from which the attack could begin. The Sixth Army would attack towards Château-Thierry, the BEF and the Fifth Army towards Montmirail supported by the Ninth Army. The Fourth Army was to hold and the Third would attack to the west. The Second and First Armies would hold the right. As the

▼ A German machine-gun team in action. The troops wear felt helmet covers; their weapon is water-cooled.

On the 30th and 31st, as von Kluck pursued his objective and von Bülow rested, the gap between the two armies continued to grow. At the same time von Moltke finally abandoned such vestiges of Schlieffen's plan that remained, opting to envelop the French armies with both flanks, the right swinging south-east of Paris instead of enveloping the French capital. Early news of this critical change of direction and plan was provided for the Allies by air reconnaissance, which thus entered the field as an important element of modern warfare. At the start of September the German view was still that the Third, Fourth and Fifth Armies would provide a decisive victory, but concern was growing about their right flank. This caused von Moltke to order the French to be driven away from Paris with the First Army following behind the Second and responsible for flank protection. This was contrary to von Kluck's perception who, not knowing about the French army assembling in Paris, chose to ignore the order. Von Kluck's army was now two days ahead of von Bülow's. His action increased the gap between the First and Second Armies and exposed the whole German flank to Maunoury's army in Paris. By 5 September, von Kluck still did not understand the threat from Paris and far from conforming to von Moltke's order he was well ahead of von Bülow and south of the Marne.

Between 1 and 5 September Joffre set in motion the actions which would prepare for the Battle of the Marne. On the 3rd he relieved the tired and worried Lanrezac of command of the Fifth Army, replacing him with Franchet d'Esperey. He also persuaded Sir

Sixth Army marched to its start line, the River Ourcq, on the 5th they found Gronau's corps of von Kluck's army west of the river and in their path. After a solid defence the Germans fell back to a new position during the night. The Battle of the Marne had begun.

The Battle of the Marne

On Sunday 6 September the Western Front stretched from north of Paris, across the Marne and on to Verdun, then across to Lorraine and south to the Alps. The balance of forces had swung dramatically in the last month. Joffre had created the Sixth and Ninth Armies which, with the Fifth Army, part of the Fourth Army and the BEF, gave him 41 infantry and eight cavalry divisions on his left. They faced the German First, Second and Third Armies with 23 infantry and five cavalry divisions. Maunoury's Sixth Army continued the fierce fighting with Gronau's corps throughout the day. Gronau called for assistance but von Kluck was still unaware of the full plight of his corps commander. D'Esperey's Fifth Army engaged von Kluck's two corps while sending a corps to help Foch on the right. Between the Sixth and Fifth Armies the BEF advanced slowly towards the gap between the Germans. The BEF had received the orders for the attack too late to prevent their continued rearward movement on the 5th and so started well behind the French line on the 6th. The French centre and right hung on meanwhile despite the gaps and numerical disadvantage.

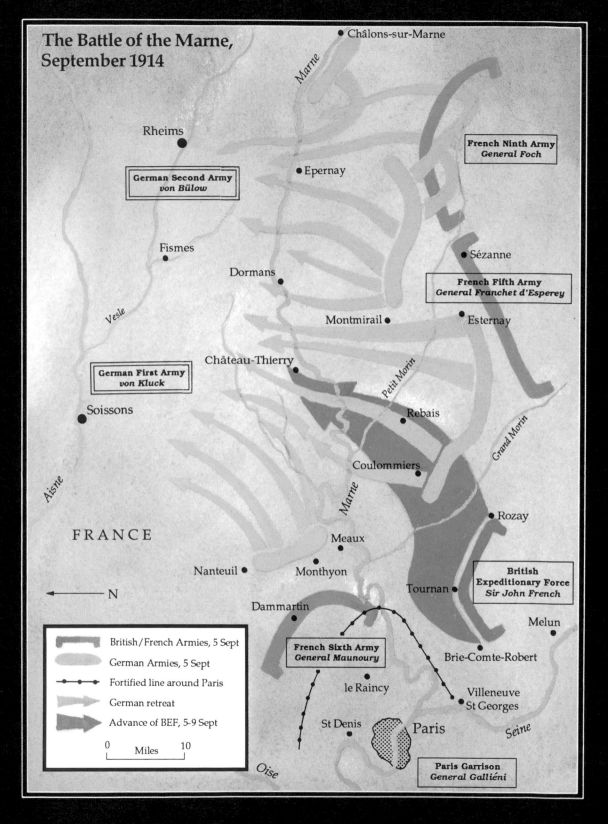

The Battle of the Marne, September 1914

Châlons-sur-Marne

Rheims

German Second Army
von Bülow

French Ninth Army
General Foch

Epernay

Fismes

Sézanne

Dormans

French Fifth Army
General Franchet d'Esperey

Montmirail

Esternay

Château-Thierry

German First Army
von Kluck

Rebais

Soissons

Coulommiers

Rozay

FRANCE

Meaux

British Expeditionary Force
Sir John French

Nanteuil

Monthyon

N

Tournan

Melun

Dammartin

Brie-Comte-Robert

French Sixth Army
General Maunoury

le Raincy

Villeneuve St Georges

Paris

St Denis

Paris Garrison
General Galliéni

British/French Armies, 5 Sept

German Armies, 5 Sept

Fortified line around Paris

German retreat

Advance of BEF, 5–9 Sept

0   Miles   10

Marne

Vesle

Aisne

Petit Morin

Grand Morin

Marne

Seine

Oise

Monday, 7 September: At last von Kluck had begun to appreciate the seriousness of his position. He now demanded that the two corps which had been on von Bülow's right and supporting his wheel should retire behind the Petit Morin river. Thus the gap between the two armies was further increased and von Bülow had no reserve left to cover his exposed right. Throughout the day Joffre ordered commanders to hold their ground and refused to give despite the pressure. A division just detrained in Paris was urgently needed by Maunoury. General Galliéni, Governor of Paris, ordered 1,000 Parisian taxi-cabs to move them to the front and in so doing earned his name a place in history. The BEF's advance on the 7th was slow; perhaps less than eight miles. Unknowingly, this was an important factor in the long term because von Bülow would not have transferred the two corps

◄ General Joseph Simon Galliéni (1849–1916). As military governor of Paris in 1914, it was his bold action in sallying forth with his garrison — many of the troops conveyed in requisitioned Paris taxi-cabs — to attack von Kluck's exposed flank on the River Ourcq, that clinched the victory of the Marne. He was posthumously created a Marshal in 1921.

▼ British heavy artillery gun in action, 1914. These pieces, often drawn by traction-engines, put down redoubtable barrages — but until late September failed to halt the German advance.

▲ An archetypical German infantry soldier, 'Kaiser moustache' included. The *pickelhaube* helmets were covered by a felt cover when in action.

▶ A grey-clad infantryman in full field service marching order.

to von Kluck if the former had been aware of the advance of the BEF into the gap between the armies.

Tuesday, 8 September: Von Moltke, in his headquarters far removed from the battle, was now aware of the gap between his two armies. Colonel Hentsch, a staff officer, was sent to the front to assess the situation. His verbal orders from von Moltke were that if a retreat on the right were necessary he should influence it in such a way as to close the gap. Hentsch paid visits to the Fifth, Fourth and Third Army Headquarters, in that order, and all were satisfactory. On the 8th he signalled von Moltke: 'Situation and point of view entirely favourable at the Third Army.' His trip to the Second Army was difficult and harrowing. On his arrival that evening he found von Bülow tired and concerned. Having explained the situation the latter pointed out the threat the BEF now posed and that he had no reserves with which to plug the gap into which the BEF were about to march; from there they could turn on the First Army or both the Second Army and the whole German flank. Foch's Ninth Army and Langle's Fourth Army held their ground despite German attacks. Farther to the French right the Third, Second and First Armies hung on. During the day the BEF advanced ten miles, opening the bridges across the Petit Morin and allowing the cavalry across. Stiff resistance was encountered but by evening the British right and centre were on their way to the Marne while the left was shelling the German positions on the far side of the river.

Wednesday, 9 September: Early on the morning of the 9th Hentsch met von Bülow's Chief of Staff, Lauenstein, and it was agreed (presumably with von Bülow's knowledge) that the Second Army would retire. Hentsch now left to persuade von Kluck to do likewise and in so doing close the gap. In the French

▼ German artillery troops manhandle a light field-gun into position.

▶ General Alexander von Kluck (1846–1934) commanded the German First Army on the extreme right flank in 1914. His error of judgement gave the Allies the chance for a telling riposte on the Marne.

◄ French *chasseur* in full dress. In Champagne in 1914, some units were sent into battle in such uniforms – often with disastrous results.

► French officer and Indian soldier. The British Empire rallied behind the mother-country, and Indian troops eventually appeared on the Western Front, to share its miseries. (Mist after Bellecour)

camp, with Maunoury's progress halted, Joffre's hopes now rested on the BEF. Special Order Number 19 was issued on the night of the 8th. It ordered Maunoury to hold but avoid decisive action on the 9th while the BEF was to cross the Marne and attack the left and rear of von Kluck's Army. The Fifth Army would cross the Marne covering the BEF on the left and supporting Foch on the right. Shortly after 8 a.m. the leading elements of the BEF were across the Marne. The right and centre found the bridges intact and crossed, but on the left the bridges had been blown and Pulteney's corps, without engineers, was held up. Despite encountering little opposition, the advance was slow and covered less than twelve miles in the day. Now was the time for speed – had they pressed on a further six to eight miles a great tactical victory lay within their grasp – but the moment passed. Meanwhile, with von Bülow retiring von Kluck had little option but to conform despite some localized advantage. Hentsch repeated the order to

◄ British cavalrymen pause to chat-up a *mademoiselle* 'somewhere in France or Belgium'.

► French infantry charge in full field service marching order, including greatcoats, late in 1914. Such bunched formations invited crippling casualties — which were duly sustained.

► British infantry manning an extemporized trench. 'Old Bill' soon learnt the need to dig. Note the lack of steel helmets in 1914.

withdraw to the line Soissons–Fismes to join von Bülow. Hausen's request to retire the Third Army also was first refused then, in the confusion, agreed by Hentsch and then countermanded by OHL. If things were going badly for the Germans on the right the same could not be said for their Fifth and Six Armies on the left. It was therefore with disbelief that they received von Moltke's order to cease the offensive.

Thursday, 10 September: by the night of the 10th the Battle of the Marne was over. On the afternoon of the 11th, von Moltke ordered the Third, Fourth and Fifth Armies to retire and by the 12th the German right wing was taking up positions behind the Aisne. The 'race to the sea' was about to begin.

The cost in casualties of the first six weeks of the war had been enormous. French casualties up to the end of the Marne were in the region of a quarter of a million. The BEF lost 12,733 men, 1,701 of them during the period 6–10 September. German records do not exist but the figures would be equally horrific.

Consequences and Observations

Despite its name, the Battle of the Marne was not just a battle won, in the classic sense, but a strategic victory achieved by manoeuvre. The combat across the front was intense, but for the key player (the BEF) the fighting was insignificant compared with its role in the game of strategic chess. It is an excellent example of the counterstroke executed at a grand level. The very presence of the BEF north of the Marne rendered the German position untenable. The single most important consequence of the Battle of the Marne was the termination of the German plan for a swift and decisive victory. With the end of this came the end of the short mobile war and the onset of four years of static positional warfare.

Lessons and observations abound and there is space here for only a few. Chief among them must be the comparison of command styles which has so far only been touched upon. Von Moltke and OHL were remote in both time and space from the realities of the front. The consequence was a lack of accurate information and the ability to influence events. The army commanders were independent and unco-ordinated with disastrous results. In contrast Joffre was everywhere, well informed and actively managing the battle. Secondly the exaggerated and embellished German reports of complete victory created a quite false impression of the state of the BEF and French armies. Thirdly, the almost total disregard by the

▲ First Battle of Ypres. A 2nd Lieutenant and a Staff Sergeant of 1st Battalion, the Cameronians, study the German line through a field of cabbages from a rudimentary trench. In the early days of the war, trenches were often only enlarged drainage ditches, and as the Germans almost invariably occupied the slightly higher ground after the 'Race to the Sea' in late 1914, the Allied trenches were often very wet. Note that the officer's badges of rank are still worn on the cuffs; they would soon be moved to the less obvious shoulder-straps.

Germans for the BEF, from start to finish, can justly be claimed as one cause of the German undoing. Finally one must note and admire the indomitable determination of the French and British troops who fought so valiantly in both retreat and attack. For this alone the 'miracle of the Marne' is justly deserving of its place among the companies of Sandhurst.

BIBLIOGRAPHY

Asprey, R. B. *The First Battle of the Marne*, London, 1962. A good analysis and account.

Edmonds, J. E. *Military Operations: France and Belgium, 1914*, Macmillan, 1933. The British Official History: a vital source of information.

Kluck, A. von. *The March on Paris 1914*, London, 1920. A fair exposition of the German view.

Liddell Hart, B. H. *History of the First World War*, London, 1970. A good over-view of the war.

Macdonald, L. *1914*, London, 1987. A good account based upon survivors' recollections.

Terraine, J. *Mons – Retreat to Victory*, London, 1960. A useful account.

SOMME COMPANY CREST
RMA SANDHURST

THE BATTLE OF THE SOMME, 1916

by Sir Anthony Farrar-Hockley

'God of battles, was ever a battle like this in the world before?'

(Alfred, Lord Tennyson, *The Revenge*)

By the end of 1915, the warring powers in Europe had come to recognize that victory would not be won speedily or cheaply. Germany, dominant among the Central Powers, had been decisively checked on the Western Front in 1914, and surprised by the success of its relatively modest forces against Russia in the east. Plan XVII had failed France: a considerable part of its northern territory had been lost as a consequence, despite the successful counter-offensive from the Marne. Subsequent extravagant hopes for a flanking advance through Belgium had collapsed when the Anglo-French forces met head-on a similar German manoeuvre coming the other way. The year ended with the establishment of trenches from the Channel to the Vosges mountains. In the spring of 1915, the Germans took away the western Allies' breath in more senses than one in a second battle round Ypres, but failed to break out into France. Repeated attacks, singly and collectively by the French and British in Artois, and by France alone in the Champagne throughout the same year, were unsuccessful in overcoming the German defences.

Attritional War

It is unfortunate that the high commanders failed to draw essential conclusions from these failures. The German and French generals were influenced by the lessons of the Franco-Prussian War of 1870–1, the British by those of the Boer War at the turn of the century. Inexperience may excuse their ineptitude during the manoeuvre phase and their early struggles to break out of trench warfare, but after eighteen months of considerable fighting all had failed to discern why their major offensives on the Western Front had been frustrated.

Among a number of problems, two were paramount. How to break into extended trench defences protected comprehensively by barbed wire? And having broken in, how to co-ordinate sufficient numbers and fire to break out into the enemy rear area? The solution lay partly in the development of tactics that made full use of the potential of modern artillery firing indirectly but with considerable accuracy, and the infantry weapons, rifles, grenades and machine-guns.

The dispatching of assault forces in column of companies or platoons across No Man's Land was a crude, ineffective and expensive method of operation.

Equally, there had to be a major improvement in the command and control of the assault forces, including reserves. Partly due to custom and organization, partly to the state of technology, commanders from brigade to army lacked the knowledge of what was happening to the soldiers they sent to close with the enemy and thus they were unable to exploit success or minimize loss. Sir Douglas Haig, who became British commander-in-chief at the end of 1915, had begun to grasp this as an army commander during the Battle of Loos, but believed that it was simply a problem of organization. Neither he nor any other senior commander pursued solutions as a matter of urgency. Similarly, many months were to pass before changes in tactics were brought about by pressure from officers who had survived the old methods of attack and were determined to replace them with something better.

As it was, in the immediate aftermath of each failure in 1915, there was a tendency in the French general headquarters to fall back upon the dreadful notion that victory would come simply by grinding away at the enemy's resources, *la guerre de l'usure*. But this was more in the nature of a mood than a policy, one which passed as common sense indicated that such methods would not bring about an early or satisfactory end to hostilities. And for France, Belgium and Luxemburg, a satisfactory end meant essentially the withdrawal of the enemy from their homelands, a consideration which frustrated German suggestions, at this time, of an armistice on the basis of territorial occupation.

Allied commanders-in-chief or their representatives met at Chantilly, 6–8 December 1915, to consider plans for the following year. General Joffre believed that the war was developing in favour of the Allies. French industry had replaced losses in arms and equipment, and was building a reserve of ammunition, most importantly artillery shells. British war production, after initial difficulties, was producing the needs of the rapidly expanding British Expeditionary Force. Russia and Italy were ready in principle to pass to the offensive. There were no proposals for further 'sideshows', such as the Dardanelles offensive, which had failed.

Rival Plans Emerge

Joffre wished to open a concerted offensive in March 1916, in order to take advantage of the spring and summer for exploitation. This was impracticable. British reinforcement would not be complete before

May. The Italians and Russians were looking towards mid-summer; the Russians lacked almost everything but men; that winter 160,000 of their soldiers were in the line without rifles. Thus 1 July was chosen as a target date.

Sir Douglas Haig became commander-in-chief of the British Expeditionary Force – the BEF – on 19 December. He had the authority of Mr Asquith's coalition government to engage in a major offensive in 1916, the time and place being left to him and to Joffre. Haig favoured Flanders, an area completely under his military control,* closed up on his lines of communication, with the Royal Navy on the Channel flank. But from the day of his appointment, the self-contained Scot, very much the professional British

The Belgian Army held the largely flooded, coastal sector but the BEF otherwise occupied and was responsible for operations in Flanders.

cavalry officer, discovered the disadvantages of being a junior partner. Joffre, 62 years of age, was 'the old man' to Haig at 54; and indeed the stout, white-haired French military engineer seemed so to those under his direction, though none doubted the power of his personality. He expected the British to field strong reserves for a strategic offensive and, simultaneously, to take over considerable sections of the trench line, involving also local 'wearing down' operations to exhaust enemy reserves. It was Haig's task to strike a balance between these two demands, which he managed well.

While developing a plan for a Flanders offensive, the British commander-in-chief struck a bargain on 14 February. The BEF would not extend its defences but would take on the major share of the offensive in the summer, attacking between Arras and Albert, north of the Somme, while the French would attack immediately north and to the south of the river. The British

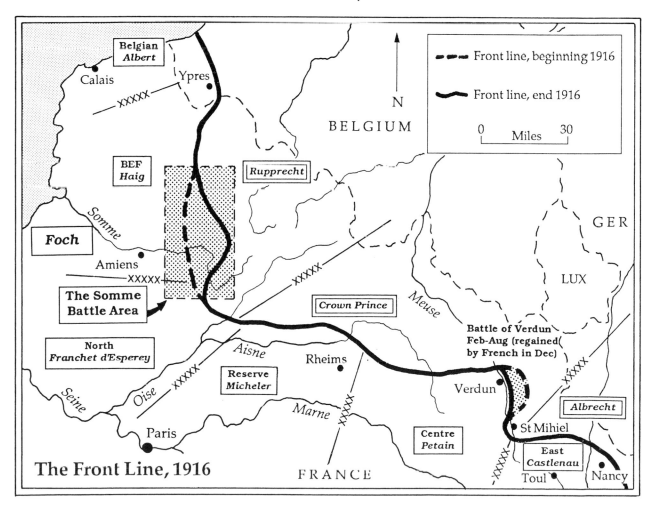

The Front Line, 1916

▲ General Erich von Falkenhayn (1861–1922) was a favourite of Kaiser Wilhelm II who from November 1914 combined the posts of Minister of War and Chief of the General Staff. Following the battles of Verdun and the Somme he was replaced in August 1916.

military power would be broken. Following the German successes in the east, some in the 'Red House' in Berlin, site of the *Oberste Heeresleitung*, the Supreme Command headquarters, began to think that it would be a better policy to defeat Russia and then turn in full strength on the Allies in France. Falkenhayn would have none of this.

It is improbable that his view was due to vexation over the success on the eastern front of Hindenburg and his arrogant chief of staff, Ludendorff. There were more compelling reasons. Heavy casualties had depleted German manpower beyond all expectations. Britain's entry into the war militated against a quick victory for Germany. The British contribution might be reduced by unrestricted submarine warfare, but the German government would not agree to this for fear of encouraging the United States to join the Allies. But France also had lost heavily: more than a million and a quarter of its officers and men were dead or missing. A further huge loss would be intolerable to the French people and war effort. France was 'England's best sword'. There were certain areas in the French sector which would be defended passionately by her soldiers and her government for emotional as well as military reasons. 'If they do so the forces of France will bleed to death . . . For an operation limited to a narrow front Germany will not be compelled to spend herself so completely that all other fronts are practically drained . . .' Thus he reasoned.

Falkenhayn's choice of objective was the fortress area of Verdun. At 4.30 on the morning of 20 February 1916, he loosed 'a hurricane of iron and steel' upon it. The fighting was intense. Rarely a day passed between the opening and 1 May without widespread close actions. By the latter date, France had lost 133,000 casualties in the area but clung still to the essential defences.

One of Joffre's strengths as a commander was his ability to judge big issues calmly. He sent just sufficient reinforcements, week by week, to sustain resistance. Even so, the divisions he mustered for the summer offensive fell from forty to thirty. He looked to this great initiative to bring the fighting at Verdun to an end; and he looked to his British Ally to make good the reserves for the operation. Haig was offering twenty divisions, principally allocated to his Fourth Army.

He had others, but they were the reserves behind each army, respectively northwards, his Third Army behind Arras, the First Army, and Second Army,

would 'wear down' the enemy, but this universally loathed form of operation would be confined to 1–15 days beforehand. 'By straightforward dealing I gained both these points,' Haig wrote in his diary on the 14th. 'But I had an anxious and difficult struggle.' Joffre feared that his plans might be upset by a renewed onslaught against the Russians by Germany and Austria-Hungary in the spring. What he did not know was that General Erich von Falkenhayn was planning to strike a mighty blow against French lines in February.

As chief of the Great General Staff, Falkenhayn was *de facto* operational commander of the forces in the field, particularly of the armies in France and Flanders, for whom there was no front headquarters. It had long been a canon of German strategic policy that, in war, France must be defeated first, whereafter Russian

northernmost, behind Armentières and Ypres. He could also have drawn back a number of divisions from the line; the British held the trenches more densely than the French and Germans. Next to Fourth Army, he wished to keep the Second strong in case he should need to switch the offensive to an alternative front if the Somme offensive slowed as it attracted German reserves. Joffre had originally hoped to employ such a strategy on the Somme between the French and British forces before the depletion of his own reserves.

However, Haig did not mention this concept in their discussions. Well aware that the struggle at Verdun had raised French political as well as military difficulties, he did not want to suggest that he was planning to renege on his commitment to the joint operation. At a meeting with members of the French government and Joffre on 31 May he protested at a remark that 'the British Army had not been attacked' in 1916: his casualties since December numbered 83,000,[*] he reminded them. He had been asked to attack on 1 July, and would be ready to do so.

Preparations

The good if surprising news of an extraordinary success by the Russians in the first half of June offset a serious reverse to the Italians in May. Of more immediate influence on Franco-British plans was the alarming loss of Fort Vaux, considered vital to the Verdun positions, early in June. Joffre proposed urgently to advance the Somme offensive. Haig said he would begin on the 25th. By the 16th, however, the crisis was over and Joffre suggested delay; Foch, the French army group commander, said his Sixth Army was not ready. Finally, the choice was to be left to Haig and Foch.

The British had been preparing for four and a half months and the time had been used well. The numbers in Fourth Army had swollen to half a million men, two hundred battalions of infantry mustered for the offensive together with an extensive support and administrative organization. The area round Amiens became a huge camp.

The original task of General Sir Henry Rawlinson, commander of Fourth Army, had been to break open

*These figures relate to killed, wounded, missing and sick in a 'defensive' line. The casualties were thus due to enemy fire, local raids, patrols, etc., and the winter weather.

▲ General (later Field Marshal) Sir Douglas Haig (1861–1928), succeeded to the command of the BEF in September 1916. His hopes for a rapid break- through on the Somme were dashed on 1 July, but he insisted on continuing the battle until November, heedless of loss.

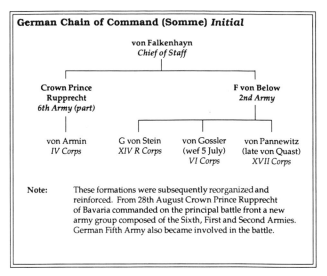

German Chain of Command (Somme) *Initial*

von Falkenhayn
Chief of Staff

Crown Prince Rupprecht
6th Army (part)

F von Below
2nd Army

von Armin
IV Corps

G von Stein
XIV R Corps

von Gossler
(wef 5 July)
VI Corps

von Pannewitz
(late von Quast)
XVII Corps

Note: These formations were subsequently reorganized and reinforced. From 28th August Crown Prince Rupprecht of Bavaria commanded on the principal battle front a new army group composed of the Sixth, First and Second Armies. German Fifth Army also became involved in the battle.

the enemy line so as to pass a mass of cavalry through the breach which, turning northwards, would attack the enemy in flank and rear, infantry and artillery reserves following. By June, however, the concept had been distinctly modified. The Army was to 'undertake offensive operations . . . in conjunction with the French Sixth Army astride the Somme, with the object of relieving the pressure on the French at Verdun and inflicting loss on the enemy'. Specifically, the aim was to seize the high ground held by the Germans, principally the Thiepval–Pozières ridge and, from that position of advantage, either continue until a breach was made, or to exploit to the limit of capability. If operations came to a halt, Rawlinson was to 'keep the enemy fully employed' while offensive operations were continued elsewhere – by which Haig meant Flanders. The frontage was twelve miles on a ruler, twenty-one miles as the trenches ran. First, Second and Third Armies were to mount operations in co-operation, 'misleading and wearing out the enemy'. Two divisions on the right flank of Third Army were to engage in Fourth Army's offensive. At a late hour, the breakout force – the cavalry corps and two divisions of infantry – was detached from Rawlinson's command, forming what was to be called the Reserve Army under Lieutenant-General Hubert Gough.

The revised general objective of the operations planned on either side of the Somme was sure to be achieved in so far as relieving pressure on Verdun and inflicting losses on the enemy were concerned. In any case, the German offensive had exhausted the better part of thirty divisions there and was, on this account, diminishing. A grand Allied offensive would evidently cause German losses. The question was, what would their own losses be, and to what extent would these overcome the German defences on the Western Front?

Although Rawlinson was an artful man, he was not stupid or unimaginative; quite the reverse. He was much concerned with the problem of breaking into the German defences lying largely on the high ground in front of him which, from prisoner-of-war information and air photographs, he knew to be heavily fortified. Von Falkenhayn expected a counter-offensive any time after he attacked at Verdun. Having stripped out the reserves elsewhere, he strengthened the defences along the front by extensive engineer works. Forward, support and reserve trenches were provided with living shelters cut deep into the chalk subsoil: beds, recreation areas, supplies, cooking, medical and sanitary facilities were disposed within them. Barbed wire barriers were multiplied. Trenches were to be kept drained and heavily revetted. Ferro-concrete strong points were built to house observers during enemy bombardment. When enemy infantry approached, these men would bring up their sheltering comrades to fire-positions in the foremost trenches. Selected batteries were to be concealed and kept temporarily inactive for counter-attack. Sufficient reserves would be kept in shelters behind to recover positions lost. No ground whatsoever was to be ceded.

The Fourth Army plan was deliberate in character. The enemy defences, artillery and communications would be painstakingly bombarded for a week by the mass of guns and howitzers, heavy, medium and field, and trench mortars, for at least a week. Barbed wire would be cut by this means, strong points demolished, the enemy's morale sapped. Royal Engineer deep mines and lesser devices would be exploded. On the assumption that these measures would crush the enemy first line, the infantry would then advance, conforming to a carefully timed programme, sweeping into the enemy trenches as soon as their own artillery lifted. Forward observation officers would be able to call for fire on new targets by tapping into telephone points. Thanks to Royal Artillery initiative, a network of telephone cables had been dug deep into the ground, a task which had taken many weeks. To regulate the infantry movement within the artillery plan, and to ensure a steady movement of men across the ground between friendly and enemy trenches, battalions were drilled to keep in line, wave by wave of platoons and companies.

Rawlinson was worried that the frontage of attack was too great. He reduced it to 20,000 yards, from the village of Serre on the left to Montauban on the right, a sector divided by the Albert–Bapaume road. Serre lay on ground rising northward from the small River Ancre. South of the river, the Thiepval–Pozières ridge rises steeply, merging into ground ascending eastward. The British trenches were at about the same level as those of the enemy opposite Serre, but south of the Ancre were overlooked from the high ground. The British could see the German front trenches and some of the second line from their observation posts on the Ancre, but elsewhere occupied the lower ground with correspondingly inferior views. Opposite la Boiselle, the enemy defences were almost entirely on a reverse slope. Air photographs showed that behind the forward maze of trenches, strongpoints and fortified villages, was a second, to a depth of 5,000 yards and more. A third line was being constructed in June, apparently to cover Bapaume.

During the months of concentration, the infantry were occupied in three ways: by turns, holding the line, labouring among the defence works and rear installations, and in training. The Royal Artillery followed their craft but spent much time in preparing defences against counter-battery fire. The Royal Engineers were occupied as much forward in mining, road maintenance, digging-in cable, as in construction work in the Army administrative area. The seventeen divisions assembling were classified as 'Regular', 'Territorial Force', or 'New Army'. Much of the old Regular Army had been lost in the fighting of 1914–15. The survivors were dispersed among the New Armies as instructors or leaders. Still, there was a residue of professionalism among the 'Regular' formations. The Territorial Force divisions had been blooded throughout 1915, had knitted together in comradeship and experience, but such expertise as they had acquired had been principally in defence. The 'New Army' divisions contained the men who had volunteered in tens of thousands as a patriotic duty; called in impulsively by Lord Kitchener but for whom there had been inadequate training or administrative resources. Their time and talent had been wasted for many months but by 1916 they had picked up the rudiments of soldiering. They were keen to show what they could do, buoyed up by comradeship, protected still by the common notion that others might be killed but not themselves.

Given full observation over the Fourth Army area, the Germans had ample evidence that an offensive was being prepared against them, evidence substantiated by lack of security among ministers in Britain and military attachés in neutral capitals. General Fritz von Below, commanding the German Second Army from the Oise to Gommecourt, asked von Falkenhayn for reserves, but received only a detachment of captured Russian 8in howitzers. When the British and French bombardments began on either side of the Somme, von Below's command braced itself for battle; and with them the army of the Bavarian Crown Prince Rupprecht immediately to the north.

The Battle Opens

Saturday, 24 June 1916, was 'U' Day. In relays, batteries expected to fire throughout each successive twenty-four hours until the morning of 'Z' Day, the 29th. But low cloud had made it difficult for the correction of the deeper artillery fire by the Royal Flying Corps. Infantry patrols also reported that, in front of the enemy trenches, much of the wire remained uncut. 'Z' Day was put back to 1 July, which pleased the French Sixth Army. The strain on the guns and gunners was high. Manhandling ammunition hour after hour was exhausting. Guns and howitzers, particularly the field guns, became unserviceable. Yet the infantry waited quietly if apprehensively. Al-

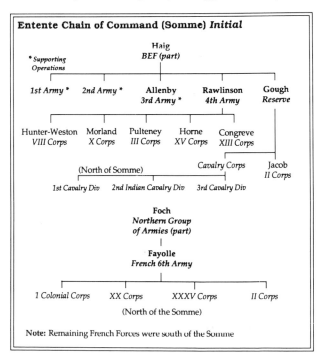

◀ Left: Attack of the 'Red-hand' Ulster Division on the Somme. (Print after J. P. Beadle)

◀ Below left: A Vickers machine-gun on the Somme. A water-cooled, belt-fed weapon, its cone of fire caused heavy German casualties. Note the raised backsight and the masks worn by the crew as a precaution against gas attack (frequently employed by both sides from 1915).

▼ Pipers of a Highland Regiment leading a charge at Longueval. The deadly nature of 'Going over the top' into 'No Man's Land' at the Battle of the Somme is graphically portrayed. Any lift to the men's morale was welcome. Troops were habitually issued with a strong rum ration before such an ordeal by fire. (Drawing by R. Caton Woodville)

though tales are now told that these men were coerced by warnings that they would be shot by 'military police' if they failed to take part in the attack, all the evidence is of a collective wish to go forward with comrades – the sick rate fell sharply during these last few days; some men left hospital of their own accord to rejoin their friends. In darkness on the Sunday morning, the assault battalions assembled in the front trenches under a clearing sky. Washed, shaved, breakfasted, bowels evacuated, they answered roll call as dawn came and remained talking quietly and smoking for zero hour at 07.30.

In the final quarter of an hour, the various mines were exploded. By this time, trench ladders were in position and, minutes later, the first wave went 'over the top' from Gommecourt to the French left flank just south of Montauban.

Mythology relates that the lines of men were rapidly mown down by German machine-gun fire across the entire front. In some sectors the plan was negated by muddled arrangements, in others the wire was inadequately cut, at points luck ran against the British. But, equally, in many places quite large numbers captured enemy strong points and trenches, penetrating sometimes to a depth of 1,000 yards. Part of the bombardment had been very effective indeed, smashing upper

works and cowing those in shelter below. Luck ran, here and there, against the Germans, sufficiently to disturb commanders all the way up to General von Below. But British success, inevitably in those localities where staff work was good, and owing much to the spirit of the infantry and their associated gunner and engineer supporters, was mostly negated by the inadequacy of communications; the inability to concentrate fire and resources where opportunity offered.

On the left flank, excessive caution and muddle in the higher echelons reduced the final bombardment of the trenches to token fire from a fraction of the 18pdrs, and sacrificed the effect of firing two great mines on Redan and Hawthorn Ridges. Left centre, an important lodgement was gained, principally by the 36th (Ulster) Division, on the Thiepval–Pozières ridge, which was lost, as elsewhere, due to prolonged isolation.

Right centre, in XV Corps, immediately below the Albert–Bapaume road, the artillery arrangements were notably unsatisfactory, despite the presence of an artilleryman as corps commander and, no fault of his, faulty British shell fuzes. Here the 7th Green Howards were indeed mown down: fifteen officers and 336 other ranks fell in three minutes. Aerial reports in this sector had provided clear and timely information that their commital was pointless. It was not heeded.

However, on the right flank of the corps, at Mametz, and yet more at Montauban, within XIII Corps, luck ran with the British. The enemy line was decisively broken. The corps commanders' caution denied the fruits of this success, exasperating their French neighbours.

On each side of the river the French Sixth Army attacked at 08.30, securing strategic and tactical surprise. Von Falkenhayn did not believe that the French would attack at all because of their Verdun losses. When more than an hour had passed after the British assault, German commanders decided that none was coming, despite a continuing intense bombardment by eighty-five heavy batteries. Having evolved at Verdun the use of small groups rather than lines in assault, the numbers of French infantry entered the enemy positions. Despite fierce resistance at some points, they won most of their objectives. The British caution on their left flank denied a sweeping Allied advance to High Wood, Ginchy and Guillemont, to the edge, perhaps, of Combles.

At Haig's headquarters, information was scant. As often in war, good news was quickly accepted, bad disregarded. When the dismal facts became known, the commander-in-chief chose to think that some of his battalions had refused to fight, an impression he retained despite the final casualty list which showed

◀ German prisoners-of-war taken on the Somme manage a wry smile for the camera. For them the war was over.

▶ Delville Wood – scene of one of the most notorious and bloody engagements of the Battle of the Somme.

that 993 officers and 18,247 other ranks had been killed, 1,337 officers and 34,156 other ranks wounded, with 2,152 missing, never traced, the great majority of whom were struck in No Man's Land or the enemy positions. Regimental stretcher-bearers and the RAMC field ambulances knew the facts.

This dreadful tally was not known to Haig when, seeking to reactivate the offensive, he placed the two northern corps under Gough's command to capture Beaumont-Hamel and Thiepval, while instructing Rawlinson to obtain a good position from which to attack the enemy second line. He was under pressure from Joffre but held to the principle of exploiting success rather than failure. And despite von Falkenhayn's reiteration that no ground was to be ceded, the Germans were, over the next ten days, driven back by a combination of tactical guile and costly battering, mostly by Lieutenant-General Horne of XV Corps.

On 14 July, a well-planned silent night attack by XIII Corps carried six brigades forward through the German second line, a method which astonished the French. It surprised corps and army headquarters also; their communications arrangements failed to carry instructions to the reserves to push through and capture the empty High Wood. The German Second Army, in process of being reorganized, was thankful to be able to occupy the wood and adjoining ground

to seal the breach.

The Russian advances in Galicia and the Anglo-French offensive on the Somme required von Falkenhayn to bring all offensive action of his own to a halt. He regrouped, placing an additional army headquarters on the Somme front, the whole being subordinated to Lieutenant-General Max von Gallwitz. Throughout the remainder of July, as the casualties on each side rose to 90,000, Gough's Reserve Army, Rawlinson's Fourth, and Fayolle's Sixth French Army drove forward into Pozières, Longueval, Delville Wood and Péronne. German garrisons remained in the crumbled remains of Serre and Thiepval. The British First Army front was tapped unimaginatively in Flanders but found to be firm. The Australians and South Africans were drawn into the reeking battlefields between the Ancre and the Somme.

The dreadful policy of 'wearing down' returned which sapped more than anything the confidence of the fighting men in their generals. Now indeed there were weary and shaken battalions whose men did not universally follow their officers out of the trenches into some of the manifestly pointless local attacks or raids.

The greatest losses had been among experienced leaders. Quick promotion did not solve this problem.

◄ Battle of the Somme. British troops in a captured trench.

◄ A German soldier's last resting place amid the poppy fields of Picardy and the Somme – a reminder that the enemy suffered almost as badly as the Allies.

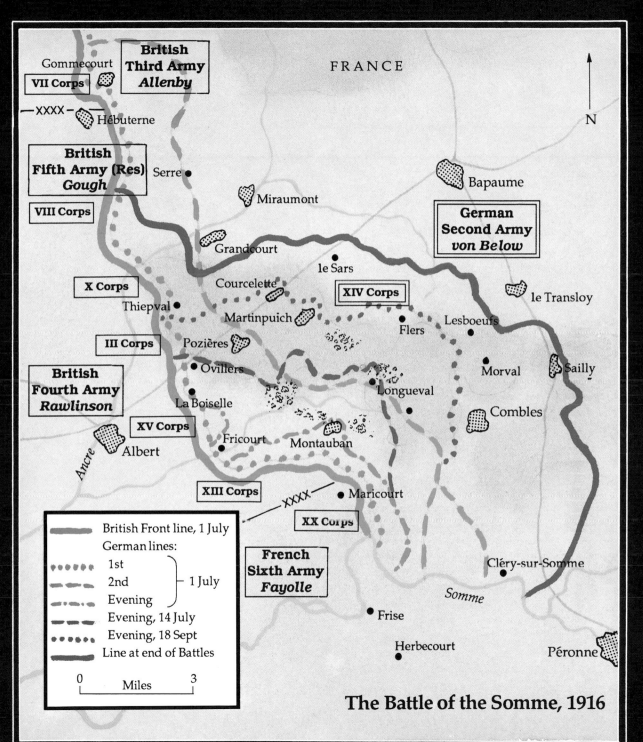

The Battle of the Somme, 1916

FRANCE

Gommecourt

British Third Army *Allenby*

VII Corps

XXXX

Hébuterne

British Fifth Army (Res) *Gough*

VIII Corps

Serre

Miraumont

Bapaume

Grandcourt

German Second Army *von Below*

X Corps

Courcelette

le Sars

XIV Corps

le Transloy

Thiepval

Martinpuich

Flers

Lesboeufs

III Corps

Pozières

Morval

Sailly

British Fourth Army *Rawlinson*

Ovillers

Longueval

XV Corps

La Boiselle

Combles

Albert

Fricourt

Montauban

Ancre

XIII Corps

XXXX

Maricourt

XX Corps

French Sixth Army *Fayolle*

Cléry-sur-Somme

Somme

Frise

Herbecourt

Péronne

British Front line, 1 July

German lines:
1st
2nd ⎬ 1 July
Evening
Evening, 14 July
Evening, 18 Sept
Line at end of Battles

0 — Miles — 3

The Battle of the Somme, 1916

N

Officer and other rank reinforcements were just sufficient to replace casualties but not to provide fresh divisions. Conscription, hitherto a political football in Britain, loomed, but with or without it, manpower for the Services was becoming increasingly short. Yet Haig was determined to persevere. The aim of relieving Verdun had been achieved, the greater part of the German Army was pinned to the Western Front and being reduced. In any case, as he and Joffre agreed, having come so far, should they now stop and allow the enemy to rebuild a new line during the autumn and winter? Much had been learned in July. Staff procedures and artillery arrangements had been overhauled; new tactics adopted – principally abandonment of the old 'wave' approach to the enemy positions. And a secret weapon was arriving: the 'tank'.

From the First Use of the Tank to the Battle's End

The crude, armed and armoured caterpillars of the Heavy Section of the Machine-Gun Corps, were an unknown quantity. 'C' and 'D' Companies – fifty tanks – reached the Somme in September for a major attack, planned to begin at 06.20 on the 15th. Mechanical and other failure reduced this to twenty-four at zero hour.

Gough's army was to force the enemy off the northern end of the main ridge, away from the Fourth. Rawlinson's task was to breach the remaining enemy trench system. The French Sixth Army had cleared the enemy from the British right flank. Northwest of the Albert-Bapaume road, the Canadians outpaced their seven tanks as they captured Courcelette. Immediately south, a similarly spirited advance by the 15th Scottish Division was helped by a single tank in taking Martinpuich. Development of the creeping barrage by the artillery was a feature of both attacks. But to the south-east, the Germans in High Wood swept the ground with fire from each end. Tanks here were of little help, a few lost direction and fired on their own infantry. But east again, progress towards Flers was enhanced by four tanks arriving at a critical moment. The ruined village fell to a single caterpillar followed by mixed platoons of Hampshires and Royal West Kents. The area was secured by Brigadier Clemson and his brigade major, Gwyn Thomas, who came into the foremost line with a party of Royal Engineers and the brigade machine-gun

company, fortuitously reinforced by New Zealanders. Courcelette, Martinpuich and Flers, the trophies of the day, resisted strong counter-attacks at the end of a rainy afternoon. But on the right, the Guards Division was forced back from some of the ground they had captured in small actions throughout the morning.

Aircraft and balloons of the Royal Flying Corps had been flying continuously throughout daylight reporting battlefield movement, spotting for artillery, and fighting off German air intervention. Rawlinson therefore had a general idea of his situation at dusk on the 15th. Although he and Gough were instructed to keep fighting, neither believed in the likelihood of breaching the enemy defences. Pressed by Joffre, who had fallen back on the strategy of *l'usure*, racked by anxiety that they would have to begin all over again in 1917, Haig kept the offensive simmering until 19th November when, in the torment of winter, Hawthorn and Redan Ridges and Beaumont-Hamel fell at last, but neither Thiepval nor 'the sinister ruins of Serre'.

The casualties totalled about 1,200,000, split roughly between the two sides. The French losses, following Verdun and all that had been endured before, contributed notably to the collapse of the Army in 1917. Conscription became a necessity in Britain. A German participant wrote later that 'The Somme was the muddy grave of the German field army.' It was certainly the grave of the patriotic ardour of the British new armies but not, fortunately, of their spirit. In the two dark years of war that remained, the greater burden of the land fighting would fall progressively on the British Army.

BIBLIOGRAPHY

Blake, R. (ed.). *The Private Papers of Douglas Haig, 1914–18*, London, 1952. These include detailed extracts of the diaries of the commander-in-chief.
Crutwell, C. R. M. F. *A History of the Great War, 1914–18*, Oxford, 1934. Perhaps the best overall book on the war. The author was an officer on the Somme and his account of the campaign brings it to life.
Falkenhayn, E. von. *General Headquarters, 1914–16*, Leipzig, 1919. Contains the view of events as seen by the Chief of the Great General Staff.

Farrar-Hockley, A. H. *The Somme*, London, 1964.
Middlebrook, M. *The First Day on the Somme*, London, 1971. A compendium based on personal experiences interwoven with details from official documents.
Miles, Captain W. *Military Operations, France and Belgium, 1916*, British Official History, vols. I & II. The two volumes provide the detail of orders and events during the campaign based on a collection of accounts, official and private documents.

THE THIRD BATTLE OF YPRES, 1917

by Donald Schurman

*'As they hurried to Pioneer Keep they heard confused calling from
the fire-trench and one running up behind shouts as he comes
nearer, for bearers.*
"Bearers at the double."
No, the last burst it was – caught 'em unexpected.
*It's Mr Donne of No. 8 who's got it and Fatty Weavel in
the sap and some Staff bloke they can't identify.*
*What brought him to this type of place, why his immaculate
legs would carry him, jodhpurs and all, so far from his
proper sphere, you simply can't conceive.'*

(David Jones, *In Parentheses*)

The few lines overleaf from a most sustained and evocative piece of writing about trench warfare by a British veteran, capture neatly the insecurity of life in the front line, and the great gulf that was fixed between trench-fighter and staff-member. It involved much more than rank as everyone knew in those days. Even French civilians in Montreuil, the location of British General Headquarters, used to joke about the effect of a hypothetical air raid destroying the British planning centre. Aside from the supposed benefit to the Germans, it was quipped, the benefit to the Franco–British cause would be incalculable. The Third Battle of Ypres did nothing to alter these acid perceptions.

The Road Past Menin Gate

English soldiers had been in Flanders before; in Elizabethan times and later under both Marlborough and Wellington. In 1914 the particular theatre around Ypres had seen the British Army strained to the utmost resisting the German great push. After fierce fighting they established positions around Ypres, a salient overlooked, unfortunately, by observation points, within gun range, and open in places to enfilading fire. This was known as the First Battle of Ypres. The Second Battle of Ypres, in 1915, involved the first use of gas by the Germans, who just failed to break through, partly because they did not fully understand their own weapons and partly because British troops, including Canadian, plugged the holes that the new weapon had created.*

The Third Battle of Ypres in 1917, also known as Passchendaele, took place from 31 July to 10 November 1917. General Sir Douglas Haig was Commander-in-Chief of the British forces involved. The German Army Group Commander was Crown Prince Rupprecht of Bavaria. The actual 1917 battle involved a British advance of some three miles over a seven-mile front east of Ypres; an area of some 21 square miles. The fighting claimed some 250,000 British and Dominion casualties and at least 202,000 German. Passchendaele village, the original tactical objective in July, and acquired at great psychological and human cost, was taken three months later. It was taken back by the Germans in their Great Offensive of 1918 although Ypres itself remained in British hands. Passchendaele village was finally recaptured by the Belgians for the Entente in the autumn of 1918.*

What kind of a general was Douglas Haig? He has been variously assessed as an insensitive driver who only knew how to push ahead; as a devious political general; as a strong, straightforward leader; and as a dull-witted, unimaginative director of war. One thing seems clear in retrospect: if Haig had not attacked it is hard to believe that he would have been applauded for either standing still or for going backwards. He may have been unwise enough to think that cavalry would win the war, but he was not inept enough to be manoeuvred out of a command position once he had got it. His loyalty to his subordinates was marked. This positive Scots trait was put down by his detractors as evidence that he was a poor judge of character.

Douglas Haig's most significant experience of war at the top military level was based on his involvement at the Somme. If Field Marshal Sir John French, whom Haig had helped to oust from his command,

Editor-in-Chief's Note

The Ypres salient saw three titanic battles between 1914 and 1917. The Third, also known as 'Passchendaele', forms the subject of this chapter. The following paragraphs by Doctor C. J. Duffy of the War Studies Department, RMAS, summarize the preceding First and Second Battles of Ypres:

'The soggy farmland and low ridges around Ypres formed nearly the extreme left flank of the Entente's front in World War One. The fighting went on without a pause from October 1914 to October 1918, but three main battles can be distinguished. The first two of which were:

First Ypres (19 October–22 November 1914): This was the last episode of the 'Race to the Sea'. The highly trained all-regular British Expeditionary Force prevented the Germans from breaking through to the Channel ports, albeit at the cost of 50,000 of its total post-Marne remaining strength of 160,000 men. From now on trench warfare gripped the entire Western Front.

Second Ypres (22 April–31 May 1915): This opened with a German gas attack (the first in warfare) against the French and Canadian sectors. The Germans were narrowly prevented from achieving a breakthrough – their generals doubting the effects of chlorine gas, and consequently failing to follow-up their initial success – but the salient was now reduced to a flat curve only two miles from Ypres itself, and all the high ground was henceforth in German possession.'

The word 'entente' was used in World War One to describe the British, French and Russians. The 'allies' were the Germans and the Austrians.

▲ Field Marshal Paul Ludwig von Hindenburg (1847–1934) and his Chief of Staff, Erich von Ludendorff (1865–1937), the formidable command team who replaced von Falkenhayn on the Western Front from September 1915. Ten years later Hindenburg would become President of the Weimar Republic. (Print after H. Voger)

failed at Loos, Haig had followed that lead on the Somme. Then the French Army exhausted itself at Verdun, and in the spring of 1917 failed miserably in offensive operations, under General Nivelle, at the Chemin des Dames fiasco. The British commander-in-chief felt it necessary for the British to mount an offensive to divert German attention from the French predicament. In June Haig was informed of the French Army's almost mutinous state by Pétain who had assumed command. The battle was to go forward despite British political suspicions that unacceptable casualties would result. In fact plans for the 1917 Flanders offensive had captured Haig's mind quite apart from the French problem, and he was determined to have his big push.

Plumer takes Messines

The curtain-raiser to the Third Battle of Ypres was the Battle of Messines which took place on 7 June when an overwhelming artillery barrage was timed to support an explosion of some huge mines. Captain T. C. Eckenstein wrote in a letter dated 9 June 1917:

'We got an hour or two of sleep that night and were called at 2 o'clock and had some breakfast. At 3.5 we went out to see the start. The guns had eased off and everything was perfectly quiet, when suddenly at 3.10 all the mines were sent off and all the guns began to fire. It's impossible to describe the sight or sound. It was one deafening roar and I've never heard or seen anything like it. Afterwards I had to go up to the new front line . . . [the] change was quite hard to realize. The Bosche line in front of Wytschaete and Messines looked right down on ours it was curious to look at our own front lines from his in the same way as the Bosche had done for so long. He could observe right behind the front line and see what was going on behind.'

What Captain Eckenstein did not say was that since the Messines ridge enfiladed British lines east and south of Ypres, the third Ypres attack would not have been possible without it. General Herbert Plumer had planned with care. It was regarded as an almost model operation both at the time and since. Nevertheless, British casualties were relatively heavy: about 25,000 men, of whom more than 12,000 were Anzac. The Germans lost an estimated 23,000!

The Battle of Messines not only made an attack east of Ypres possible, it determined its character; for the Germans clearly understood from the Messines battle that more was to follow. Also the Messines method, heavy bombardment followed by short rushes, came to dominate the general pattern of the tactics for the Third Battle of Ypres. Haig's intention was not a limited one. He intended to punch a hole through which cavalry would stream through to Roulers, and perhaps the sea, to free Channel ports which – it was authoritatively claimed – menaced British sea com-

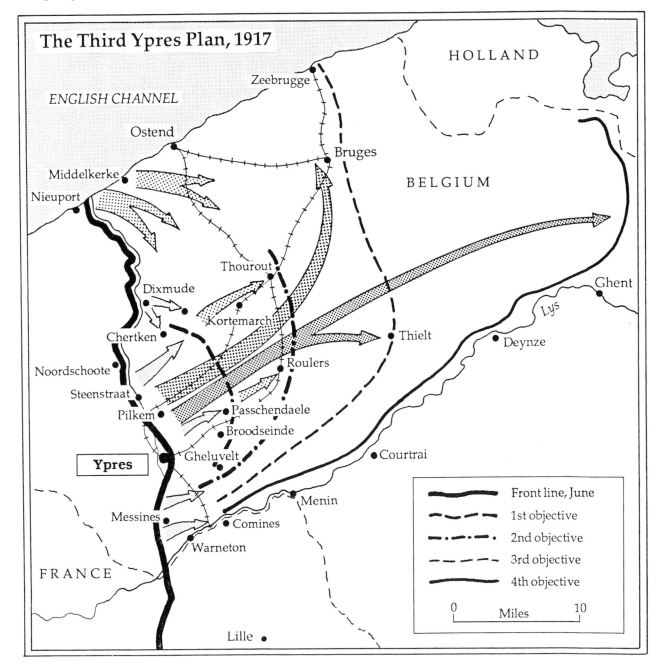

The Third Ypres Plan, 1917

HOLLAND

ENGLISH CHANNEL

Zeebrugge

Ostend

Bruges

BELGIUM

Middelkerke

Nieuport

Thourout

Ghent

Dixmude

Lys

Kortemarch

Thielt

Deynze

Chertken

Roulers

Noordschoote

Steenstraat

Passchendaele

Pilkem

Broodseinde

Courtrai

Gheluvelt

Ypres

▬▬▬▬	Front line, June
▬ ▬ ▬ ▬	1st objective
▬·▬·▬·	2nd objective
▬ ▬ ▬ ▬	3rd objective
▬▬▬▬	4th objective

Menin

Messines

Comines

Warneton

0   Miles   10

FRANCE

Lille

munications. He planned to push to Passchendaele relatively swiftly by the use of carefully phased attacks, the success of which would be predetermined by saturation and counter-battery artillery work. Not only did Messines telegraph the intention of the next move, but GHQ further emphasized it with a colossal expenditure of shells which began on 22 July and only ended shortly before the attack (originally scheduled for the 25th). The first tactical objective of the offensive was the Passchendaele–Westroosebeke ridge. The left wing would fight through the old 1915 battlefield around St Julien and the right would endeavour to use the Messines success to shake itself loose from the strong German Menin Road defences, fight clear of Hooge, Sanctuary Wood, through Polygon Wood, Tower Hamlets and thence move eastwards across the Gheluvelt Plateau through Zonnebeke and Broodseinde. This last was rough

▶ British troops in a trench. Despite the ever-present danger of lice, short haircuts do not appear to have been mandatory for all. Note the use of the trench-periscope by the sentry; also the water in the bottom of the trench.

▼ A German wiring-party caught by artillery-fire. Wiring tasks and patrolling took up much of the time for both sides during 'quiet' periods in the line – particularly at night. (Print after Felix Schwormsttadt)

▲ Canadian troops fix bayonets preparatory to 'going over the top'. From 1915 onwards steel helmets were on almost universal issue.

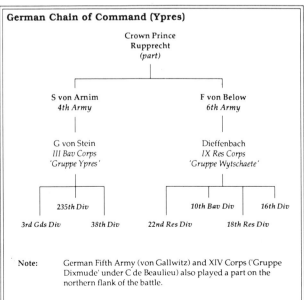

German Chain of Command (Ypres)

Crown Prince
Rupprecht
(part)

S von Arnim
4th Army

F von Below
6th Army

G von Stein
III Bav Corps
'Gruppe Ypres'

Dieffenbach
IX Res Corps
'Gruppe Wytschaete'

235th Div

10th Bav Div   16th Div

3rd Gds Div   38th Div   22nd Res Div   18th Res Div

Note: German Fifth Army (von Gallwitz) and XIV Corps ('Gruppe Dixmude' under C de Beaulieu) also played a part on the northern flank of the battle.

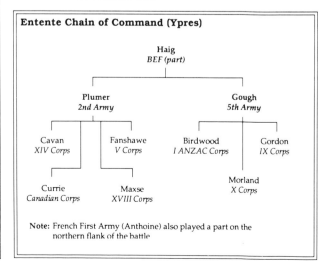

Entente Chain of Command (Ypres)

Haig
BEF (part)

Plumer
2nd Army

Gough
5th Army

Cavan
XIV Corps

Fanshawe
V Corps

Birdwood
I ANZAC Corps

Gordon
IX Corps

Currie
Canadian Corps

Maxse
XVIII Corps

Morland
X Corps

Note: French First Army (Anthoine) also played a part on the northern flank of the battle

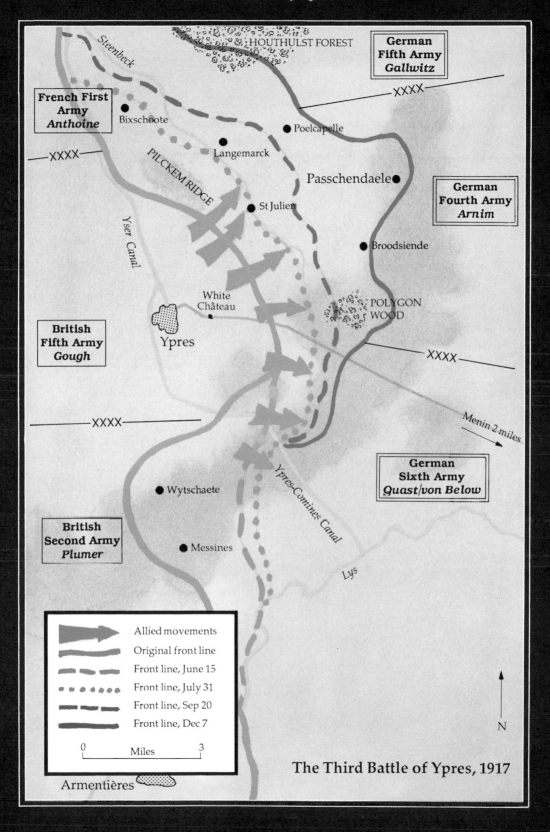

The Third Battle of Ypres, 1917

HOUTHULST FOREST

German Fifth Army *Gallwitz*

XXXX

French First Army *Anthoine*

Bixschoote

Steenbeck

XXXX

PILCKEM RIDGE

Yser Canal

Langemarck

Poelcapelle

Passchendaele

German Fourth Army *Arnim*

St Julien

Broodsiende

White Château

POLYGON WOOD

British Fifth Army *Gough*

Ypres

XXXX

XXXX

Menin 2 miles

German Sixth Army *Quast/von Below*

Wytschaete

Ypres-Comines Canal

British Second Army *Plumer*

Messines

Lys

Legend

➤	Allied movements
	Original front line
	Front line, June 15
	Front line, July 31
	Front line, Sep 20
	Front line, Dec 7

0 — Miles — 3

Armentières

N

The Third Battle of Ypres, 1917

ground in any sense of the term. The movement of guns even in the dry was difficult, and the British target calibrations were graven on the German gunners' minds like the Ten Commandments.

The situation was further complicated by the fact that the left wing, and commanding control of the battle, was given to General Hubert Gough and V Corps. Plumer, the victor of Messines and commander of II Corps, who was on Gough's right, wanted to keep going after the success of 7 June, on the assumption that momentum was an unusual but exploitable possibility in Flanders. He was frustrated when Haig took Gough's advice to go slowly. In retrospect this appears to have been a mistake.

On to Passchendaele

Thus the offensive which Haig began on 31 July aimed at a successful breakthrough to the east. The rain struck almost at once as the troops moved forward against a well-alerted foe. While there were some successes in a limited way along Pilkem Ridge on Haig's left, on his right along the Menin Road they were negligible. By 2 August they had captured 3,000 yards at the cost of 30,150 men. Further gains were made at the Battle of Langemarck, past Pilkem in the St Julien area, by the middle of the month. It ought to have been clear then that the notion of a gigantic breakthrough was exploded. But the fighting con-

tinued and it was tough along the British right where they fought for Inverness Copse. Sometimes they aimed at objectives beyond the woods, sometimes at the woods themselves, sometimes at the troublesome strongholds between them, always the Germans counter-attacked. These strokes, aimed at the morale of the German Army, were wearing down the morale of the British. Whether British commanders were aware of the facts or not, it was the August fighting that gave the Third Battle of Ypres its baneful reputation. The fighting at Passchendaele two months later merely added to this. Also, it was the August battering that convinced Lloyd George that Haig was irresponsible in his objectives and offensive activities.

Haig, for his part, had been impressed by what had been achieved in August, and he determined to adopt a more step-by-step approach, as opposed to the big breakthrough idea. It was ironic that he launched the first successful one just as the Prime Minister was seriously attempting to block him. Viewed in retrospect, the end of August was, in fact, the crucial point of the campaign. The weather was turning fine. Also the decision to go on with the battle by the short rush method had then been firmly embraced at GHQ. Strategically, it could have been a time to re-evaluate the uses of artillery, tanks and aircraft for long-term goals. Strong points have been made about the sophisticated capacities of the artillery stemming from

◄ Sappers at work on Messines Ridge, June 1917. Royal Engineers look up almost nonchalantly as a shell explodes nearby. The water-logged nature of the Ypres Salient — caused by the destruction of field irrigation — is well brought out.

▶ The tools of modern war at Ypres in August 1917. From the 'Race to the sea' in late 1914 to the final advances in 1918, 'spades' were very much 'trumps' under the difficult conditions of trench warfare on the Western Front. A little humour helped as well.

▶ Work party at Zillebeke, August 1917. Supervised by a lance-corporal, troops attempt to dig a drainage trench.

the use of electronic techniques and aircraft. The counter-battery capabilities were far in advance of what the Command seems to have realized, although the discipline of aircrews for such work is not so easy to assess. Nevertheless, this was when Haig decided to go ahead, using short rushes following a rolling barrage instead of searching, selective artillery target work. Lloyd George's opposition resulted in material deliberately being diverted to the Italian Front. Pressed, Haig defended his 'limited objectives only' rationale. He also played the French incapacity card once more although in fact the French were much stronger.

Although they were costly, and limited, the next two battles in September took the Gheluvelt plateau and Polygon wood. Anzacs were heavily committed to this battle as a corps, and they were the spearhead of the attack that took the door to Passchendaele, Broodseinde, on 12 October. By this time the rains were pouring steadily once more. Rather than give up the offensive, however, Haig decided to bring fresh troops in the form of the Canadian Corps, to capture the elusive ridge. Three rushes, on a reasonably narrow front between October 26 and November 6, saw the spearhead in what had once been Passchendaele village, and after a further exploitive but difficult run on 10 November, the battle was over. It is true that Australian and Canadian troops were prominent in the latter attacks in the Third Battle of Ypres, but

▲ General Sir Hubert Gough (1870–1963) was commander of the British Fifth Army at the battles of the Somme and at Third Ypres. Known as 'Goughie' to his men, he was removed from command after the Germans broke though his sector in their Spring Offensive in 1918.

◄ Dig, dig, dig, dig! Soldiers in a shallow communication trench at Menin Road Bridge on 20 September 1917, the date of the opening of the third phase of the Third Battle of Ypres. The strain of combat fatigue is plain in the light infantryman's face. Note what appears to be a skull at the top of the picture.

► Heavy howitzer of 194 Siege Battery, Royal Artillery, in action on 24 September 1917. Note the slogan 'Make Peace' chalked on the shell about to be loaded.

both were heavily dependent upon British preparation and support. There were some 51 British divisions engaged in this battle. Many were engaged more than once, for instance, two Australian divisions, like many British, were there five times. Some, like the Canadians, who finally took Passchendaele village, were only engaged for one spell. The Germans may have had 78 divisions engaged. Thus the nature of the ground and the magnitude of the effort do not allow for any comments about prowess or national characteristics. Towards the end the worst problem of the Anzacs and the Canadians had been to get their artillery to required positions and keep the batteries supported in the almost quicksand ground conditions. For the rest, square yards of mud were gained from time to time.

A somewhat laconic approach to this tragic encounter has been deliberately adopted in order to avoid too much concentration on the evils of the site, although something must be said of it. It was vile, but battle sites are often inherited rather than selected. This was the case at Ypres. The quicksand mud existed in August and October–November and produced appalling conditions in the salient. It was wet on the Somme, it snowed at Vimy, and casualties were

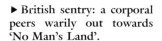
▶ British sentry: a corporal peers warily out towards 'No Man's Land'.

relatively as high, month for month in the final offensive of 1918, as they were at Ypres.

An Assessment

What seems clear is that Haig began with a strategic objective that lay well past Passchendaele, and he had certain forces pressuring him towards such goals. It is true that he had bad luck with rain in August. Furthermore, the fact of the rain has been hung around Haig's neck by historians almost as if he had willed it. It is hard to fault completely his September offensive tactically. On the other hand his strategic objectives were, by then, gone forever. This gave the campaign the kind of unreality Lloyd George saw.

His artillery and tank leaders had the doctrinal understanding and the capacity to give him a good chance of something more substantial strategically. But at that moment he opted for the tactical method of short rushes following a rolling barrage. They worked, despite the rain, all the way to Passchendaele village. They also produced heavy casualties. In the end there was an improved tactical position, on the ridge, on which to sit the winter out. The question

about the Third Battle of Ypres is, were the tactical successes worth the casualties?

It is easy to answer this question from a so-called moral viewpoint, but not so easy to recognize that at a transitional period in the use of weapons of war, decisions about means and the linkages between tactics and strategy were hard. It is not very surprising that a man with Haig's training and cavalry outlook took the decisions he did. His qualities of loyalty to subordinates, tenacity of purpose and strong sense of commitment were qualities admired by many who had been brought up in the old, pre-1914, army. How-

▼ The end of the battle. A field gun almost immersed in the mud of Flanders, November 1917.

▶ Right: When the shelling stopped. Moonscape, Passchendaele, November 1917. Survivors recall the all-pervading stench of the battlefield. Small wonder a song popular in the trenches went: 'And when

we tell them, they'll never believe us'.

▶ Below right: German storm or assault detachment. From the latter stages of Cambrai in early December 1917, German 'Hutier' tactics – based upon storm troopers penetrating deep into Allied defence systems, bypassing serious centres of opposition – had become standard.

ever, they were not the qualities of innovation, based on knowledge of modern equipment that might have transformed a slog through the mud into the breakthrough everybody wanted.

The other question is, was the offensive productive of something, aside from the misery of the participants? It is rather like trying to assess the impact of the bombing of Germany in 1942–5 on the outcome of the war, or the effect of the British blockade on Germany, 1914–18. It has been suggested that the economic power and manpower capacities of all the Allied Powers (excluding the USA) were in rapid decline in 1917–18. If this was so, the 1917 campaign could have had heavy, perhaps decisive, consequences for Germany. But the margin cannot have been great between the Allied and the Central Powers.

▲ Troops of the East Lancashire Regiment (today the Queen's Lancashire Regiment) on the march 'somewhere in Belgium'. The light blanket of snow would date it as approaching winter, sometime after the end of the Third Battle of Ypres.

The Third Battle of Ypres was not a battle to delight those who admire Napoleonic modes and methods, or devotees of civilized behaviour. It clearly did not delight the modernists who held, and hold, that modern techniques oriented to new methods could have overcome the slogging match on the Western Front. The battle was fought by a strong-willed but quite conventional general who commanded fairly conventional troops at a transitional time for weapons and concepts of war. It left behind memories of an impossible battlefield and men who showed unbelievable endurance – on both sides of Passchendaele Ridge. Part of David Jones's dedication to *In Parenthesis* was to 'the enemy front-line fighters who shared our pains against whom we found ourselves by misadventure'. It forms a fitting epilogue to the story of the Third Battle of Ypres.

BIBLIOGRAPHY

Bean, C. E. W. *The Australian Imperial Force in France, 1917*, Sydney, 1934. The best account of the battle.

Bidwell, S., and Graham, D. *Firepower: British Weapons and Theories of War, 1904–1945*, London, 1982. The most rewarding of new interpretations.

Blake, R. *The Private Papers of Douglas Haig, 1914–1919*, London, 1952. The standard supporting work.

Edmonds, J. E. *Military Operations: France and Flanders, 1917*, London, 1948, vol. 2. The official history.

Nicholson, G. W. L. *The Canadian Expeditionary Force, 1914–1919*, Ottawa, 1962. A balanced account.

Ferro, M. *The Great War, 1914–1919*, Newton Abbot, 1974. Social realism.

Pulteneny, W. *The Immortal Salient*, London, 1925. Much useful information available with difficulty elsewhere.

Warner, P. *Passchendaele: the Tragic Victory of 1917*, New York, 1988. A comprehensive account.

Wolff, L. *In Flanders Fields*, New York, 1958. A piece of brilliant historical debunking.

GAZA COMPANY CREST
RMA SANDHURST

THE BATTLE OF GAZA, 1917

by Jeffrey Grey

'He who can modify his tactics in relation to his opponent, and thereby succeed in winning, may be called a Heaven-born Captain.'

(Sun Tsu, *The Art of War*, c.500 BC)

In contrast to the fighting on the Western Front, which provides still the most common popular image of the First World War, the operations in Sinai and Palestine against the Turks demonstrated that mobility still had a place in modern industrial warfare. No one arm dominated the battlefield here, as arguably did the artillery in France, and military operations provided opportunities for the deployment of forces of all arms. The climate and terrain posed as many problems for British commanders as did the enemy, with the provision of water for men and animals being the principal limiting factor in the planning and conduct of the war. Nowhere are the various elements of the fighting in the Middle East better demonstrated than in the offensive to capture the Turkish positions at Gaza in 1917.

The War with Turkey

As allies of the Germans, the Ottoman Empire had entered the war against the Entente Powers on 5 November 1914. For most of the war the Turks fought on several fronts simultaneously, against the Russians in the Caucasus and against the British, Australians, New Zealanders and Indians in Sinai, Palestine, Mesopotamia and during the Dardanelles campaign in 1915. Turkish attempts to capture the Suez Canal, thus cutting the lines of communication between Britain and India, Australia and New Zealand, were unsuccessful. After the Battle of Romani (4 August 1916) the Egyptian Expeditionary Force (EEF) went over to the offensive, gradually clearing Turkish forces from the Sinai peninsula and ending the first phase of the campaign in this theatre. By January 1917 the forces of General Sir Archibald Murray had reached the southern frontier of Palestine, effectively beginning the second phase of the campaign which was to last throughout 1917 and to culminate in the capture of Jerusalem in December.

The Turkish positions at Gaza presented formidable problems for Murray and his commanders. Gaza occupies a naturally strong position, made stronger still by the Turks. With Beersheba, 25 miles to the east, it forms 'the gateway of southern Palestine'. The town dominates the coast road running to the north while Beersheba, little more than a village in 1917, offers the last water base on the edge of a wilderness stretching to the south and east. (The advance through Sinai had been accompanied by the construction of a railway and a pipeline, ensuring the supply of water, both of which were considerable engineering feats, but the result was that the EEF was tied to an operational radius based on the railheads and pumping stations.) Having been forced out of Sinai the enemy commander, the German Colonel Friedrich Freiherr Kress von Kressenstein, reinforced Gaza in mid-March and concentrated his forces in southern Palestine, ready to meet an Allied assault the direction of which was clearly apparent to him.

The plan for the first battle of Gaza sought to repeat the earlier manoeuvres at Rafa and Magdhaba in 1916 on a larger scale. The mounted troops were to be dispersed to the north and east both to prevent reinforcement of the garrison and to cut off its retreat, while the main force assaulted the town. Supplies, especially of the ever-precious water, were strictly limited and this meant that the town had to be taken by nightfall, or the attacking force would have to retreat or face disaster. This was the plan's fundamental weakness, but it was in other respects a well thought-out scheme given the lack of co-ordination in the Turkish defences beyond Gaza itself.

The attack was launched on 26 March, and fighting lasted all day. Early morning fog caused delays in launching the assault, and the stout resistance of the enemy further complicated an already tight timetable. To make matters worse, staff work broke down at crucial levels and higher headquarters were unaware of the gains made by various units and formations, not least the cavalry. By nightfall the key Turkish positions on the Ali Muntar ridge to the east of the town were in British hands, but General Sir Charles Dobell, commanding Eastern Force, and General Sir Philip Chetwode, commanding the Desert Column, reluctantly ordered the withdrawal. Worried by the threat posed by lack of supplies and the approach of fresh Turkish forces from the north, they let slip the opportunity to take Gaza. Too late it was learned that the relieving force had halted at nightfall, and that the garrison had been on the point of surrender. British casualties were about 4,000.

Having survived by great good fortune, von Kressenstein rapidly strengthened the defences around

▶ **Top right: Australian Light Horse at Alexandria, Egypt, in early 1916.**

▶ **Below right: British troops holding a post close to the sea at Gaza. The near** desert conditions were a great contrast to those pertaining on the Western Front. Note the neck-shields to protect against sun-stroke.

▲ General Sir Edmund Allenby (1861–1936), nicknamed 'the Bull', was one of the most successful British commanders of the First World War. Transferred from command of British Third Army in France to Palestine, he masterminded the great victories at Gaza (which led to the capture of Jerusalem) and then Megiddo in 1918, which caused the collapse of the Turkish front and led to the occupation of Damascus.

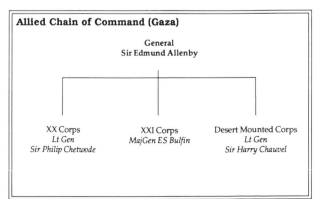

Allied Chain of Command (Gaza)

General
Sir Edmund Allenby

XX Corps	XXI Corps	Desert Mounted Corps
Lt Gen	*MajGen ES Bulfin*	*Lt Gen*
Sir Philip Chetwode		*Sir Harry Chauvel*

Gaza and closed the gaps between Gaza and Beersheba, erecting a series of redoubts to cover the whole front against penetration as far as Sheria. The garrison at Beersheba was reinforced and the open ground between there and the main defensive line was covered by a cavalry screen. Any further attempts to storm Gaza would now involve frontal attacks against a stronger and thoroughly aroused defence. In reply, Dobell increased the weight of artillery to be deployed in support of his forces and introduced two weapons previously unknown in this theatre – tanks and gas. Attacking in two stages from 17 to 19 April, the British enjoyed no more success than previously, indeed rather less. Only eight tanks had been sent to Egypt, and these either broke down or were disabled by Turkish artillery fire; the gas had little effect, and the artillery had only 170 guns (of which only sixteen were medium or heavier pieces) to provide fire support along a front of some 15,000 yards. Turkish defensive fire was unaffected, and this second failure to take Gaza resulted in a further 6,500 British casualties. It resulted also in the relief of both Murray and Dobell.

Opposing Commanders and Forces

At midnight on 28 June 1917, General Sir Edmund Allenby assumed command of the EEF, having come from the successful command of the Third Army on the Western Front. The victor of Arras, his success there had been overshadowed by the failures which followed from pressing the attacks beyond the point of success and at least initially he regarded his new appointment as a demotion. Nicknamed 'the Bull', he had a reputation as an aloof, taciturn and imperious man. Although less often on public display, his character was marked equally by patience, tolerance and compassion. Combined with a driving, ruthless energy and a solid military professionalism, he was the ideal man to invigorate a command grown cynical and listless by successive failures before Gaza. His biographer notes that Allenby's arrival 'made a remarkable change'. Headquarters moved from Cairo to the front, but above all, 'it was Allenby's personality that stirred [his soldiers'] imagination and roused their hope'.

There were other changes. Eastern Force was abolished and the divisions reorganized into three corps in August. Lieutenant-General Sir Harry Chauvel, an Australian regular officer with service in

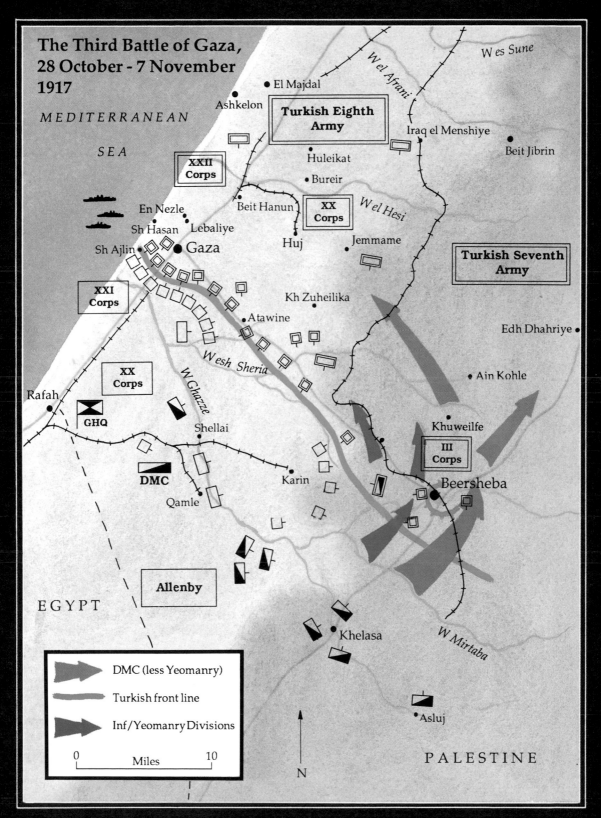

The Third Battle of Gaza, 28 October - 7 November 1917

MEDITERRANEAN SEA

Turkish Eighth Army

Turkish Seventh Army

El Majdal
Ashkelon
W el Afrani
W es Sune
Iraq el Menshiye
Beit Jibrin
Huleikat
Bureir
XXII Corps
En Nezle
Sh Hasan
Lebaliye
Beit Hanun
XX Corps
W el Hesi
Sh Ajlin
Gaza
Huj
Jemmame
XXI Corps
Kh Zuheilika
Atawine
Edh Dhahriye
W esh Sheria
Ain Kohle
Rafah
XX Corps
W Ghazze
GHQ
Shellai
Khuweilfe
III Corps
DMC
Karin
Beersheba
Qamle
Allenby
EGYPT
Khelasa
W Mirtaba
PALESTINE
Asluj

DMC (less Yeomanry)

Turkish front line

Inf/Yeomanry Divisions

0   Miles   10

N

◀ 'Johnny Turks' wearing field uniform. They were respected by their opponents as hard-fighting if cruel adversaries.

◀ Turkish field-gun detachment in action at Gaza.

the South African War, was given command of the Desert Mounted Corps comprising the Anzac, Australian, and Yeomanry Mounted Divisions and the Camel Brigade. The infantry divisions were allotted to XX Corps (four divisions) under Chetwode and XXI Corps (three divisions) under Major-General Edward Bulfin, recently arrived from the Salonika theatre. He had brought with him the 60th Division as reinforcements, and a further division, the 75th, was in process of formation in Egypt. Not the least consequence of Allenby's arrival was the new priority accorded to the theatre by the government in London.

Changes were under way on the Turkish side also. The Turkish high command was torn between the demands of the southern front in Palestine and the desire to recapture Baghdad, one of the holy cities of Islam, which had been taken by British forces in Mesopotamia in March 1917. General Erich von Falkenhayn, the former chief of the German high command who had been superseded after the disaster

at Verdun, was sent by the Germans in April to assist the Turks in the recapture of Baghdad. The projected offensive into Mesopotamia was named Yilderim, 'Lightning', and the Yilderim force of two army corps was concentrated around Aleppo. It was the intention of the British government that a renewed offensive in southern Palestine should draw this force south from Aleppo, causing the abandonment of the offensive against Baghdad and leading, it was hoped, to a blow which would knock Turkey out of the war. Divisions within the enemy high command, between different personalities within the Turkish army and between Turks and Germans, led to the abandonment of this plan and in any case von Falkenhayn had decided in September that the Palestine front was the crucial one. When Allenby's offensive against Gaza came in October–November, it found the enemy still in the process of reorganizing his forces.

Under von Falkenhayn's overall command the forces in southern Palestine were divided into the

Seventh and Eighth Armies under Fevsi Pasha and von Kressenstein respectively. The Eighth Army disposed of XXII Corps (two divisions) in Gaza itself and XX Corps (three divisions with one more in reserve) at Sheria. A further division was held in Army reserve, for a total of approximately **35,000** men and **260** guns. Beersheba was defended by III Corps under Ismet Bey, who could call upon two divisions in the town itself, and two regiments on the flank towards Gaza, a total of **5,000** men, **60** machine-guns and **28** artillery pieces. The Yilderim reserve, of one division, was held 25 miles north of Gaza. In contrast to Allenby, von Falkenhayn was well to the rear and did not even reach Jerusalem until 5 November.

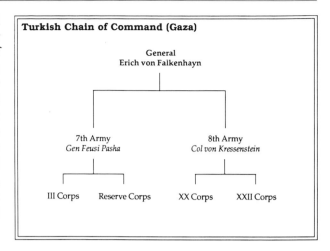

Turkish Chain of Command (Gaza)

General
Erich von Falkenhayn

7th Army
Gen Feusi Pasha

8th Army
Col von Kressenstein

III Corps   Reserve Corps   XX Corps   XXII Corps

The Plan and its Execution

The British enjoyed a preponderance in infantry of about three to one; in mounted troops eight to one; in guns about three to two. This numerical advantage was countered to some extent by the greatly strengthened defences of the Gaza position, too strong to be broken directly by other than a long and costly siege. The enemy centre was strong also, but his defences on his left flank were weaker and the open flank here provided an opportunity for the mounted divisions as well. The plan for the third battle of Gaza, devised by Chetwode, called for a preliminary operation against Beersheba to enable a force to be pushed on to the high ground between there and Hareira which would then re-deploy to roll up the Turkish flank. XX Corps and the Desert Mounted Corps would form the striking force, while XXI Corps made a secondary attack against Gaza itself to keep the enemy's attention focused there. The Yeomanry Mounted Division, detached from Desert Mounted Corps, would operate in the twenty-mile gap in the centre between the other formations.

The plan had three weaknesses. Supply would rely on pack animals, since the EEF would be operating beyond the range of both railhead and pipeline. Food and ammunition could be supplied beyond Beersheba in limited quantities, but not water. It would be a vital prerequisite for the success of the operation that the wells and pumps at Beersheba be captured intact and on the first day. Finally, it was imperative that the enemy be convinced that the move on his left was a feint and that the main assault would come at Gaza, as before. This last process was an outstanding Intelligence success, ensured in large part by the famed

▲ General Otto Liman von Sanders (1855–1929). Seconded to Turkey in 1913, he commanded the Turkish Fifth Army with great distinction and success at Gallipoli in 1915– 16, and in 1918 commanded three Turkish armies pitted against Allenby in Palestine and Syria – with less success. He was indubitably a very gifted commander.

▲ The Charge of the Light Horse at Beersheba. (Painting by G. W. Lambert)

◄ A Turkish machine-gun detachment near Beersheba, scene of the crucial Allied breakthrough. Note the optical range-finder in use.

Meinertzhagen ruse,* but assisted also by the activities of recently arrived squadrons of the Royal Flying Corps in new Bristol Fighters which swept the skies of the enemy's aircraft and further confused his Intelligence-gathering effort.

On the night of 30/31 October some 40,000 troops of all arms moved into position for the attack on Beersheba. The mounted divisions had farthest to go, making a night march of some 25–30 miles in order to attack the town from the east. The diversionary action before Gaza was timed to begin once the result at Beersheba was known, but 24–48 hours before the attack on Sheria began in the hope that this would lead the Turks to reinforce their right at the expense of their left and further facilitate the task of XX Corps.

Meinertzhagen was a very organized Intelligence officer who managed to fool the Turks by dropping a satchel of marked maps in a convincing manner while conducting a reconnaissance.

The bombardment of the Gaza defences began on 27 October as part of this deception, the guns of Bulfin's corps aided by naval gunfire from French and British ships offshore. At Beersheba the British deployed just 116 guns, all but sixteen being light pieces, for support along a 5,000-yard front and for counter-battery work.

The first phase of the assault on Beersheba began early on the morning of 31 October, when a brigade of the 60th Division took the enemy defences on Point 1069 to the south-west with little loss. Other attacks by units of the 60th and 74th Divisions followed. By later afternoon the infantry's objectives in the outer defences south and south-west of Beersheba had been secured and the Turks had been driven back into the town. To the east and north-east units of the Anzac Mounted Division took the enemy defences at Tel es Sakaty and Tel es Saba, although the New Zealand Mounted Brigade was held up by

▲ An armoured car attached to the Royal Artillery on patrol in the Palestinian desert.

◄ General Allenby inspecting a captured German Albatros D scout-fighter aircraft, 'somewhere in Syria' towards the end of the campaign. Note the 'Aero Tyre' marking in English on the aircraft's tyre. The aperture cut in the upper wing was to enable the pilot to watch for enemy aircraft above him.

enemy machine-guns in front of the latter and Chauvel had to commit two Australian Light Horse Regiments to assist them. By 1500 these positions had been taken after some fierce fighting. Half an hour later, 1 and 2 Light Horse Brigades moved on positions immediately to the north of Beersheba so as to isolate the garrison and begin the infiltration of the town itself.

Time was running out, however, and progress was too deliberate. The success of the whole plan hinged upon the capture of the town and the securing of the water supplies therein. Chauvel now drew in 4 Light Horse Brigade, kept in reserve until that moment. They were chosen because they were nearer than the Yeomanry units of 5 Mounted Brigade, but the decision to charge the defences in cavalry style appears to have been made by Brigadier Grant, the brigade commander. Chauvel's order was simple: 'Put Grant straight at it.' At 1630 Grant led the 4th and 12th Light Horse Regiments, on a front of two regiments, against the eastern defences of the town. The light horse were not issued with swords, and so carried their long bayonets unsheathed in their hands. The 11th Light Horse Regiment moved up in reserve

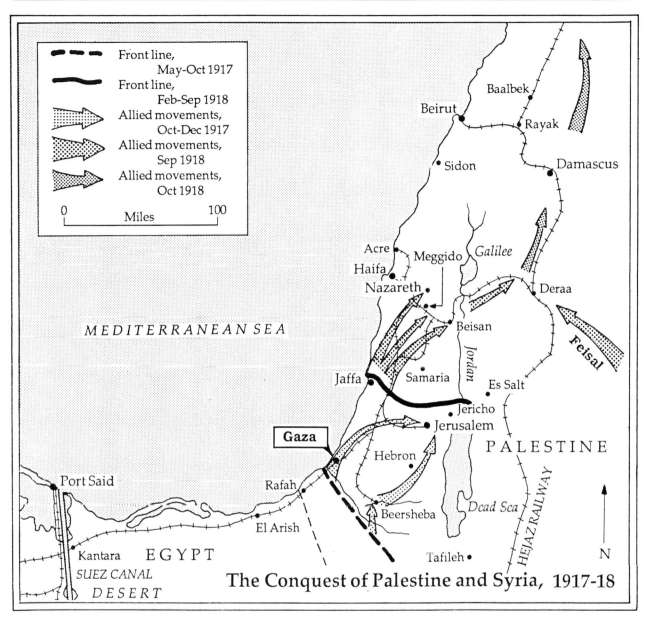

The Conquest of Palestine and Syria, 1917-18

behind the main body of the charge while the machine-gun squadron advanced on the left rear of the brigade to neutralize Turkish machine-guns in the trenches (which were much more extensive and better developed than the maps in the British official history indicate). Five Mounted Brigade was ordered to move in support also, as were 7 Mounted Brigade from the south and 1 and 3 Light Horse Brigades from the north. Thus nearly two mounted divisions were on the move against the Turks as part of 4 Brigade's charge.

The pace of the charge carried the light horse through the 'beaten zone' of enemy machine-gun, rifle and artillery fire with few casualties. Two squadrons of the 12th Regiment galloped straight on into the town, but the majority of the men crossed the trenches, dismounted and cleared the positions of the enemy with the bayonet. It was an intense, hand-to-hand struggle, and most of the Australian casualties of 31 killed and 32 wounded occurred here. The Turkish plans to destroy the wells and evacuate the town collapsed; Ismet Bey barely escaped capture, and the Australians alone took more than 1,000 prisoners and nine guns. The effect upon Turkish morale was considerable. A German officer, taken prisoner by the

▲ 'Lieutenant, McNamara winning the VC' – a dramatic rescue in the Syrian desert of a shot-down pilot. Lieutenant M. H. McNamara's award was dated 20 March 1917. He flew with 1st Squadron, Australian Flying Corps; but in the Second World War he transferred to the RAF. (Painting by Stuart Reid)

◄ Be2c aircraft of 30 Squadron, the Royal Flying Corps, at Nasiriyeh.

Light Horse, concluded after the charge that 'they are not soldiers at all; they are madmen'.

'The capture of Beersheba with its wells mainly intact, and the almost complete destruction of the enemy's 27th Division, formed an auspicious opening to . . . Allenby's operations' (Wavell, *The Palestine Campaigns*). But Beersheba was only the preliminary to the main event, and the forces on the British right needed now to strike at and round the enemy's flank before he could withdraw or reinforce his threatened positions. Allenby had foreseen a 48-hour delay between the two phases, and it was more necessary than ever to maintain the enemy's attention on the feint before Gaza. The assault on the Turkish left was timed for 3 or 4 November; the assault on Gaza was fixed therefore for the night of 1/2 November.

The bombardment here had begun on 27 October, and brought the fire of 218 guns to bear on a front of some 5,000 yards between Umbrella Hill and the sea. The assault was to be undertaken in two phases, entrusted to the 54th Division and one brigade of the 52nd, with six tanks in support. Umbrella Hill was taken by the 7th Scottish Rifles on 1 November, all objectives being secured before midnight. After a four-hour pause the main assault was launched early the following morning, its objectives being taken by 0630. The attack penetrated some 3,000 yards at its furthest point, obliging the Turkish command to reinforce the garrison while the depth of the British success here had effectively turned the flank of many of the carefully prepared defences of the town.

Chetwode had thrown out strong forces to protect his flank north of Beersheba, the 53rd Division, the Camel Brigade and the Anzac Mounted Division moving towards Khuweilfe and along the Hebron Road. These formations became locked in a drawn-out battle with Turkish forces over the next few days, preventing the enemy from mounting a counter-stroke against what he mistakenly believed to be an attempted push up the Hebron road towards Jerusalem. The fighting here did not end until 7 November, when the Turks withdrew as part of their general retreat from the Gaza–Beersheba line.

Meanwhile, the main attack against the Turkish left was timed for 6 November, the delay occasioned once more by difficulties in keeping so large a force watered at a distance from the pipeline. The Turkish trenches of the Qawuqa system ran for eight miles eastward from Sheria to Hareira, and the 74th, 60th and 10th Divisions were positioned from right to left with the Australian Mounted Division on the left flank to cover the 15-mile gap between XX and XXI Corps. The intention was to roll the enemy up from east to west, taking the entrenchments in enfilade as much as possible. The 74th Division led off on the right, advancing five miles overall against well-sited trenches which were defended stubbornly. All objectives had been taken by mid-afternoon. The 60th and 10th Divisions then worked across the main Qawuqa system, assisted by the concerted bombardment of the divisional artillery of both formations which cut the wire in front of the assault. At 1630 two brigades of the 60th Division were able to turn north against the Sheria defences, but stout resistance from Turkish machine-gunners and the coming of darkness, together with the confusion engendered by the wholesale burning of his stores by the enemy, led to the postponement of a night assault on the position.

By that evening the Turks were beginning to retreat, and the EEF was able to go over to the pursuit next morning. Sheria was taken at dawn by the 60th Division and the Hareira redoubt by the 10th after a short, costly assault largely unsupported by artillery. Chauvel was ordered to launch his mounted formations through the enemy's fractured centre towards Jemmame and Huj in order to secure the water supply and thus extend once again the operational radius of his units. XXI Corps had found Gaza abandoned on the morning of 7 November. Its garrison, faced by a double envelopment, was in full retreat.

Allenby had intended that the mounted units should cut off the Turkish retirement in the plain of Philistria to the north, but once again the problems of water frustrated expectations. Although Beersheba's wells had been taken largely intact, they could not meet the needs of the whole force alone. One mounted division had to be sent back to its starting-point for water after the capture of the town. In addition, four of Chauvel's ten mounted brigades had been engaged in the fighting to the north around Khuweilfe, and could not disengage quickly enough to join the pursuit, leaving just four brigades to intercept the enemy's retreat. And although that enemy was in retreat, he was by no means yet thoroughly beaten. His rearguards fought stubbornly over the next few days, and the tired men and horses of the mounted units, short of water, had come to a standstill by 9 November, having failed to set the final seal on the victory through no fault of their own.

Consequences

The first and most obvious consequence of the victory at Gaza was that it unlocked the defences of southern Palestine, defended stoutly by the Turks for the preceding nine months. In the weeks immediately afterwards the enemy fell back 75 miles with heavy losses. Jerusalem was taken on 9 December, the 'Christmas present for the British nation' for which Lloyd George had pressed Allenby in June that year. Yet this was not achieved without more hard fighting. Von Kressenstein described his Turkish army at this time as being 'still in good order and capable of fighting effectively'. Turkish resistance was stubborn until the end of the year, despite the manpower problems which plagued the Turkish Army and the

increasingly acrimonious disputes between the German and Turkish high commands. British and Empire casualties during the period October to December numbered 19,702. The Turkish losses were higher and that, together with the growing hopelessness of their strategic position, was what now counted.

On a personal level, the victories in the latter part of 1917 retrieved Allenby's reputation, and the successes of the following year merely confirmed his abilities as a skilled commander of mobile operations. His forces likewise thrived upon success. Chauvel wrote at the end of the year that '[l]ots of decorations have been earned by my people since [Beersheba] . . . they have rather come into their own in that way under the new regime'. Kress von Kressenstein was less fortunate; relieved of his command before the end of the year, the enemy lost the services of an able general who was one of the few Germans in Palestine to have much empathy with his Turkish allies.

While Gaza was of great significance for the prosecution of the war in the Middle East, it had little or no importance in terms of the wider war beyond. The decision to pursue a course which diverted resources from the main theatre and the main enemy – the Western Front and the Germans – was part of Lloyd George's continuing search for a less costly solution to the tactical problems of the Western Front. That the 'sideshow' in Palestine affected that outcome not at all is suggested strongly by the Turkish surrender just a fortnight before the end of the war in Europe.

BIBLIOGRAPHY

Falls, Cyril. *Military Operations, Egypt and Palestine from June 1917 to the end of the war*, part I, London, 1930. The relevant volume of the British official history, valuable for its extensive use of still untranslated Turkish sources.

Gullett, H. S. *The Australian Imperial Force in Sinai and Palestine. Official History of Australia in the War of 1914–18*, vol. 7, Sydney, 1923. The relevant volume of the Australian official history. Gullett was an official correspondent in Palestine during the last year of the war.

Hill, A. J. *Chauvel of the Light Horse*, Melbourne, 1978.

Meticulous and scholarly biography based on extensive private papers.

Powles, C. Guy. *The New Zealanders in Sinai and Palestine*, Wellington, 1922. The relevant volume of the semi-official New Zealand history.

Wavell, F. M. Lord. *Allenby, Soldier and Statesman*, London, 1944. An admiring but not uncritical biography of one desert general by another.

— *The Palestine Campaigns*, London, 1968. Still the best short guide to the war in Palestine.

AMIENS COMPANY CREST
RMA SANDHURST

THE BATTLE OF AMIENS, 1918

by Sir Martin Farndale

'August 8th was the black day of the German Army in the history of war.'

(General von Ludendorff, Chief of the German General Staff)

By the middle of 1918 both sides in the Great War appeared to have fought each other to a standstill. The German offensive of March of that year had been held by the Allies and using all their power they had, by July, regained most of what they had lost. But it had not been easy and after four years of war they were weary enough. Nevertheless the American effort was building up and plans were being made for a major offensive in 1919 to end the war. Thus it was not surprising that at the end of July 1918, Ludendorff wrote, 'Full-dress attacks by the enemy are as little to be expected as a counter-attack by us!' How wrong he was!

The Setting

Before looking at the great Allied victory at Amiens it is necessary to see how it all came about. On 12 July Marshal Foch proposed an offensive on the British front between Festubert and Rebecq. Five days later Haig replied that he saw no point in such an attack but that a much better idea would be to, 'Make a combined Franco-British operation, the French attacking south of Moreuil and the British north of the Luce . . .' He went on to say that the British should advance in an easterly direction, 'To free that town [Amiens] and the railway'. Thus Haig only envisaged a limited operation. Nevertheless Foch agreed and the French First Army was put under command of Haig for offensive operations.

General Rawlinson was to command the British and Debeney the French. It was to be a frontal attack so surprise was essential and the methods used to achieve it are still an object lesson in what can be done when the situation does not look promising. The first problem was that the British were going to rely on the massed use of some 465 tanks and a massive predicted fireplan by 1,300 field and 160 heavy guns but with no preliminary bombardment. The French, however, had few tanks available and could not dispense with a preliminary bombardment; this produced a problem of co-ordination. After some discussion it was agreed that the French would not start until the British advance had begun.

The Plan is Proposed

The British gunners had perfected the predicted artillery attack at Cambrai in November 1917 when they fired the first such attack in history and achieved complete surprise. By August 1918 they had perfected this technique even further. First, it was necessary to survey in all guns and targets on to the same map grid. Then the barrels of all guns when laid on the same bearing had to be precisely parallel, no easy task when almost 1,500 guns were involved. Field Survey Companies of the Royal Engineers established 'Bearing Pickets' right across the battlefield. Artillery Boards, or accurate blank maps, enabled the guns and targets to be plotted with great accuracy; this in turn enabled Gun Position Officers to read off accurate bearing and range to the targets. Next, thanks to the work of Lieutenant-Colonel (later Professor) W. L. Bragg on sound ranging, enemy guns were being fixed with an astonishing 90 per cent accuracy. He had also worked out a method of measuring the velocity of shells on discharge, thus enabling each gun's variation from the normal muzzle velocity to be calculated. By

▲ General Sir Henry Rawlinson (1864–1925), GOC Fourth Army, who had turned a body of volunteer troops – which bore the brunt of some heavy fighting in 1916 – into a veteran army which in large measure won the battle of Amiens two years later.

August 1918 all guns were well-calibrated and a method had been perfected of measuring meterological conditions and for circulating them round all gun positions every few hours as the conditions changed. Thus, provided the calculations for each individual gun were correctly worked out on the gun position it was possible to hit targets without prior registration.

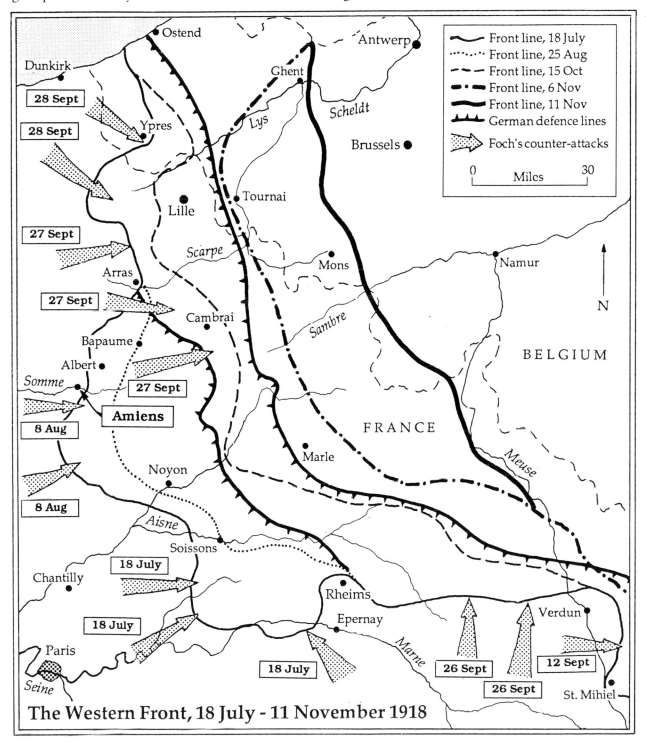

The Western Front, 18 July - 11 November 1918

◀ King George V talking to General Sir Douglas Haig, with General Rawlinson, commander Fourth Army, in the background.

▶ Field Marshal Paul von Hindenburg (left) and General Erich von Ludendorff, his First Quartermaster (or chief of staff). The victorious command team of Tannenberg (1914), were to adopt a different role at Amiens four years later.

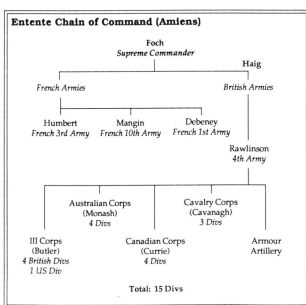

Entente Chain of Command (Amiens)

Foch
Supreme Commander

French Armies

British Armies

Haig

Humbert
French 3rd Army

Mangin
French 10th Army

Debeney
French 1st Army

Rawlinson
4th Army

Australian Corps
(Monash)
4 Divs

Cavalry Corps
(Cavanagh)
3 Divs

III Corps
(Butler)
4 British Divs
1 US Div

Canadian Corps
(Currie)
4 Divs

Armour
Artillery

Total: 15 Divs

But secrecy was necessary in the build-up to battle. Conferences were always held in different places to deceive the ever watchful spies. Dates and timings were top secret and only released to very few, the plans themselves were known to a few more and only released at the latest possible moment. For example, divisional commanders did not know that an attack was intended until 31 July and below that level not until 36 hours before Zero-Hour. Even the War Cabinet was kept in the dark. All preparatory movement was by night, artillery fire was maintained at normal rates especially at night to cover the noise of movement; guns were moved into their positions and concealed before dawn each day. Great quantities of ammunition were stockpiled. By 7 August Fourth Army had been raised in strength to thirteen infantry divisions, three cavalry divisions, ten heavy and two 'whippet' tank battalions. A total of 30,000 rounds of HE and 10,000 rounds of gas shell was dumped for the 18-pounders and 24,000 rounds of smoke alone was dumped beside the ubiquitous 4.5in howitzers. The final act of deception was to dispatch a force of Canadians north to Kemmel in Flanders knowing that they would be reported. The Germans recognized the fact that wherever the Canadians were usually meant an attack before long. These moves were coupled with a series of false messages and air activity. So as the rest of the Canadian corps was secretly moved south to the Somme, the Germans were convinced that, if anything, there might be an attack much farther north.

The fireplan was to start at Zero-Hour and as the guns opened up the tanks were to move forward. The 18-pounder barrage was to move forward in lifts of 100 yards. The opening line was to be 200 yards ahead of the Start Line. Lifts were to be at three-minute intervals for eight lifts and then to slow to

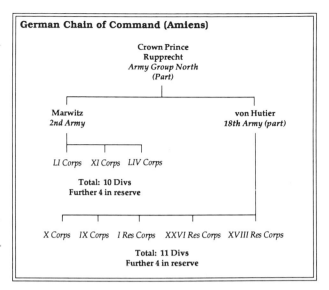

German Chain of Command (Amiens)

Crown Prince
Rupprecht
Army Group North
(Part)

Marwitz
2nd Army

von Hutier
18th Army (part)

LI Corps XI Corps LIV Corps

Total: 10 Divs
Further 4 in reserve

X Corps IX Corps I Res Corps XXVI Res Corps XVIII Res Corps

Total: 11 Divs
Further 4 in reserve

intervals of four minutes. A deep barrage was to be fired by some of the heavies from Zero to plus four hours while two-thirds of the heavy guns were to be committed to counter-battery tasks. On capture of the first objective specified field and howitzer batteries were to move forward on orders of Infantry Brigades and horses were moved up to be ready.

The whole attack front was fourteen miles long. The German line was held by six skeleton divisions, their morale was low and their defences weak. German aircraft could not penetrate the British air superiority. Nevertheless we now know that on several occasions German forward troops reported hearing tanks at night but they were ridiculed by the Staff who were convinced that the British were not strong enough to go on to the offensive.

The Battle Opens

Thus as the tension grew during the night of 7/8 August 1918, with commanders asking themselves whether security had held, the men waited for the mighty crash of the guns to herald yet another attack. On the guns 10,000 gunners waited too; would their calculations be right, would it all work again, and this time could they also move forward with the battle? Then in a great sheet of flame the ground shook as rank after rank of guns opened fire and at the same moment the 450 tanks rolled forward as the infantry also left their trenches and made best speed for their first objectives. A thick ground mist had risen overnight and this added to the enemy's confusion; soon the Australians and the Canadians had captured their objectives, describing the barrage as quite excellent. The mist made it difficult for the leading waves to keep up with it as they could not see the bursting shells in the swirling mist until dangerously close, but the shooting was very accurate and the infantry had learned long ago to follow close and the guns would lead them to their objectives. Soon the tanks were over the front trenches and armoured cars were racing on ahead; at Proyart they shot up a German Corps Headquarters at breakfast.

Next came the advance of the guns, first the field guns galloping forward over the enemy's front trenches and swinging into action often under machine-gun fire from pockets of enemy not yet defeated. Then came the heavies, the great 60-pounders and the 6-inch howitzers and finally the field howitzers, the 4.5s, great lines of guns surging forward and stirring the hearts of the infantry and

tank crews already made buoyant by their success. (The advance of the artillery before Harbonières on 8 August 1918 is one of the great moments of British history and has been dramatically painted by Septimus Power; it hangs at the Royal School of Artillery, Larkhill.)

At 1400 hours that day a very special visitor arrived at the 471st Super Heavy Battery RGA. The battery had recently taken over two of the biggest guns ever manned by the Royal Artillery – 14-inch, 270-ton railway guns firing shells weighing three-quarters of a ton to a range of 20 miles. The Battery had christened them 'HMG' (His Majesty's Gun) 'Bosche Buster' and 'Scene Shifter', and it was King George V himself who

▲ Field artillery in action at Harbonnières, 8 August 1918. This was 'The Black Day' of the German army: at zero hour, 4.20 a.m., more than a thousand guns opened fire and the infantry began the advance. (Painting by H. Septimus Power)

▶ Crews of three 4.5in pieces of 112th Howitzer Battery, Australian Field Artillery in action near Hamel, August 1918.

was their special visitor that day. In his presence one gun was fired as part of the attack on Douai. It fired twelve rounds and subsequently it was found that with its first round it had hit the railway causing enormous destruction and preventing its use by the Germans to move reinforcements forward. This became known as 'The King's Shot' and was said by the Gunners to mark the actual turning-point in the war.

Even after the move forward of the guns communications were somehow maintained, to the everlasting credit of the line parties. This was a major feature in maintaining the ability to concentrate artillery as the attacks moved forward in order to keep up momentum. The fire was visually directed by the forward observers moving with the leading infantry, reeling out cable behind them as they went along, although at Amiens one or two bulky and somewhat unreliable wireless sets were also used. As the victorious tanks

and infantry rolled on they passed evidence of some of the most effective counter-battery fire of the war. Whole batteries were knocked out, some still with their muzzle caps on, showing how complete had been the surprise. The British counter-battery policy was to attack each enemy battery with three or four heavy batteries systematically, and in turn then to swing off them on to others before swinging back on to each on a sporadic basis to catch the enemy gunners as they struggled to sort out the mess. So effective was this and so accurate was the fire that the attacking infantry were never hampered by German gunfire at Amiens. A sound-ranging base and observation parties went forward on 9 August and were soon reporting new enemy gun positions.

Artillery casualties on the first day of the battle of Amiens were actually nil! But more than a thousand horses were hit as the enemy bombed a great concentration waiting to move the guns forward. At the end of the first day it was clear that the great majority of the German casualties were caused by shellfire. It is probable that on 'eight, eight, eighteen' the British artillery reached its peak of perfection, every aspect of the plan being a success. The guns lifted the assault on to its objectives, protected its flanks, broke up counter-attacks, prevented the enemy from using his guns and then moved forward with the

◄ **Men of 93rd Siege Battery, Royal Garrison Artillery, loading a 9.2in howitzer near Bayencourt, 8 August 1918. Some idea of shell consumption is given in this picture.**

◄ **Below left: A 6in howitzer at Merris 12 April 1918.**

▼ **A battery of 60pdr guns in action on 10 August 1918. Note the limbers and ammunition caissons.**

assault and repeated the process for the next two phases.

There were many gallant and splendid actions by all arms. As the 17th Lancers swept forward 'K' Battery RHA dropped into action on the move and destroyed a German counter-attack at Cayeux Wood. Three Brigade RCFA advanced to positions just west of Beaucourt at 1500 hours, covering its infantry forward. At 2030 hours, the Germans attempted a counter-attack from Beaucourt and ran straight into the guns of 'C' Battery RHA which crushed it before it started. The Canadians captured 114 officers, 5,000 men and 161 guns. In the Australian sector the barrage was so thick that they had their objectives by 0700 hours, 10 Brigade RAFA giving magnificent support for the attack on Cérisy. Scarcely a German shell fell after 0540 hours.

◄ Marshal Ferdinand Foch (1851–1929), one of the most notable senior commanders of the First World War, who was appointed Supreme Commander of the Entente's armies during the so nearly successful major German offensive in the spring of 1918. In August he was awarded his baton as a Marshal of France.

▼ A detachment of Highlanders moving up into the line from the rear, 'somewhere in France'. Periods out of the front line for training and rest purposes were interspersed at regular intervals.

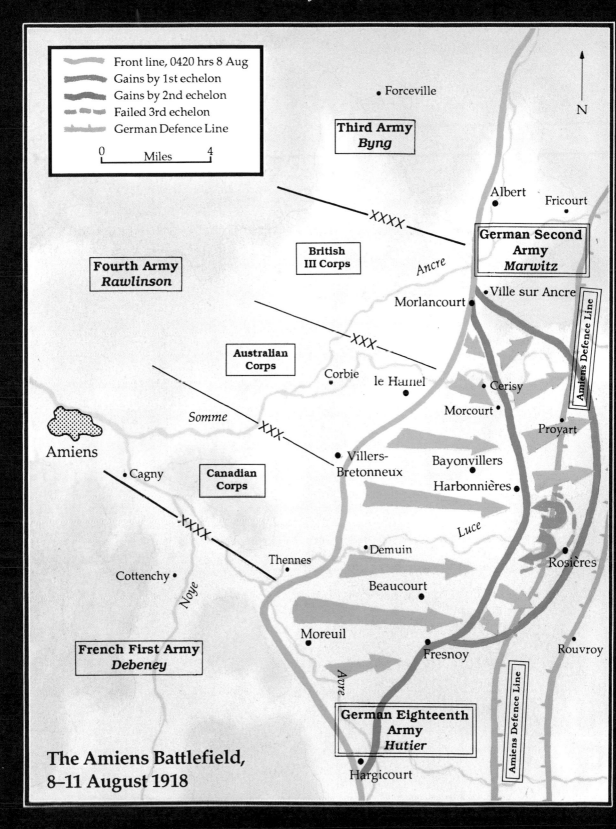

Legend:
- Front line, 0420 hrs 8 Aug
- Gains by 1st echelon
- Gains by 2nd echelon
- Failed 3rd echelon
- German Defence Line

0 Miles 4

• Forceville

Third Army
Byng

N

Albert •   Fricourt •

German Second Army
Marwitz

Fourth Army
Rawlinson

British III Corps

Ancre

• Ville sur Ancre

XXXX

Morlancourt •

Australian Corps

XXX

Corbie •   • le Hamel

• Cerisy

Morcourt •

Amiens Defence Line

Somme

XXX

Proyart •

Villers-Bretonneux •

Bayonvillers •

• Cagny

Canadian Corps

Harbonnières •

Amiens

Rosières •

XXXX

Luce

Thennes •

• Demuin

Cottenchy •

Noye

Beaucourt •

French First Army
Debeney

Moreuil •

Avre

Fresnoy •

Rouvroy •

German Eighteenth Army
Hutier

Amiens Defence Line

The Amiens Battlefield, 8–11 August 1918

Hargicourt •

attack. Being frontal, the more it pushed the more the enemy were concentrated. On the 10th Haig visited the front and stopped the attack, telling Foch that he had gone far enough and that he next intended to attack with Third Army north of Albert; this he did on 21 August. Fourth Army seized the opportunity and continued their attack on 28 August against St Quentin and Péronne.

At this stage General Rawlinson ordered his guns, including the heavies, right forward. These were to attack enemy positions in depth. Even the 12- and 14-inch guns came forward to bombard the bridges over the Somme. Subsequent German records show how these tactics caused great disorganization and demoralization. As the advance continued all arms learnt quickly how to work together in the more mobile operations that had eluded them for almost four years; rapid fireplans, tanks and infantry working as battlegroups and often with air support. All-arms mobile tactics of a remarkably high standard were developed and these improved until the end of the war. So much was then forgotten when peace came, and it all had to

▲ Mount Kemmel, 2 September 1918; an 18pdr battery, RA, in action.

◀ The price of defeat: German prisoners of war being escorted to the rear past a section of 13pdr anti-aircraft guns near Mericourt l'Abbé.

▶ Wilhelm II (1859–1941), Kaiser and King of Prussia, grandson of Queen Victoria, and sometime honorary Field Marshal in the British Army. For him, after Amiens, the future only held exile in Holland.

The Measure of Victory

What a success it had been, an advance of six to eight miles and all objectives taken. Why then did it all slow down, why was the initiative not seized and a breakout achieved? There seem to be many reasons. First, as always, was the problem of supply once the battle had reached the edge of the Somme battlefields with all its trenches, wire and mines, and movement became extremely difficult. Then once again there was a lack of reserves ready to push on and by last light the Germans were beginning to reinforce; by 11 August they had moved forward eighteen divisions. Then there was the reason inherent in the form of

be learnt again the hard way when war broke out in 1939.

Amiens was a very great victory, possibly the most significant in the Great War. Sixteen thousand prisoners on the first day and 21,000 in all was a considerable haul. But the advance of twelve miles was not as great as it might have been had the objectives not been so limited or had better preparations been made to commit reserves to exploit the initial success and to maintain momentum. However the surprise achieved was most significant and it forced the German High Command to use up all their available reinforcements. By 16 August they had only nine reserve divisions between the Somme and the sea. The rapid move of these reserves stopped the British, but in the end their use hastened the end of the war. Once again the great value of surprise was demonstrated and it had a very great effect on German morale. It led the Kaiser to say '. . . We are at the end of our resources, the war must be ended . . .' After the war Ludendorff said that in his opinion, 'August 8th was the black day of the German army in the history of war.' The success at Amiens certainly made it possible to achieve victory in 1918 at a time when the War Council was making plans for operations in 1919.

BIBLIOGRAPHY

Blaxland, G. *Amiens 1918*, London, 1968. Probably the best overall coverage of the whole campaign and battle.

Edmonds, J. E. *Military Operations, France and Belgium, 1918*, vol. 4, London, 1947. The official history. Of great value.

Farndale, M. *History of the Royal Regiment of Artillery – Western Front 1914–1918*, London, 1987. The most recent overall survey and account.

Monash, Sir J. *The Australian Victories in France*, Sydney, 1936. A full account of the Australian contribution by one of the First World War's ablest commanders.

Pitt, B. *1918 – the Last Act*, London, 1962. A vivid coverage of the whole campaign on the Western Front.

Terraine, J. *To Win a Way: 1918 – the Year of Victory*, London, 1978. A sound study by a noted historian of the First World War.

Editor-in-Chief's note:
RCFA = Royal Canadian Field Artillery
RAFA = Royal Australian Field Artillery

ALAMEIN COMPANY CREST
RMA SANDHURST

THE FIRST AND SECOND BATTLES OF ALAMEIN, 1942

by Lord Carver

'Fret not to roam the desert now, with all thy winged speed.'

(Caroline Norton, *The Arab's Farewell to His Steed*)

The battle which raged from 23 October to 4 November 1942 in the desert seventy miles west of Alexandria marked the turning-point not only of the campaign in the Western Desert of Egypt and Libya, but of Britain's fortunes in the Second World War. The strategic aim of the campaign, and of the naval and air operations in the Mediterranean of which it formed a part, was never entirely clear. It resulted from a number of *ad hoc* decisions arising out of Italy's entry into the war as France collapsed under German attack in June 1940. Britain's links with India and the oil supplies of the Persian Gulf through the Mediterranean, the Suez Canal and the Red Sea were threatened by the Italian fleet and aircraft based in Sicily and the Italian colony of Libya, and by large Italian garrisons in Libya, Abyssinia and Somaliland.

The Strategy

Initially the task of General Sir Archibald Wavell and his naval and air colleagues was limited to securing their base in Egypt; but their success against the Italian forces and Mussolini's attack on Greece in October 1940 led both to German involvement and to a more ambitious British strategy. A severe shock to that was administered in the spring of 1941 by the successful German operations in Greece and Crete and Lieutenant-General Erwin Rommel's rout of the British Army in Cyrenaica, culminating in the arrival of his forces on the Egyptian frontier in April 1941, encircling Tobruk in the process. Malta, important as an air and naval base from which to operate against shipping supplying Italian and German forces in Libya, was now under severe threat.

General Sir Claude Auchinleck, Commander-in-Chief in India, changed places with Wavell in July 1941 and, in November, launched an offensive which, after some set-backs, relieved Tobruk and drove the Italian and German forces back to the border of Tripolitania, so that the Royal Air Force could base aircraft in Cyrenaica to give cover to convoys sailing from Alexandria to Malta.

The 1942 Reverse

In January 1942 Rommel repeated his performance of a year before and drove Lieutenant-General Neil Ritchie's Eighth Army back to Gazala, forty miles west of Tobruk, depriving the RAF of their airfields in northern Cyrenaica. There the two sides remained until May, Auchinleck under constant pressure from Churchill and the Chiefs of Staff to regain them, as Malta was in dire straits and unable seriously to affect the build-up of forces facing Ritchie. The latter was himself building-up Eighth Army and a base at Tobruk to support a counter-offensive.

He had not launched it when Rommel attacked on 27 May, and, in a series of hard-fought actions over two weeks, reversed Ritchie's significant superiority in numbers of tanks, so that the latter's immobile infantry became hostages to fortune. He was forced to withdraw from Gazala and, before his forces could be adequately reorganized, Rommel attacked and captured Tobruk, and then threatened to outflank Ritchie's positions on the Egyptian frontier. Ordered to hold Mersa Matruh, 140 miles within Egypt, to which reinforcements had been sent, Ritchie was dismissed, replaced by Auchinleck himself, who abandoned the position and ordered a confused and disorganized Eighth Army back to the line of El Alamein, only seventy miles from Alexandria, from which the fleet had been withdrawn to the Red Sea.

Auchinleck at El Alamein

A line running south from the railway halt at El Alamein was the obvious place at which to make a stand to defend the Nile delta. There, only thirty miles of desert lay between the coast and the Qattara Depression, an area of salt-marsh impassable to a large force. This limited the ability of a mobile force to outflank a defence, provided that sufficient forces could be deployed to fill the gap. But the experience of the previous nine months had persuaded Auchinleck that static positions in the desert, manned by immobile infantry, became liabilities unless the threat of the enemy's mobile forces could be removed. He therefore tried to make his army mobile by reducing the strength of the infantry to only that needed to escort the artillery, which he regarded as his principal arm of offence, to be moved around the battlefield under the personal direction of divisional, or even corps, commanders.

However, Rommel did not give him time to effect the change, which in any case was resisted by the Australian and New Zealand Divisions which had been brought from Palestine to reinforce Eighth Army. His leading troops reached the defences of El Alamein on 30 June, having overtaken some of the

▶ Lieutenant-General Oliver Leese, commander of XXX Corps, with three of his divisional commanders: (left to right) Major-Generals Morshead, Wimberley and Pienaar.

▶ A near-miss for an Eighth Army bren-gun carrier. The rolled-up sand mats carried on the rear of the carrier illustrate one problem of battle in the Western Desert – namely soft sand. Much of the surface was uneven rock, with very rare outcrops as in the background. Water, fuel and ammunition were the key requirements – in that order.

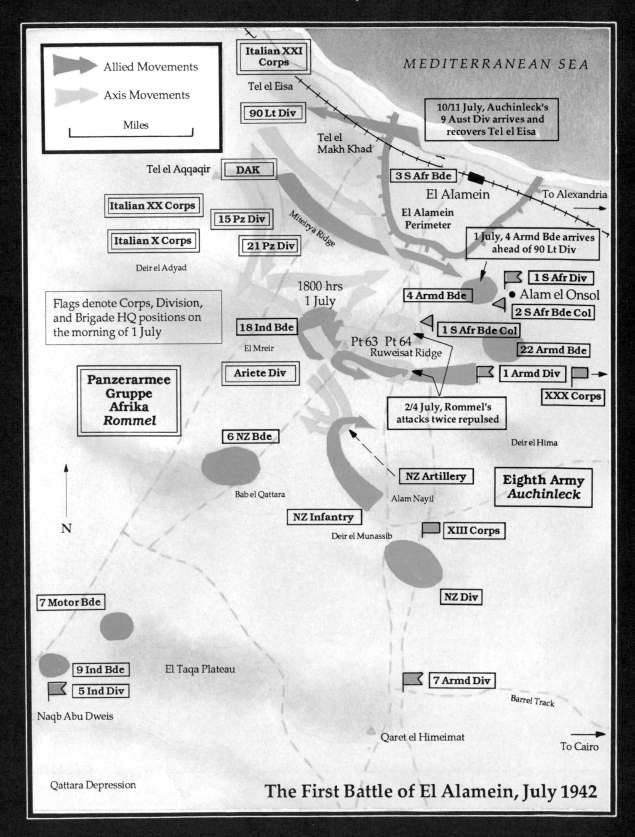

Allied Movements

Axis Movements

Miles

Italian XXI Corps

Tel el Eisa

90 Lt Div

MEDITERRANEAN SEA

10/11 July, Auchinleck's 9 Aust Div arrives and recovers Tel el Eisa

Tel el Makh Khad

Tel el Aqqaqir

DAK

3 S Afr Bde

El Alamein

To Alexandria

El Alamein Perimeter

Italian XX Corps

15 Pz Div

Miteirya Ridge

1 July, 4 Armd Bde arrives ahead of 90 Lt Div

Italian X Corps

21 Pz Div

Deir el Adyad

Flags denote Corps, Division, and Brigade HQ positions on the morning of 1 July

1800 hrs 1 July

4 Armd Bde

1 S Afr Div

Alam el Onsol

2 S Afr Bde Col

18 Ind Bde

El Mreir

1 S Afr Bde Col

Pt 63   Pt 64

Ruweisat Ridge

22 Armd Bde

1 Armd Div

XXX Corps

Panzerarmee Gruppe Afrika *Rommel*

Ariete Div

2/4 July, Rommel's attacks twice repulsed

Deir el Hima

6 NZ Bde

Bab el Qattara

NZ Artillery

Alam Nayil

Eighth Army *Auchinleck*

N

NZ Infantry

Deir el Munassib

XIII Corps

NZ Div

7 Motor Bde

9 Ind Bde

5 Ind Div

El Taqa Plateau

7 Armd Div

Barrel Track

Naqb Abu Dweis

Qaret el Himeimat

To Cairo

Qattara Depression

The First Battle of El Alamein, July 1942

DAVID COBB

retreating British forces on the way. Rommel decided to attack next day, having 55 German and 30 Italian tanks, 330 German and 200 Italian guns of all kinds, and about 1,500 German and 5,500 Italian infantry. Auchinleck had about the same number of tanks, but they were still disorganized as a result of their withdrawal from Mersa Matruh.

Rommel's attack followed the pattern that had been successful there: encirclement of the fixed defences on the coast, while driving away and getting behind the mobile forces to the south. He failed, thanks largely to the stubborn defence of its position south of the main defences of a newly arrived Indian infantry brigade in its first action, and after two days of fighting Rommel had only 26 tanks fit for battle.

Plentifully supplied with Intelligence from radio intercept of his opponent's weakness and dispositions, Auchinleck attempted to exploit it in a series of counter-attacks, as his forces were strengthened and

▲ A painting by David Cobb showing the action by Captain W. M. Nicholl that won him the DSO. On 30 June 1942, he managed to return twenty tanks to British lines despite their being under considerable fire from German positions.

strongly supported by Air Vice-Marshal 'Maori' Coningham's Desert Air Force. But co-operation between tanks and infantry, complicated by the enemy's rapid deployment of minefields, was poor; and, having failed to exploit the tantalizing opportunities which his Intelligence had offered him, Auchinleck, at the end of July, concluded that there must be a pause in which Eighth Army could be strengthened, reorganized and retrained on the lines he had tried to introduce.

He was not to be given the chance. The succession of failures demanded a change in command. Churchill's first choice was General Sir Harold Alexander to replace him and the promotion of Lieutenant-

General W. H. E. ('Strafer') Gott from command of XIII Corps to that of Eighth Army, Churchill and the CIGS, General Sir Alan Brooke, flying to Cairo to judge for themselves and effect the changes. On his way to meet them in Cairo, Gott's aircraft was shot down and he was killed. Lieutenant-General Bernard Montgomery, who a few days before had been chosen to replace Alexander as Commander of First Army, assigned to the Anglo-American expedition to French North Africa under the US Lieutenant-General Dwight D. Eisenhower, was flown out to succeed him and assumed command of Eighth Army (before he was officially supposed to) on 13 August 1942.

The Impact of Montgomery

Just short of his 55th birthday, Montgomery was old for his rank by Second World War standards. Gott and Ritchie were ten years younger: his superior,

▲ In August 1942 Churchill decided to move General Sir Claude Auchinleck from the Middle East to India, and to bring in a new command team. Sir Harold Alexander was the designated new overall commander, but Bernard Montgomery only received Eighth Army because of the death of 'Strafer' Gott.

▲ Above right: Montgomery and his corps commanders − (left to right) Oliver Leese, Herbert Lumsden and Brian Horrocks − who were to prove a formidable team.

Alexander, was four years his junior and had been a student under his instruction at the Staff College. He was not a typical British general, having no social graces or influential connections. His family background was that of the clergy. Supremely confident in his own ability and opinions, he was rudely intolerant of those of others. Wounded while gallantly leading his platoon at the Third Battle of Ypres in October 1914, he spent the rest of that war on the staff, finishing it as GSO1 of a division. Between the wars,

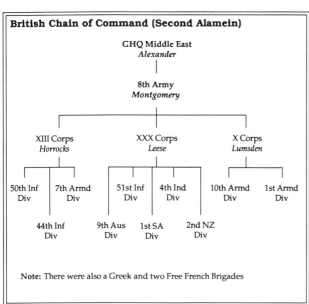

British Chain of Command (Second Alamein)

GHQ Middle East
Alexander

8th Army
Montgomery

XIII Corps
Horrocks

XXX Corps
Leese

X Corps
Lumsden

50th Inf Div · 7th Armd Div

51st Inf Div · 4th Ind Div

10th Armd Div · 1st Armd Div

44th Inf Div

9th Aus Div · 1st SA Div · 2nd NZ Div

Note: There were also a Greek and two Free French Brigades

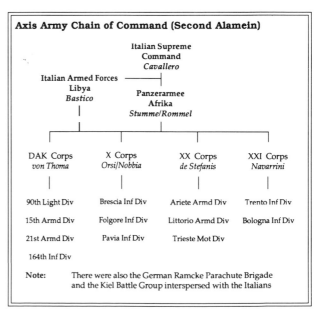

Axis Army Chain of Command (Second Alamein)

Italian Supreme Command
Cavallero

Italian Armed Forces Libya
Bastico

Panzerarmee Afrika
Stumme/Rommel

DAK Corps
von Thoma

X Corps
Orsi/Nobbia

XX Corps
de Stefanis

XXI Corps
Navarrini

90th Light Div · Brescia Inf Div · Ariete Armd Div · Trento Inf Div

15th Armd Div · Folgore Inf Div · Littorio Armd Div · Bologna Inf Div

21st Armd Div · Pavia Inf Div · Trieste Mot Div

164th Inf Div

Note: There were also the German Ramcke Parachute Brigade and the Kiel Battle Group interspersed with the Italians

he earned a high reputation as an instructor and trainer of infantry. His performance in command of the 3rd Division in the retreat to Dunkirk in May 1940 had greatly impressed his corps commander, Brooke, as did his vigorous and ruthless command of formations at higher level in England thereafter. Brooke 'had absolute faith in Montgomery's tactical ability'. He knew that '. . . he was self-confident to a fault, thoroughly resilient and ruthless in getting his way. Eighth Army needed such a man.'

On assuming command, Montgomery decided immediately to cancel all Auchinleck's orders for a 'mobile defence' and to form a continuous front, twenty miles long, as far south as Bare Ridge, held by four infantry divisions, from north to south: 9th Australian, 1st South African, 5th Indian (later relieved by 4th Indian) and 2nd New Zealand. He knew that the recently arrived 44th Division was being held back to man the defences of the Nile delta. If they were sent up to him, he could use them to hold the Alam el Halfa ridge ten miles east of the New

▲ '25-Pounder Gun and Team in Action on the El Alamein Front'. In many ways the second Battle of Alamein proved the apogee of the Royal Artillery. After the battle the tank became the leading weapon, a position it has held to the present time, although today the helicopter gun-ship is challenging the main battle tank's supremacy. (Painting by John Berry)

Zealanders, thus refusing his left flank and covering the gap of some fifteen miles between it and the lip of the Qattara Depression with minefields and the light armoured forces of 7th Armoured Division. His main armoured strength, which by the end of the month should rise to some 800 tanks, would be disposed on either side of Alam el Halfa. GHQ, where Auchinleck was in process of handing over to Alexander, agreed to send up 44th Division, and, having arranged for two new corps commanders of his own choice to be flown from England, Lieutenant-Generals Oliver Leese to replace Ramsden in command of the 30th and Brian Horrocks to take Gott's place with the 13th,

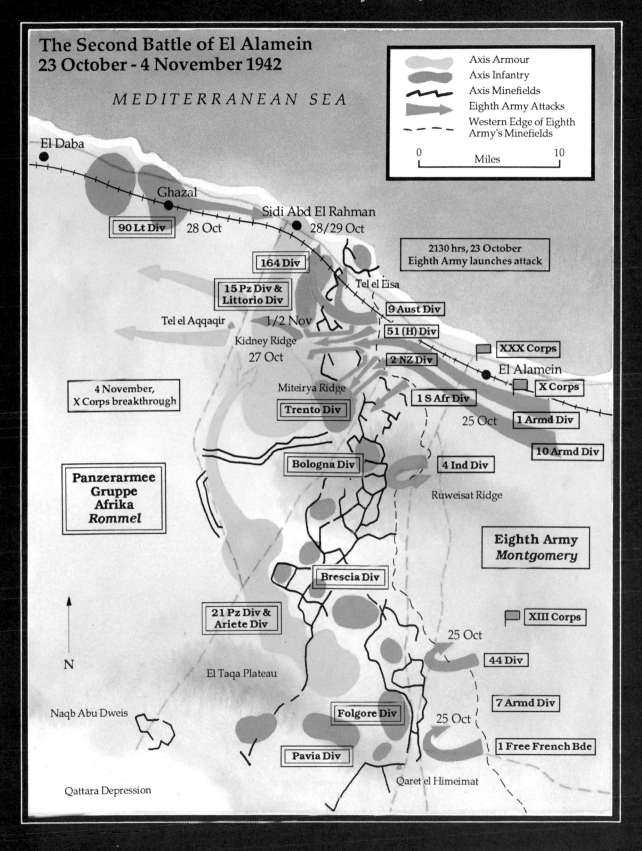

The Second Battle of El Alamein
23 October - 4 November 1942

MEDITERRANEAN SEA

Legend:
- Axis Armour
- Axis Infantry
- Axis Minefields
- Eighth Army Attacks
- Western Edge of Eighth Army's Minefields

0 — Miles — 10

El Daba

Ghazal

Sidi Abd El Rahman
28/29 Oct

90 Lt Div 28 Oct

2130 hrs, 23 October
Eighth Army launches attack

164 Div

15 Pz Div &
Littorio Div

Tel el Eisa

Tel el Aqqaqir
1/2 Nov

9 Aust Div

51 (H) Div

Kidney Ridge
27 Oct

2 NZ Div

XXX Corps

El Alamein

4 November,
X Corps breakthrough

Miteirya Ridge

1 S Afr Div

X Corps

Trento Div

25 Oct

1 Armd Div

10 Armd Div

**Panzerarmee
Gruppe
Afrika**
Rommel

Bologna Div

4 Ind Div

Ruweisat Ridge

Eighth Army
Montgomery

Brescia Div

N

XIII Corps

21 Pz Div &
Ariete Div

25 Oct

El Taqa Plateau

44 Div

7 Armd Div

Naqb Abu Dweis

Folgore Div

25 Oct

Pavia Div

1 Free French Bde

Qaret el Himeimat

Qattara Depression

he faced with confidence the attack which it was clear that Rommel was preparing.

Erwin Rommel, promoted Field Marshal after his capture of Tobruk, a schoolmaster's son from Württemberg, was, almost to the day, four years younger than his opponent. He had fought as an infantry platoon and company commander in France, Roumania and Italy in the First World War, gaining several awards for gallantry. He remained in the post-war army of 100,000 and did not reach the rank of major until 1933, when, after four years as an instructor at the infantry school, he gained command of a mountain infantry battalion. His chance came in 1938, when he was chosen to command the special battalion assigned to escort the Chancellor, Hitler, at the time of the invasion of Austria, a post he held until the end of the campaign in Poland. Hitler's high regard for him resulted in his obtaining command, for the invasion of France, of the 7th Panzer Division, which he drove forward with all the vigour, boldness and total disregard for any form of caution which he

was to demonstrate in North Africa, and which led General Halder to describe him in 1941 as 'this soldier gone stark mad'.

By the end of August 1942, commanding Panzerarmee Afrika, technically under the command of the Italian Marshal Cavallero, Rommel had some 200 German and about 250 Italian tanks, his principal anxiety being the precariousness of his fuel supplies. Montgomery had a clear warning from Ultra and other radio intercepts and was not surprised when Rommel launched his attack on the night of 31 August through the minefields south of Bare Ridge, delayed by the resistance of 7th Armoured Division, continuous air attack, a dust storm and the even slower progress of the Italian Mobile Corps on the left of the Afrika Korps, whose commander, Major-General Nehring, was wounded. The attack was brought to a halt in the last hour of daylight on 1 September, short of Alam el Halfa, by a resolute defence by Roberts's 22 Armoured Brigade. Battered from the air all night, Rommel made a half-hearted and unsuccessful attempt to renew his advance next day. After another night of continuous air bombardment, he decided to withdraw. Montgomery planned to cut him off by a counter-attack south from Bare

▼ Special equipment was available for dealing with the Axis minefields: here a Matilda 'Scorpion' tank with its revolving roller of thrashing chains.

Ridge, reinforcing Major-General Bernard Freyberg's New Zealand Division with an infantry brigade from the 44th Division and tanks from 23 Armoured Brigade for the operation. But it was successfully resisted by the Italians, and Rommel withdrew without further loss to what had been 7th Armoured Division's forward positions, from which he could overlook the whole area south of Bare Ridge.

Preparations for Battle

The Battle of Alam el Halfa gave Eighth Army great confidence in its new commander, but his failure to exploit it reinforced Montgomery in his conviction that an intense period of training and preparation was needed if he was to be able to attack successfully; and that he must have time for this, even if it allowed Rommel to strengthen and develop his defences, especially with minefields. He therefore resisted pressure from Churchill to attack before the full moon period in the third week of October. First, he set up an organization to develop a detailed drill for gapping minefields and train troops to apply it. Secondly he formed a third corps, as a *corps de chasse*, to consist of three armoured divisions, 1st, 8th and 10th, and the New Zealand Division with two of its own infantry brigades made mobile and one British armoured brigade. Against his wish, he was forced to accept Herbert Lumsden, promoted Lieutenant-General, as commander of this X Corps. In the end, no infantry for the 8th could be found, and its armoured brigade, the 24th, joined Major-General Alec Gatehouse's 10th Division as an additional brigade.

Montgomery's original plan was for Leese's XXX Corps (9th Australian, 51st Highland, initially 2nd New Zealand, and 1st South African) to force a gap in the northern sector of Rommel's defences through which Lumsden's armoured divisions would pass and position themselves 'astride the enemy's supply routes'. This would force Rommel to use his armoured divisions to attack them, in the course of which they would be destroyed. Horrocks's XIII Corps in the south would offer a diversionary threat to tie down 21st Panzer Division in that area. He stressed that Leese's infantry must secure and his engineers clear gaps through all the minefields by dawn, so that Lumsden's tanks could pass through them by that time without becoming themselves embroiled in the battle to clear a way through.

Doubts about the ability of both the infantry and the armour to meet these demands led Montgomery, on 6 October, to change his plan to a less ambitious one. It would still remain Leese's task to secure and clear the minefield gaps, but Lumsden, instead of 'positioning his tanks astride the enemy's supply routes', would stand guard beyond the minefields while Leese's infantry 'crumbled' the enemy's within their defences. Rommel's tanks would be forced to come to their rescue and be destroyed. Montgomery finally resisted suggestions that Leese's task should be spread over two nights, but an unfortunate lack of clarity resulted about whether or not, if Leese's task had not been fully completed by dawn, Lumsden's divisions had to fight their own way out of the minefields.

A Famous Victory

Montgomery's attack, launched after dark on 23 October 1942 with the highly organized support in Leese's sector of 426 field and 48 medium guns, took Panzerarmee Afrika by surprise. Rommel was on sick leave in Austria, his place taken by the 56-year-old General Stumme, who, driving to the front line to find out what was happening, died of a heart attack. In spite of actions of great gallantry by 51st Highland and the New Zealand Divisions, through whose sectors the gaps of respectively 1st and 10th Armoured Divisions were to be driven, there was doubt and argument in both cases as to whether they had been cleared sufficiently for the tanks to drive through. Montgomery's chief of staff, Brigadier de Guingand, had to summon Lumsden to meet his chief, allergic to interruption of his sleep, to be given a sharp order for him to get Gatehouse to push his tanks through the New Zealanders. In the event it made no difference, and Montgomery had to face the fact, on the 24th, that in none of the sectors, including Horrocks's, had the tanks been able to break out. The progress of Major-General Leslie Morshead's 9th Australian Division in the extreme north, however, showed greater promise; and, for 25 October, Montgomery switched his major effort to them and to Major-General Raymond Briggs's 1st Armoured Division (to which one of Gatehouse's brigades had been transferred), which had managed to emerge from the minefields. Rommel, who returned on that day, reacted by concentrated counter-attack which cost him dear. But, despite constant attacks over the next four days, in which his infantry suffered heavy losses,

Montgomery could detect no sign of a breakout, and Horrocks's attempts to break through in the south had come to nothing. In fact Rommel's losses in counter-attacking both 1st Armoured Division and the Australians had left him fatally weakened.

Churchill's spirits fell and Brooke concealed his anxiety about the trust he had placed in his choice. Alexander flew from Cairo to consult. Montgomery, impressed by the achievements of the Australians, had decided to switch his main effort to their sector astride the coast road; but Rommel had reacted and strengthened his forces there. De Guingand, backed by Intelligence, persuaded him to switch his thrust to the sector just south of the Australians, which, erroneously, was thought to be held only by Italians. Freyberg was chosen to deliver the blow, reinforced by two brigades from 51st Highland Division and the Valentine tanks of 23 Armoured Brigade. This operation, postponed at Freyberg's request for 24 hours and launched on the night of 1/2 November, proved to be the decisive act of the battle, opening the way to the break-through, although that did not come immediately. Rommel however acknowledged defeat and decided that evening to withdraw, informing Hitler, whose counter-order had no effect. Nevertheless hard fighting continued on 3 and 4 November before a true breakout was achieved.

Seventh Armoured Division had been brought up from the south to join Lumsden's *corps de chasse*, the great moment for which had at last arrived; but the mass of vehicles of several different divisions struggling to start the pursuit led to confusion. Montgomery's plan was for Lumsden's armoured divisions to swing north in a wide arc to press the retreating

▶ 'The Opening of the Minefields, El Alamein' by Terence Cuneo.

▼ Below: 'Breaking through the last of the German Minefields at El Alamein, 4 October 1942'. The existence of the second, or westerly, German minefields came as a nasty surprise on the first day of Eighth Army's great offensive. Only after eleven days' heavy fighting did the armour break through into the open desert beyond – forcing Rommel to concede defeat. (Painting by Alex J. Ingram)

▼ Below right: A Diamond 'T' Tank Transporter of the RASC carrying a tank in the Western Desert. These vehicles gave sterling service in North Africa, Italy and north-west Europe, and remained in use until the 1970s. Together with the newly formed REME Mobile Field Workshops, the RASC Tank Transporter Squadrons made it possible to recover and repair many damaged armoured vehicles, and return them to the battle – a lesson the British Army had learnt from the *Afrika Korps*. (Painting by D Summerville)

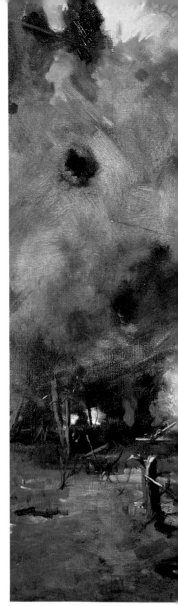

enemy up against the coast, while Freyberg, still under Leese's command, would thrust to Fuka, forty miles behind the front, to act as a backstop. It underestimated the speed at which Rommel would get the remnant of the Afrika Korps away, abandoning most of their allies. When Montgomery tried to change his orders, Lumsden was deliberately out of touch, and he missed the opportunity to put all Rommel's forces 'in the bag'. Montgomery blamed it on the heavy rain which fell on 6 November, but the Germans had by then escaped. A direct thrust through the desert with a smaller force, aimed at the frontier, might have succeeded, if it could have been kept supplied.

Although, in that respect, disappointing, it was a 'famous victory'. Of Rommel's total strength of probably a little more than 100,000 men at the beginning of the battle, 30,000, of whom 10,000 were German, were taken prisoner. Estimates of their killed and wounded vary from 8,000 to 20,000. Rommel lost almost all of the 220 German and 320 Italian tanks with which he had started the battle: he had only twenty German tanks left, when he withdrew from Mersa Matruh on 8 November. He had abandoned 1,000 guns on the battlefield. Eighth Army suffered 13,500 casualties, eight per cent of its initial strength, of whom 2,500 were killed. Of its 1,350 tanks, 500 had been put out of action, but only 150 destroyed beyond repair, as were 111 guns.

◄ The dreaded German 88mm, with Eighth Army souvenir hunters. This weapon – originally designed as a heavy anti-aircraft gun – proved even more effective in the anti-tank role.

◄ First Battle of Alamein. A knocked-out Italian M13 tank. The Italian armour was not on a par with either German or Allied equipment. Italian infantry, on the other hand, fought valiantly at Second Alamein – only to be deserted when the Germans commandeered all their transport for the retreat towards Tripoli. Note the 'jerrycan' to the front left: a crucial piece of basic equipment for petrol or water which entered the English language.

▶ The Second Battle of Alamein was to be the last all-British victory of the war. With the landings in North-West Africa (Operation 'Torch'), an American Supreme Commander over all forces in North Africa was appointed. Here General Dwight D. Eisenhower chats with the victorious Montgomery. Their relationship was not destined to be of the easiest.

▲ The author of this chapter, John Carver, as a brigadier in 1946, aged 31. At the Second Battle of Alamein he held the staff appointment of GSO1 in 7th Armoured Division (the 'Desert Rats') in Lieutenant-General Horrocks's XIII Corps.

succeeded later in forcing his withdrawal, as it would not have been possible for the Germans and Italians to have maintained an effective defence for long at both ends of North Africa. The principal significance of Montgomery's victory was its effect on both British and American confidence in the British Army. Before the battle it had been low. Montgomery transformed it, and thus made an essential contribution to national, Commonwealth and Allied morale, greatly strengthening Churchill's political position at home and in his relations with both the USA and the Soviet Union. Churchill also took the view that a victory in Egypt would help to dissuade Franco's Spain from interfering with the Anglo-American expedition to Morocco and Algeria. These politico-military factors were more important than the actual losses inflicted on Panzerarmee Afrika, great as they were.

On the day that Rommel withdrew from Mersa Matruh to the Libyan frontier, 8 November, the Anglo-American forces under Eisenhower landed in French North Africa at the other end of the Mediterranean. Had Montgomery failed to break Rommel's position at El Alamein, he would certainly have

BIBLIOGRAPHY

Carver, M. *Dilemmas of the Desert War*, London, 1953. An analysis of the major problems encountered.
— *El Alamein*, London, 1962. A full treatment of both battles of El Alamein and Alam Halfa.
Connell, J. *Auchinleck*, London, 1959. The official biography, based on Auchinleck's papers.
Guingand, F. de. *Operation Victory*, London, 1947. Valuable insights by Montgomery's chief of staff.
Lewin, R. *Montgomery*, London, 1971. One of the most balanced accounts of the victor of the Second Battle of Alamein.
Hamilton, N. *Monty: the Making of a General*, London, 1981.

The standard biography; it concludes with the Second Battle of Alamein and North Africa.
Hinsley, F. H. (ed.). *British Intelligence in the Second World War*, vol. 2, London, 1981. Includes the *Ultra* contribution to the Desert War.
Liddell Hart, B. H. *The Rommel Papers*, London, 1953. Provides insights into the German commander's view of events.
Pitt, B. *The Crucible of War. Year of Alamein, 1942*, London, 1982. A generally sound overall account.
Playfair, I. S. O. (ed.). *The Mediterranean and the Middle East*, vols. 3 and 4, London, 1960 and 1966). The Official History.

SALERNO COMPANY CREST
RMA SANDHURST

THE BATTLE OF SALERNO, 1943

by Eric Morris

'Why,' Churchill asked, 'crawl up the leg of
Italy like a harvest bug from the ankle upwards?
Let us strike at the knee.'

(Winston Churchill to General Sir Alan Brooke,
July 1943)

On 3 September 1943, General Sir Bernard Montgomery took Eighth Army across the Straits of Messina and landed on the very toe of Italy. Nearly a week later, in the early hours of 9 September Lieutenant-General Mark Clark took the US Fifth Army into battle for the first time when they assaulted the Bay of Salerno, what might be regarded as the ankle.

The Strategic Setting

The Italian campaign was a compromise, it produced bitter argument and rancour among the Allies and the men who fought in Italy suffered in consequence. Even the decision to invade Italy was taken very late in the day and Salerno shows all the hallmarks of hasty and compromised planning.

When the Allied leaders met in Washington during May 1943, for the Trident Conference, the war in North Africa had reached its successful climax. Planning was already far advanced for the invasion of Sicily, the objective being to open the Mediterranean sea lanes and, it was hoped, deliver a mortal blow to Mussolini. But where next?

The British favoured Italy. Churchill believed that an early defeat of Mussolini would open the door to profitable ventures in the Balkans and even entice Turkey off its neutralist perch. The Americans were opposed. Reluctant converts to Operation 'Husky' and the Sicilian invasion, Roosevelt was adamant that nothing else should stand in the way of the earliest possible date for 'Overlord'. He did accept, however, that the latter could not take place before May 1944. In which case a Mediterranean strategy concentrating on southern France by way of Sardinia and Corsica made more sense.

As a compromise, planning teams were set up to work on all these contingencies and it wasn't until mid July, when the Allies were firmly ashore in Sicily, that attention focused on Italy. The mainland became the priority a week later after a *coup d'état* had removed Mussolini from power. Even so, resources were scarce as men and equipment began the long journey to England in preparation for 'Overlord'. Assault craft in particular were in short supply and dictated the timing and location of the landing in Italy. In the first, code-named 'Baytown', Montgomery was to lead his Eighth Army across the Straits of Messina. The second aimed to secure the port of Naples from where the Allied would launch their march on Rome.

Along that rock-strewn western coast of Italy there were really only two beaches which were suitable, Gaeta to the north and Salerno to the south of Naples. Once the combat ranges of fighters operating from Sicily were included in the equation, Salerno appeared the only suitable choice.

The Battleground

The British 46th Infantry Division fought the Italian campaign from beginning to end. Before disbanding, an official history was produced which described the ground at Salerno through a veteran's eye:

'The Sele plain, which lay south of Salerno and was the selected place for the landings, stretched down to a 23-mile-long sandy beach, cut up by the broad gravel channels of evenly spaced rivers and streams. Especially to the south, the plain was criss-crossed with irrigation canals and dikes. Moving inland – its greatest depth was sixteen miles – the ground rose in a series of cultivated terraces mounting step-like to the circle of hills. It was an open countryside, except where thick orchards and olive groves provided a low screen of greenness, and from the hills the whole plain could be seen spread out to view against the blue sea. To the north, bare brown hills closed down on the coast behind the flourishing seaside town of Salerno. Through this barrier of hills two steep-sided corridors led northwards towards Naples, the western corridor from Vietri, a little town jammed between rocky hills and the sea, through Cava, and the second itself to Sanseverino. For three miles south of Salerno there was only a narrow strip of flat, wooded country between the town and Pontecagnano. Beyond Vietri the mountainous Sorrento peninsula jutted out to the west with its fringe of terraces and small resorts along the twisting coast road.'

D-Day was selected as 9 September because the moon cycle suited the conflicting needs of both an airborne and amphibious landing, and by then it was hoped that Montgomery would be sufficiently close to influence the battle.

The Allied Fifth Army was under command of Lieutenant-General Mark Clark of whom a senior officer was to write:

'Clark impresses me, as always . . . with his energy and intelligence, you cannot help but like him. He certainly is not afraid to take rather desperate chances, which after all, is the only way to win the war.'

At Salerno Clark took a number of desperate chances. He had sufficient assault craft to land as his main force the British 46th and 56th Infantry Divisions from X

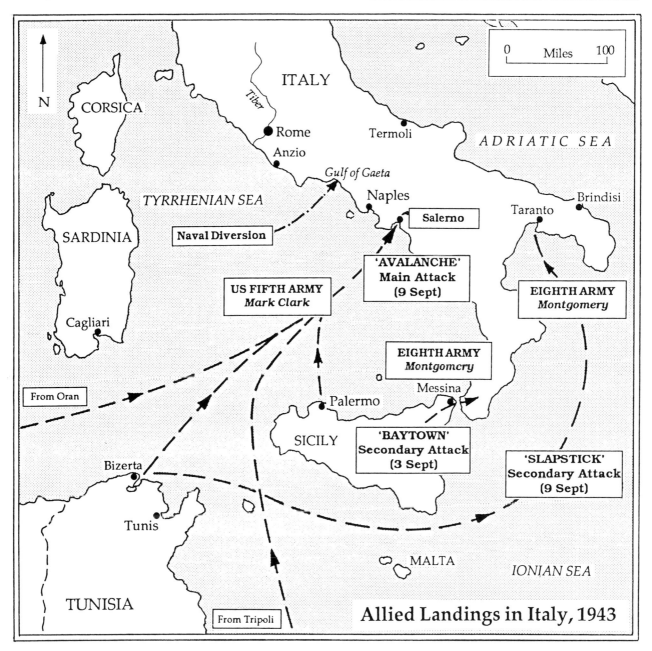

Allied Landings in Italy, 1943

Corps, and the US 36th Infantry Division plus an RCT (Regimental Combat Team) from US 45th Infantry Division. While the British were to spearhead the advance to Naples the Americans were to guard their right flank and link up with Montgomery. Three weak battalions of US Rangers and two British Commandos were to land first and secure the high ground and defiles of the road that led to Naples.

Clark's plan called for the port's capture by D+5 at the latest. The Army Commander laid great emphasis upon surprise and therefore dispensed with any prolonged naval bombardment of the beachhead. The British insisted on at least an accompanying fire as their landing craft headed inshore, but for the Americans there was to be none at all. Clark regarded the 82nd Airborne Division as his trump card upon whose deployment the fate of the landings depended. They were to be dropped north of Naples to secure the bridges across the Volturno and thereby prevent the enemy from reinforcing the beach-head.

▲ Lieutenant General Mark Wayne Clark (1896–1984), commander of US Fifth Army. In this role he supervised the Allied invasion of western Italy at Salerno and the subsequent capture of Naples and the west coast advance towards the Gustav Line. Ahead of him lay Monte Cassino, Anzio and the eventual capture of Rome.

Ultra decryptions gave the Allied High Command an accurate account of enemy deployment and an insight into their intentions, although on this occasion Hitler was uncharacteristically undecided. A contingency plan, 'Asche', had been prepared to occupy Italy and disarm Italians abroad in the event of their government's surrender. Thereafter, Rommel, who was to command Army Group 'B', favoured a phased withdrawal to the northern Apennines. The more optimistic Field Marshal Albert Kesselring, at OB South in Rome, believed the Allies could be held in the south at least until the following spring.

A new German army, the Tenth, had been formed in August 1943 to defend southern Italy. Under the experienced Panzer leader *General Oberst* Heinrich von Vietinghoff, it had more than 90,000 men with a further 45,000 in Kesselring's strategic reserve. In southern Calabria the 26th Panzer and 29th Panzer Grenadier Divisions slowed Montgomery's advance to a crawl and the 1st Parachute Division guarded the airfields at Foggia. At Eboli, behind the Salerno beaches, the 16th Panzer Division, reformed after Stalingrad, established its headquarters. North of Gaeta were the 15th Panzer Grenadier Division and Hermann Goering Division was close at hand near Naples.

The Italians surrendered twice. The first occasion was to the Allies in a clandestine, protracted and bizarre negotiation which had three influences on the battle of Salerno. Their surrender was broadcast to the invasion forces on the eve of the landings; an act of crass misjudgement which blunted the fighting edge of many of the troops in their euphoria of an anticipated easy victory. Secondly the timing signalled clearly to the Germans that Salerno, rather than Gaeta, was the objective of the invasion armada which the Luftwaffe has been so assiduously shadowing. Plan 'Asche' was activated and the 16th Panzers quietly took over the positions manned by the Italian 222nd Coast Division and sent the latter home. Finally, Mark Clark lost the immediate services of 82nd Airborne; they were stood by to drop on Rome and bolster the resistance of the Italian garrison against their German masters, a tortuous strategy which begged more questions than it answered.

The Landings

It is usual to divide Salerno into three phases: the landings, consolidation and the battle for the beachhead. None of the Allied units achieved their objective on D-Day. The Rangers under Colonel Darby secured the coast road along the Sorrento peninsula and occupied the high ground at the Chiunzi pass which looked down on the highway to Rome. But within hours they were fiercely engaged by elements of 1st Parachute and Hermann Goering Divisions and were destined to fight their own war for the next ten days.

The British Commandos, No 2 Army, led by the eccentric but legendary 'Mad Jack' Churchill and No 41 Royal Marines, stormed ashore but failed to dislodge the Germans from the defiles. The highway to Naples was blocked and the American Rangers isolated.

The 46th British Infantry was a territorial division comprising two North Midland brigades and one with three battalions of the Royal Hampshires. Their objective was to secure Salerno, the town and its port, link up with the Commandos and send mechanized

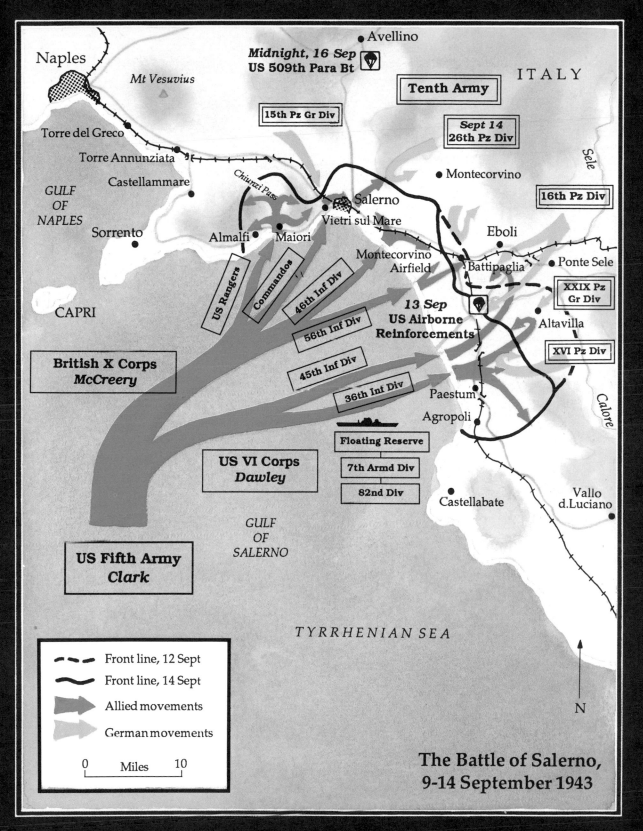

The Battle of Salerno, 1943

units to relieve the Americans. After a torrid day of street fighting the Germans were pushed out and, although their mortars and artillery were to dominate Salerno for days to come, a tenuous corridor was opened to the Commandos.

The 56th (City of London) Infantry Division comprised territorials and the 201st Guards Brigade. Their objectives were the all-important Montecorvino airfield and the town of Battapaglia, while their armoured reconnaissance units were to rendezvous with the Americans on their right flank at Ponte Sele, some nine miles inland. The airfield was captured and lost to local counter-attacks and, worse still, there was no link with the Americans.

The Sele was a wide river whose estuary was in the lower third of the bay; it was the corps boundary on D-Day. Across the Sele the US 36th Infantry Division had the worst time of all. The National Guard outfit, drawn largely from Texas, had to contest every foot of the way from the shore inland against a murderous German fire from batteries and pillboxes left intact by the absence of any preliminary bombardment.

The Allies were ashore on D-Day but well short of all their objectives, in a shallow beach-head and, ominously, with a yawning gap between the British and Americans astride the River Sele. The gap in places, was five miles wide.

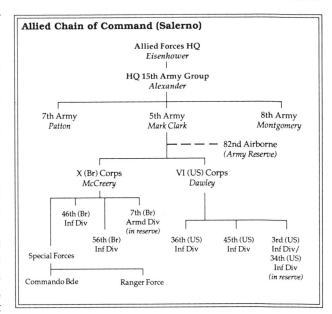

Allied Chain of Command (Salerno)

Allied Forces HQ
Eisenhower

HQ 15th Army Group
Alexander

7th Army — 5th Army — 8th Army
Patton — *Mark Clark* — *Montgomery*

82nd Airborne
(Army Reserve)

X (Br) Corps — VI (US) Corps
McCreery — *Dawley*

46th (Br) Inf Div — 7th (Br) Armd Div *(in reserve)*

56th (Br) Inf Div

36th (US) Inf Div — 45th (US) Inf Div — 3rd (US) Inf Div/ 34th (US) Inf Div *(in reserve)*

Special Forces

Commando Bde — Ranger Force

▼ Landing Ships Infantry (or LCIs) of the Allied invasion fleet head for the Italian shore while fighter aircraft patrol overhead.

▶ Tracer streaks the sky as Royal Navy vessels supporting the landing operations at Salerno fight off a low-level torpedo-bomber attack which lasted two hours on the night of 8/9 September 1943. One raider was accounted for.

◄ British troops forming part of US Fifth Army come ashore from a Landing Ship Tank (or LST) in the bay of Salerno on 9 September 1943 to help consolidate the bridgehead which was already experiencing strong German counter-attacks. Although Italy had surrendered that morning, German troops responded all too effectively.

► A machine-gun crew laying down fire during the fighting on 'Amber' Beach.

▼ A painting of the scene on the beaches as Allied troops of the Black Watch and their supplies land in Italy. (Painting by Ian Eadi)

Consolidation

The Germans won the second round. Determined to 'throw the Allies into the sea', Kesselring ordered Tenth Army to deploy all its resources against the beach-head before the Eighth Army could intervene. Leaving sufficient rearguards to hold Montgomery, who was still some 100 miles to the south in the Calabrian hills, the 26th Panzers and 29th Panzer Grenadiers hurried north to join the fray. The 1st Parachute Division all but abandoned Foggia and hastened westwards to join the Hermann Goering Division, already in action.

From an Allied perception Salerno became two separate battles. While some attempt was made, through the landing of a second RCT from the US 45th Infantry Division, to close the gap in the Allied line, the River Sele was to remain an international as well as a Corps boundary for the remainder of the battle. In the north Mark Clark allowed the X Corps Commander, Lieutenant-General Sir Richard McCreery, gifted and battle-wise, to direct his own affairs. Army headquarters was established across the Sele, in the Villa Rosa, and close to where Major-

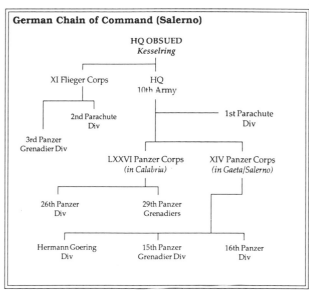

General Ernest Dawley directed the operations of his own VI Corps.

Try as they might neither the British nor the Americans could find a way off their cramped beach-heads and into the hills. In the succeeding days the enemy continued to hold the high ground and bring

▲ At the same time as the Salerno landings started near Naples, the British Eighth Army crossed the Catanian Straits from Sicily into the 'toe' of the Italian mainland. Here General Montgomery watches a Scottish unit marching into Reggio.

◄ German infantry use the wall of a road-bridge to secure cover as the Allies attempt to deepen their bridgehead by moving inland.

down heavy fire on anything that moved during the daylight hours. Mark Clark was convinced that the key lay in the high ground, and expended men and resources to secure such hilltop towns as Altavilla, destined to change hands over and over again in bloody fighting.

▲ Come to see for himself after the landings were completed, General Sir Harold Alexander (left), commander of operations on the Italian mainland, tours the beaches at Salerno accompanied by Lieutenant General Mark Clark, GOC US Fifth Army, and Lieutenant General R. McCreery, commanding British X Corps.

The Germans Counter-Attack

In this closely fought encounter battle Ultra was unable to serve Allied needs and the German counter-attack caught them off balance and ill-prepared to defend the beach-head. The main weight of the enemy attacks fell during the four days after Saturday 11 September. Making full use of the high ground, position and mobility, *ad hoc* battlegroups, at which the Germans were so good, probed for a weakness and once found, heavier formations of tanks and assault guns closely supported by Panzer Grenadiers and

assault pioneers in halftracks fanned out in attack. A battalion of Royal Fusiliers clung tenaciously to Battapaglia, but, surrounded, they were overwhelmed once their anti-tank guns had been destroyed. The Scots Guards suffered heavily in a local attack to capture a key strong point called the 'Tobacco Factory', in the same sector.

The heaviest attacks fell on 'Black Monday', 13 September. The battle rippled along the entire beach-head. The British infantry fought with that dogged determination for which they were renowned, but it was the Americans who bore the brunt of the German

▲ Castel de Rio, one of the coastal towns taken by the Allies as they pushed forward out of the Salerno area. (Painting by George Meddemmen)

◀ By 26 September the Allies had reached Cava. Here a column of Shermans – clearly not expecting to be attacked from the air – prepares for a triumphal entry into the Italian town.

▶ By 13 September the fighting had moved inland from Salerno. Here men of the 9th Royal Fusiliers man an observation post in a battered building.

assault. Von Vietinghoff had made the correct appreciation. The key ground was the Sele corridor, still only thinly held by the Americans. Panzer battlegroups spearheaded by Mark IV tanks poured down the corridor towards the sea. A single battalion of Texans, the 2nd Battalion of the 143rd Infantry Division barred their way at Persano and was overwhelmed. Then the Germans came up against the gun line of the 189th and 158th Artillery Battalions of the 45th Infantry Division. The guns were served by skeleton crews while the remainder, together with clerks, mechanics and the divisional band, deployed as infantry and held the German advance until dusk when the enemy retreated.

There was a hasty scramble for reinforcements. The 82nd Airborne, which had not after all gone to Rome, successfully dropped a parachute battalion into the American lines that night. A second battalion was dropped into the hills behind Salerno to raid the enemy lines of communication and ease some of the pressure off the British; but they were so dispersed, that those who were not captured could only hide in the hills until they could rejoin the Allied line.

General Sir Harold Alexander, the Fifteenth Army Group Commander, dispatched three fast cruisers loaded with 1,500 British infantry (these were men, veterans, for the most part, of North Africa and Sicily where they had been wounded and were awaiting drafts to their units. Most came from the 51st (Highland) Division and the 52nd (Tyne and Tees) Division. Resentment at being sent to reinforce strange units, together with shoddy treatment at the bridgehead, caused some to mutiny) as reinforcements from camps in North Africa. Battleships sailed from Malta to lend their firepower. Alexander also cajoled Eighth Army into greater activity but the ever cautious Montgomery was still 75 miles from Salerno, his progress dictated by stubborn rearguards and an unwillingness to take risks.

Mark Clark ordered contingency plans for the evacuation of the American corps but this was quickly discounted by his subordinate commanders as quite impracticable. As darkness fell on that Monday night and the guns grew silent, the Americans withdrew to a new defence line on the La Cosa creek, a tributary stream of the Sele, running parallel to the sea and in places just a few miles inland. There they planned to make a last stand.

The Germans attacked with the dawn, confident they would indeed reach the sea. But overwhelming artillery fire from warships offshore and batteries on land tore the heart out of the Panzer battlegroups before they could even come within small-arms range of the La Cosa defences. Desperate to succeed, von Vietinghoff redirected attacks against the British despite the advice of his field commanders who reported that they had no answer to the sheer weight and volume of fire from the Royal Artillery. In a series of attacks battalions of the Queen's and the Guards, Leicesters, Lincolns, Sherwood Foresters and the redoubtable Fusiliers, withstood the onslaught: though the line buckled it remained firm.

The Commandos, who had been relieved from their outposts on 11 September and now represented the last reinforcements in the British Corps beach-head, found themselves back in the line on 14 September and under heavy pressure. It was in this action, for a village called Pigoletti, that the Duke of Wellington, a company commander with No 2 Commando, was killed. Late in the afternoon of Wednesday 15 September the Germans made a final attempt to break the British line. A task force from 26th Panzer Division, tanks, self-propelled guns and halftracks with Panzer Grenadiers, swung west out of Eboli, skirted the ruins of Battapaglia only to be repulsed by the Royal Fusiliers with the Shermans of the Royal Scots Greys in support.

So the crisis passed. Gun barrels elevated and the bombardment dropped further inland. Von Vietinghoff's troops began an orderly withdrawal, still dictating the pace of the Allied advance as they were indeed to do until the final offensive in the spring of 1945. In the meantime new uniforms and fresh faces appeared in the beach-head. Seventh Armoured Division came ashore in the British sector and the US 3rd Infantry Division landed south of the Sele. To this point German casualties stood at 3,472, American at 1,649 and British at 5,259.

On Saturday 18 September the first set of D-Day objectives were achieved when British and American forces linked at Ponte Sele. Later that same afternoon a liaison party from 5th British Infantry Division appeared at the 36th Infantry Division Command Post, emissaries from the Eighth Army still 40 miles to the south. The Eighth Army had marched and fought their way over 200 miles of mountains against a tough and resilient rearguard. This was a considerable achievement but the Eighth Army, contrary to British belief, did not save the day at Salerno.

There were still some weeks of bitter fighting ahead before the Allied Fifth Army broke free of the hills around Salerno and it was not until 5 October that American Rangers and paratroopers, riding the tanks of the Royal Scots Greys, trundled into Naples. By that time British casualties had risen to 7,000 and the Americans had lost 5,000 men, dead, wounded and prisoners.

There were other casualties too. A number of American senior commanders whose leadership had been found wanting at Salerno were sacked by Mark Clark. They included General Dawley, the corps commander. He was replaced by Major General John Lucas who was later to suffer a similar fate at Anzio.

For a final verdict on Salerno the comments of the fair-minded and phlegmatic Alexander in the War Diary of Fifteenth Army Group in an entry dated 25 September said it all:

'The Germans may claim with some justification to have won, if not a victory at least an important success over us.'

Early in October Ultra decryptions were faithfully recording future strategies. Encouraged by Kesselring's success and convinced that the Allies would deploy only limited resources and cautious generals, Hitler ordered the Gustav Line to be readied in the high Appenines. Anchored on Cassino the Germans planned a winter campaign south of Rome. The battle for Italy had still very much to be won – but at least the southern third had been rendered safe by the Allies thanks to the stalwart fighting at Salerno and elsewhere.

BIBLIOGRAPHY

Jackson, W. G. F. *The Battle for Italy*, London, 1967. An excellent overall account of the campaign.
Morison, S. E. *Sicily, Salerno, Anzio*, Boston, 1975. A useful American view of the major combined operations.
Morris, E. *Salerno*, London, 1983. A full account and analysis.
Shepperd, A. *The Italian Campaign*, London, 1968. A useful account and analysis by the former Librarian at Sandhurst. Strawson, J. *The Italian Campaign*, London, 1987. The latest book devoted to the subject.

THE BATTLE OF NORMANDY, 1944

by Richard Holmes

*'Under the command of General Eisenhower, Allied
naval forces, supported by strong air forces,
began landing Allied armies this morning.'*

(BBC broadcast, 6 June 1944)

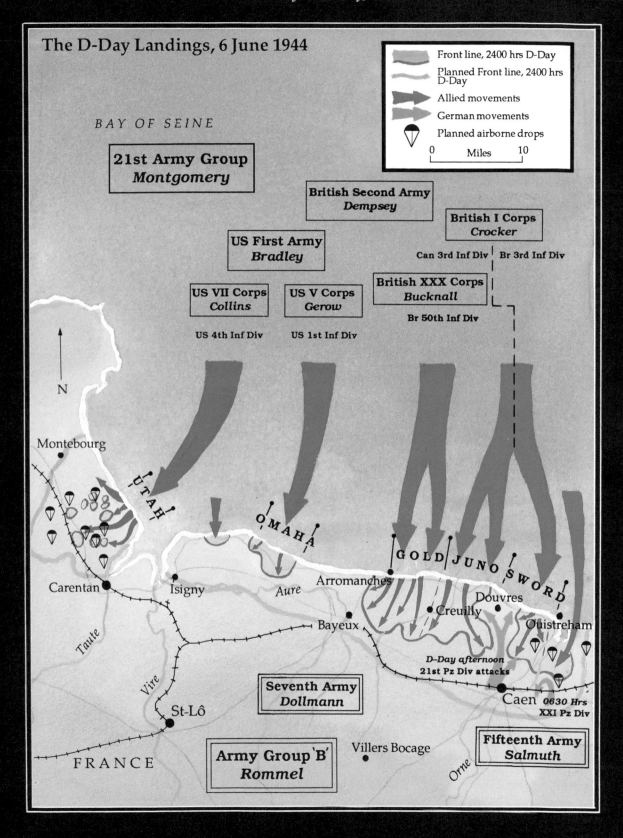

The D-Day Landings, 6 June 1944

Front line, 2400 hrs D-Day
Planned Front line, 2400 hrs D-Day
Allied movements
German movements
Planned airborne drops

0   Miles   10

BAY OF SEINE

21st Army Group
Montgomery

British Second Army
Dempsey

British I Corps
Crocker

US First Army
Bradley

Can 3rd Inf Div | Br 3rd Inf Div

British XXX Corps
Bucknall

US VII Corps
Collins

US V Corps
Gerow

Br 50th Inf Div

US 4th Inf Div   US 1st Inf Div

N

Montebourg

UTAH

OMAHA

GOLD | JUNO | SWORD

Carentan

Isigny

Arromanches

Douvres

Creuilly

Ouistreham

Aure

Bayeux

Taute

Vire

D-Day afternoon
21st Pz Div attacks

Seventh Army
Dollmann

Caen   0630 Hrs
XXI Pz Div

St-Lô

Villers Bocage

Fifteenth Army
Salmuth

Army Group 'B'
Rommel

Orne

FRANCE

At sixteen minutes past midnight on 6 June 1944 Staff-Sergeant Jim Wallwork brought his Horsa glider down a few yards east of the bridge over the Canal de Caen in the Normandy village of Bénouville. After a brief pause, for the shock of landing had knocked them unconscious, the aircraft's occupants – men of Major John Howard's 'D' Company, 2nd Battalion The Oxfordshire and Buckinghamshire Light Infantry – poured out as two other gliders crunched along the canal bank behind them. Lieutenant Den Brotheridge led his platoon across the bridge, only to fall mortally wounded at its west end. As sappers checked the bridge for explosives, the platoon from the second glider seized the defences on its near side, while the third platoon crossed the bridge to secure the far bank.

Major Howard's two remaining platoons swooped down on the nearby bridge over the River Orne at Ranville, taking it without loss. Howard had established his headquarters in a trench at the north-east end of the canal bridge, and there he received the bad news about Brotheridge, followed by the unwelcome tidings that the other two platoon commanders at Bénouville had been wounded. But then his luck changed. Captain Jock Neilson of the sappers reported that there were no explosives under the bridge (they were later found nearby) and his men had removed the firing mechanisms. Then came word that the river bridge, too, had been captured intact. Howard turned to his radio operator, Corporal Tappenden, and told him to send the code-words for success at both objectives. 'Ham and Jam, Ham and Jam,' repeated Tappenden, announcing that the first act of the Allied liberation of Europe had gone according to plan.

Towards 'Overlord'

The first steps towards the Normandy invasion were taken in the winter of 1941–2 at the Anglo-American conference code-named 'Arcadia'. It was then that the United States agreed to throw the weight of her ground forces against Germany and Italy, and to embark upon 'Bolero', the large-scale build-up of these forces in Britain. Yet the path from 'Arcadia' to 'Overlord' (the eventual code-word for the invasion) was neither smooth nor easy. The British were reluctant to mount an early assault, preferring to devote resources to more modest objectives in North Africa and Italy. The 'Torch' landings in North Africa

in November 1942 were followed by the Casablanca conference, at which the Americans agreed to Operation 'Husky', the invasion of Sicily, and 'Pointblank', the strategic bombing offensive against Germany.

Growing strength and experience made American policy-makers anxious to avoid what they saw as sideshows, and at the 'Trident' conference in May 1943 it was provisionally agreed that north-west Europe would be invaded on 1 May 1944. The Americans also insisted that Operation 'Anvil', a landing in southern France, would be carried out soon after 'Overlord', even if this meant diverting resources from the Italian campaign. This policy was endorsed by Stalin at the Teheran conference in November 1943, and the Russian leader's approval gave further impetus to American desire to press on despite British reservations. These were not altogether unreasonable. Churchill fully accepted the necessity of invasion, but feared that it might result in beaches choked with Allied dead, while the Chief of the Imperial General Staff, Sir Alan Brooke, was concerned with conflicting priorities of which the invasion of Europe was but one.

In April 1943 Lieutenant-General Sir Frederick Morgan was appointed Chief of Staff to the Supreme Allied Commander (Designate) – COSSAC. His planning was to suffer from the fact that limited landing craft allowed him to put only three divisions ashore in the first wave. Nevertheless, it is important to recognize the invaluable work done by Morgan and his staff. They considered four possible invasion sites. The nearest was the Pas-de-Calais, just across the Channel from England, but well-defended and so obvious as to make surprise difficult. Brittany, despite its excellent beaches, was too far from England, and a landing on the Cotentin Peninsula could easily be contained by the Germans. The COSSAC staff decided that Normandy offered the best prospects, and attention was concentrated on a landing in the Caen sector.

Morgan's staff started work long before a Supreme Commander had been appointed. It was widely believed that General George G. Marshall, Chairman of the US Joint Chiefs of Staff, would take up the post, but fears that the change would weaken American planning encouraged President Roosevelt to look elsewhere. His choice was General Dwight D. Eisenhower, Allied commander in North Africa. A 54-year-old Kansan, Eisenhower had seen no action in the First World War but had subsequently attracted

Marshall's attention by his talent as a staff officer. His lack of battlefield command experience was a disadvantage, but there could be no doubting his skill as an alliance manager. Brooke wondered if this would suffice. 'Just a co-ordinator,' he wrote, 'a good mixer, a champion of inter-Allied co-operation, and in those respects few can hold a candle to him. But is that enough?' Events were to prove Eisenhower equal to his task, though it was made no easier by senior subordinates whose strong personalities sometimes pulled hard in different directions.

Air Chief Marshal Sir Arthur Tedder, Eisenhower's deputy, had commanded the Desert Air Force and had served as Allied air commander in the Mediterranean. He got on well with Eisenhower but was on poor terms with General Sir Bernard Montgomery, the flamboyant victor of El Alamein, who was to command all ground forces in the invasion. Admiral Sir Bertram Ramsay and Air Chief Marshal Sir Trafford Leigh-Mallory served as naval and air commanders. British predominance in the chain of command was resented by many Americans, and plans were made to alter arrangements once the build-up in Normandy was complete. For the landings, Montgomery's Headquarters 21st Army Group was to control both Lieutenant General Omar N. Bradley's US First Army and Lieutenant-General Miles Dempsey's British Second Army. In due course the American contingent would form 12th Army Group and Montgomery would cease to exercise overall command over ground forces.

Although Eisenhower had reservations about Montgomery's appointment – he would have preferred General Sir Harold Alexander – he agreed with him over the COSSAC plan. Montgomery had already seen the document, and when he heard the formal exposition of the COSSAC scheme on 3 January 1944 he pointed out its weaknesses, demanding a five-divisional assault, flanked by divisional strength airborne landings, on a fifty-mile front. He presented the revised plan to Eisenhower on 21 January, and it was accepted two days later. The COSSAC team was eclipsed as Montgomery's men moved into key appointments: the gentlemen were out, it was said, and the players were in.

Montgomery briefed his senior commanders on 7 April. US First Army was to land on Omaha and Utah beaches, with the 82nd and 101st Airborne Divisions securing its right flank. The Americans were to capture the port of Cherbourg, and then push down to St-Lô. British Second Army would go ashore on Gold, Juno and Sword Beaches, taking Caen before moving south and south-east to seize airfield sites and protect Bradley's army. The British left flank was to be covered by the 6th Airborne Division, whose tasks included securing bridges over the Caen canal and the Orne. The landing forces would be reinforced by Canadian First Army, which was to take over the left of the bridgehead, and US Third Army, which would clear Brittany and shield the southern flank when First Army eventually swung eastwards for the Seine.

The sheer scale of the exploit was prodigious. On its first two days the Allies planned to put 150,000 men and 1,500 tanks ashore, supported by nearly 7,000 naval vessels and 12,000 aircraft. Two huge prefabricated harbours, code-named 'Mulberries', were to be installed, and PLUTO – Pipeline Under The Ocean – was intended (over-optimistically) to supply the bridgehead with fuel. Operation 'Fortitude' was designed to make the Germans believe that the invasion would come in the Pas-de-Calais, and their deployment showed just how well this deception had worked.

The defence of France, Belgium and Holland was the responsibility of Field Marshal Gerd von Rundstedt, Commander-in-Chief West. His 57 divisions formed two army groups, Colonel-General von Blaskowitz's 'G', south of the Loire, and Field Marshal Rommel's 'B', its Seventh Army between Seine and Loire and its Fifteenth Army on the Channel coast. Rommel had done much to strengthen the seaward defences, and his experience of Allied air power led him to doubt the conventional wisdom, favoured by Rundstedt and General Geyr von Scheweppenburg of Panzer Group West, of sealing off the landing and then crushing it with armoured reserves. In any event, neither Rommel nor von Rundstedt enjoyed operational independence, for reserve armoured divisions could not be committed without the permission of the Armed Forces High Command (OKW).

The Battle of the Beaches

Invasion was dependent on the weather, and D-Day had already been postponed for 24 hours when the decision was taken to launch the operation on 6 June. The airborne assault began shortly after midnight. Low cloud and anti-aircraft fire disrupted the drop of the two American divisions, whose members were scattered, although they managed to secure many of

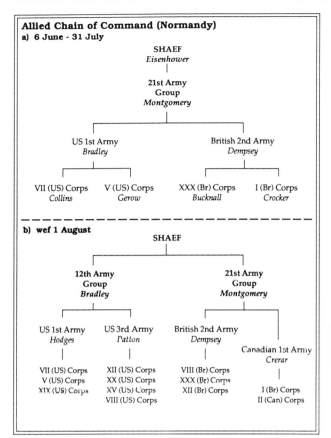

Allied Chain of Command (Normandy)

a) 6 June - 31 July

SHAEF
Eisenhower

21st Army Group
Montgomery

US 1st Army
Bradley

British 2nd Army
Dempsey

VII (US) Corps
Collins

V (US) Corps
Gerow

XXX (Br) Corps
Bucknall

I (Br) Corps
Crocker

b) wef 1 August

SHAEF

12th Army Group
Bradley

21st Army Group
Montgomery

US 1st Army
Hodges

US 3rd Army
Patton

British 2nd Army
Dempsey

Canadian 1st Army
Crerar

VII (US) Corps
V (US) Corps
XIX (US) Corps

XII (US) Corps
XX (US) Corps
XV (US) Corps
VIII (US) Corps

VIII (Br) Corps
XXX (Br) Corps
XII (Br) Corps

I (Br) Corps
II (Can) Corps

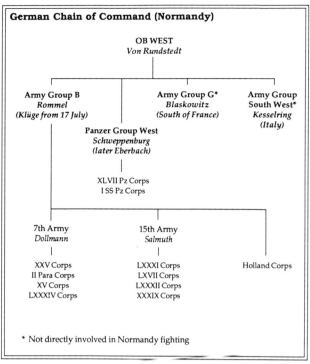

German Chain of Command (Normandy)

OB WEST
Von Rundstedt

Army Group B
Rommel
(*Klüge from 17 July*)

Army Group G*
Blaskowitz
(South of France)

Army Group South West*
Kesselring
(Italy)

Panzer Group West
Schweppenburg
(*later Eberbach*)

XLVII Pz Corps
I SS Pz Corps

7th Army
Dollmann

15th Army
Salmuth

XXV Corps
II Para Corps
XV Corps
LXXXIV Corps

LXXXI Corps
LXVII Corps
LXXXII Corps
XXXIX Corps

Holland Corps

* Not directly involved in Normandy fighting

▼ The preliminary 'soften-ing-up' of the Normandy coastal defences was partly undertaken by the Allied air forces, and partly by heavy naval units. Here the RN battleship, HMS *Rodney*, sends her 16in shells hurt-ling inland.

▲ The amphibious attack on the Normandy beaches was headed by Duplex-Drive (DD) Sherman tanks, tasked with providing close fire-support against the German defences for the first waves of assault troops.

▼ DD tank, rear view, with canvas shield erected. Note the propellers – the subject of an inter-Service wrangle as to whether the vehicle should be classed as an armoured fighting vehicle or a ship. When at sea, the freeboard was very low, and many tanks were swamped in the considerable swell, especially off Omaha Beach.

their objectives. The British 6th Airborne Division was also widely spread by its drop, but it secured the bridges at Bénouville and Ranville, blew five of the bridges over the Dives, and by nightfall, reinforced by an air-landing brigade and a commando brigade, had the eastern flank of the bridgehead in its grasp.

The seaborne landings went in under cover of an awesome bombardment by warships and aircraft. On Utah Beach, the US 4th Infantry Division spearheaded the attack of VII Corps. Its first wave of landing craft hit the wrong beach, but pressed on to secure objectives inland. The 1st and 29th Infantry Divisions of V Corps, landing on Omaha Beach, found that the division defending that sector had been reinforced by another, and this, coupled with bluffs which dominated the beach, an ineffective naval bombardment, and the loss of armour and engineers in heavy seas off the coast, produced an ugly stalemate as those troops who managed to make their way ashore were pinned down by intense fire at the water's edge. Gallant leadership eventually got them off the beach, but 'Bloody Omaha' cost V Corps more than two thousand men.

In the British sector, XXX Corps' 50th Division and 8 Armoured Brigade went ashore on Gold Beach, facing heavy resistance which Crabs (flail tanks) and

▲ 'D-Day', by Terence Cuneo.

AVRES (Armoured Vehicles Royal Engineers) – invaluable ingredients of the British landings – were instrumental in breaking. By nightfall the division was on the outskirts of Bayeux. Juno Beach was the objective of the Canadian 3rd infantry Division, supported by the Canadian 2 Armoured Brigade. The landing was complicated by reefs at the mouth of the River Seulles and rough seas which swept landing craft on to beach obstacles. Despite this, the Canadians got almost six miles inland, and only congestion on the beach prevented a further advance. The British 3rd Division, assisted by 27 Armoured Brigade, stormed ashore on Sword Beach, but made

slow progress clearing strongpoints around Hermanville and Colleville further inland.

Rommel was on leave when the invasion began. It took his staff some time to accept that the attack was not a feint, and communication difficulties further reduced the speed of response. In mid-afternoon 21st Panzer Division was ordered to counter-attack, and jabbed into the gap between British 3rd and Canadian 3rd Divisions. Its most notable achievement was to halt the advancing 2nd Battalion, The King's Own

◄ A landing craft prepares to drop its gangways as it beaches on 6 June 1944, somewhere in British Second Army's sector. Already ashore are commando units and an assortment of 'funnies' (special assault armour) including Sherman DD (duplex-drive) amphibious tanks.

▶ D-Day, 6 June 1944: the busy scene on the beaches as Landing Ships Tank (LSTs) disgorge their cargoes of tanks and lorries while 'Liberty ships' await their turn to unload.

◄ Heavily laden infantrymen organize themselves on the Normandy beaches. Note the smoke-screen concealing the scene from enemy aircraft – although in fact the Luftwaffe was notable by its absence on D-Day – and the gas capes (never required) worn on top of the troops' backpacks.

▶ Expanding the bridgehead: a Sherman tank and Scottish infantry pass through the village of Reviers.

◀ Pointe-du-Hoc, Normandy: the forbidding cliffs stormed by American Rangers at heavy cost to silence a German heavy battery – which in the event was found to be dismantled.

▲ Frank Wootton's 'Gliders at Caen' shows the aircraft debris resulting from the glider landings of 6th Airborne Division near Pegasus Bridge and the Caen Canal. The paratroopers involved were a spearhead force engaging in a vital task, and this they had accomplished by dawn of D-Day itself.

▶ Arromanches, the scene today. Considerable remnants of the breakwater of sunken, concrete-filled ships are still to be seen offshore. The picture was taken at half-tide.

▲ American infantrymen at the foot of the sea-wall on Omaha Beach. This was the least satisfactory of the five landing beaches. The German defenders were at their posts, General Gerow chose not to use the specialized British armour on offer, and the DD tanks were launched too far out to sea, so most were swamped. The results were 2,000 casualties, scant gains on 6 June, and eventually a Congressional Inquiry into the near-failure.

◀ Parts of the Arromanches Mulberry Harbour being assembled on 14 June. A caliper wall is being built around the end of a 'Shore Float Ramp', connecting a 'Whale' to the end of the first pier. A major Channel gale would soon destroy the American Mulberry and badly damage the British one.

Shropshire Light Infantry, near Lébisey Wood, effectively blunting 3rd Division's diffident thrust for Caen. For the Allies, results of the day were not unsatisfactory, despite the agony of Omaha and the fact that none of the final D-Day objectives had been reached. They were ashore: it remained to be seen whether they could retain their grip, and what use they would make of it.

Battle for the Breakout

The Allies consolidated their hold in the days following the assault, taking Bayeux on 7 June, and going on to link all bridgeheads. The expected counter-attack was delayed and diluted. Allied air forces enjoyed mastery of the skies, and German troops moving by day were at the mercy of prowling fighter-bombers. The fate of Headquarters Panzer Group West is illustrative: no sooner had it taken three panzer divisions under command with a view to counter-attacking to split the Allied front than the British located it by radio direction-finding. The resultant air attack left its command vehicles blazing in an orchard: Geyr von Schweppenburg himself was wounded and his chief of staff and many other officers killed. No less serious was the effect of air interdiction on bridges and railway junctions leading to the front. The French

▲ A Centaur tank moves into action at Tilly-sur-Seulles in one of the early British Second Army attempts to outflank the city and communications centre of Caen – just one week after D-Day. Note the compass card painted around the turret.

Resistance, too, played its own dangerous part in harrying the march of units bound for Normandy.

The absence of a co-ordinated counter-attack made the fighting no less bitter. The British failed to take Caen by direct attack on 7–8 June, and their attempts to pinch it out by outflanking – at Villers-Bocage on 13 June and Operation 'Epsom' on the 25th – were unsuccessful. It was difficult for German armour to move up into Normandy, but it fought with grim determination when it arrived. Twelfth SS Panzer Division and the Canadian 3rd Division fought one another to a bloody standstill outside Caen, and at Villers-Bocage SS Captain Michael Wittman lacerated 7 Armoured Brigade in a close-range brawl where German experience and combat power paid dividends. Indeed, it was becoming clear that while some British formations lacked experience, others had rather too much. Both the 7th Armoured and 51st Highland Divisions, lions of the desert, contained many soldiers who felt that they had done their bit, and the disappointing results of the fighting around Caen were to lead to the dismissal of Lieutenant-General

◀ Establishing the bridgehead, British troops move at the double though a coastal town in the combat zone. They carry only their rifles, ammunition and entrenching tools. The soldier in the foreground is probably a member of a mortar detachment as he carries mortar-bombs as well as his .303in rifle.

▶ Once the Normandy break-out had been achieved, the German Seventh Army sustained massive casualties in the Falaise pocket. Allied rocket-firing Typhoons decimated the German armour and transport. The long and hard-fought Battle of Normandy was at last over and won. (Painting by Frank Wooton)

◀ Allied chiefs meet at 21st Army Group's Headquarters at Creully, 15 June 1944. Left to right: General Eisenhower (Supreme Commander), Lieutenant-General G. C. Bucknell (XXX Corps commander), General Dempsey (Commander-in-Chief British Second Army) and Air Chief Marshal Tedder (Deputy Supreme Commander). Missing (most unusually): General Montgomery.

▶ His Majesty King George VI presenting the CBE to Major-General R. F. L. Keller, GOC, 3rd Canadian Division, for distinguished service in Normandy, 16 June.

Bucknall of XXX Corps and three divisional commanders. Max Hastings is right to observe that:

'There was nothing cowardly about the performance of the British Army in Normandy. But it proved too much to ask a citizen army, with the certainty of victory in the distance, to display the same sacrificial courage as Hitler's legions, faced with the collapse of everything that in the perversion of nazism they held dear.'

With the British locked fast about Caen, the Americans pushed on into the *bocage* – close country, with small fields and high, banked hedgerows – of the Cotentin. Cherbourg fell on 27 June, and though its harbour did not reach full capacity until late September, it was a welcome prize. On 19–22 June a fierce storm had wrecked numerous vessels, destroyed the American Mulberry and damaged its British cousin: many supplies were landed straight over open beaches, but proper port facilities were urgently required. With Cherbourg secured, Bradley swung south towards Coutances, St-Lô and Caumont, making slow progress against unrelenting opposition before wresting a grip on the height of St-Lô on 18 July.

Interpretation of the events that followed polarizes

opinion amongst historians and veterans alike. Montgomery's supporters argue that he had always planned to 'write down' German resources around Caen to permit the Americans to break out. In mid-July he had mounted Operation 'Goodwood', a concentrated attack by three armoured divisions against the Bourguébus ridge south-east of Caen, delivered in the wake of stupendous air and artillery bombardment. The advance made slow and costly progress in the face of determined and well-sited defenders. Many attackers certainly believed that 'Goodwood' was expected to produce a breakout, and Montgomery was less than forthright to aver:

'We had . . . largely attained our purpose . . . and the enemy had thrown in his available resources . . . we had drawn the German armour east of the Orne again and caused heavy losses to the enemy.'

'Goodwood' had indeed maintained pressure on the British flank and so assisted Bradley, but there are grounds for believing that it was designed to bring more tangible gains. And, although Montgomery had long thought in terms of an American offensive from the western flank of the bridgehead, Operation 'Cobra', the drive to Avranches which began on 25 July, was conceived and executed by Bradley.

'Cobra' bit sharply into over-stretched defences. To the Germans, fighting on under the merciless flail of air power, came new troubles. Field Marshal von Kluge had replaced von Rundstedt on 1 July, and Rommel had been wounded when a British fighter strafed his car on the 17th. On the 20th came the bomb plot against Hitler, which darkened the German mood, and was to cost the lives of von Kluge and Rommel, both of whom committed suicide rather than stand trial for alleged involvement.

On 1 August Bradley's 12th Army Group came into being, its First Army joined by Lieutenant General George S. Patton's Third Army. The momentum generated by 'Cobra' spilled out into Brittany as Patton jabbed down to Rennes and Brest, before turning, on 3 August, towards the Seine. His swing was not the result of a long-established plan on Montgomery's part, although, to his credit, Montgomery was flexible enough to recognize the opportunities offered by exploitation of the open flank. On 7 August a counter-attack east of Mortain, specifically ordered by Hitler, was roughly handled, and on the 8th it was decided that Lieutenant-General Harry Crerar's Canadian First Army would stab down towards Falaise, while Patton swung up to Argentan, pocketing the remnants of Seventh and Fifth Panzer Armies. The Canadians took Falaise on 16 August, but Bradley, concerned about an accidental collision, ordered Patton to halt at Argentan. The neck of the pocket was not sealed until 19 August, and about 20,000 Germans had managed to escape.

But there was no escape for most of the defenders of Normandy. Some had died in their bunkers on D-Day, or in the hedgerows and orchards inland. Others had fallen victim to fighter-bombers on the roads, or been obliterated by the carpet-bombing that preceded 'Goodwood' and 'Cobra'. About 10,000 perished in the Falaise pocket, and another 50,000 were captured. Of the fifty divisions in action in June, only ten remained as fighting units, and perhaps less than 120 armoured vehicles clattered back across the Seine. The walls of Fortress Europe had been breached, and the defeat of Germany was now only a matter of time, although the tensions which had shown themselves in Normandy would continue to bedevil inter-Allied relations as the war in the west entered its final phase.

Retrospect

To the battles of the beaches and the breakout has been added that of the memoirs. Montgomery, who relinquished overall ground forces command on 1 September, and was promoted field marshal on the same day, interpreted the campaign in a way which suggested a higher degree of pre-planning than most analysts would recognize. 'Goodwood' undoubtedly tarnished his reputation, and both he and Bradley have been criticized, less reasonably, for their failure to close the Falaise pocket sooner.

The historical battle will grind on, its intensity diminished as the years whittle away those men whose youth was marked by bodies stacked like cordwood on a beach, or the oily smoke of burning Shermans amongst the *bocage*. Yet they were the real victors of Normandy. The soldiers of a citizen army are not imbued with fanaticism; political slogans ring hollow in the heat of battle, and draconian discipline sits uncomfortably alongside democratic values. That Eisenhower, Montgomery and Bradley had their faults as commanders is undeniable. Equally undeniable is the fact that each grasped, in his own way, the limitations imposed by the armies they commanded and the enemy they fought. As Brigadier Bill Williams, Montgomery's chief Intelligence officer, put it:

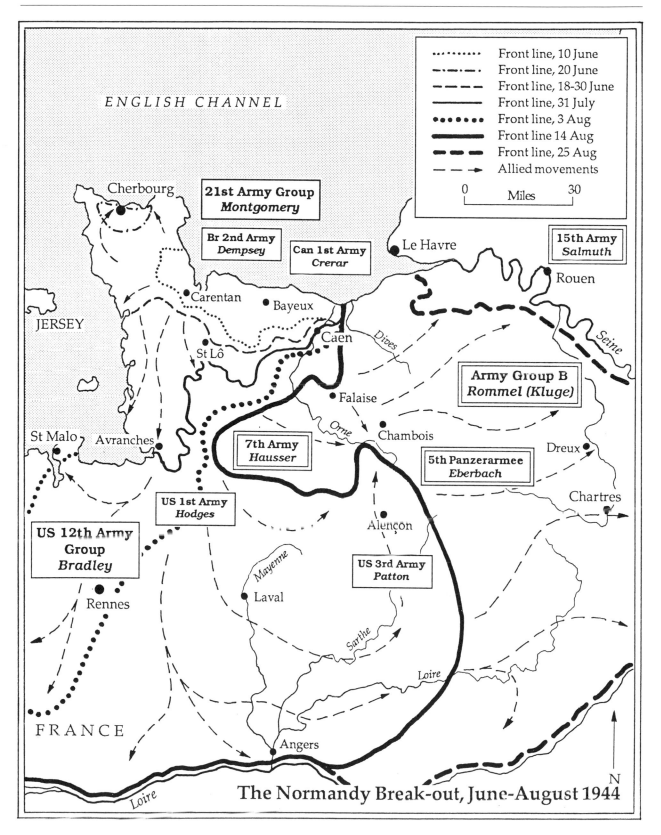

The Normandy Break-out, June–August 1944

'We were always very well aware of the doctrine "Let metal do it rather than flesh". The morale of our troops depended on this. We always said – "Waste all the ammunition you like, but not lives."'

This principle may not guarantee swift victory, but it is no dishonourable preoccupation for men charged with the greatest responsibility that any state can confer. In retrospect it is easy to condemn the Allies for over-caution in Normandy. But at the time it might have proved harder to generate, or to justify, a more rapid decision at a greater price.

BIBLIOGRAPHY

D'Este, Carlo. *Decision in Normandy: The unwritten story of Montgomery and the Allied campaign*, London, 1983. In this, the most penetrating study of Allied strategy yet published, d'Este provides balanced criticism of Montgomery.

Hamilton, Nigel. *Monty: Master of the Battlefield 1942–1944*, London, 1983. The second volume of the invaluable official biography of Montgomery. Hamilton does not shrink from criticism where he thinks his subject deserves it, but is far more restrained than Carlo d'Este.

Hastings, Max. *Overlord: D-Day and the Battle for Normandy 1944*, London, 1984. A well-written popular account of the campaign which combines evocative personal narratives with solid analysis.

Keegan, John. *Six Armies in Normandy*, London, 1982. The face of the Normandy battle through the eyes of its American, Canadian, British, German, Polish and French participants.

Lucas, James, and Barker, James. *The Killing Ground: The Battle of the Falaise Gap, August 1944*, London, 1978. The most useful account of the fighting around Falaise, whose authors make good use of German sources.

Wilmot, Chester. *The Struggle for Europe*, London, 1952. A classic account of the campaign in NW Europe, 1944–5, which stands the test of time unusually well.

ARNHEM COMPANY CREST
RMA SANDHURST

THE BATTLE OF ARNHEM, 1944

by Sir John Hackett

'I saw men who were hungry, exhausted, hopelessly outnumbered, men who by all the rules of warfare should have gladly surrendered to have it all over with, who were shelled until they were helpless psychopathics; and through it all they laughed, sang, and died, and kept fighting.'

(Report by Lieutenant Bruce E. Davis, US Signals. In US Archives)

T here were many holding their breath in late September 1944 as the drama unfolded in Holland of the battle to force a crossing over the Lower Rhine and, with a right hook into industrial Germany, bring the Second World War to an early end. The battle was lost, but, like many another lost battle, it will not soon be forgotten.

Search for a Solution

The summer had seen the Allied invasion in Normandy, the breakout from the beach-head and the thunderous advance across north-western Europe of a triumphant army, under air superiority, exploiting success against an enemy army defeated but by no means yet destroyed. What next? The Axis had lost the war, but the Allies would not yet have won it until Germany, still doggedly fighting, laid down her arms.

The Supreme Allied Commander, the American Dwight Eisenhower, tended to favour a general advance of British and American troops towards the Rhine along the whole front, exploiting success wherever it could be found. Field Marshal Montgomery, British C-in-C of 21st Army Group, reasoned that to advance everywhere was likely to bring success nowhere and favoured instead a single powerful, narrow, deep thrust across the river obstacles in north Germany, to penetrate and turn what we called the Siegfried Line and then sweep down to destroy the enemy's industrial base in the Ruhr. George Patton, the forceful commander of the US Third Army and star performer in Bradley's US 12th Army Group was, however, making good progress in the centre, so good

in fact that although Eisenhower adopted Montgomery's plan for a single thrust in the north, he was unwilling to deprive Patton of the logistical support whose transfer to 21st Army Group was essential to its success.

With hindsight it is clear that the opening of the Scheldt estuary and the port of Antwerp should have preceded any major offensive in the north, and that without the logistical support which was still going to Patton, despite Eisenhower's preference for Montgomery's plan, the single deep thrust was in jeopardy from the start.

The Plan Emerges

The plan for operation 'Market Garden' was to seize crossings over three major water obstacles, the Waal, the Maas and the Lower Rhine, with two US Airborne Divisions (82nd and 101st) and one British (1st), and for the three divisions of the British XXX Corps, strong in armour, to follow up from Nijmegen and relieve in two days the British airborne force, put down on the farthest crossing, at Arnhem.

With insufficient Allied aircraft to land the whole force on one day, priority was given to the two US divisions, whose early seizure of the two southern crossings, over Maas and Waal, was vital to the follow-up. British 1st Airborne Division, of two parachute and one glider-borne infantry brigades, with support-

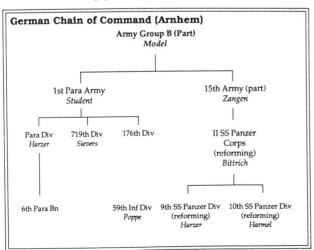

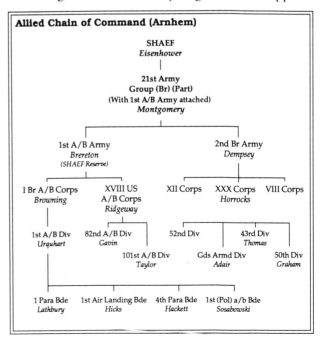

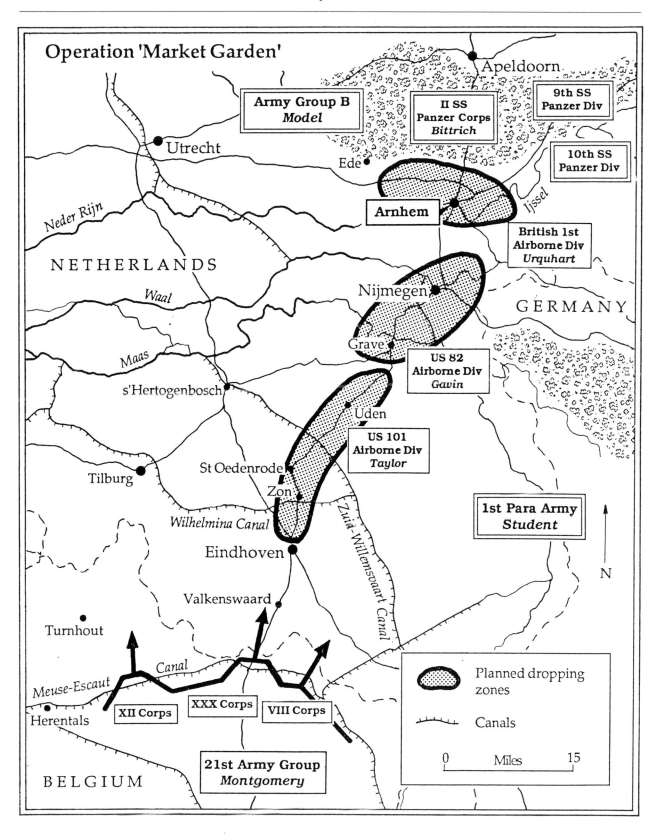

Operation 'Market Garden'

Army Group B
Model

II SS
Panzer Corps
Bittrich

9th SS
Panzer Div

10th SS
Panzer Div

Apeldoorn

Utrecht

Ede

Neder Rijn

Arnhem

British 1st
Airborne Div
Urquhart

NETHERLANDS

Waal

Nijmegen

Ijssel

GERMANY

Maas

Grave

US 82
Airborne Div
Gavin

s'Hertogenbosch

Uden

US 101
Airborne Div
Taylor

Tilburg

St Oedenrode

Zon

1st Para Army
Student

Wilhelmina Canal

Zuid-Willemsvaart Canal

Eindhoven

N

Valkenswaard

Turnhout

Meuse-Escaut

Canal

Herentals

XII Corps

XXX Corps

VIII Corps

Planned dropping
zones

Canals

21st Army Group
Montgomery

0   Miles   15

BELGIUM

ing arms and services (but of course no armour), with a Polish parachute brigade under command, could not therefore all be brought in on the first day. It could not in fact, be completely deployed in less than three days, with surprise already lost on the first. Good weather, good communications and a slow German reaction would have given 'Market Garden' a better chance. None of these three conditions was satisfied. Bad weather delayed later drops and hampered both re-supply and air support operations. Communications ran into early difficulties and never fully recovered. German reaction was swift and effective, greatly aided by the presence in the area of cadres of both the 9th and 10th SS Panzer Divisions, moving back into Germany to refit and now very weak in armour, but still strong enough to defeat lightly armed airborne attack. A final stroke of ill luck pinned down Major-General Roy Urquhart, the Divisional Commander who, though with poor communications, had on his arrival gone forward, and remained out of touch with his HQ for nearly 36 vital hours, during which urgent decisions had to be taken.

Operation 'Garden'

On the first day, 17 September, 1 Para Brigade (Brigadier G. Lathbury) arrived as planned and Frost's 2nd Para Battalion moved in and secured the northern end of the vital Arnhem road bridge. Frost and his force of little more than a company, with some

▲ Departure. A Stirling bomber 'tug' prepares to take off 'from an air-base somewhere in England' with a Horsa glider 'tow' as the Allied Airborne Army (the Supreme Commander's reserve) sets out for Holland, waved away by paratroops and RAF personnel.

additions from other units, was to stay there under heavy and increasing enemy pressure for the best part of five days, until the few men remaining, blown out of one burning house after another by SP and tank gun fire, were overwhelmed. The action of 2nd Para Battalion and its additional detachments at the Arnhem road bridge was a truly classic example of the tremendous impact that airborne troops, under the sort of command they always deserve, can have in battle.

Four Parachute Brigade (Brigadier J. W. Hackett), delayed by bad weather, came in several hours late on the next day, the 18th, its dropping zones defended against increasing opposition by infantry from the 1 Airlanding Brigade (Brigadier P. H. Hicks), who might otherwise have been pressing on to the bridge. Put down six miles from its objective, which German armour would prevent it from reaching, 4 Para Brigade was brought in, greatly reduced, when Urquhart was once more in charge, to help defend the bridgehead on the Rhine bank, around Oosterbeek, which was to be the Division's final position. This, in fact, had only been the GOC's choice as a staging area, but by 20 September it was clear that we were here

The Battle of Arnhem, 1944

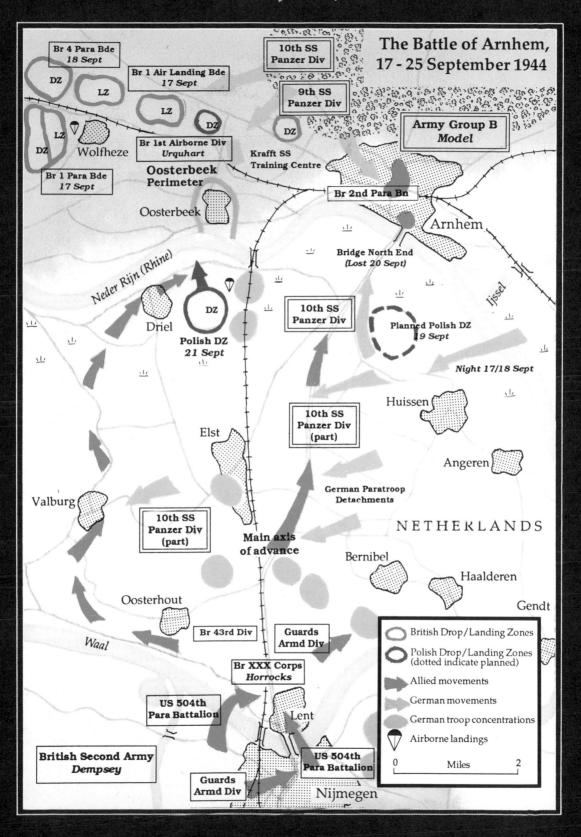

The Battle of Arnhem,
17 - 25 September 1944

Br 4 Para Bde
18 Sept

DZ

LZ

10th SS
Panzer Div

Br 1 Air Landing Bde
17 Sept

LZ

9th SS
Panzer Div

DZ

LZ

LZ

Army Group B
Model

DZ

DZ

Wolfheze

Br 1st Airborne Div
Urquhart

Krafft SS
Training Centre

Oosterbeek
Perimeter

Br 2nd Para Bn

Br 1 Para Bde
17 Sept

Oosterbeek

Arnhem

Neder Rijn (Rhine)

Bridge North End
(Lost 20 Sept)

IJssel

DZ

Driel

10th SS
Panzer Div

Planned Polish DZ
19 Sept

Polish DZ
21 Sept

Night 17/18 Sept

Huissen

10th SS
Panzer Div
(part)

Elst

Angeren

German Paratroop
Detachments

Valburg

NETHERLANDS

10th SS
Panzer Div
(part)

Main axis
of advance

Bernibel

Oosterhout

Haalderen

Gendt

Waal

Br 43rd Div

Guards
Armd Div

Br XXX Corps
Horrocks

British Drop/Landing Zones

Polish Drop/Landing Zones
(dotted indicate planned)

US 504th
Para Battalion

Lent

Allied movements

German movements

German troop concentrations

British Second Army
Dempsey

US 504th
Para Battalion

Airborne landings

0   Miles   2

Guards
Armd Div

Nijmegen

► Paratroopers and glider-borne troops landing on the 'DZ's and 'LZ's on the north-west outskirts of Arnhem while formations of Dakotas fly overhead. Note how the tails of Horsa gliders were designed to break off upon landing – permitting their human cargoes to deplane rapidly.

► Below right: Resembling from the air a swarm of locusts that have shed their wings, a broad and open 'Dropping Zone' near Arnhem receives a fresh wave of paratroops on the afternoon of 17 September 1944. A small number have in error landed in the forest (centre left).

▲ Putting on a brave face – although many eyes reveal deeper thoughts – a Dakota-load of paratroopers from an undisclosed British airborne unit depart for what for many of them would prove 'a bridge too far' – Arnhem.

for keeps – Divisional HQ and Divisional troops; the Independent Company (Boy Wilson's splendid lot); what survived of Fred Gough's Recce Squadron; the Light Regiment RA; the great fighting men of the Glider Pilot Regiment, who took higher casualties in the whole action than any; the RAMC manning two much fought-over dressing-stations and much else besides; and two brigades, more or less, the Airlanding Brigade and 4 Para Brigade, with their appropriate elements in support such as some wonderful gunners and sappers.

So there we stayed in and around Oosterbeek, in a cauldron narrowed daily as the enemy pressed in, under shell and mortar fire and air attack, with SP guns and tanks, and even with the loud speaker on a tank which got into the position one evening. 'Tommy, for you the war is over. Think of your loved ones. Raise a white handkerchief . . .' To my dying day I shall recall the roar of catcalls and abuse that greeted this invitation: who *had* a white handkerchief? Anything that would serve was already in use,

wrapped around an injury. The company just there was terrific, the best I have ever known.

The bridge was finally lost on 21 September, after three days and four nights of fierce defence by a force reduced towards the end to less than a hundred men, mostly members of 2nd Para Battalion and the Recce Squadron, with gunners, sappers, RASC and other components of 1 Para Brigade. Urquhart was now concentrating on holding a tight bridgehead perimeter around Oosterbeek. Of the 10,095 airborne soldiers brought in, he still had some 3,000 disposed in two sectors: the western under the Airlanding Brigade, the eastern under a sadly depleted 4 Para Brigade, with the addition of some Polish parachute infantry and elements rallied from the fighting near the bridge. Under heavy and increasing German pressure it was clear that only the early arrival of relief from XXX Corps could save the bridgehead. The unsuitability for tanks, however, of the single main road running across Polder land north from Nijmegen, easily cut by anti-tank fire, so delayed the Guards Armoured Division that, with casualties high and mounting and ammunition and other supplies almost exhausted, there was no alternative course for the remnant of 1st Airborne Division to withdrawal. Urquhart finally, on the night of 24/25 September, got some 2,000 men back across the river.

▲ Landed paratroops hasten to collect their weaponry (most of it dropped in containers rather than in drop-bags suspended beneath them in the modern practice), before regrouping and setting off for their first RVs, Arnhem, 1944.

▼ Paratroops unpacking ammunition canisters and other stores dropped at Arnhem. Unfortunately many valve radio sets proved unworkable, and in later stages of the battle many supply drops fell straight into German hands, so fluid and confused was the fighting.

▶ 'Arnhem Bridge, 5 p.m. the Second Day'. This dramatic picture depicts the intensity of the fighting around the key bridge as Frost's men weather the German onslaught and inflict heavy casualties upon their opponents. (Painting by David Shepherd)

ARNHEM BRIDGE, from THE SECOND DAY — David Shepherd

▶ Local Dutch people greet their liberators with refreshments. What the bucket contains can only be conjectured, but its contents appear to be acceptable.

▲ A 6pdr anti-tank gun in action against a German self-propelled gun about 80 yards away. The presence of German armour close to Arnhem on the first day was a particularly unpleasant surprise.

◄ Troops dug-in in a wood, ready to defend their Brigade Headquarters – 18 September 1944. Already Operation 'Market Garden' was running into difficulties.

▶ A paratrooper patrol advances cautiously through ruined houses in Oosterbeek as the perimeter begins to contract.

▼ The vital bridge at Arnhem. Lieutenant-Colonel Frost's First Parachute Battalion occupied the northern end but arrived just too late on the evening of the 17th to forestall the German arrival at the southern end. A heroic battle ensued, which cost the Germans heavy casualties. An armoured column that tried to rush the bridge was wiped out.

Points of View

Let others speak of what happened in this battle. Here are extracts from a report in US archives by Lieutenant Bruce E. Davis, a young US officer of signals, put in to HQ 1st Airborne to direct the air support that never came.

'. . . *I am not trying to sound courageous, for courage was commonplace and heroism was the rule. God knows I was badly scared a good deal of the time.*

. . . I learned this from the Arnhem operation, that men, born and bred as freemen, have a great strength and will power which they distrust until they need it. I saw men who were hungry, exhausted, hopelessly outnumbered, men who by all the rules of warfare should have gladly surrendered to have it all over with, who were shelled until they were helpless psychopathics; and through it all they laughed, sang, and died, and kept fighting.

. . . The greatest tribute that I think could be paid to the 1st Airborne Division was paid by a German prisoner, a major, the old Prussian type of officer, who saw service in the last war and in this one. The prisoners were in a cage about 200 yards from division headquarters. They were complaining that they were not getting enough food. At that, they were getting more than we were, and they could sleep. The major called them together and dressed them down severely, concluding with something like this: These men have stood up under the most terrible artillery bombardment I have ever seen. They have fought on without food or sleep for several days. Even though they are our enemies, I never saw braver men. When you complain you make me feel

◄ Top left: Lance-Sergeant J. D. Baskeyfield (South Staffordshire Regiment) manning a 6pdr antitank gun as he bravely resists enemy armour at Oosterbeck, 20 September 1944, despite being gravely wounded. He was awarded a posthumous VC on 23 November – the last of four Victoria Crosses earned at Arnhem. (Painting by Terence Cuneo)

◄ Below left: On 21 September 1944, British tanks of the Guards Armoured Division (wearing the white star identification mark of Allied Forces Europe) cross the Nijmegen Bridge over the River Waal (which had been taken by paratroopers of the US 82nd Airborne Division and British troops of XXX Corps after a tough two days' battle) and advance towards Arnhem. But it was already almost too late.

► Major-General Robert Urquhart, General Officer Commanding the British First Airborne Division, poses outside his headquarters in the Hartenstein Hotel near Arnhem, beside the Airborne Forces flag, on 22 September – in defiance of enemy shell, mortar and machine-gun fire.

◄ 'Down, but far from out'. A group of the 2,200 paratroops who successfully evacuated to the south bank of the Rhine after the abandonment of Operation 'Market Garden' on 26 September 1944. But 7,000 comrades were not so fortunate.

ashamed of our being German. I suggest that you be quiet and follow their example.

. . . The amazing thing about the British infantry was that they carried on with the light-hearted abandon of a Sunday school class on their first spring picnic.'

A wounded airborne soldier lying in St Elizabeth's hospital in Arnhem a few days later heard marching men outside. They were singing in lusty chorus as the column moved down the street. Was this XXX Corps, arriving at long last to relieve us? They were British voices. It was a column of prisoners, being marched off into captivity, defeated but not down. For even when we knew we were beat we knew we were better. I was that airborne soldier and shall never forget the singing.

There is another, deeper thought. As time has gone by many who were there realize more and more clearly what was already beginning to dawn upon some of us during the last tumultuous days in the sad groves of Oosterbeek. This was a battle, but its significance as an event in human experience transcended the military. Strategic aspects of it have attracted attention. The tactical, the technical, the logistical problems it raised are often of high and absorbing interest. More and more, however, those of us who fought through this battle and have thought about it over the years, have become aware that what remains with us can best be described as a spiritual experience. To see Dutch children, who were not born when all this happened, most of whose parents were not born either, laying their flowers year after year on the quiet graves in the Airborne cemetery, at Oosterbeek, teaches a lesson not easily forgotten.

BIBLIOGRAPHY

Urquhart, Major-General R. E. *Arnhem*, Cassell, 1958. Remains the best and most authoritative account of the battle by the GOC 1st Airborne Division, though more recent writing fills it out.

Tugwell, Maurice. *Arnhem: a case study*, Thornton Cox, 1975. Probably the best short account, with an excellent bibliography, maps, photographs and an order of battle for 1st Airborne Division.

Other titles:

Powell, Geoffrey. *The Devil's Birthday: the Bridges to Arnhem*, Buchan & Enright, 1984. An admirable account by a first-rate company commander who fought all the way through. Good bibliography, maps and illustrations.

Golden, Lewis. *Echoes from Arnhem*, William Kimber, 1984. A valuable book by the Adjutant of the 1st Airborne Division Signal Regiment. Particularly good on communications. Excellent bibliography and notes, maps and illustrations.

Special Aspects:

For 1st Airborne Division's Order of Battles 17 September 1944, see Appendix 1 from Tugwell, pp. 53–5.

For Allotment of aircraft and gliders to Units, see Appendix 2 from Tugwell, pp. 56–8.

For Victoria Crosses awarded for gallantry at Arnhem, see Appendix 3 from Tugwell, p. 59.

Editor-in-Chief's Note: readers' attention is also drawn to Sir John Hackett's own book, *I was a Stranger* (London, 1977 and 1988), the dramatic and moving account of what happened to him after Arnhem.

THE CROSSING OF THE RIVER RHINE, 1945

by John Pimlott

'Over the Rhine, then, let us go. And good hunting to you all on the other side.'

((Field Marshal Montgomery to the troops of 21st Army Group, 23 March 1945)

At 4 p.m. on Wednesday, 7 March 1945, American soldiers achieved the impossible – they captured intact a bridge across the Rhine at Remagen, shattering the myth of the river's impregnability and dealing a mortal blow to German morale. The Ludendorff railway bridge, built during the First World War and named after a famous German commander of the time, had been sighted three hours earlier by the lead platoon of Company 'A', 27th Armored Infantry Battalion, part of Brigadier General William M. Hoge's Combat Command 'B', 9th Armored Division. Tasked to do no more than close to the Rhine in the Remagen sector, Hoge ignored his orders and urged his men across. German defences were weak and, although demolition charges went off, the bridge remained in place. By nightfall, as news of the *coup* travelled up the command chain to the Supreme Allied Commander, General Dwight D. Eisenhower, all available forces were being rushed to Remagen to secure the east-bank bridgehead.

The Original Plan

Not everyone on the Allied side was pleased. Major General Harold R. Bull, Eisenhower's operations officer, reacted to the news by pointing out that 'it just doesn't fit into the overall plan'. Lieutenant General Omar N. Bradley, in whose 12th Army Group sector the seizure had taken place, retorted 'Plan, hell! A bridge is a bridge, and mighty damn good anywhere across the Rhine,' but it is not difficult to appreciate Bull's reservations. The formidable barrier of the Rhine – western Europe's greatest river, rising in Switzerland and flowing 1,320 kilometres (825 miles) through Germany and the Netherlands to the North Sea – had obsessed Allied commanders since the breakout from the D-Day beaches in Normandy the previous August. Field Marshal Sir Bernard Montgomery's failure to secure a bridge over the lower Rhine at Arnhem by airborne assault as part of Operation 'Market Garden' in September had reinforced a growing apprehension, helping to persuade Eisenhower to adopt a more deliberate approach.

The result was a 'broad-front' strategy, in which all Allied armies – divided between Montgomery's 21st Army Group in the north, Bradley's 12th Army Group in the centre and Lieutenant General Jacob M. Devers' 6th Army Group in the south – would advance in unison to the Rhine, clearing German opposition from the west bank before mounting a carefully planned assault crossing. This was to be concentrated in the northern sector, with subsidiary crossings farther south to surround and destroy the Ruhr industrial area. With that gone, Germany would be finished, allowing Montgomery to advance across the north German plain in the direction of Berlin, while Bradley entered central Germany and Devers swung south to link up with Allied forces advancing through northern Italy.

Closing to the Rhine

Closing to the Rhine was not easy. Although elements of 6th Army Group reached the west bank around Strasburg in late 1944, the river proved too difficult to cross. Even if an assault could have been mounted, Allied forces would have been too far away from the heart of Germany to pose any meaningful threat. The key to eventual victory lay in the centre and north, but here a combination of factors delayed the advance: the failure of 'Market Garden', the onset of an extremely wet autumn and the unexpectedly rapid recovery of the German Army in the wake of recent Allied advances. In addition, on 16 December 1944 Hitler suddenly unleashed nearly 300,000 men and 1,000 armoured vehicles in a surprise attack through the weakly held Ardennes, threatening to split the Allied armies apart. It took until mid-January 1945 for the resultant 'bulge' in the Allied line to be squeezed out, and this inevitably delayed the push to the Rhine until February. Even then, a co-ordinated campaign proved difficult to achieve.

Montgomery made the first move, committing Lieutenant-General Henry Crerar's Canadian First Army to an assault to the east of Nijmegen. Code-named 'Veritable', it opened on 8 February in appalling conditions of rain and mud which, together with tenacious opposition from the Germans, guaranteed slow progress. The plan was for the Canadians to strike south-east towards Wesel to meet up with a similar thrust north-east from the River Roer – code-named 'Grenade' – by the US Ninth Army (part of 21st Army Group), but floods in the Roer valley, caused by the incessant rain, delayed the American attack until 23 February.

By then the Canadians, with British XXX Corps in attendance, had struggled through the forests of the Reichswald to capture Cleve and Goch against a formidable total of ten enemy divisions, three of

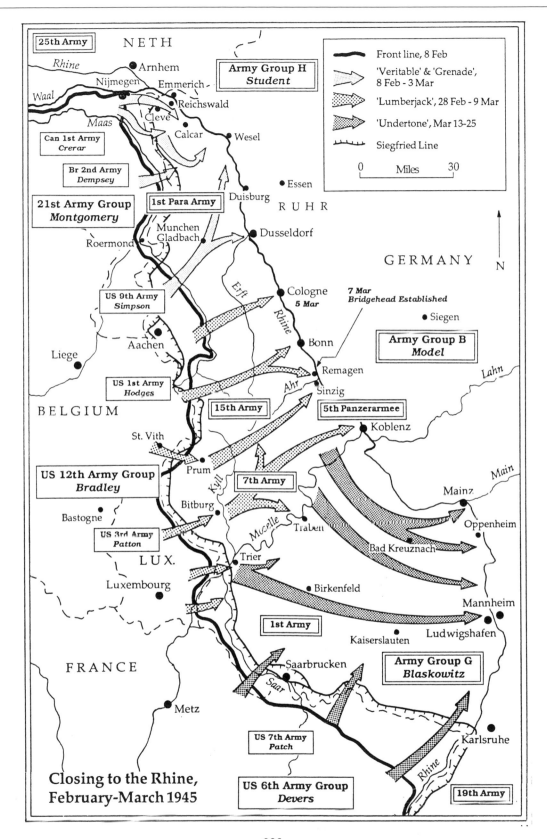

Closing to the Rhine, February–March 1945

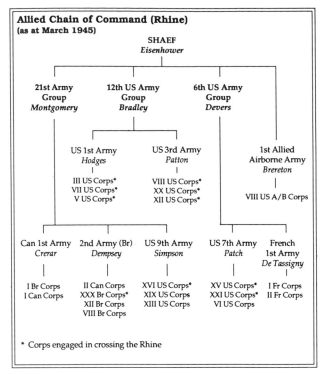

Allied Chain of Command (Rhine)
(as at March 1945)

SHAEF
Eisenhower

- 21st Army Group — *Montgomery*
- 12th US Army Group — *Bradley*
- 6th US Army Group — *Devers*

US 1st Army — *Hodges*
US 3rd Army — *Patton*
1st Allied Airborne Army — *Brereton*

III US Corps*
VII US Corps*
V US Corps*

VIII US Corps*
XX US Corps*
XII US Corps*

VIII A/B Corps

Can 1st Army — *Crerar*
2nd Army (Br) — *Dempsey*
US 9th Army — *Simpson*
US 7th Army — *Patch*
French 1st Army — *De Tassigny*

I Br Corps
I Can Corps

II Can Corps
XXX Br Corps*
XII Br Corps
VIII Br Corps

XVI US Corps*
XIX US Corps
XIII US Corps

XV US Corps*
XXI US Corps*
VI US Corps

I Fr Corps
II Fr Corps

* Corps engaged in crossing the Rhine

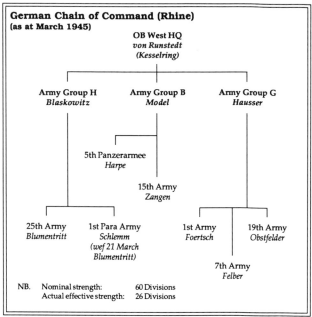

German Chain of Command (Rhine)
(as at March 1945)

OB West HQ
von Runstedt
(Kesselring)

- Army Group H — *Blaskowitz*
- Army Group B — *Model*
- Army Group G — *Hausser*

5th Panzerarmee — *Harpe*

15th Army — *Zangen*

25th Army — *Blumentritt*
1st Para Army — *Schlemm* (wef 21 March *Blumentritt*)
1st Army — *Foertsch*
19th Army — *Obstfelder*

7th Army — *Felber*

NB. Nominal strength: 60 Divisions
     Actual effective strength: 26 Divisions

---

which were armoured. The only advantage was that when the Americans did strike, they encountered dwindling opposition – from four weak infantry divisions – and were able to advance with relative ease. 'Veritable' and 'Grenade' linked up at Geldorn on 3 March, forcing the last pockets of enemy troops to hurry across the Rhine, destroying bridges and ferries behind them. American spearheads tried to seize intact bridges at Obercassel and Urlingen on the night of 2/3 March, only to see them blown up as they approached.

Farther south, in 12th Army Group sector, Bradley's two US armies – Lieutenant General Courtney H. Hodges' First and Lieutenant General George S. Patton's Third – did not open their assault until 28 February, under the code-name 'Lumberjack'. This was a far more expansive operation than Montgomery's, extending from Cologne right down to Mainz. On the left, First Army crossed the Roer as the floodwaters receded and, once beyond the river, found the going comparatively easy, crossing the Cologne plain at some speed. Cologne itself was taken on 5/6 March and Remagen, on the extreme right of First Army's advance, the following day. Meanwhile, elements of Patton's army had moved north-east to link up with Hodges just south of Remagen and,

when that was achieved on 9 March, the Rhine was clear along much of its length, with the added bonus of a bridgehead on the east bank. This allowed the fourth and final attack – Operation 'Undertone' – to begin, with Patton's forces co-operating with those of Major General Alexander M. Patch's US Seventh Army (part of 6th Army Group) to clear the west bank south of Mainz. In the process, on 22/23 March, Patton ordered his forward troops to seize crossings over the Rhine at Nierstein and Oppenheim.

Preparing for 'Plunder'

Patton was more than pleased to have beaten his old rival Montgomery to the east bank, but in reality the crossings in Third Army's sector and at Remagen could never be more than secondary. Third Army was too far south to have any decisive impact, while the Remagen bridgehead led into the difficult country of the Westerwald. Regardless of American success, the key to breaching the Rhine barrier lay firmly in the north, where Montgomery had been preparing his assault for months under the code-name 'Plunder'. He may have gained a reputation (despite 'Market Garden') for extreme caution, building up his forces and preparing for every contingency before committing them to a battle they were virtually guaranteed to win by sheer weight of firepower and numbers, but this was exactly what was needed in March 1945. The

Germans, aware of the growing threat to the Ruhr, had kept significant forces in the northern sector and were likely to defend the Rhine with a tenacity born of desperation. In such circumstances, any Allied attack had to be meticulously planned; failure would only prolong the war.

Montgomery viewed the projected assault in much the same way as the D-Day landings – as an amphibious operation requiring sound Intelligence, close air-ground and inter-arm co-operation and maximum preliminary firepower to soften up enemy positions, preparatory to the projection of sufficient infantry and armour on to the far shore to carve out a viable bridgehead, secure against counter-attack. This was reflected in the final plan, issued to 21st Army Group on 9 March. The assault, preceded by massive air and artillery bombardments, was to be carried out on the night of 23/24 March by British Second Army (under Lieutenant-General Sir Miles Dempsey) on the left, seizing Wesel and Rees, and by the US Ninth Army (under Lieutenant General William H. Simpson) on the right, between Wesel and Duisburg. As soon as the first waves of infantry had crossed, engineers would construct raft ferries and Bailey bridges for follow-up units and supplies.

In daylight on 24 March, in a subsidiary operation code-named 'Varsity', Major General Matthew B. Ridgway's US XVIII Airborne Corps, comprising the British 6th and US 17th Airborne Divisions, would

▼ **The Ludendorff Railway Bridge at Remagen: its dramatic capture intact by Lieutenant Timermann and a task force of US 9th** Armored Division on 7 March 1945 gave the Allies an unanticipated crossing over the Rhine.

THE LONGEST TACTICAL BRIDGE BUILT
THE FIRST ACROSS THE RHINE
CONSTRUCTED BY
· 291 ENGR C BN
· 988 TDWY CO
· 998 TDWY CO

▲ The Ludendorff Bridge, weakened by bombing and V2 near-misses, collapsed on 17 March. By that time, however, it had been supplemented by two long pontoon bridges built by US Army Combat Engineers, linking Remagen (west bank) with Erpel (east bank).

land as immediate reinforcements on the east bank. The immediate aim was to create a bridgehead 64 kilometres (40 miles) long and 16 kilometres (ten miles) deep, out of which the bulk of 21st Army Group would push east to begin the encirclement of the Ruhr, eventually linking up with US forces from the Remagen area. Canadian troops, on Montgomery's extreme left, would cross the Rhine at Emmerich once the main assault was complete,

advancing north and west to trap enemy forces in northern Holland.

Gathering the Forces

It was an elaborate plan, requiring a mountain of preparatory work. The Rhine in the assault area was normally about 305 metres (1,000 feet) wide, with a current running at between three and five and a half knots. However, because of the winter rains, the river had widened in places to 453 metres (1,500 feet), with sodden, slippery approach routes. This made the task of the engineers – 37,000 men of the Second Army and 22,000 of the Ninth – extremely difficult.

The Allied Crossing of the Rhine,
7–13 March 1945

GERMANY

Haldern

Dingden

SONSFELD FOREST

WITTENHORST
WOODS

First Para Army
Schlemm

Rees

Rhine

Issel

Bellinghoven

Hamminkeln

Haffen

Mehr

Br 51st (H) Div
Rennie

Br 6 A/B Div
Bols

Bislicher Ley

DIERSFORDER WALD

Vyman

Vissel

Schuttwick

US 17 A/B Div
Miley

Br 15th Div
Barber

Diersfordt

Wardt

HOCHWALD

Bislich

Luttingen

Loh

Wesel

Allied assaults

Allied drop
zones

Rhine

0   Miles   2

Xanten

Br 1 Commando
Brigade
Mills-Roberts

Br Second Army
Dempsey

Roads leading to the assault areas had to be reconstructed after the recent west-bank fighting, hard standings for supplies erected and, most important of all, bridging and ferrying equipment stockpiled. By 19 March suitable sites for raft ferries and Bailey bridges had been selected and more than 25,000 tons of bridging equipment brought forward. Engineer units were also to accompany the assault waves to set up landing stages on the east bank and to clear minefields, while others (aided by naval personnel) supervised the assault craft and Buffalo amphibious vehicles needed in the initial crossing.

Fire support was to be provided by Allied air forces and artillery. Air Chief Marshal Sir Arthur Tedder, Deputy Supreme Commander, organized the air side, committing heavy bombers from strategic fleets in England as early as February. They concentrated on transportation targets, effectively interdicting the Ruhr. As the assault drew closer, fighter-bombers were to suppress enemy anti-aircraft guns and destroy more tactical targets. On the ground, Montgomery gathered more than 2,000 field, medium and heavy artillery pieces (each with an allocation of 600 rounds) on the west bank, backed by 3,000 anti-tank, anti-aircraft and rocket projectors. They would be used to give close support to the infantry as they crossed the river; in addition, for ten days before the assault, a massive smokescreen was to be laid down all along the front. With more than a million Allied troops packed into a relatively small area, enemy pre-emptive bombardments had to be avoided.

To the Germans on the opposite bank – about 85,000 men belonging to Lieutenant-General Alfred Schlemm's First Parachute Army – the build-up must have been obvious. During the pause between 'Veritable' and 'Plunder', they struggled to improve their defences, but there was little they could do. Tedder's air-interdiction campaign left them desperately short of equipment and supplies, morale was low and, to top it all, the command chain was in chaos. On 8 March, in the aftermath of Remagen, Field Marshal Gerd von Rundstedt was sacked as Commander-in-Chief West, and replaced by Field Marshal Albert

◄ View from the railway tunnel (east bank), in which German soldiers and civilians took shelter during the fighting. The failure of the demolition charges fired from here was described by Dr Goebbels as 'a screaming scandal'. Five German officers were subsequently sentenced to death by court-martial for dereliction of duty.

◄ Michael Burnett's 'Horsa Gliders at the Rhine Crossing, 24 March 1945'. Airborne landings played a vital role in the Allied advance into Germany, just as they had during D-Day. The resistance encountered by Horsa gliders and their occupants, however, was often far fiercer than before.

▲ A bomber crew preparing to embark on another dangerous mission over Germany. Allied aircraft inflicted many casualties and great damage on Germany's population and landscape – but proportionately the aircrew ran daunting risks themselves. (Painting by Dame Laura Knight)

Kesselring. He had a formidable reputation as a master of defence, gained in Italy, but he knew nothing of the situation along the Rhine. Beneath him were the remnants of once-proud field formations, none up to strength and few retaining cohesion. When, on 22 March, Schlemm was wounded by an artillery strike on his headquarters, disruption was complete.

By then, the Allied assault formations – 15th Scottish and 51st Highland Divisions, plus 1 Commando Brigade, in the British sector, 30th and 79th Infantry Divisions in the American – had moved up to their assembly areas. Morale was high as the men prepared for the last great battle of the war in the west, confident in their numerical and material superiority

▶ Troops of 6th Battalion, the King's Own Scottish Borderers, move forward, accompanied by bren-gun carriers and anti-tank guns, through wooded country near the Rhine on 25 March 1945.

▼ Airborne drops formed an important part of the Rhine Crossings. Here paratroops take a quick breather near the east bank of the Rhine.

and aware of their part in a meticulous plan. Indeed, Montgomery was so confident that he raised no objection to a visit by the Prime Minister, Winston Churchill, determined to be in on the final act. On 23 March Churchill, accompanied by the Chief of the Imperial General Staff, Field Marshal Sir Alan Brooke, flew to 21st Army Group headquarters at Venlo. While they were airborne, Montgomery issued his final attack order.

Crossing the Rhine

The artillery barrage in the British sector began at 6 p.m. and gradually built up to a stunning crescendo. As the east bank disappeared in a pall of smoke, interspersed by flashes of high-explosives, the lead battalions calmly filed aboard an assortment of assault craft, Buffalo and DUKW amphibious vehicles, supported by Sherman amphibious tanks of the 79th Armoured Division, packaged out among all elements of the crossing force. Major Martin Lindsay, commanding the 1st Battalion, Gordon Highlanders, witnessed the scene:

It is a lovely night with a three-quarter moon. I shall always remember the scene in the loading area: the massive bulk of the 'buffaloes'; the long ghostly files of men marching up to them . . . a few busy figures darting here and there in the moonlight directing people into this and that buffalo; a chink of light

▶ A jeep crosses over the 1,400-foot 'Class Nine' Bailey Bridge built over the Rhine near Rees in just 12 hours on 27 March 1945. It was christened 'Waterloo Bridge'.

▼ Fifth Battalion, the Dorsetshire Regiment, crossing the Rhine in Buffaloes on 28 March 1945, to support 51st Highland Division already engaging the Germans in Rees.

shining up from the slit entrance to the command post . . . All this against the background of the guns firing with the steady rhythm of African drums.'

At 9 p.m. the first assault wave, comprising four battalions of the 51st Highland Division, entered the water. Seven minutes later the men landed to the south-east of Rees against minimal opposition, and although some of the amphibious tanks had problems with mud on the east bank, ferries soon began to operate. Within twelve hours, all three brigades of the 51st were across and lead elements were fighting for possession of Rees against dug-in self-propelled guns.

Similar success was achieved farther south at Wesel, where 1 Commando Brigade made a relatively smooth crossing at 10 p.m., carving out a bridgehead to the west of the town. Some assault boats and a Buffalo were hit by German artillery fire but the Commandos consolidated in time to witness an air bombardment of Wesel by 212 Lancasters and Mosquitoes. As the last of the bombers departed, having deposited more than 1,000 tons of high-explosives on to streets already devastated by artillery and air attack, the Commandos burst into the shattered town. Reinforced by the 1st Battalion, Cheshire Regiment, they fought a bitter battle among the ruins that was to continue until 25 March.

While this was going on, the spearhead battalions of the 15th Scottish Division stormed ashore opposite Xanten, between Rees and Wesel, after a renewed artillery barrage. At the same time – 2 a.m. on 24 March – the American assault farther south began, having been presaged by a hurricane artillery bombardment in which 2,070 guns fired 65,261 rounds in an hour. Men of the US 30th Division encountered few problems as they crossed at Büderich, Wallach and Rheinburg, creating bridgeheads at little cost. At 3 a.m. elements of the US 79th Division landed farther south, around Walsum and Orsay, and although they encountered some difficulties with a strong current (to the extent that at least one assault boat inadvertently turned completely round in midstream to conduct a dramatic landing back at its original start-point), similar success was achieved. As one of the Americans noted, 'There was no real fight to it. The artillery had done the job for us.'

Throughout the remainder of the night, engineers struggled to ferry reinforcements across and to construct more permanent bridges, often under fire. By dawn, five bridgeheads had been firmly established and only at Rees and Wesel was strong opposition still being encountered. But any German hopes of survival were soon to be shattered: at 10 a.m. the skies began

◀ Cameronians crossing the Dortmund–Ems Canal in a canvas collapsible assault boat on 3 April 1945, to take part in the battle for the town of Rheine.

▶ Top right: A soldier of No. 1 Commando Brigade looking back over the River Elbe from Lauenberg, April 1945. The Elbe was the last major river crossing required in exploitation of the earlier Rhine Crossings. Soon link-ups would take place with the Russian Red armies arriving from the east.

▶ Below right: A picture showing an unnamed German town – illustrating the typical destruction wrought by Allied bomber aircraft upon the German homeland. (Painting by E. A. Eales)

to fill with an armada of 1,700 transport planes, towing 1,300 gliders. Operation 'Varsity' was under way.

The airborne landing was witnessed by Churchill from a vantage point near Xanten on the west bank, and what he saw was the largest (and most successful) such operation of the war. German anti-aircraft fire was heavy – by noon 44 transports and more than 50 gliders had been brought down – but there was little the enemy could do against such overwhelming force. Paratroops of the British 6th and US 17th Airborne Divisions took the towns of Diersfordt and Dinlaken, seized crossings over the River Issel (the eastern boundary of the bridgehead) and established a firm base between Xanten and Wesel. As an exercise in instant and devastating reinforcement to ground troops, it was a stunning success.

But the fighting was not yet over. In Rees the Gordons and Black Watch had a tough battle to clear the town, house by shattered house, slowly flushing out the diehard remnant of the First Parachute Army. In the process the commander of the 51st Highland Division, Major-General Thomas Rennie, was killed, although this did nothing to stop (and probably a great deal to accelerate) the final clearance. By 28 March, Montgomery had 20 divisions and more than 1,000 tanks on the east bank and, as German defences crumbled, he prepared to exploit his success.

The Impact of 'Plunder'

He was not to do so in the fashion he had envisaged, for although his immediate objective of the Ruhr remained (elements of 21st Army Group linked up with the US First Army at Lippstadt on 2 April, taking the surrender of the Ruhr three weeks later), he was not allowed to go for Berlin. On 28 March Eisenhower issued a new directive by which the main emphasis of the Allied advance was shifted to Bradley's armies in the centre, aiming for Leipzig and Dresden. Montgomery was to be content with a drive towards Hamburg and Bremen, leaving Berlin to the Russians. He was to remain convinced that he could have got there first.

Nevertheless, the Rhine crossings were an unqualified operational success, indicating how professional the Allied armies had become by March 1945. Whether seizing fleeting opportunities like Remagen or preparing for and carrying out meticulous crossings as in the north, a combination of flexible command, inter-Allied, inter-service and inter-arm co-operation, good leadership and numerical and material superiority produced a momentum for victory that was overwhelming. The final surrender of the Germans in early May owed much to the successes on the Rhine, which remain among the most impressive Allied operations of the war.

BIBLIOGRAPHY

Ellis, L. F. and Warhurst, A. E. *Victory in the West*, vol. II *The Defeat of Germany*, London, 1968. The British Official History of the campaign, full of fact and occasionally quite readable, but it is very detailed and sometimes difficult to follow. Even so, an essential source.

Essame, H. *The Battle for Germany*, London, 1969. A readable history of the British side of the campaign against Germany in 1945. Now a little dated, but useful on the planning for the Rhine crossing in the north.

Lindsay, M. *So Few Got Through*, London, 1946. Although written more than 40 years ago, this remains one of the best first-hand accounts of the north-west Europe campaign. The author was commanding 1st Gordons at the time of the Rhine crossings.

MacDonald, C. B. *US Army in World War II European Theater of Operations. The Last Offensive*, Washington, 1973. The US Official History of the final attacks on Germany in 1945. Remarkably readable and full of information.

Toland, J. *The Last 100 Days*, London, 1965. Very much a journalistic, anecdotal account of the final months of the war in Europe, taken from all sides. The sections on the Rhine make exciting reading.

Weigley, R. F. *Eisenhower's Lieutenants*, London, 1981. An excellent overview of the Allied campaign in north-west Europe, 1944–5. For obvious reasons, it is American-biased, but it is the best general history available.

Whiting, C. *Battle of the Ruhr Pocket*, London, 1970. One of the few detailed histories of the Ruhr battles available, with a good introductory chapter on the crossing of the Rhine.

THE
BURMA CAMPAIGN,
1942–1945

by Antony Brett-James

*'Personally, I consider Slim was the finest
general the Second World War produced.'*

(Admiral of the Fleet, Lord Mountbatten)

Until a few weeks before it happened on 15 January 1942, senior civil and military authorities had not expected Burma to be invaded. In the previous eighteen months five headquarters in turn had been made responsible for defending the country, and administrative control had mostly been divorced from operational. Since much of the manpower raised in the initial expansion of India's armed forces had been sent to the Middle East or Malaya, little could be spared for Burma. Indeed, two divisions only were available – hurriedly assembled, inexperienced, the one specially trained for desert rather than jungle warfare, the other containing many raw Burmese troops, of whom some, under the stress of defeat and retreat, were to desert in order to protect their families left behind in Japanese-occupied territory.

The Japanese Onslaught

The first Burma campaign lasted four months. The Japanese quickly captured three airfields on the Tennasserim coast, from which they could give fighter escort to their bombers attacking Rangoon. Against their better judgement the British commanders had to hold the line of the River Salween, then of the Bilin, in order to allow time for reinforcements to reach Rangoon by sea; such a policy incurred the risk of not being able to disengage the troops involved, and several fighting withdrawals were as hazardous as they were skilful. Particularly vital at this stage was Wavell's decision, having noted the suitability for tanks of dry ricefields behind the River Sittang, to ask for 7 Armoured Brigade, then *en route* from the Middle East to Malaya, to be diverted to Rangoon. Its tanks were to play a vital role in breaking enemy roadblocks and extricating the army.

The blowing of the Sittang Bridge on 23 February, when two brigades were still on the east bank – a very difficult decision coming after grievous mishaps had delayed the retreat of the vehicles – meant that 17th Indian Division almost ceased for a while to exist as a fighting force, most of its transport and equipment having been lost.

Once the Sittang line was given up, the fall of Rangoon became inevitable. And once Rangoon port fell into their hands, the Japanese could land supplies and reinforcements and could fly in their aircraft from Malaya, where the fighting had ceased (Singapore surrendered on 28 February). They thus brought overwhelming strength to bear against the small Anglo–American air force which, hampered by being based in areas where sufficient warning of the approach of enemy aircraft could not be given, had to pull right back at the end of March, having held air supremacy over Rangoon till the end and having destroyed 233 Japanese aircraft in the air and 58 on the ground – or a ratio of five to one in our favour. At one stage the total Allied fighter strength facing 230 enemy aircraft was six flyable machines.

With the loss of Rangoon on 7 March – only through a grave Japanese error did our troops get clear – the army, now commanded by Alexander, was virtually isolated from its base in India, since no roads had been built to link Assam with Burma; it depended for reinforcements on the few that could be flown in and, for supplies, on such stocks as had wisely been backloaded to Mandalay. The security of this new base, of the Yenangyaung oilfields, and of the Mandalay–Lashio link with China now became the main object of our defence.

The retreating army was seriously hampered by tens of thousands of refugees; by the unexpected unfriendliness of the Burmese, some of whom joined the Japanese or indulged in sabotage on their own initiative; by the enemy's trick of disguising soldiers as peaceful villagers. The few maps available were small-scale and sometimes obsolete. Lack of signals equipment and a shortage of doctors and ambulances added to the difficulties. Lack of air support adversely affected morale and deprived our commanders of aerial reconnaissance and early information of Japanese reinforcements; units became daily weaker, until some battalions had lost their L of C, and troops had to hold off mounting pressure on their front and at the same time turn round in order to battle against threats to their rear. Then co-operation with the Chinese divisions sent in by Chiang Kai-shek under Stilwell's command presented considerable problems.

After the destruction of the oilfields on 15 April, Alexander hoped to hold a line at Meiktila, but realized the danger of hanging on too long and so

▶ The famous General Sir William Slim (1891–1970), General Officer Commanding-in-Chief, of 'the Forgotten' Fourteenth Army. A brilliant soldier who converted defeat in 1942 to victory in 1945, and who was promoted field marshal and created Viscount Slim of Burma. He was probably the finest British general of the Second World War. (Painting by Amy Katherine Browning)

being forced to fight in the loop of the Irrawaddy below Mandalay. A superb rearguard action at Kyaukse imposed enough delay on the Japanese to allow the safe crossing of the river at the end of April. Thereafter, the retreat to the Chindwin and so to Assam was a race against Japanese and monsoon alike.

This retreat of nearly 1,000 miles was the longest ever carried out by a British army (three times the length of Moore's retreat to Corunna, for instance). Whereas Japanese casualties during the campaign were given as 4,597, British and Indian losses numbered 13,463, almost half of them 'missing': and the proportion of sick among the returning troops was appalling. Slim, who commanded Burcorps, summed up in one phrase: 'We, the Allies, had been out-manoeuvred, outfought, and outgeneralled.'

The Creation of Fourteenth Army

The fifteen months' period after this campaign was spent by both sides in consolidation and planning. The Japanese did not follow up in force west of the Chindwin. We had two weak corps with which to hold the Burma frontier, defend against probable invasion 700 miles of the Bengal–Orissa coastline, uncovered by naval forces, and to control a huge area and a population of many millions at a time when the Congress Party was inciting anti-Allied feeling, campaigning against recruiting for the army and against support of the war effort. That summer of 1942 civil disobedience was proclaimed throughout India, rebellion broke out in Bengal and Bihar, and armed gangs attacked railways, halting the flow of supplies to the Burma front for days at a time. It took some anxious weeks to bring the trouble under control.

Since the closing of the Burma Road (Rangoon–Mandalay–Lashio–Yunnan), opened in December 1938, China had been all but isolated from Allied aid, except for what could be sent over the 'Hump' – the mountain range between Assam and China and some of the world's most difficult flying country. It being doubtful whether the Chinese will to resist would survive this isolation – failure to do so would mean the release of huge Japanese forces to fight outside China – the efforts of the Allies turned to securing enough of northern Burma to keep open the air route and, if possible, to open a new land route for supplying China, this time from Ledo.

Attempts, early in 1943, to recapture Akyab and its important airfield by means of an overland advance down the Arakan coast, even after the landing craft for a seaborne assault had not been forthcoming, failed completely. Errors and miscalculations were made; the troops were inexperienced and prone to fear the jungle more than the enemy; frontal attacks against skilfully sited and camouflaged 'bunker' strongpoints proved unavailing and costly; the L of C was tenuous; artillery and air support were inadequate for the ambitious task in hand.

Our reverses at Donbaik and Rathedaung in March gave the Japanese time to bring up reinforcements and take the offensive, driving us back behind the Maungdaw–Buthidaung line. On the credit side must be set the fact that the Japanese were obliged to move troops to Arakan from central Burma, leaving insufficient for their contemplated advance into Assam.

This grim failure in Arakan, which further lowered morale, was partially offset by the first Chindit operation commanded by Wingate. It was originally to have been co-ordinated with a Chinese–American advance from Ledo and a British–Indian thrust from Imphal and Tamu; but when, for lack of supplies, this main offensive had to be abandoned, Wavell decided to continue with the Chindit expedition. Its object was to cut the railway between Shwebo and Myit-kyina, harass the Japanese, and if possible cross the Irrawaddy and attack enemy communications southwest of Bhama. Of the 3,000 men who marched beyond the Chindwin in February, some 2,180 had returned to India four months later, having covered between 1,000 and 1,500 miles across terrible country. Perhaps the military damage and casualties inflicted on the enemy were small in proportion to the effort, hardship and cost involved – most of the mules and equipment had to be left behind. Moreover, the operation had no immediate effect on Japanese troop dispositions or plans. But the troops, who were supplied by air on wireless demand, had operated in the heart of the enemy-held territory, had damaged the railway, and brought back many valuable lessons in jungle warfare, travel and subsistence. The exploit, widely publicized, affected training and raised morale.

Throughout this period training was designed to teach soldiers to believe that they were as good as or superior to the Japanese as fighting men in the jungle: the myth of the Japanese as supermen had to be destroyed. They had to learn to live and move in the jungle, to patrol there with boldness and cunning – this was the basis of success, though exhausting in the climate and harsh mountain-river country. Troops had to get used to having Japanese parties in their rear; there could be no non-combattants in jungle warfare, and every unit had to be responsible for its own all-round defence. Men had to learn not to allow ruses to frighten them or induce them to disclose their positions or waste ammunition in 'trigger-happy' panic firing, especially at night.

It was essential to raise morale, above all in rear areas, in reinforcement camps, and along the L of C. Bitterness over being the 'Forgotten Army' and the all too prevalent hopelessness of expecting ever to beat the Japanese had to be dispelled. A passive, defensive attitude had to make way for something more positive and aggressive. In Slim's words: 'Our object became not to defend India, to stop the Japanese advance, or even to occupy Burma, but to destroy the Japanese Army, to smash it as an evil thing.'

One way to raise morale was to improve the army's health – a tremendous problem, since, to begin with, for every man evacuated with wounds, 120 went on account of illness, principally malaria, dysentery, skin troubles and mite typhus. In some units the few men who remained on their feet barely sufficed to look after the mules or to drive the vehicles. At the end of 1942 one forward division was 5,000 men under strength, out of 17,000.

Discipline being vital not only for success but for survival too, very strict health precautions were imposed, in particular against malaria. Research into tropical diseases; the introduction of mepacrine and other drugs; the treatment of the sick in forward areas

▼ A railway bridge over the River Salween mined by 'Burcorps' in early 1942 as it commenced its 1,000-mile retreat to the Indian frontier region.

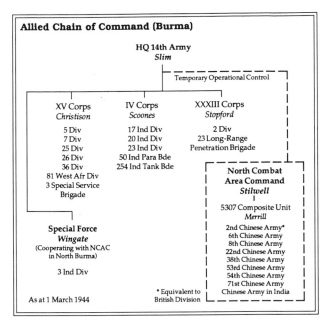

Allied Chain of Command (Burma)

HQ 14th Army
Slim

Temporary Operational Control

XV Corps *Christison*	IV Corps *Scoones*	XXXIII Corps *Stopford*
5 Div	17 Ind Div	2 Div
7 Div	20 Ind Div	23 Long-Range
25 Div	23 Ind Div	Penetration Brigade
26 Div	50 Ind Para Bde	
36 Div	254 Ind Tank Bde	
81 West Afr Div		
3 Special Service Brigade		

North Combat Area Command *Stilwell*

5307 Composite Unit *Merrill*

2nd Chinese Army*
6th Chinese Army
8th Chinese Army
22nd Chinese Army
38th Chinese Army
53rd Chinese Army
54th Chinese Army
71st Chinese Army
Chinese Army in India

Special Force *Wingate* (Cooperating with NCAC in North Burma)

3 Ind Div

As at 1 March 1944

* Equivalent to British Division

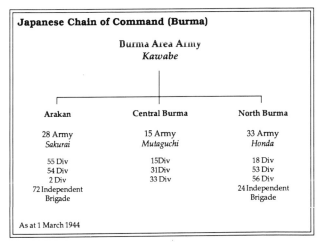

Japanese Chain of Command (Burma)

Burma Area Army
Kawabe

Arakan	Central Burma	North Burma
28 Army *Sakurai*	15 Army *Mutaguchi*	33 Army *Honda*
55 Div	15 Div	18 Div
54 Div	31 Div	53 Div
2 Div	33 Div	56 Div
72 Independent Brigade		24 Independent Brigade

As at 1 March 1944

▲ 'The Battle of the Tennis Court', at Kohima, by Terence Cuneo.

◄ When elephants were not available, sheer human muscle-power had to be called in to assist light transport to master a steep river bank, 'somewhere in Burma'.

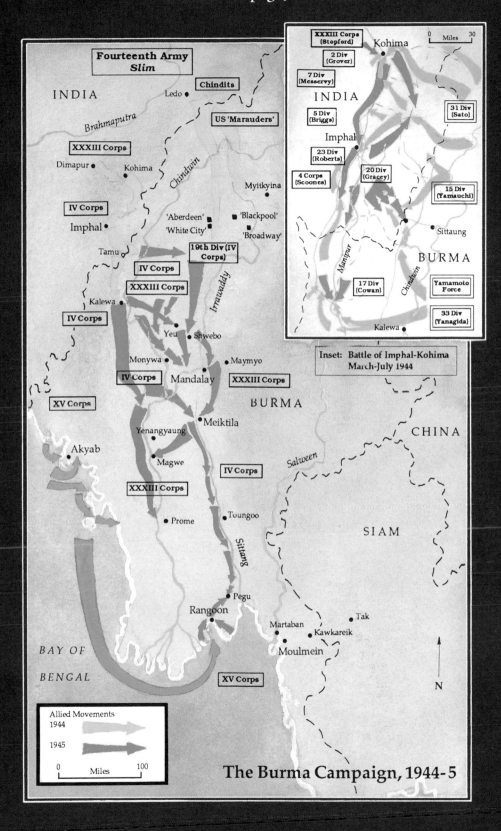

The Burma Campaign, 1942–1945

The Burma Campaign, 1944-5

Inset: **Battle of Imphal-Kohima March-July 1944**

instead of evacuating them to India – this meant an absence from duty of weeks instead of months; the arrival forward of surgical teams; evacuation by light aircraft from airstrips cut out of jungle or ricefield; the innovation of jeep ambulances and the gallant, devoted work of doctors, nurses, the American Field Service volunteers and others – all served to diminish the ravages of disease and to increase the chances of recovery for the wounded.

In this process of rebuilding morale the personal contributions of Slim as Fourteenth Army Commander and of Mountbatten, when he became Supreme Commander, South-east Asia, in August 1943, were immense. The former, applying the

lessons learnt in adversity and defeat, encouraged resourcefulness, ingenuity and improvisation: *vide* his motto, 'God helps those who help themselves'. Very effective also was the ability of both leaders to talk to troops – British, Indian, Gurkha, West African, East African – in sincere, forthright, homely, informed, yet inspiring, terms.

They had much to worry them, not least the movement of men and supplies, thanks to shortage of transport, inadequate railways, and few roads – and those alarmingly vulnerable to rain and landslides. The Fourteenth Army, at the bottom of the priority list and stretched over a 700-mile front from the Chinese border to the Bay of Bengal, was short of everything. Aircraft on loan might always be taken away at short notice. Landing craft were seldom available. Indeed, the supply situation was for a time serious enough to threaten the possibility of any offensive. Then the railhead at Dimapur lay 600 miles from Calcutta, and no bridges spanned the wide Brahmaputra. However, three main all-weather roads were built during 1942 and 1943 to bridge the gap between railheads and the

▼ Air supply came to play a vital role in Burma, enabling isolated positions or 'boxes' to hold out against remorseless Japanese attacks. As parachute silk was at a premium, a substitute 'parajute' (made of plant fibres) was developed following an idea first put forward by General 'Bill' Slim. Here we see one such drop from a Dakota falling close to the crew of a Bofors fast-firing anti-aircraft gun.

fighting troops. Besides the sappers and miners, who worked magnificently at a great variety of tasks during the campaigns ahead, the roadbuilding and repair was done by thousands of coolies from the Assam tea estates and by local Naga or Arakanese labour. Forward all-weather airstrips were also constructed, using the invaluable 'bithiess' – bitumenized hessian.

Meeting the Renewed Japanese Attack – Kohima and Imphal

Allied preparations did not go unnoticed by the Japanese. In early 1942 the Japanese had toyed with the idea of invading eastern India by means of an overland offensive from Upper Burma, but in the second half of that year had discounted this option; the difficulty of operating across the border, plus the requirements of other theatres, forced the Japanese to accept a defensive stance in this theatre. The 1942 Chindit operation, however, illustrated that the border areas were not impenetrable, and with the Allies clearly preparing to carry the war into Upper Burma the Japanese high command came to the conclusion that it was better to mount a pre-emptive attack than to await an attack by a vastly superior enemy. Such a course of action carried obvious risks, but with defeats mounting in the Pacific Tokyo needed a victory to steady morale and stop the rot. In January 1944, therefore, Tokyo sanctioned 'The March on Delhi'.

To divert Slim's attention, and hold Fourteenth Army's reserves away from the main battlefield, an attack was launched in Arakan, where the British had recently fought their way forward to recapture Maungdaw. The ferocious battle lasted for most of February and was a turning-point in the Burma Campaign. For the first time we held and trounced a major Japanese assault, and the troops cut off in the Ngakyedauk 'Admin Box' stood their ground, being supplied by parachute. For the first time, too, the enemy's infiltration and enveloping tactics did not produce the results (hitherto almost invariably successful) he anticipated. Broken was the Japanese legend of invincibility. Having begun their 'March on Delhi', they left more than 5,000 dead on the battlefield. Greatly enhanced was the morale of Southeast Asia Command.

The Japanese main offensive against Imphal, Kohima and Dimapur began in March. Defence of our front, which had the disadvantages of running from north to south over 300 miles, was liable to be cut at any point by enemy forces advancing westwards over the Chindwin. It was decided to withdraw our two outlying divisions and fight the battle of Imphal on and around the Imphal Plain, on ground of our own choosing, and with the Japanese at the end of a very difficult L of C, without benefit of air supply. The 17th Indian Division was recalled rather late, and had to make a fighting withdrawal along a tortuous mountain road, which the enemy blocked in several places. As a result, other troops had to be sent to the rescue. To redress the balance, most of the 5th Indian Division was flown urgently from Arakan to Imphal, complete with mules, jeeps and 25-pounders.

The Japanese soon severed all land communication with Imphal. But supplies and reinforcements were flown in throughout the siege, and returning planes flew out 43,000 non-combatants and 13,000 casualties. Flying sortie after sortie over the mountains and through treacherous cloud formations imposed a great strain upon air crews and planes alike. Yet Dakotas delivered to the troops at Imphal 14,317,000 pounds of rations, including 423 tons of sugar and 919 tons of food grain, 5,000 live chickens and 27,000 eggs (solely for use in hospitals), 5,250,000 vitamin tablets, as well as 1,303 tons of grain for the mules, 835,000 gallons of fuel and lubricants, 12,000 bags of mail, and well over 43 million cigarettes – a formidable achievement of 'Q' planning, providing and packing, and of maintenance by ground crews. And other fronts simultaneously required to be supplied by air. All this was made possible by the supremacy gained by the Allied air force, which not only protected the supply routes and gave close support to the Army, but also attacked ports and shipping, roads and railways, far into Burma and even beyond.

Eighty miles north from Imphal the garrison of Kohima, against which the strength of the Japanese thrust had been under-estimated, put up an epic defence and held out in a dwindling perimeter until relieved on 18 April, having gained time for reserves to come up and for a counter-offensive to be prepared. The struggle there continued for weeks, with numerous setbacks and heavy casualties. Meanwhile, fierce fighting raged all round the circumference of the Imphal plain as the Japanese sought desperately to break in, often with suicidal attacks. Not until 22 June was the enemy's ring broken.

Whereas British casualties in the fighting at Kohima and Imphal totalled close on 16,700, the Japanese lost

◄ Falling back from Kohima-Imphal in mid-1944, the Japanese abandoned Tiddim – but left troublesome snipers in the surrounding jungle. Here a medium machine-gun detachment keeps a wary eye open for any such activity.

▶ A column of the 1st South Staffordshire Regiment marching with the Chindits in Burma. (Painting by Cecil Lawson)

◄ Hard pressed during their retreat towards Mandalay in 1945, the Japanese tried to make a stand at the village of Payan. they were first subjected to a demoralizing artillery bombardment, and then cleared out by infantry, including these men of the Royal Scots, proudly displaying a captured Japanese battle flag.

53,000, of which more than 30,000 were killed or died. Imphal was the greatest defeat on land ever suffered by the Japanese Army. To quote one Japanese general: 'On this one battle rests the fate of the Empire.' A British reverse would have caused a débâcle of great magnitude, with repercussions in India and to the Allied cause as a whole that are hard to calculate.

Something should be said here about the Japanese soldier. He displayed astonishing fighting qualities, tenacity and powers of endurance; and nothing but death would stop him from gaining his objective or defending his positions. Sustained by an unusual attitude to death on the battlefield, and imbued with a sense of shame at being taken prisoner, he was a formidable, often fanatical opponent. What he

achieved in 1944 despite inadequate supplies of all kinds, inferior guns and tanks, negligible air support after March, and scanty medical services was extraordinary. Yet on the whole his marksmanship was poor. Japanese patrols often moved carelessly, noisily, through the jungle. The few other-rank prisoners, having rarely received any security training, would answer questions truthfully when interrogated, and even volunteered information. The Japanese were careless, too, about carrying into action orders, marked maps, and other vital documents.

Their commanders tended to follow plans to the letter, even when circumstances had altered, and they rarely showed flexibility. In Arakan in February, and again at Imphal, their administrative arrangements were based on capturing our supplies and transport; and if events did not keep pace with the pre-arranged timetable, difficulties arose. Then, at Imphal, the senior generals refused to admit that their plans had

failed, and, rather than avert a disaster by a withdrawal, they drove their exhausted, emaciated, starving soldiers, already battered by artillery and aircraft, beyond the limits of even their exceptional endurance and stoicism. Their spirit broke, and the defeat became a veritable rout.

On the isolated northern front every effort was being made to build the new supply route to China. To the Americans the reopening of land communications with Chiang Kai-shek was more important than the reconquest of Burma, even though Rangoon, once recaptured, might have provided a better means of achieving this object. Stilwell's task was to occupy northern Burma as far south as Mogaung and Myitkyina, so as to cover the construction of the road and pipelines in which he had such faith. Although the advance from Ledo began in October 1943, it was not until August 1944 that Myitkyina was captured, after a grim siege lasting ten weeks.

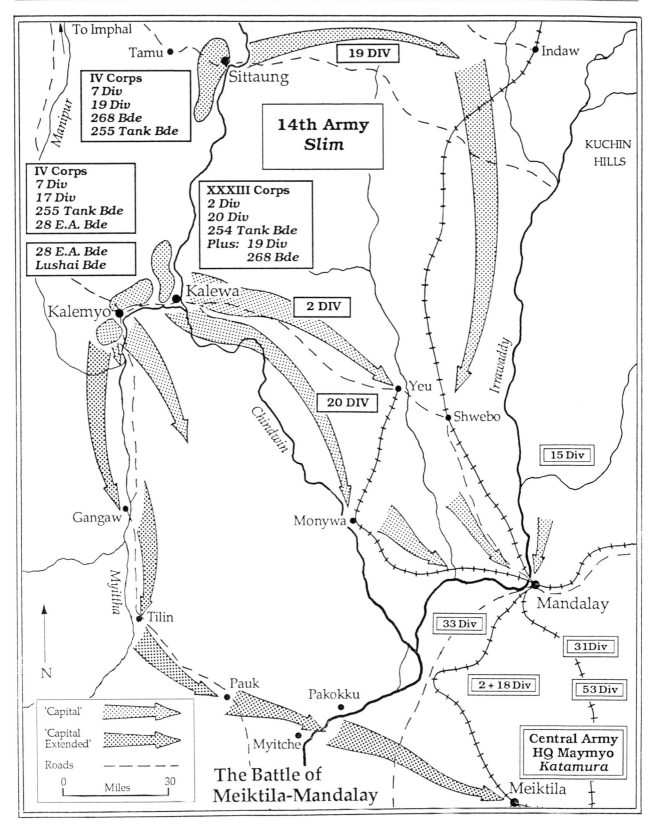

To Imphal

Tamu

Sittaung

19 DIV

Indaw

IV Corps
7 Div
19 Div
268 Bde
255 Tank Bde

14th Army
Slim

KUCHIN
HILLS

Manipur

IV Corps
7 Div
17 Div
255 Tank Bde
28 E.A. Bde

XXXIII Corps
2 Div
20 Div
254 Tank Bde
Plus: 19 Div
268 Bde

28 E.A. Bde
Lushai Bde

Kalewa

Kalemyo

2 DIV

Yeu

Irrawaddy

20 DIV

Shwebo

Chindwin

15 Div

Gangaw

Monywa

Myittha

Mandalay

Tilin

33 Div

31 Div

N

Pauk

Pakokku

2 + 18 Div

53 Div

'Capital'

'Capital
Extended'

Roads

Myitche

0   Miles   30

**The Battle of
Meiktila-Mandalay**

**Central Army
HQ Maymyo**
Katamura

Meiktila

▲ A Grant tank of the 3rd Carabineers inches its way down the river bank to a motor pontoon, prior to crossing the wide Irrawaddy. The bridgehead established here opened the way for an all-out attack against Meiktila, the centre of Japanese military power in Burma. Note on the right a Sikh soldier of the Punjab Regiment.

▼ A Priest self-propelled-gun, armed with a 105mm howitzer and a .50in Browning machine-gun. This manoeuvrable vehicle was well-suited for blasting Japanese defence bunkers, often from point-blank range. 'Somewhere in Burma', summer 1945.

The second Chindit operation, in March – the largest airborne operation of the war, with 30,000 men and 5,000 animals landed far behind the enemy lines and maintained by air for months – was designed to help the American–Chinese advance by cutting road and rail communications south of Mogaung, which fell in June, and by creating confusion and preventing the movement of reinforcements. Farther east, Chinese divisions attacked across the Salween and fought a desperate two months' battle on the Yunnan front around Tungling.

Fourteenth Army takes the Offensive – Mandalay and Meiktila

After the victory at Imphal the vital decision was taken to break precedent by fighting on through the monsoon and to pursue the Japanese without respite. This pursuit to the Chindwin followed two routes: one along a mountain road via Tiddim and Kennedy Peak, nearly 9,000 feet high, the other down the malarial Kabaw valley. Slim planned to force another major battle on the enemy at the earliest feasible moment, probably near Shwebo. But the new Japanese commander, Kimura, being surprised by the speed of our offensive over the Chindwin, decided to withdraw behind the Irrawaddy and fight what he termed 'the battle of the Irrawaddy shore'. In Slim's amended plan the ostensibly main crossings were to

be forced by XXXIII Corps, north and west of Mandalay, thus drawing the greatest possible concentration of enemy troops. When Kimura was committed there to the hilt, IV Corps would advance secretly, cross at Pakakku to the south and seize Meiktila, the main Japanese administrative base in central Burma. This master-stroke would catch the enemy off balance; it would be like squeezing a wrist when all the fingers are active, and paralysing them for want of blood.

Once again, the whole operation – the opposed crossing of a great river and a major battle – had to be conducted at the end of an L of C which stretched 500 miles from railhead. Equipment was, as usual, short and much of it was 'part-worn'. There were too few outboard motors and power-craft for river crossings. And shortage of manpower in British infantry, due to lack of reinforcements from home, had led to the amalgamation of battalions and even, in several divisions, to the substitution of Indian troops.

However, surprise was achieved at Meiktila. Although the garrison fought ferociously, its defence

aided by wide lakes, the town was taken in four days and its fate sealed the fate of the Japanese army in Burma. But the enemy launched such effective counter-attacks that he reached the airfield, and only after very severe fighting was he repulsed at the end

▶ **Men of the Dorsetshire Regiment moving up towards Mount Popa** – one of several defensive positions north of Rangoon held with determination by the Japanese in 1945.

▼ **Troops of the 19th Indian Division and a Grant tank in the streets of Mandalay, 1945.** Although reduced to only a number of strongpoints, the Japanese fought back tenaciously. To destroy armoured vehicles, some would sit in a disguised hole dug in the road, clutching a live shell, until a tank drove

over them whereupon they would drive the impact fuse into its underside.

▶ **Below right: Burmese resistance fighters lie ready to ambush any Japanese presenting themselves as targets across the river.** (Painting by Leslie Cole)

of March, having lost most of his guns and incurred disastrous casualties. Mandalay was recaptured on 20 March.

The next task was to rush the Japanese off their feet before they had time to regain balance. In any case, speed was essential so as to reach Rangoon and open the port before the main monsoon rains turned the roads to mud and the streams into raging torrents, and before the air lift of supplies became greatly reduced. While XXXIII Corps headed south down the Prome road, two divisions of 4 Corps, in mechanized columns, leap-frogged to Pegu, where strong resistance and a swollen river halted a hitherto rapid advance – 221 miles in fourteen days. But on 1 May Rangoon was subjected to an amphibious and airborne assault and was entered two days later – by troops that had earlier captured Akyab and Ramree Islands as sea-supplied air-bases for Fourteenth Army on its dash to Rangoon.

The Arakan offensive had opened on 12 December 1944, Buthidaung had been captured, and on 2 January the Japanese were found to have pulled out of Akyab. Next XV Corps set about cutting their retreat route, first at Myebo, then at Kangaw, where 3 Commando Brigade and 25th Indian Division had to fight very hard by muddy *chaungs* (tidal waterways) and mangrove swamps, and repulse fierce counter-attacks. When 82nd West African Division appeared on their flank the Japanese were forced to take to the hills, abandoning their heavy equipment. The garrison of Ramree was eventually defeated at the end of February.

In the north, the Chinese took Lashio and thereafter ceased, for all practical purposes, to participate in the Burma War.

Now Burma was ours. All that remained was to destroy the large enemy force seeking to escape eastwards across the Sittang and Salween, and faced by a country already flooded by the violent rains, the ricefields deep in mud. Roaming over a wide area, thousands of Japanese, often scattered in small groups, were cut off in roadless jungles, and intercepted and killed when they broke from cover. The 'Battle of the Break-out' raged during June and early July, in which month 11,500 Japanese were killed or captured for a loss of ninety-six. Indeed, more prisoners were taken than ever before in Burma. At the same time, Slim's troops had to regroup and prepare for the impending invasion of Malaya and Singapore – a major assault which became a peaceful occupation once the two atomic bombs had been dropped and Japan had surrendered in August.

▼ The price of failure. Japanese officers are required to surrender their swords – many of great value and antiquity – to the British Second Division under the supervision of a watchful British armoured car. General Kimura's ended up on the wall of Lord Slim's study, '. . . as I had always intended it should'. The war in the Far East was over.

BIBLIOGRAPHY

Brett-James, E. A., and Evans, G. *Imphal*, London, 1962. A comprehensive treatment of this great and critical battle.

Draper, A. *Dawns like Thunder – the Retreat from Burma*, London, 1987. A notable study of the longest retreat ever conducted by a British army and the price of unpreparedness.

Evans, G. *Slim as Military Commander*, London, 1969. An excellent biographical study of the great commander of the Fourteenth ('Forgotten') Army.

Kirby, S. W. *The War against Japan*, vol. 4, London, 1956. A good, overall treatment of the campaigns in the Far Eastern theatres of war.

Masters, J. *The Road Past Mandalay*, London, 1961. A vivid account of the Second Chindit operation by a participant.

Slim, W. *Defeat into Victory*, London, 1956. The classic account of the Burma Campaigns: a model of how a general should describe his achievements and failures.

Swinson, A. *Kohima*, London, 1966. A first-class account of a dramatic and crucial battle.

EPILOGUE

by Sir William Jackson

▲ The author of the Epilogue, General Sir William Jackson, GBE, KCB, MC, a distinguished Royal Engineer commissioned from 'the Shop' in 1937, and from 1978–82 Commander-in-Chief and Governor of the Rock of Gibraltar.

As I write this postscript to *Great Battles of the British Army* after 45 years' service to the Crown, memories come flooding back of my days at Woolwich and Sandhurst: as a Gentleman Cadet at the former in the late 1930s, and as Commander of Somme Company at the latter in the early 1950s.

My memories of the Shop and Sandhurst do not fade. They highlight the constancy and yet ever-changing nature of our Army. In 1937, we were still being trained at the Shop to fight on horseback, and we spent more time in the riding schools than on anything else. As I joined the 55th Field Company RE of the 5th Divisional Engineers at Catterick on the outbreak of the Second World War, the horses and limbers were being led out of the barrack gates and trucks were being driven in. In the Second World War we had to learn to master the *Blitzkrieg* in Europe, armoured warfare in the Western Desert, and jungle warfare in the Far East; and, in the end, we gave our enemies greater punishment than we had received from them in the early years of the conflict.

After the war came the unprecedented stationing of a British Army on the Continent of Europe in peacetime, and in a nuclear deterrent posture; and in the world at large we fought the politico-military actions of our long withdrawal from Empire –

Palestine, Malaya, Korea, Cyprus, Suez, Borneo, the Radfan, Aden and Oman to name only the main campaigns. More recently we have been faced with the challenge of terrorism in Ulster and in the Middle East: at each change of direction, we needed to acquire new and different military techniques.

Every time that we have been faced with major change, many of us have uttered the words *'The Army will never be the same again'*. Nor has it been; but in my experience it has always changed for the better. It is this constant change that is our greatest challenge, and gives us the greatest sense of achievement.

Nevertheless, the fundamentals of military service do not alter. We bear arms on behalf of our country. No other profession carries such a grave and challenging responsibility. As junior officers, we are directly responsible for the lives of our men; and as we become more senior, the safety of our country and its interests depend more upon the soundness of our military judgement, and upon our organizational and administrative skills. On the one hand, we need the power of leadership and command; and on the other, the intellectual capacity to handle the complexities and uncertainties of war.

These two sides of the coin of training for a military career were reflected, for good historical reasons, in RMC Sandhurst, and the RMA Woolwich, before the war. Both instilled the basic military values needed for successful military leadership, but while Sandhurst emphasized the command requirements of the cavalry and infantry, 'the Shop' added the technological needs of the gunners, sappers and signals. Regrettably, Sandhurst cadets saw us at 'the Shop' as a bunch of intellectual snobs, and we looked down on them as 'Donkey Wallopers' and 'Gravel Crunchers'!

Indeed, the Shop did take the Scholarship stream of each year's intake of Gentleman Cadets into the Army. The attractions of a free university education and of Corps pay led the top third of those successful in the Army Entrance Exam to opt for Woolwich and the chance of going to Cambridge if they could pass out high enough in the order of merit to be commissioned into the sappers.

The difference between the careers of the two streams was epitomized by our respective pantheons. We, at the Shop, gloried in the names of our politico-military saints such as Augustus Eliott (the old 'Cock o' the Rock' of Gibraltar), Napier of Magdala, 'Chinese' Gordon, 'Bobs' Roberts of Kandahar, and Kitchener of Khartoum; and in those imperial pioneers such as Colonel Bigh who founded Ottawa, and Colonel Light who built the foundations of Adelaide. Sandhurst looked to great cavalry and infantry commanders like Garnet Wolseley, Redvers Buller, John French, Douglas Haig and Henry Rawlinson.

There was, moreover, an undoubted trend for the Shop to provide the ablest senior staff officers of the Army, while Sandhurst provided the great commanders: indeed, it was relatively rare in the two World Wars to find a gunner or a sapper in chief operational command. The Shop's Alanbrooke, Churchill's great Chief of the Imperial General Staff, and Sandhurst's Montgomery of Alamein, exemplify the point. The Shop provided the organizers of victory; Sandhurst produced its pre-eminent leaders. The trend was still evident until the last Shop gentleman cadet left the Service in the early 1980s.

The reasoning behind the pre-war decision of 1937 to amalgate the Shop and Sandhurst was, as ever, primarily financial – the reduction of overheads in cadet training. War broke out before the decision could be implemented, but by the time it was over the case for amalgamation had been greatly strengthened by operational experience. The Second World War had shown that close co-operation between all arms was a battle-winning factor. Its achievement would be made easier if all army officers were trained together in their most formative years. There were, however, doubts as to whether it was practicable to train cadets for so wide a spectrum of requirements, and with such varied abilities, in one establishment. It was like trying to combine the training of young Napoleons with that needed for nascent Berthiers.

When I started to instruct at the newly combined Royal Military Academy, Sandhurst, in 1951, I must confess that I thought the amalgamation was unwise and impracticable. Unwise because the army lost its intellectually biased scholarship stream. And impracticable because the span of ability in each class was too great: at the top end the brighter cadets often wasted their time, while at the other end the slower ones were left behind and were too discouraged to try to catch up.

This was certainly true in the 1950s, but with the continuous re-organisations and constant fine tuning of the curriculum over the post-war years, both these weaknesses have been largely eradicated by the introduction of the graduate and the school-entry pre-commissioning streams, together with the follow-up Junior Command and Staff Courses. Although major changes in the Academic Departments are pending, the overall military and intellectual standards that produced 'the Shop' style of young officer will be preserved for the benefit of the whole army instead of concentrating them in the three Shop corps – the Royal Artillery, Royal Engineers and Royal Corps of Signals.

With the collapse of the old certainties of the Cold War in the wake of the political revolutions in eastern Europe during 1989, the army will be faced once more with radical change. The Royal Military Academy, Sandhurst, embracing the mottoes of its two illustrious predecessors – *Sua Tella Tonanti* (To the warrior his weapons), and *Vires acquirit eundo* (He gains strength as he goes along) – is well established to provide the potential commanders and staff officers that will be needed to meet the unpredictable challenges of the future, under its motto, 'Serve to Lead'.

Plus ça change, plus c'est la même chose.

APPENDIX A: THE CADET COMPANIES
by Tony Heathcote,
Curator of the Sandhurst Collection

THE ROYAL MILITARY ACADEMY SANDHURST is, like most regiments of the modern British Army, the product of several amalgamations, and, like those regiments, commences its history with the earliest of the components from which the modern Academy is descended. This was the Royal Military Academy founded at Woolwich on 30 April 1741 by authority of a Royal Warrant granted to John, Duke of Montagu, Master-General of the Ordnance. Whereas at this time, and indeed for some sixty years to come, the British Army considered it quite needless to insist upon, or even provide, training for the officers of its cavalry or infantry, it had at least come to appreciate the necessity for the training of officers in the scientific branches.

This Academy replaced an earlier school or seminary, founded in 1719, three years after the establishment of the Royal Regiment of Artillery as a regiment of the army in place of the various units, companies, and fortress gunners existing prior to that time. The Board of Ordnance, as a Department of State, dated from the fourteenth century, and was responsible for supplying the army with all the munitions of war, and the personnel to control their supply and use. Thus the new Academy was intended to train not only gunnery officers, but military engineers. As the first set of Academy Rules and Orders put it, 'An Academy or School shall forthwith be established and opened at the Warren at Woolwich in Kent for instructing the people of

the Military branch of the Ordnance, wherein shall be taught, both in theory and practice, whatever may be necessary or useful to form good Officers of Artillery and perfect Engineers.'

The syllabus of the new Academy was divided into Theory and Practice, each taught for three days respectively in a six-day working week. The Theory covered arithmetic, algebra, geometry, trigonometry, mechanics, levelling and the draining of morasses, fortification, mining, ballistics, and 'the names of the several pieces of Ordnance, their dimensions, as likewise the names and dimensions of their Carriages, and other warlike Engines, the Composition of the Metal of which the Ordnance is made; the Composition of Gunpowder; and the several sorts of Fireworks'. The Practice, which in the early days was attended not only by the Cadets but by all other members of the Royal Regiment at Woolwich, covered all aspects of artillery and military engineering. These included laying, loading and firing every type of gun, the construction of batteries, trenches, mines and other earthworks, bridging, the operation of an ordnance field park, the making of gunpowder, the design of magazines, and the formation of a train of artillery, either for field service or a siege. As is still the case at RMAS to this day, the theoretical subjects were taught by academic lecturers, now officially referred to as 'civilian instructors', and then, rather more graciously, as 'Professors and

▶ The Royal Military Academy, Woolwich. Founded in April 1741 by order of George II, Woolwich trained Gentleman Cadets for the Regiment of Royal Artillery and the Corps of Royal Engineers (and later for the Royal Corps of Signals) until its closure in September 1939.

Masters', while the practical classes were taken by serving officers or senior NCOs. One further custom instituted in 1741 which has continued is that of rewarding those students who distinguish themselves in the various subjects with 'some prize of honour if an Engineer, Officer, or Cadet; or some pecuniary premium, if a Private Man, as an encouragement'.

The system of training cadets and soldiers at the same time was found to be unsatisfactory, and in 1744 the RMA became an academy solely for gentlemen cadets. The twenty or so cadets were increased in number and formed into a separate 'Company of Gentlemen Cadets', the senior company of the Royal Artillery, with its own Command structure consisting of a Captain (who was in fact the Master General of the Ordnance, and so confined his duties to collecting the extra pay in return for exercising general supervision), a Captain-Lieutenant (who acted as the company commander), three subalterns, and a drum-major.

The new Academy soon proved its worth, by the higher quality of officer it produced for the Royal Artillery, which in its early days had still tended to be thought of as a body of tradesmen or civilian specialists in uniform rather than a corps of highly skilled soldiers. Colonel Forbes Macbean, one of the first cadets to join the Regiment from the RMA, later wrote, of the campaigns of 1747 and 1748, that in this period the artillery first began to bear a regular military appearance and 'great attention was paid to good order, and strict discipline and subordination; a change that was far from agreeable to the older Officers who, being promoted from the ranks, had grown up with erroneous notions and bad habits, inconsistent with any Military system; but the junior Officers, who of late had been promoted from the cadet Company, being now in the majority, entered with great zeal and military spirit into the newly adapted alterations and improvements'.

The very nature of a military officer's duties is such that members of the Academy (staff as well as students) have always needed to be robust and resilient. At no time was this more the case than in the Georgian and early Victorian period, an age in many ways of great refinement, but in others of great brutality, affecting all classes of society. The ruling elements had, in order to maintain their position, to be just as physically tough as those whom they ruled, and gentlemen were expected to participate in all kinds of hazardous leisure pursuits as a matter of course.

The British Army has always reflected the basic values of the nation it exists to protect, and the Academy reflects the contemporary values of the army. Thus, at a time when life was, by modern standards, marked by much harshness, conditions at the Academy could be very harsh indeed. Accommodation, in dormitories or barrack rooms, was spartan, and rations were inadequate and unappetising, a matter of special importance bearing in mind that the gentlemen cadets were, until the middle of the nineteenth century, mostly boys in their mid-teens.

Nevertheless, the Academy, though sometimes a hard school, was always a good one, and no cadet was granted his commission until he had reached the specified standard in each of the subjects studied. There was every incentive to study, since progress from level to level depended upon completing each course. If a cadet did not gain sufficient marks, he stayed in the same class until he was discharged. Moreover, a posting to the élite Corps of Royal Engineers, with its prospects of higher pay and more varied employment than that offered by the Royal Artillery, was dependent on passing out in the top third in the final order of merit.

The nineteenth century saw many changes and improvements in the lot of the gentleman cadet. The original premises of the Academy had been in an estate, known as 'the Warren', which formed the nucleus of the Royal Arsenal at Woolwich. The many workshops in the area gave to the Academy its familiar name, 'The Shop', which it retained for as long as it was located in the Woolwich area. Its first move, however, was merely up the hill to Woolwich Common, to a new Academy, built in 1806, and thereafter occupied by the RMA until the outbreak of war in 1939. A high standard of instruction was provided, with several of the professors becoming eminent men in their own fields of study. The most famous of these was probably Michael Faraday, the great scientist who made many important discoveries associated with electricity and magnetism, and who was from 1829 to 1849, Lecturer in Chemistry at the RMA. At a more basic level, Captain F. W. Eardley Wilmot, RA, who commanded the company of Gentlemen Cadets from 1847 to 1854, made many improvements in the conditions in which the cadets lived and presented a silver bugle, still awarded annually at Sandhurst, for the best athlete of the Academy, in what was the first regular athletics competition to take place in England.

In 1862 came the first of the amalgamations in the Academy's history. It had been decided that, with the reorganization of the Indian Army after the Bengal Mutiny of 1857–8, all the East India Company's troops should be transferred to the service of the British Crown. The Royal Engineers and Royal Artillery became responsible for providing officers to serve with the few remaining units of Indian sappers and gunners, while the Royal Regiment itself was greatly enlarged by the transfer to it of the European-manned units of the East India Company's artillery. The East India Company's Military Seminary at Addiscombe House, Croydon, was closed, and its primary role, of training cadets for service as engineers or artillery officers in India, was transferred to the RMA (which had in fact provided a few places for East India cadets prior to Addiscombe being opened in 1809). At the same period the average age of entry was increased to about 18.

By the beginning of the present century life at the RMA, though still spartan in many respects, would have been familiar to the modern officer cadet. From reveille to 'lights-out' the day was crammed with military training or sports, together with activities which are no longer considered necessary during cadet training, such as instruction in science or foreign languages. There was a library, which

▲The Front Parade, Wool-
wich. The buildings on the
right were occupied by the
Royal Military Academy
Woolwich until 1939. In the left distance is the steep
roof of the Rotunda, hous-
ing a collection of artillery.
(Painting by Lieutenant-
Colonel I. W. McLaughlan)

contained light reading as well as text books. Balls were
organized, attended by young ladies and their chaperons.
Various clubs and societies were formed, and a pattern of
life established which, except for the period of the First
World War, when emergency conditions were in force,
remained much the same until the ending of 'The Shop' as
a separate body.

The decision to amalgamate the RMA with its sister
establishment, the Royal Miliary College, at Sandhurst, was
first made in 1858, though it was not finally put into effect
until ninety years later. The most powerful argument against
the idea was that which had led to the establishment of the
RMA in the first place, i.e., that future engineer and artillery
officers needed a higher level of scientific education than did
those of the rest of the army. There was no point in wasting
time and money in training cavalry and infantry cadets in
subjects which they did not require for the efficient
performance of their duties, and which, it was often broadly
hinted by gunner and sapper officers, they in any case lacked
the intellectual capacity to master. On the other hand, it
became increasingly difficult to justify the maintenance of
two separate officer training establishments, especially as
many subjects were common to both the RMA and RMC
courses, such as equitation (and, after 1920, the internal
combustion engine), musketry, drill, modern and military
history, languages, military sketching and field engineering.
Moreover, after the First World War the RMA ceased to

turn out officers fully qualified for their arms, but instead
sent them on to further courses at the Schools of Artillery
or Military Engineering. Although supporters of a separate
'Shop' suspected that the final decision to amalgamate, made
in 1938, rested purely on the grounds of the financial
savings to be achieved, the official reason was that, in
modern warfare, all arms needed to work so closely together
that regular officers should all share the same cadet training,
before diverging to their separate arms schools.

The orderly transition to this arrangement, planned to
take place in 1940, was disrupted by the outbreak of war in
September 1939. It had already been decided that, unlike in
all previous wars, neither the RMA nor RMC would
continue to train gentlemen cadets. This was partly because
those who were commissioned from these two establishments were entitled to regular commissions, but as the
courses were shortened during war-time, more officers were
produced than the Regular Army could employ when
hostilities were over. Moreover, with the introduction of
conscription it was anomalous to have one group of future
officers, the gentlemen cadets, who were still paying fees for
their tuition, serving alongside another group, officer
cadets, who were soldiers in the ranks, paid, rationed and
clothed by the State.

On the outbreak of war, gentlemen cadets of the RMA
and the RMC who had satisfactorily completed most of
their course were granted their regular commission. The
remainder were sworn in as private soldiers in the Territorial
Army, were called up for war service, and then dispatched
(still wearing their RMA or RMC uniforms) to Officer
Cadet Training Units of which one or more was established
for each arm , branch or service. The buildings at Woolwich
were allotted to other purposes, as it was thought the danger

from bombing made it unsuitable for an OCTU. The military staff dispersed to other posts, those civilians who were reservists reported for duty, and the remainder were dismissed. But although 'The Shop' ceased to exist, the Royal Military Academy did not, and eight years later remustered in its future home, adding to its own ancient role and traditions those of the old Royal Military College under the proud title 'Royal Military Academy Sandhurst'.

Although 'Sandhurst' had commonly been used as a synonym for the Royal Military College, just as it is at the present time for the RMAS, the College occupied a number of different locations during its own history as a separate establishment. The Royal Military College was the brain-child of Colonel John Gaspard Le Marchant, a cavalry officer of great vision, ability, and energy, who from his experience of war in the Low Countries in the 1793 campaign, had become convinced of the need to provide a system of training officers of the Line, comparable to that which the RMA provided for those of the two Ordnance corps. His original plan was for a tripartite College, consisting of a Senior Department, where officers could, after a period of regimental service, be trained in the duties of a staff officer; a Junior Department, where gentlemen cadets could be trained in the duties of a subaltern; and a Legion, where the sons of serving soldiers could be given an education that would make them potential NCOs, and which would be used to provide what in modern terms is called a 'demonstration company' trained to show the cadets how troops should manoeuvre. The Legion was also to provide squads on whom the cadets would practise giving orders and drill commands. In the event it was never

formed, as the Duke of York, then the Commander-in-Chief, felt it would be injurious to that social separation between officers and men on which discipline in the army rested, if the two were to be trained together. Nevertheless the idea of offering education to the sons of soldiers survived and the 'Legion' was formed at the same time as the Royal Military College, but under another guise, that of the Royal Military Asylum, at Chelsea. It later became the Duke of York's School, now at Dover, with its original premises in King's Road more familiar to Londoners as the Duke of York's Headquarters of the Territorial Army. Though never part of the Royal Military College, the 'Duke of York's' building bears a strong architectural resemblance to the RMC building at Sandhurst, now Old College of the RMAS.

The two Divisions of the RMC were originally formed in quite separate locations. The first students who were officers wishing to learn staff duties, assembled in May 1799, and were quartered at the Antelope Inn, High Wycombe, under the command of Colonel Le Marchant, with an *émigré* French officer, General Jarry, as Director of Studies.

▼ **The Royal Military College, High Wycombe.** Founded in 1799 as a temporary junior officer training establishment (a 'senior department' for the training of staff officers came into existence at Marlow in 1801), the first RMC's Gentlemen Cadets were transferred to what is today Old College at Sandhurst in 1812 on its completion. In due course the 'Senior Department' became the Staff College, Camberley, in 1861.

Originally the establishment at High Wycombe had no official standing and General Jarry and his staff were simply contractors supplying instruction and support to military students in return for government funds. The manifest disadvantages of such a system to both the army and the public soon became evident even to the venal politicians of Regency England and in 1800 a Royal Warrant was issued, recognizing the school at High Wycombe as The Royal Military College. A year later a further warrant established the College's Junior Department, and on 17 May 1802 the first batch of gentlemen cadets assembled, at Remnatz, a large house on the edge of Great Marlow, Buckinghamshire, and within easy reach of High Wycombe.

With the College offically established, and proving to be a success, there was a need for it to move to larger premises. Twenty miles due south of Marlow lay an infertile tract of land, whose unpromising soil gave the name to one of the villages located there of Sandhurst. This area, composed of low hills of sands and gravels left behind by the melting ice sheet as it began to retreat from its farthest southern limit during the last Ice Age, was generally referred to as Bagshot Heath. Near Blackwater village, where the River Blackwater is crossed by the main London to Exeter road, and where the three counties of Surrey, Hampshire and Berkshire meet, a small area of heathland in the Royal Forest of Windsor was 'emparked', or enclosed, during the period of the Commonwealth. About a hundred and fifty years later, this area, Sandhurst Park, comprising a recently built 'manor house' and a much older farmstead, came on to the market and was bought by John Tekel, an army lieutenant who had sold his commission and decided to invest in land. His wife, Lady Griselda, was one of the three daughters of the Earl Stanhope. He had married again on the death, in childbirth, of their mother, and had rather neglected his three little girls. As they grew up, they turned to their mother's family, that of the Earl of Chatham, and in particular to their uncle, the Prime Minister, William Pitt the Younger. When Lady Griselda's husband wished to dispose of Sandhurst Park, Pitt bought the land himself, and then a few months later sold it to the government as the site on which the recently formed Royal Military College could be concentrated.

The choice was an ideal one. The poverty of the land was such that the area was sparsely inhabited, with a density of population comparable to that of modern Dartmoor or the Borders. It was hoped that this would prevent the gentlemen cadets being exposed to the temptations of life in a large garrison or dockyard town such as those which caused constant anxiety to the authorities at the Royal Military Academy. Nevertheless, the gentlemen cadets of the RMC had already proved themselves in every way the equals of their brothers-in-arms at the RMA in what is politely called 'high spirits', and within a few years of their arrival at Sandhurst had established a record of indiscipline and disputes with the few local inhabitants that would last well throughout the first half of the nineteenth century. The grounds of the new estate were large enough, nevertheless,

to provide ample space for military activity, especially as those of the original estate were soon increased by the grant of neighbouring Crown lands, and the College's share of the adjacent common lands when these were divided up and 'enclosed', shortly after its arrival in the area.

After the usual delays, fraudulent contracting, changes in design, cancellations, re-ordering and profiteering which historically seem inseparable from any kind of defence project, the new RMC building was completed sufficiently for the first batch of gentlemen cadets to move from Marlow to Sandhurst in 1812. Other events which took place that year make it an easy date to remember – Napoleon's retreat from Moscow, British involvement in a war with the infant United States of America, and one of Wellington's most brilliant victories in the Peninsular War, Salamanca, where Le Marchant, heading the cavalry charge that helped decide the day, became the first ex-member of the RMC staff to fall in battle. As the Lieutenant Governor (and effectively, in modern terms, Commandant) of the College, he had overseen the foundation and design of both its courses and its first buildings.

The pattern of life and training for gentlemen cadets in the Junior Division of the RMC in many ways resembled that at the RMA. Science and mathematics were not, however, studied to the same level, and there was, naturally, more emphasis on cavalry and infantry training than upon artillery and engineering. Like the RMA, the RMC required its cadets to pay fees towards the cost of their board and accommodation, usually with reduced charges for the sons of military and naval officers. The major difference between officers of the Line and the Ordnance was that whereas the latter could not obtain their commissions except by successfully completing the RMA course, and were thereafter promoted by seniority, those of the Line normally obtained their first commissions and all subsequent promotion by purchase. Thus attendance at the RMC was not, in its early years, mandatory. Those students who chose to attend did so, in the Senior Division, because it increased their chances of appointment to the staff (which was decided by selection not by purchase) and in the Junior Department, because gentlemen cadets who obtained a certificate of having satisfactorily completed their studies could claim their first commission without purchase, and had priority over all others when there were more applicants than vacant commissions available.

The College's first expansion after settling at Sandhurst came in 1860. This stemmed from the reorganization of the Indian Army at that time, as already mentioned in connection with the simultaneous expansion of the Academy. The reformed Indian Army required officers only for cavalry and infantry, as its engineer and artillery components were absorbed into the Royal Artillery and Royal Engineers. This meant that officers wishing to spend their entire career in India could no longer join these two technical arms. Previously, all cavalry officers and most infantry officers of the East India Company's army (the exceptions being those who had attended Addiscombe but failed to pass out high enough for the artillery) had joined their regiments as cadets and learned their duties in post. As part of the post-Mutiny reorganization, it was decided that in future, future officers of the Indian Army should be trained as gentlemen cadets at the junior Division of the Royal Military College, alongside those who would be joining the British cavalry and infantry. This led to an accommodation problem, solved by the construction of a new trident-shaped complex on the edge of the back square (now Chapel Square), and a completely separate building for the Senior Division (now the Staff College) in the south-east corner of the College estate.

The College had already provided a focus of settlement in the area, which had previously had no particular name. At first the College address had been RMC Blackwater, but as this was in Hampshire and most of the College estate lay in the Berkshire parish of Sandhurst, the latter name was adopted, though the centre of Sandhurst village is two miles away. The College faced towards the London to Exeter road, which ran through empty heathland in the northern part of the parish of Frimley, Surrey. The arrival of the College led to the establishment of small villages at each of its three entrances. That at the Sandhurst gate took the name College Town and that at the Frimley gate was called York Town after the Duke of York, brother of George III, Commander-in-Chief of the British Army, and a strong supporter of the plan to set up the Royal Military College. The main gate, or Grand Lodge, situated at the side of the estate nearest to London, at first was too far from the College's central complex to give rise to a settlement, but with the building of the Senior Division's own premises, the Staff College, there in 1862, a development began, named Cambridge Town, after the then Commander-in-Chief, the Duke of Cambridge, Queen Victoria's cousin. Later, as the 'town' expanded, it became necessary to change its name to avoid confusion with the university town and a new name was made up combining the 'ley' of its neighbouring old Saxon villages with the first syllable of Cambridge to give the euphonious and now well-known place-name 'Camberley'.

The army reforms of 1870, though eventually leading to a further expansion of the College, at first led to the closure of its Junior Department. The purchase system had long been under attack as having outlived its original usefulness, and the government of the day therefore decided to replace it with one in which officers were promoted by seniority. First commissions in the Line were to be granted directly to those passing out highest in open competitive examination, and the gentlemen cadet system, which had existed as an alternative to the purchase system, was discontinued. The ranks of cornet (in the cavalry), second-lieutenant (in fusilier and rifle regiments) and ensign (in the rest of the infantry) were abolished, and replaced by that of sub-lieutenant. Rifle regiments had not called their junior subalterns 'ensigns' because they had no Colours to carry. Fusilier regiments had used the rank second-lieutenant, to conform to the Royal Artillery, as originally they were raised as close-escort troops for the artillery, armed with the fusil or flintlock, which

posed less hazard to the gunners' powder barrels than the matchlocks then carried by the rest of the infantry.

In 1875, sub-lieutenants were ordered to attend the then empty RMC for instruction in subjects relating directly to the examinations set for their subsequent promotion. This proved unsatisfactory. The students resented being disciplined and accommodated as if they were cadets, attended classes with reluctance, and in some instances claimed that they were not being taught the correct subjects. After further trials, the War Office decided in 1877 that the old system should be revived, and that all Regular officers of the British and Indian Line should, normally, be trained as gentlemen cadets, at the Royal Military College. To house the increased numbers, an additional trident block was built in the back square, and a new chapel built in the centre. This chapel, greatly enlarged and altered during the 1930s, is now the Royal Memorial Chapel of the RMAS and the Staff College. The original chapel, just inside the Grand Entrance of the original RMC building, became the College Museum, and, after several subsequent changes of use is now the Indian Army Memorial Room.

For more than two centuries, the combat units of the British Army were organized almost on a decimal system. Battalions corresponded to a thousand men, and were each divided into ten companies corresponding to a century, in which each private soldier was a 'centinel'. At the head of each company was its captain and his two lieutenants. In practice, at most periods the infantry company was only 80 strong, divided into two half-companies of 40, each allotted to one of the two subaltern officers. Each half-company was made up of two sections, commanded by a serjeant, and each section consisted of two sub-sections consisting of a corporal and nine men. Each company had a colour-serjeant, and each battalion was commanded by a lieutenant-colonel and with two majors as his wing commanders. (The 'wing' was a tactical sub-unit or detachment of up to four companies.) For most of its history, the cadet element of the Royal Military College was divided into companies organized along these lines, without junior NCOs, but with a captain, lieutenants and serjeants from the permanent staff. Internal discipline was exercised by a system of Under Officers and Corporals, who were really cadet captains and lieutenants, and who wore the dress distinctions of these ranks. The use of the term corporal to indicate an officer rather than an NCO was a historic survival of its original meaning, as for example in 'Corporal Nym', the lieutenant of Shakespeare's Sir John Falstaff and his company. In the same way, the junior officers of the Boer Commandos were called 'Corporals', to the confusion of their British enemies.

The cadets of the Royal Military Academy were organized in much the same way. The reorganization of the Royal Artillery after the Crimean War included the replacement of the artillery companies (commanded by captains with 2nd captains as their seconds in command) by batteries (commanded by majors with captains as their seconds in command). Each battery was made up of three divisions, which were commanded by subalterns, and the RMA was similarly reorganized into divisions, each of twenty-five gentlemen cadets. The RMC adopted the divisional system for its own cadets when these were once more admitted to the College in 1877.

Companies were re-instituted at both the RMA and RMC in 1903. At the same time the Staff College was formally separated from the RMC, which thereafter was solely a college of gentlemen cadets. A proposal to call RMA companies 'batteries' was negated, on the grounds that the Academy was a school not only for future gunners but also for future Royal Engineers, whose sub-units (except those in cavalry formations) were known as companies. There were at first three companies at the RMA, numbered 1 to 3, with the addition between 1905 and 1911 of No 4 Company, consisting of gentlemen cadets destined for the Line for whom there was during that period insufficient accommodation at the RMC.

The 1903 reforms led to the RMC cadets being reorganized to resemble an infantry battalion. The Under Officers and Corporals were replaced by cadet NCOs, though shortly afterwards the Cadet Serjeant Major and Cadet Colour Serjeants were replaced by a Senior Under Officer and Junior Under Officers. At the same time, command of a company of gentlemen cadets was graded as a General Staff Grade Two post, held by a major, entitled to the red gorget patches which all General Staff officers at that period normally wore.

In 1910 an inter-company competition was instituted, with the winners styled 'Champion Company at Arms' and given the place of honour as right flank company of the battalion for their next term. In 1918, HM King George V presented a banner to be carried by the Champion company at the RMC. The completion of New Building at Sandhurst in 1912 allowed the total of companies (which at this time were distinguished by letters rather than numbers) to be increased to eight.

In 1912 the internal organization of British infantry units was completely changed. It was felt that with the advent of new weapons and tactics the ideal size of a sub-unit would be about 200 men, half the size of the 'wing', which in any case had no permanent existence as a formed body, but twice the size of the traditional type of company. A complicating factor was that whereas in continental and American armies the infantry regiment was a combat unit divided into two or three battalions, in the British Army an infantry regiment was an administrative organization composed of several different types of units, and its battalions themselves were combat units, commanded by lieutenant-colonels, not by majors as in the continental and American systems (an arrangement which to this day causes problems in establishing an equivalent level of command when operating with allied forces). In 1912 it was decided that the companies in every British infantry battalion should be doubled in strength but halved in quantity, to provide four companies of 160 men each under a major rather than eight of 80, each under a captain. Captains ceased to be 'captains' of anything in the literal sense, and while the senior ones were promoted

▲ The Royal Military College Sandhurst's greatest son. Winston Spencer Churchill (a Gentleman-Cadet from 1893–4) who only gained a place at his third attempt at the 'Further' (or Civil Service Entrance) Examination. Nevertheless, he passed out 20th in the Order of Merit out of a class of 130. He is shown in the uniform of a second-lieutenant in the 4th Queen's Own Hussars in 1895, aged 21 years.

to major (of which each battalion now had five instead of two) the juniors were posted to the new appointment of 'company second in command'. Old style 'half-companies' became 'platoons' under a subaltern, with a serjeant as 2IC. Thus infantry serjeants, like their captains, ceased to be junior commanders. The old-style 'section' of 20 men was replaced by two small new sections (the old-style 'sub-sections' renamed) each under a corporal. Of the two colour-serjeants in each pair of old-style companies, the junior became a staff-serjeant with the new appointment of company quarter-master serjeant, and the senior became a Warrant Officer, 2nd Class, with the appointment of Company Serjeant Major, thus dividing the two functions both previously carried out by the Colour Serjeant. The

Serjeant Major became the Regimental Serjeant Major. The new-style company organization did not come into force at the RMC until the post-war reorganization of 1920. The ten companies then existing, lettered A to J, were remustered as five, numbered 1 to 5, later reduced to four, numbered 1, 3, 4 and 5. The total of four sections in each infantry platoon, and four platoons in each company had been reduced to three in 1918, when the British Army no longer had the manpower to maintain the original organization.

Between 1939 and 1945 the buildings of the Royal Military College were occupied by a series of Officer Cadet Training Units. These were divided into sub-units, but unlike those of the pre-war College, these had no continuity. Each company was composed of officer cadets at the same stage in their training, and when they finished the course the company was completely reformed with the next intake. No 161 Infantry OCTU was allowed to retain the sub-title RMC and its cadets wore the RMC badge even while this OCTU was transferred in 1942, to Mons Barracks at Aldershot. The companies of 161 OCTU were lettered A to D, and one passed out in rotation every month. No 101 Royal Armoured Corps OCTU (remustered in 1942 as No 100) remained at Sandhurst throughout the war, divided into squadrons (lettered A to D).

When the Academy reformed in 1947 under its new title, the Royal Military Academy Sandhurst, it was organized into three Colleges (corresponding to battalions) each of four companies. The Colleges were named Old, New and Victory, and their companies were neither numbered nor lettered, but, as then had become the fashion within training units, named. Those of Old College were Blenheim, Dettingen, Waterloo and Inkerman; those of New College were Marne, Ypres, The Somme and Gaza; and those of Victory were Alamein, Normandy, Rhine and Burma. Each company, commanded by a major with his 2IC and CSM, consisted of three platoons, each under a captain and staff-serjeant. Each platoon consisted of officer cadets at different stages in their training, so that every term those of the senior division passed out, and those junior to them moved up to take their place and hand on the torch in their turn. The senior cadets provided one Senior Under Officer per company, assisted by a Company Junior Under Officer, and one Junior Under Officer per platoon, assisted by Cadet Serjeants. On exercises, each company took the field as a complete sub-unit, with the seniors practising command skills over their juniors. Each company had attached to it not only its own members of the academic staff, but a share of the other senior military and civilian staff, who were not involved in the company's training, but supported it on social and sporting occasions, and helped contribute to the atmosphere of continuity.

This organization lasted for twenty years, in what was for the Academy a golden age during which future regular officers of all arms and services received both a military and an academic education. Gradually, however, changes in the outside world began to have their effect. Conscription had

been continued into the post-war era, and two Officer Cadet Schools, the successors to the war-time OCTUs, had been set up to train suitable candidates for commissions as junior officers during their period of National Service. Those who volunteered for three years' service with the Colours instead of the compulsory two were granted Short Service Commissions, and paid at the same rates as Regular officers. The OCS at Eaton Hall was closed in 1958 when National Service came to an end, but that at Mons Barracks was retained, as the concept of the Short Service commission had proved very useful. It brought into the Army gentlemen who wished only to spend a few years in soldiering before going on to their chosen career, and it meant that as a high proportion of junior officers left after three years, those who remained had the benefit of improved chances of promotion to the higher appointments. Mons OCS trained officer cadets for commissions in six months, instead of the twenty-four required by RMAS, so that, of two officer cadets joining the Army together, the one who chose to go to Mons became an officer, with all the benefits arising therefrom, eighteen months before the one who chose Sandhurst. Although in theory the Mons officer cadet received only a short service commission, in practice so many preferred the short-term advantages of the Mons route rather than the long-term ones offered by RMAS, that the Academy became unable to fill all the Regular vacancies, and officers from Mons therefore had a good chance of being granted regular commissions after a short period of regimental service.

Thus the numbers of cadets attending Sandhurst began to dwindle. In 1968 it became necessary to disband three companies and Inkerman, The Somme and Normandy, respectively the junior in each college, were selected. In 1971 further cuts were called for, and one college had to disband. Normally the junior unit is selected when such reductions are demanded, but Victory College had just moved into a newly completed and expensive, though ungracious building, typical of the 60s brutalist style. New College was therefore chosen in its stead. Ypres Company was disbanded, Gaza was posted to Old College and Marne to Victory.

This arrangement lasted only for a year, after which came the most sweeping reorganization of officer cadet training in the British Army since the end of the Second World War. It was decided that Mons Officer Cadet School should move into the vacant New Building at Sandhurst, to become Mons College of the RMAS. The OCS course was renamed the Standard Military Course, and was to be undertaken by all officer cadets, regular or short service. The special courses for university entrants, specialists, and Territorials previously provided at Mons became the responsibility of Victory College, while Old College became responsible for the Regular Careers Course, the remnant of the academic element of the old RMAS course. This became obligatory both for regulars on completion of the Standard Military Course, or short service officers wishing to obtain Regular commissions after a tour of regimental duty. The companies of Old College under this system were Dettingen (for officers returning after regimental duty), Blenheim and Waterloo. Those of Mons College were Salerno and Arnhem (both from Mons OCS), Rhine, Burma and Alamein (transferred from Victory) and Normandy (a former Victory College company re-raised). Victory College was allotted Amiens Company (from Mons), Gaza (originally in New, but by this time in Old College), Marne, and Ypres. When a fifth company was required, this was raised as Salamanca Company, in allusion to the great victory at which Le Marchant, founder of the RMC, was killed.

Since 1972 there have been several reorganizations of the courses at RMAS, each intended by their originators to set the pattern of junior officer education for a generation, but each lasting for only a few years before being changed to meet the Army's own changing requirements. The companies of the Academy, each composed of individuals at the same stage of training on the same one of the several different courses now offered at Sandhurst, tended to be disbanded, reformed, or have their names changed with a bewildering rapidity, as the Academy met the challenge of these protean arrangements. Salamanca, being continually confused with Salerno, was renamed The Somme. Ypres was re-raised, and Victory College became an all 'First World War' college, just as New had once been, except for Amiens

in place of Gaza. Mons College was renamed New College, and became an all 'Second World War' college, consisting of Victory's four former companies, plus the two companies from Mons OCS, Salerno and Arnhem, which were later disbanded and replaced by Blenheim and Waterloo, in Old College, re-roled as cadet companies.

The most recent amalgamation of another establishment with the Academy took place in 1981. In that year the Women's Royal Army Corps College, Camberley, was incorporated as a College of the RMAS. This College was subsequently closed and its land sold for housing development; the officer cadet courses of the WRAC College were transferred to Old College, and formed into Richmond Wing, named after the location of the WRAC Depot. At first the officer cadets of Richmond Wing continued to wear the badges of the WRAC but in 1988 they became women officer cadets of RMAS. Richmond Wing was divided into two companies, Windsor and Edinburgh, commemorating the location of the two wartime OCTUs of the Auxiliary Territorial Service, the predecessor of the WRAC. These companies moved from Old to Victory College to permit Blenheim and Waterloo companies to be re-mustered. At the same time Dettingen Company was revived to enable Old College to take over from Victory College the various short specialist courses for which the Academy had become responsible in 1972.

Without doubt, further changes will occur as the Academy responds to changing needs. And equally without doubt Sandhurst's companies will respond in the spirit of the motto of the old Royal Military College, *Vires acquirit eundo*, 'He gains strength as he goes along'.

▼ **An aerial photograph of today's Old College, RMA Sandhurst, with the 'King's Walk' and 'sacred turf' of the parade ground to the** fore, and the Byzantine-style Memorial Chapel, completed in 1937, in the square behind.

◄ Saxon bronze cannon with a 6in calibre; cast in 1733, it fired an approximately 32pdr ball, and was probably a siege gun.

◄ British bronze 6pdr cannon. Weighing 12cwt, with a calibre of 3.7in, it was a gun much used by horse artillery, and saw service at Waterloo.

◄ French 12pdr taken at Waterloo. Guns of this calibre were nicknamed 'the Emperor's Lovely Daughters', and were stationed at *corps d'armée* and Artillery Reserve levels. Cast during the French Revolution (*l'an 2. 1794*), it has a 120mm calibre and was capable of firing ball to 1,800 metres. Guns of this type were the feared killers of the Napoleonic battlefield.

APPENDIX B: THE SANDHURST GUNS
by 'Buck' Ryan (late RA)

A VARIETY OF GUNS can be found in the grounds of the RMA Sandhurst. These pieces date from the first half of the eighteenth century up to the time of modern artillery, some of which was in active service as late as the early 1970s. Most are situated outside the three Colleges (Old, New and Victory) and the present location of the remainder will be described below. With the exception of the modern guns, the Kurnool Mortar and the Russian 64pdr guns, none of the remainder is thought to be on its original carriage.

On approaching Old College from Queen Victoria's statue, six central guns will be seen with three deployed on each side of the Grand Entrance. Four further guns will be noticed, two being in front of the East and West Wings of Old College respectively. The six central guns were all used at Waterloo. Two of these, plus another at Yorktown Gate, were taken from the French and are inscribed accordingly. The remainder are British 6pdrs weighing 12cwt, being made of bronze, which confusingly are referred to normally as 'brass guns'. These light, smooth-bore cannon with a calibre of 95mm (3.7in) were highly manoeuvrable and are a type which was in service from 1750 to 1860. Firing solid shot, they had a maximum range of 1,189 metres (1,300 yards). Unlike mortars, which were fired at high elevations, these guns were often fired from the flanks of troops supported, aiming at the enemy over open sights. Although solid or roundshot was the normal ammunition (70–80 per cent of that carried), case-shot was also used as explosive projectiles.

Lieutenant Henry Shrapnel, RA invented an improved type, introduced into service in 1804, in which the hollow shell was filled with small shot. A time fuze set the bursting charge to explode over the heads of the enemy. The effect of such shrapnel, as it became known, was devastating to troops in the open. The heavier French cannon were used in a similar fashion. Napoleon, being a gunner himself, frequently concentrated his artillery and, at Waterloo, used his guns to fire over the heads of the French troops. The calibre of the French gun at the Yorktown Gate is 120mm (4.745in), and like the other French guns at Sandhurst it can be recognized by the rather ugly handles (see photograph). This is a 12pdr brass cannon.

In front of Le Marchant House there is one Russian 64pdr iron fortress gun with the double-headed Tsarist eagle clearly visible. It was taken at Sebastopol in 1855 and this is recorded on a plate on its iron carriage. Repeated coats of black paint largely obscure other detail. Alongside it is a Saxon bronze gun dated 1733 with a calibre of 153mm (6in). The arms of Saxony and other details are particularly clear and this is a fine specimen of its genre. Its weight of shot would have been *circa* 32 pounds.

At the east end of Old College, in front of College Headquarters, two further guns are to be seen. One is a Russian gun identical with the 64pdr described above, taken at Bomarsund in the Aaland Islands in Finland. In the last century the islands were part of the Russian Grand Duchy of Finland. At the time of the Russian War (1854–6), while the major battles were being fought in the Crimea, subsidiary naval and amphibious operations were mounted in the Baltic by a British fleet and 11,000 French troops. In the course of hostilities, the port of Bomarsund was taken and since twelve of its 51 guns were undamaged, they were removed as trophies. It was one such gun that eventually came to Sandhurst. The plate inscribed 'Taken at Bomarsund' is clearly displayed.

The second gun adjacent to the Bomarsund gun, is a Dutch cannon cast in bronze at the Hague in 1734 with the coat of arms of the Dutch Republic and other detail. It bears the inscription 'Taken by storm on the batteries within the Lines of Fort Cornelis on the Island of Java'. The battle concerned took place near Batavia in August 1811 when the Dutch East Indies were conquered in an operation sanctioned by the Governor-General of India, designed to eliminate French influence in the area. No fewer than 280 guns were captured in a short and successful campaign. At the moment of writing, this cannon is dismounted and is lying on the grass outside Mons Hall awaiting a new carriage. Next to it is another 64pdr Russian fortress gun with no detail other than a double-headed eagle. There is no plate saying where it was taken, but it is likely that it came from Sebastopol.

Moving to New College, two 'tiger guns' are to be seen outside the Officers' Mess of the RMA Sandhurst. They are highly ornamental brass 3pdrs of 70mm calibre (2¾in) and were taken in 1799 at the storming of Seringapatam. The muzzle of each gun is shaped as a tiger's mouth, hence the nickname. The carriages of the guns were recently rebuilt. They have been on loan from the Royal Artillery Institute since 1902. An identical gun can be seen at Woolwich at the RA Museum (the Rotunda).

At Lake Corner stands the Kurnool Mortar. Purists would argue that it is a howitzer as the trunnions are not situated at the breech end of the piece. It was found buried in a garden in Kurnool in India (1839) by British troops in the course of a search following information that the Nawab

▼Rear-view of the same Russian 64pdr, showing the commemorative plate. The iron display carriage would not be employed on active service.

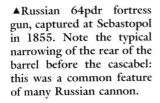

▲Russian 64pdr fortress gun, captured at Sebastopol in 1855. Note the typical narrowing of the rear of the barrel before the cascabel: this was a common feature of many Russian cannon.

▶ The Kurnool 'mortar' (in fact a howitzer), found buried in India, 1839. Weighing almost nine tons and with a 27in calibre, it has never been fired. It was probably cast as a siege-train weapon.

of Kurnool was storing arms and ammunition in contravention of the Treaty he had signed. It weighs 8¾ tons, is 7 feet long, and has a calibre of 675mm (27in). There are no records of its having been used and an examination of the bore shows no signs of firing. If not the finest, it is certainly the most conspicuous of the artillery pieces at Sandhurst.

It may be thought appropriate that the modern guns are to be found outside the more recent buildings at Sandhurst. Outside Victory College, there are two British 25pdr, Mark II gun-howitzers. These have a calibre of 88mm (3.45in) and a maximum range of 12,195 metres (13,400 yards). The 25pdr was first used in action in the Norwegian Campaign in 1940 and was last fired in anger in 1972 during the Dhofar Campaign in Oman. The workhorse of the Royal Artillery during the Second World War and in Korea, it performed well in both low- and high-angle fire. Until the 6pdr anti-tank gun was issued, the 25pdr was frequently employed in the Western Desert as an anti-tank gun over open sights. Self-propelled versions of the gun were also used extensively during the latter part of the Second World War.

Outside Churchill Hall, two 5.5in medium guns will be seen. This was the standard towed medium gun of the British Army from May 1942 until replaced in this role by the FH70 155mm (6.1in) in 1979. With a maximum range of 16,470 metres (18,100 yards) when firing the 80-pound

shell, the 'Five Five' was an accurate and well-regarded gun, the performance of which was outstanding during the Second World War and in Korea. A few are still used at the Royal School of Artillery, Larkhill, for training purposes.

The Faraday Hall on Hospital Hill is the home of the Academic Departments at Sandhurst. Outside the Hall is a Bofors 40mm L70 which was the last form in which this versatile air defence gun was used by the Royal Artillery. The original Bofors 40mm was developed initially for the Swedish Navy in 1932. In 1937 Britain made an initial purchase of 100 Bofors guns to be employed in the light anti-aircraft role. Subsequent guns were produced under licence in the United Kingdom. The Bofors was employed in the British Army for some 40 years and it is still in service in a variety of forms in many armies today.

SELECT BIBLIOGRAPHY

Hogg, Brigadier O. F. G. *Artillery: Its Origin, Hey-day and Decline*, Hurst, London, 1970.
Hughes, Major-General B. P. *British Smooth-Bore Artillery: The Muzzle Loading Artillery of the 18th and 19th Centuries*, Arms & Armour Press, London, 1969.
Bidwell, Brigadier Shelford. *Gunners at War*, Arms & Armour Press, London, 1970.
(Both Hogg and Hughes include extensive lists of tables and references).

APPENDIX C:
AWARDS OF THE VICTORIA CROSS
made to former Woolwich and
Sandhurst Gentlemen and Officer Cadets

The Victoria Cross *'for valour'* was instituted by Queen Victoria in 1856, but made retrospective to late 1854. There have been 1,348 awards to date. Former cadets of Sandhurst have won 91, and former cadets of Woolwich 37 – making a total of 128. The most recent award was made posthumously to Lieutenant-Colonel H. Jones, OBE, the Parachute Regiment, for valour in The Falklands, 1982.

Before the First World War

1854   Brevet Lieutenant-Colonel E. W. D. Bell (Sandhurst) 23rd Regt, Crimea
Lieutenant-Colonel C. Dickson (Woolwich) RA, Crimea
Lieutenant F. Miller (Woolwich) RA, Crimea
Lieutenant W. O. Lennox (Woolwich) RE, Crimea

1855   Captain M. C. Dixon (Woolwich) RA, Crimea
Captain H. C. Elphinstone (Woolwich) RE, Crimea
Lieutenant G. Graham (Woolwich) RE, Crimea
Captain G. Davies (Woolwich) RA, Crimea
Lieutenant-Colonel F. F. Maude (Woolwich) The Buffs, Crimea
Lieutenant C. C. Teesdale (Woolwich) RA, Crimea

1857   Lieutenant-Colonel H. Toombs (Sandhurst) Bengal Artillery, Delhi
Captain F. C. Maude (Woolwich) RA, Lucknow, Indian Mutiny
Lieutenant J. C. C. Daunt (Sandhurst) 11th Bengal Inf, India
Major J. C. Guise (Sandhurst) 90th Regt, Lucknow

1858   Lieutenant F. S. Roberts (Sandhurst) Bengal Artillery, India
Captain H. E. Jerome (Sandhurst) 86th Regt, Jhansi

1863   Ensign J. T. Down (Sandhurst) 57th Regt, New Zealand
Lieutenant A. F. Pickard (Woolwich) RA, New Zealand

1865   Captain H. Shaw (Sandhurst) 18th Regt, New Zealand

1874   Lieutenant M. S. Bell (Woolwich) RE, Ashanti

1879   Lieutenant N. J. A. Coghill (Sandhurst) 24th Foot, Zululand

Lieutenant J. R. M. Chard (Woolwich) RE, Zululand
Lieutenant R. C. Hart (Woolwich) RE, Afghanistan

1879   Captain E. P. Leach (Woolwich) RE, Afghanistan
Lieutenant E. S. Browne (Sandhurst) 24th Foot, Zululand
Captain O. M. Creagh (Sandhurst) Bombay Staff Corps, Afghanistan
Major G. S. White, CB (Sandhurst) 92nd Foot, Afghanistan
Captain E. H. Sartorius (Sandhurst) 59th Foot, Afghanistan
Captain R. K. Ridgeway (Sandhurst) Bengal Staff Corps, Eastern Frontier, India
Lieutenant W. H. Dick-Cunyngham (Sandhurst) Gordon Highlanders, Afghanistan
Captain W. J. Vousden (Sandhurst) Bengal Staff Corps, Afghanistan

1882   Lieutenant W. M. M. Edwards (Sandhurst) Highland Light Infantry, Egypt

1884   Lieutenant P. S. Marling (Sandhurst) KRRC, Sudan

1891   Lieutenant C. J. W. Grant (Sandhurst) Indian Staff Corps, Manipur
Captain F. J. Aylmer (Woolwich) RE, Hunza Nagar
Lieutenant G. H. Boisragon (Sandhurst) Indian Staff Corps, Gilgit Frontier
Lieutenant J. Manners-Smith (Sandhurst) Indian Staff Corps, Gilgit Frontier

1897   Lieutenant E. W. Costello (Sandhurst) Indian Staff Corps, NW Frontier
Lieutenant H. L. S. Maclean (Sandhurst) Indian Staff Corps, Upper Swat, India
Lieutenant J. M. C. Colvin (Woolwich), RE, Punjab Frontier
Lieutenant T. C. Watson (Woolwich) RE, Punjab Frontier
Lieutenant H. S. Pennell (Sandhurst) Sherwood Foresters, Tirah

1898   Captain P. A. Kenna (Sandhurst) 21st Lancers, Sudan
Lieutenant Hon R. H. L. J. De Montgomery (Sandhurst) 21st Lancers, Sudan
Captain N. M. Smyth (Sandhurst) 2nd Dragoon Guards, Sudan

1899 Captain M. F. M. Meiklejohn (Sandhurst) Gordon Highlanders, S. Africa
Captain W. N. Congreve (Sandhurst) Rifle Brigade, S. Africa
Lieutenant Hon F. H. S. Roberts (Sandhurst) KRRC, S. Africa
Captain H. L. Reed (Woolwich) RA, S. Africa
Captain H. M. Schofield (Woolwich) RA, S. Africa

1900 Lieutenant R. J. T. D. Jones (Woolwich) RE, S. Africa
Lieutenant F. N. Parsons (Sandhurst) Essex Regt, S. Africa
Captain C. Mansel-Jones (Sandhurst) West Yorkshire Regt, S. Africa
Major E. J. Phipps-Hornby (Woolwich) RA, S. Africa
Lieutenant F. A. Maxwell, DSO (Sandhurst) Indian Staff Corps, S. Africa
Captain C. J. Melliss (Sandhurst) Indian Staff Corps, W. Africa

1901 Lieutenant L. A. E. Price-Davies, DSO (Sandhurst) KRRC, S. Africa

1902 Captain A. S. Cobbe, DSO (Sandhurst) Indian Staff Corps, Somaliland

1903 Captain W. G. Walker (Sandhurst) Indian Staff Corps, Somaliland
Captain G. M. Rolland (Sandhurst) Indian Staff Corps, Somaliland
Brevet Major J. E. Gough (Sandhurst) Rifle Brigade, Somaliland

1904 Lieutenant J. D. Grant (Sandhurst) 8th Gurkha Rifles, Tibet

During the First World War

1914 Lieutenant M. J. Dease (Sandhurst) Royal Fusiliers, France
Captain T. Wright (Woolwich) RE, France
Lieutenant-Colonel E. W. Alexander (Woolwich) RA, France
Major C. A. L. Yate (Sandhurst) KOYLI, France
Captain D. Reynolds (Woolwich) RA, France
Captain E. K. Bradbury (Woolwich) RA, France
Captain W. H. Johnston (Woolwich) RA, France
Lieutenant J. A. O. Brooke (Sandhurst) Gord, France
Lieutenant W. L. Brodie (Sandhurst) HLI, France
Captain J. F. P. Butler (Sandhurst) KRRC, Cameroons
Lieutenant F. A. De Pass (Woolwich) Indian Army Poona Horse, France
Lieutenant P. Neame (Woolwich) RE, France
Lieutenant W. A. McC Bruce (Sandhurst) 59th Scinde Rifles, France

1915 Captain E. Jotham (Sandhurst) 51st Sikhs, NW Frontier
Captain C. C. Foss, DSO (Sandhurst) Bedfordshire Regt, France
Lieutenant C. C. Martin, DSO (Woolwich) RE, France
Major G. G. M. Wheeler (Sandhurst) 7th Hariana Lancers, Mesopotamia
Lieutenant G. R. P. Roupell (Sandhurst) East Surrey Regt, France
Captain R. R. Willis (Sandhurst) Lancashire Fusiliers, Gallipoli
Lieutenant-Colonel C. H. M. Doughty-Wylie, CB, CMG (Sandhurst) Royal Welsh Fusiliers, Gallipoli
Lieutenant J. G. Smyth (Sandhurst) 15th Ludhiana Sikhs, France
Captain G. R. O'Sullivan (Sandhurst) Royal Inniskilling Fusiliers, Gallipoli
Captain L. G. Hawker, DSO (Woolwich) RE Att RFC, France
Captain P. H. Hansen (Sandhurst) Lincolnshire Regt, Gallipoli
Captain A. F. G. Kilby (Sandhurst) South Stafford Regt, France
Captain A. M. Read (Sandhurst) Northampton Regt, France
Major A. F. Douglas-Hamilton (Sandhurst) Cameron Highlanders, France
Captain E. D. Bellew (Sandhurst) 7 Canadian Infantry, France

1916 Major L. W. B. Rees (Woolwich) RA Att RFC, France
Brevet Major W. La T. Congreve, DSO, MC (Sandhurst) Rifle Brigade, France
Lieutenant W. L. Robinson (Sandhurst) Worcestershire Regt, RFC, England
Brevet Lieutenant Colonel J. V. Campbell, DSO (Sandhurst) Coldstream Guards, France

1917 Major G. C. Wheeler (Sandhurst) 9th Gurkha Rifles, Mesopotamia
2nd-Lieutenant T. H. B. Maufe (Woolwich) RA, France
Brigadier-General C. Coffin, DSO (Woolwich) RE, France
2nd-Lieutenant D. G. W. Hewitt (Sandhurst) Hampshire Regt, France
2nd-Lieutenant M. S. S. Moore (Sandhurst) Hampshire Regt, Belgium
Major L. P. Evans, DSO (Sandhurst) Royal Highlanders, Belgium
Lieutenant-Colonel A. D. Borton, DSO (Sandhurst) London Regt, Palestine
Captain N. B. Elliott-Cooper, DSO, MC (Sandhurst) Royal Fusiliers, France
Lieutenant W. M. Stone (Sandhurst) Royal Fusiliers, France

1918 Lieutenant J. R. Gribble (Sandhurst) Royal Warwick Regt, France
Major O. C. S. Watson, DSO (Sandhurst) County of London Yeomanry, France

Captain F. C. Roberts, DSO, MC (Sandhurst) Worcestershire Regt, France

Captain J. Forbes-Robertson, DSO, MC (Sandhurst) Border Regt, France

Brevet Lieutenant-Colonel G. W. St G. Grogan, CMG, DSO (Sandhurst) Worcestershire Regt, France

Captain C. E. Hudson, DSO, MC (Sandhurst) Notts & Derbyshire Regt, Italy

Major D. Burgess, DSO (Sandhurst) Gloucestershire Regt, Balkans

Brevet Major J. S. S. P. V. Viscount Gort, DSO, MVO, MC (Sandhurst) Grenadier Guards, France

Major G. de C. E. Findlay, MC (Woolwich) RE, France

Between the World Wars

1920   Captain G. S. Henderson, DSO, MC (Sandhurst) Manchester Regt, Mesopotamia

Captain G. Meynell, MC (Sandhurst) 5th/12th FF Regt, NW Frontier

During the Second World War

1940   Captain H. M. Ervine-Andrews (Sandhurst) East Lancashire Regt, France

Captain E. C. T. Wilson (Sandhurst) East Surrey Regt, Somaliland

1941   Lieutenant-Colonel G. C. T. Keyes, MC (Sandhurst) Royal Scots Greys, Middle East

Brigadier J. C. Campbell, DSO, MC (Woolwich) RHA, Middle East

Captain J. J. B. Jackman (Sandhurst) Royal Northumberland Fusiliers, Tobruk

1942   Lieutenant-Colonel H. R. B. Foote, DSO (Sandhurst) Royal Tank Regt, Middle East

Captain P. A. Porteous (Woolwich) RA, Dieppe

Lieutenant-Colonel V. B. Turner (Sandhurst) Rifle Brigade, Western Desert

1943   Lieutenant-Colonel D. A. Seagrim (Sandhurst) Green Howards, Middle East

1944   Major C. F. Hoey, MC (Sandhurst) Lincolnshire Regt, Burma

Captain L. E. Queripel (Sandhurst) Royal Sussex Regt, Arnhem

After the Second World War

1950   Major K. Muir (Sandhurst) Argyll & Sutherland Highlanders, Korea

1951   Lieutenant-Colonel J. P. Carne, DSO (Sandhurst) Gloucestershire Regt, Korea

1982   Lieutenant-Colonel H. Jones, OBE (Sandhurst) The Parachute Regt, The Falklands

APPENDIX D:
AWARDS OF THE GEORGE CROSS
made to former Woolwich and Sandhurst Gentlemen and Officer Cadets

THE GEORGE CROSS was created by King George VI on 23 September 1940, '. . . to rank next to the Victoria Cross and to be awarded to men and women for acts of supreme gallantry'. It was arranged in 1940 that surviving holders of an earlier award, the Empire Gallantry Medal (dating from 1920 as part of the Order of the British Empire), should send in these decorations and receive in return the GC. In 1971 this arrangement was extended on a voluntary basis to living holders of the Albert and Edward Medals (both being earlier distinctions awarded for the saving of life on land and sea, or for bravery in industrial accidents, respectively). The GC was of course awardable to both military and civilian recipients, in the former case for acts of great heroism conducted out of contact with the enemy (during bomb disposal for example), or in time of peace. Down to 1985, there had been 396 actual or transferred awards of the GC.

We have been at pains to gain accurate information on which regular Army Officers received these awards serving or posthumously; but there being, alas, no full records maintained at Woolwich or Sandhurst of all former Gentlemen or Officer Cadets who gained this distinction, there may be errors and omissions in the following list, which is integrated.*

Year	Date of Gazette**	Recipient	Regiment
1924	30 June	Major H. E. Burton (Woolwich)	Royal Engineers
1935	19 Nov	Lieutenant J. G. Cowley (Woolwich)	Madras Sappers & Miners (RE)
1937	9 July	Captain P. G. Taylor (Woolwich)	(former RFC/RE)
1937	24 December	Captain R. L. Japhson-Jones (Sandhurst)	Royal Army Ordnance Corps
1946	1 March	Brigadier A. F. C. Nicholls (Sandhurst)	Coldstream Guards
1946	18 March	Captain L. A. Newnham (Sandhurst)	Middlesex Regiment
1946	12 September	***Major H. P. Seagrim (Sandhurst)	19th Hyderabad Regiment
1954	13 April	Lieutenant T. E. Waters (Sandhurst)	West Yorkshire Regiment
1979	11 February	Captain R. L. Nairac (Sandhurst)	Grenadier Guards

*See F. G. Carroll. *The Register of the Geroge Cross*, London, 1985.
**Date of *London Gazette* entry was invariably much later than the deed of heroism itself.
***The brother of Lieutenant-Colonel D. A. Seagrim, VC, Green Howards (see page 269).

APPENDIX E:
GOVERNORS AND COMMANDANTS

1. The Royal Military Academy, Woolwich, 1764–1939

(The title was changed from Lieutenant-Governor to Governor in 1870, to Governor and Commandant in 1897 and to Commandant only in 1904.)

1764–77	Lieutenant-Colonel J. B. Pattison (RA)
1777–81	Lieutenant-Colonel Bramham (RE)
1781–95	Major B. Stehelin (RA)
1795–09	Lieutenant-Colonel W. Twiss (RE)
1809–20	Lieutenant-Colonel W. Mudge (RA)
1820–9	Captain W. H. Ford (RE)
1829–40	Colonel P. Drummond, CB (RA)
1840–6	Major-General Sir G. Whitworth, KCB (RE)
1846–51	Colonel J. B. Parker, CB (RA)
1851–6	Colonel G. C. Lewis, CB (RE)
1856–62	Colonel E. N. Wilford (RA)
1862–7	Major-General H. Sandham (RE)
1867–9	Major-General J. W. Ormsby (RA)
1869–75	Major-General Sir Lintorn Simmons, KCB (RE)
1875–80	Major-General Sir John Adye, KCB (RA)
1880–7	Major-General J. F. M. Browne, CB (RE)
1887–9	Major-General R. Hay, CB (RA)
1889–90	Major-General Sir Richard Harrison, KCB, CMG (RE)
1890–5	Major-General W. Stirling, CB (RA)
1895–7	Major-General E. O. Hewitt, CMG (RE)
1897–1901	Major-General F. T. Lloyd, CB (RA)
1901–4	Major-General R. H. Jelf, CMG (RE)
1904–8	Colonel H. V. Cowan, CVO (RA)
1908–12	Colonel A. G. Thompson, CB (RE)
1912–14	Brigadier-General A. E. A. Holland, MVO, DSO (RA)
1914–18	Major-General W. F. Cleave, CB (RA)
1918–20	Major-General G. H. A. White, CB, CMG, DSO (RA)
1920–4	Major-General Sir Webb Gillman, KCMG, CB, DSO (RA)
1924–6	Major-General J. R. E. Charles, CB, CMG, DSO (RE)
1926–30	Major-General H. D. De Pree, CB, CMG, DSO (RA)
1930–4	Major-General C. M. Wagstaff, CB, CIE, DSO (RE)
1934–8	Major-General A. A. Goschen, CB, DSO (RA)
1938–9	Major-General P. Neame, VC, DSO (RE)

2. The Royal Military College, Sandhurst (and its predecessors), 1800–1939

1800	Lieutenant-Governor	Lieutenant-Colonel J. G. Le Marchant
1801–11	Governor	General The Hon (from 1809, Earl) William Harcourt
1811–19	Governor	Major-General the Hon Alexander Hope
1819–23	Governor	Major-General Sir G. Murray, GCB
1824–5	Governor	Lieutenant-General the Hon Sir A. Hope, GCB
1826–36	Governor	General Hon Sir E. Paget, GCB
1837–55	Governor	Major-General Sir G. Scovell, KCB (later Lieutenant-General and General)*
1856–66	Governor	Major-General Sir H. D. Jones, KCB (later General)
1867–8	Governor	General Sir G. A. Wetherall, GCB, KH
1869–75	Governor	Lieutenant-General Sir D. A. Cameron, KCB (later General)
1876–82	Governor	Lieutenant-General W. C. E. Napier (later General)
1883–6	Governor	Lieutenant-General Sir R. C. H. Taylor, KCB (later General)
1887–8	Governor	Lieutenant-General D. Anderson
1889–93	Governor &	Major-General E. H. Clive,

*Editor-in-Chief's note: senior officers promoted to higher rank while on post at RMC are shown as such in parentheses.

	Commandant	psc
1894–8	Governor & Commandant	Major-General C. J. East, CB, psc (later Lieutenant-General)
1899–1902	Governor & Commandant	Lieutenant-General Sir E. Markham, KCB
1903–6	Commandant	Colonel G. C. Kitson, CMG, psc
1907–10	Commandant	Colonel W. B. Capper, psc
1911–14	Commandant	Colonel L. A. M. Stopford, psc
1915–16	Commandant	Colonel (Temp Brigadier-General) S. P. Rolt, CB
1917–19	Commandant	Colonel (Temp Brigadier-General) L. A. M. Stopford, CB, psc (later Major-General)
1920–3	Commandant	Major-General Sir R. B. Stephens, KCB, CMG, psc
1923	Commandant	Major-General T. H. Shoubridge, CB, CMG, DSO, psc (died at Government House)
1923–7	Commandant	Major-General C. E. Corkran, CB, CMG, psc
1928–31	Commandant	Major-General E. S. Girdwood, CB, CMG
1931–4	Commandant	Major-General Sir Reginald S. May, KBE, CB, CMG, DSO, psc (later Lieutenant-General)
1935–7	Commandant	Major-General B. D. Fisher, CB, CMG, DSO, psc
1938–9	Commandant	Major-General T. R. Eastwood, DSO, MC, psc
1939	Commandant	Brigadier M. Kemp-Welch, DSO, MC

3. OCTU Sandhurst

1939–41 Brigadier M. Kemp-Welch, DSO, MC
1941–2 Brigadier J. G. Bruxner-Randall

No 100 (RAC) OCTU
1942–3 Colonel G. E. Prior-Palmer
1943–4 Brigadier W. G. Carr, DSO
1944–6 Colonel W. M. Hutton, DSO, MC

No 161 (Inf) OCTU
1945–6 Lieutenant-Colonel Sir W. V. M. Akins, Bart, WG

Editor-in-Chief's note: OCTU Sandhurst comprised Nos 101 (RAC) and 161 (Inf) OCTUs until August 1942, when No 161 moved to Mons Barracks, Aldershot, and No 101 was renumbered 100. In early 1946, No 161 was moved back to Sandhurst and No 100 (RAC) moved away. The nucleus of what became the newly named Royal Military *Academy* Sandhurst dates from October 1946.

4. The Royal Military Academy, Sandhurst

1946–8 Major-General F. R. G. Matthews, DSO
1948–51 Major-General H. C. Stockwell, CB, DSO
1951–4 Major-General D. Dawnay, CB, DSO
1954–6 Major-General R. G. S. Hobbs, CB, DSO, OBE
1956–9 Major-General R. W. Urquhart, CB, DSO
1960–3 Major-General G. C. Gordon Lennox, CB, CVO, DSO

1963–6 Major-General H. J. Mogg, CB, CBE, DSO
1966–8 Major-General P. M. Hunt, CB, DSO, OBE
1968–72 Major-General P. T. Tower, CB, DSO, MBE
1972–3 Major-General J. W. Harman, CBE, MC
1973–6 Major-General R. C. Ford, CB, CBE
1976–9 Major-General Sir Philip Ward, KCVO, CBE
1979–82 Major-General R. M. H.

Vickers, MVO, OBE
1982–3 Major-General G. W. H. Howlett, OBE, MC
1983–7 Major-General R. C. Keightley, CB
1987–9 Major-General S. C. Cooper
1989–91 Major-General P. W. Graham, CBE
1991– Major-General T. P. Toyne-Sewell

APPENDIX F: AWARDS OF THE SWORD OF HONOUR AND THE QUEEN'S (LATER KING'S) MEDAL, 1836–1939
made to former Woolwich Gentlemen Cadets

WE ARE INDEBTED to Lieutenant-Colonel (Retd) W. N. D. Turner, Royal Artillery (who was a Gentleman Cadet at 'The Shop' from 1932 to 1934) for the following paragraphs:

'At the Royal Military Academy Woolwich the two top awards were officially the Sword of Honour and the Queen's (later King's) Medal [from 1897]. The former was given for 'exemplary conduct' and the latter went to the Gentleman Cadet best qualified in Military Subjects. In the opinion of many Gentleman Cadets, however, both awards ranked after the 'Saddle' prize for equestrian ability.

From 1900 until the closure of the 'Shop' in 1939, eighty-seven swords and seventy-eight medals were presented. In only nine cases did one recipient receive both awards; six Sappers and three Gunners. Not all recipients achieved high rank and in four cases military careers lasted less than five years. The following awards were made from 1836:

Year	Sword of Honour		Year	Sword of Honour		Year	Sword of Honour	
1836	C. A. Broke	RE	1854	R. O'Hara	RA	1869	C. C. Lindsay	RA
1837	F. W. D'Alton	RE		W. G. Martin	RA		C. H. Johnston	RE
1838	G. C. Bailie	RE		A. E. de V. Tupper	RA	1870	M. K. Brady	RE
1839	J. Bayly	RE		C. D. Bevan	RA		P. Cardew	RE
1840	J. B. Lukyen	RE	1855	O. H. Goodenough	RA	1871	H. G. Kunhardt	RE
	H. W. Barlow	RE		J. A. Papillon	RE	1872	J. H. C. Harrison	RE
	H. Y. D. Scott	RE		R. Sandham	RA		J. J. Leverson	RE
1841	No award recorded			L. C. A. A. de Cetto	RA		R. C. Maxwell	RE
1842	V. T. Mairis	RE	1856	F. B. Mainguy	RE	1873	J. C. Campbell	RE
	C. R. Binney	RE	1857	W. S. Brown	RA		M. H. P. R. Sankey	RE
1843	F. R. Chesney	RE		H. M. Moorsom	RA	1874	C. F. Hadden	RA
	B. H. Martindale	RE		H. G. Sitwell	RE		H. M. Sinclair	RE
	J. Stokes	RE	1858	R. H. B. Beaumont	RE	1875	M. A. Cameron	RE
1844	A. E. H. Anson	RA		L. Gye	RA		H. J. Foster	RE
	Hon E. T. Gage	RA		S. Anderson	RE	1876	W. T. Hawkins	RE
1845	C. B. Ewart	RE	1859	T. Howard	RE		J. H. Cowan	RE
	E. C. A. Gordon	RE		A. L. Buckle	RE	1877	J. A. Henderson	RE
1846	A. R. V. Crease	RE	1860	J. H. Urquhart	RE		W. C. Hussey	RE
	F. E. Cox	RE		J. M. Saunders	RA	1878	S. R. Rice	RE
	G. C. Henry	RA	1861	G. E. Townsend	RA		E. Druitt	RE
1847	G. H. Gordon	RE		G. A. L. Whitmore	RE		E. H. Armitage	RA
	H. R. Pelly	RE	1862	T. Fraser	RE	1879	S. G. Burrard	RE
	A. B. Tyers	RE		W. G. Ross	RE		J. Dallas	RE
	S. Carden	RA	1863	F. Q. Edmonds	RE	1880	R. S. Maclagan	RE
1848	A. Leahy	RE		J. M. Hunter	RA		M. Nathan	RE
	W. O. Lennox	RE	1864	J. C. Menzies	RE		F. J. Aylmer	RE
	W. Crossman	RE		J. J. Curling	RE	1881	J. E. Edmondes	RE
1849	C. Carpenter	RE	1865	S. L. Jacob	RE	1882	J. R. L. Macdonald	RE
1850	W. Stirling	RA		H. Jekyll	RE		R. J. H. Mackenzie	RE
	W. A. Fox-Strangways	RA	1866	S. Buckle	RE	1883	G. A. S. Stone	RE
				H. G. L. Turnbull	RA		W. G. Lawrie	RE
1851	C. N. Martin	RE	1867	F. R. de Wolski	RE	1884	T. Harrison	RE
	R. C. Longey	RA		R. Gardiner	RE		E. A. C. Jones	RE
1852	F. G. Ravenhill	RA	1868	J. C. McGregor	RE		E. A. Edgell	RE
	F. G. E. Warren	RA		H. H. S. Cunynghame	RE	1885	H. B. Williams	RE
1853	A. Walsham	RA					G. P. Lenox-	

Year	Sword of Honour		Year	Sword of Honour		Year	Sword of Honour	
	Conyngham	RE		J. M. C. Colvin	RE		A. J. Savage	RE
1886	H. M. St A. Wade	RE	1890	S. H. Sheppard	RE	1894	F. B. Tillard	RE
	W. S. Nathan	RE		R. P. T. Hawksley	RE		J. R. E. Charles	RE
1887	E. C. Ogilvie	RE	1891	H. F. E. Freeland	RE	1895	F. W. Robertson	RE
	P. T. Bourne	RE		J. G. Austin	RA		W. Stirling	RA
1888	E. G. Godfrey-Faussett	RE	1892	E. C. Tylden-Pattenson	RE	1896	J. O'H Moore	RE
	H. Coningham	RA		E. B. Macnaghten	RA		L. W. Melan	RE
1889	H. M. Thomas	RA	1893	W. C. Syman	RE			

Year	Sword of Honour		Queen Victoria's Medal		Year	Sword of Honour		The King's Medal	
1897	W. C. E. Twidale	RA	C. M. Wagstaff	RE	1915	J. A. E. Frend	RA	–	
	A. J. Turner	RA	R. F. A. Hobbs	RE		D. H. MacDonald	RE	–	
1898	S. F. Newcombe	RE	L. Evans	RE	1916	W. G. Frend	RA	T. F. M. Gayford	RE
	L. N. F. J. King	RE	E. F. J. Hill	RE		J. L. Howell	RA	R. T. Williams	RE
1899	C. Hordern	RE	T. H. L. Spaight	RE		T. L. G. Tod	RA	–	
	A. H. Du Boulay	RE	C. C. Trench	RE		G. A. N. Swiney	RA	–	
1900	F. A. Finnis	RA	M. N. Macleod	RE	1917	R. L. Holmes	RE	W. Porter	RE
	C. S. Rich	RA	E. W. Cox	RE		E. A. L. Gueterbock	RE	T. C. Barker	RE
	A. J. G. Bird	RA	–			C. A. de Linde	RE	–	
			The King's Medal		1918	L. W. R. Roberston	RA	S. W. Joslin	RE
						C. H. F. D'A McCarthy	RE	W. G. C. Glossop	RA
1901	D. A. Strachan	RA	W. Garforth	RE	1919	J. A. Sinclair	RA	A. H. Napier	RE
	A. B. Ogle	RE	C. W. Bushell	RE		M. J. Renton	RE	W. H. Ray	RE
1902	E. H. Kelly	RE	E. St G Kirke	RE		A. Murray	RA	–	
	C. R. Satterthwaite	RE	J. S. Richardson	RE	1920	H. G. Wainwright	RE	E. V. Daldy	RE
1903	L. V. Bond	RE	L. V. Bond	RE		F. E. Robertson	RA	M. Stephen	RA
	R. H. Stallard	RE	L. C. B. Deed	RE	1921	G. N. Tuck	RE	G. N. Tuck	RE
1904	D. E. Courtney	RE	A. A. Chase	RE		H. S. Kay	RE	N. A. M. Swettenham	RE
	C. S. Lewis	RE	R. S. Ryan	RA	1922	E. S. De Brett	RE	A. J. H. Dove	RE
1905	G. C. H. White	RE	E. M. Sinauer	RE		B. E. Whitman	RE	J. B. Tupman	RA
	G. G. Waterhouse	RE	G. G. Waterhouse	RE	1923	L. G. Thomas	RE	L. R. E. Fayle	RE
1906	R. W. Ling	RA	R. A. Cammell	RE		R. H. M. Hill	RA	E. L. Kellett	RE
	M. Everett	RE	A. F. Day	RE	1924	R. N. Foster	RE	A. W. Kiggell	RE
1907	A. J. Woodhouse	RA	F. V. B. Witts	RE		G. D. McK Sutherland	RE	J. C. R. FitzGerald-Lombard	RE
	F. H. Huleatt	RA	M. F. G. White	RE	1925	C. D. T. Pope	RA	W. F. Anderson	RE
1908	G. G. Rawson	RE	J. P. S. Greig	RE		J. P. Chapman	RE	J. P. Chapman	RE
	R. P. Pakenham-Walsh	RE	R. P. Pakenham-Walsh	RE		R. W. Urquhart	RE	J. McC Smith	RE
1909	J. N. Thomson	RA	C. L. T. Matheson	RE	1926	F. M. Hill	RE	W. B. Sallitt	RE
	J. N. Fletcher	RE	R. E. Gordon	RE		M. C. Perceval	RE	M. C. Perceval	RE
1910	C. J. S. King	RE	C. J. S. King	RE	1927	M. T. G. Wood	RA	R. W. Ewbank	RE
	H. C. B. Wemyss	RE	W. O. Winter	RE		S. S. Fielden	RA	A. E. H. Hamilton	RA
1911	E. E. Calthrop	RE	E. De S. Rideout	RE	1928	R. G. S. Hobbs	RA	C. L. Richardson	RE
	A. C. L. Perkins	RE	I. C. Reid	RE		M. A. W. Rowlandson	RA	D. W. Price	RE
1912	G. E. Mansergh	RE	G. E. Mansergh	RE	1929	N. L. Foster	RA	K. R. Brazier-Creagh	RA
	F. L. V. Mills	RA	G. L. Miller	RE		R. K. Page	RA	P. G. Hatch	RE
1913	A. A. M. Durand	RA	E. F. Tickell	RE	1930	G. C. Grimshaw	RA	J. G. McKendrick	RE
	E. R. Culverwell	RA	H. P. W. Hutson	RE		W. A. R. Sumner	RA	A. P. Lavies	RA
1914	J. C. Tyler	RA	A. D. Pank	RE	1931	M. StJ Oswald	RA	M. StJ Oswald	RA
	G. L. Reid	RE	R. T. Harmer	RE		C. H. Baker	RA	H. C. R. Gillman	RA
	J. M. Mayne	RA	–						
	E. E. Nott-Bower	RE	–						
1915	M. M. Jeakes	RE	H. A. Kenyon	RE					
	R. Mansell	RA	O. C. H. Osmaston	RE					

Year	Sword of Honour		The King's Medal		Year	Sword of Honour		The King's Medal	
1932	J. R. H. Robertson	RE	A. F. Bell	RE	1935	A. F. Stanton	RA	G. A. P. N. Barlow	RE
	P. C. Williams	RE	H. L. Lloyd	RE	1936	N. C. G. Charteris	RE	R. N. K. Barge	RE
1933	A. F. M. Jack	RE	J. R. Graeme	RA		J. D. L. Dickson	RA	P. M. Ronaldson	RE
	R. K. Jones	RA	C. Belfield	RE	1937	G. T. A. Armitage	RA	W. G. F. Jackson	RE
1934	W. A. M. Miller	RA	H. C. G. Cartwright-Taylor	RE		R. H. W. Dunn	RA	R. F. Harris	RE
	W. M. Inglis	RE	A. F. Coombe	RE	1938	J. A. Goschen	RA	M. H. D. Lovell	RA
1935	J. D. C. Ellison	RE	J. D. C. Ellison	RE		J. G. Palmer	RA	J. G. Palmer	RA
					1939	R. J. G. Heaven	RA	F. G. Burns	RE

Information from printed lists kindly provided by Philip Annis, Manager of the Regimental History Project of the Royal Artillery Institution, Old Royal Military Academy, Woolwich.

It is clear that sappers tended to predominate over gunners in both awards – the totals to 1939 being:

Sword of Honour:	RE 144 :	RA 78
Queen's/King's Medal:	RE 72 :	RA 13

There were four other major awards given at Woolwich:

1. The Pollock Medal (commemorating Major-General Sir George Pollock), originally issued at Addiscombe College to '. . . the most Distinguished Cadet of the season' with the sum of sixteen guineas by the Court of Directors of the East India Company, and transferred to Woolwich in 1862. From that date the award was made to 'the most Distinguished Cadet at RMA Woolwich' (later described as 'the Best Qualified Cadet') with a rationalized sum of only ten guineas.

2. The Toombs Memorial Prize (commemorating Major-General Sir Henry Toombs d.1874), first awarded at RMAW in 1877 to '. . . the Best Qualified Cadet entering the Royal Artillery'.

3. The Benson Memorial Prize first awarded in 1903 to the '. . . Cadet entering the Royal Artillery with highest marks in War Material, Tactics and Riding'.

4. The Armstrong Memorial Prize awarded to the 'Best Cadet in Advanced Electricity'.

It has not been practicable to list the winners of these four prestigious prizes for reasons of space – priority being given to winners of the Sword and the Medal as there were roughly equivalent awards at Sandhurst.

In addition there was the *British Phillpotts Memorial Prize* for Military History from 1921 (still awarded at RMA Sandhurst), the *Rainey Anderson Memorial Prize* (from 1912) for the best RE entrant in French (from 1934 in Advanced Mathematics in lieu); and the *Agar Memorial Prize* (from 1934) for the 'Best Qualified Cadet entering the Royal Corps of Signals'.

APPENDIX G: AWARDS OF THE SWORD OF HONOUR AND THE QUEEN'S (LATER KING'S) MEDAL, 1890–1939
made to former Sandhurst Gentleman Cadets

The Sword of Honour has long been awarded to the individual considered by the Governor or Commandant to be the best of his course. The Medal similarly goes to the individual who achieved the best overall results (or, in earlier years, who came top in the final Order of Merit).

Although there were certainly awards of merit at the Royal Military College long before 1890 – it is known, for example, that the selected young men were allowed to choose between a Sword and a Revolver in the 1880s – there appears to have been no Sword of Honour as such

before 1890, and no Queen's (later King's) Medal before 1897. The names that follow are taken from the Honours Boards displayed in the Central Library at Sandhurst, and I am grateful to the Senior Librarian, Andrew Orgill Esq., MA, Dip Lib, ALA, for permitting me to transcribe them.

There were generally two awards a year of both Sword and (when instituted) Medal, reflecting the two Passing Out Parades. In some years (as in 1901, 1914 and 1915) there was only a single award of the Sword made, but in others there were three (see, for example, 1917 and 1918).

Year	The Sword of Honour	
1890	H. G. McL Amos	WIR
	H. E. B. Leach	NF
1891	A. D. Macpherson	Mid
	D. R. Napier	OLI
1892	W. E. Skyes	Y&L
	C. R. Bradshaw	RWK
1893	J. A. S. Balmain	15th H
	The Viscount Crichton	RHG
1894	Hon J. F. Gaythorne-Hardy	Gren G
	W. H. Greenly	12th Line
1895	C. S. Rome	11th H
	C. Bonham-Carter	RWK
1896	N. N. Ramsay	BW
	B. F. Burnett-Hitchcock	SF
1897	W. H. V. Darell	CG
	G. O. Turnbull	26th PunjR
1898	G. C. Cobden	9th L
	C. A. G. P. Meadows	7th RajR

Queen Victoria's Medal	
J. C. Freeland	36th SI
G. H. Walford	Suf
H. R. von D. Hardinge	Hamp
C. J. Buchanan	35th SI
R. Johnston	4th BL
G. G. J. Sankey	38th SI
L. S. Gurney-Whitchurch	1st PunjC
P. B. Maxwell	35th SI
G. L. Blair	36th SI
G. N. Shea	RMR

1899	G. A. Sullivan	OLI
	J. R. F. Stansfeld	Gord
1900	B. Maclear	RDF
	P. V. Holberton	Man

Year	Sword of Honour	
1901	Hon M. V. B. Brett	CG
1902	J. Gray	SIKR
	H. W. M. Yates	LF
1903	R. Houstun	Roy
	R. E. K. Leatham	Gren G
1904	H. I. E. Ripley	Wor
	D. Harvey	31st PunjR
1905	J. A. C. Brooke	Gordon
	D. C. Boles	17th L

The King's Medal	
D. B. Ross	19th PunjR
Hon M. W. R. de Courcy	CR
J. L. Ranking	46th PunjR
A. T. Wilson	32nd SP
J. B. W. Hay	36th SI
D. F. Anderson	Devon
J. J. P. Evans	RWF
G de la Poer-Beresford	10 DCOL

Year	Sword of Honour		The King's Medal	
1906	C. F. F. Moore	DR	W. A. C. Saunders-Knox-Gore	KRRC
	W. M. Parker	RB	H. J. Daniell	20th DCOI
1907	I. C. Macfadyen	IA	C. F. T. Swan	RB
	B. Osborne	15th H	A. E. Barstow	15th Ludhiana Sikhs
1908	H. V. Lewis	129th Bal	H. V. Lewis	129th DCO Bal
	C. E. H. Tempest-Hicks	16th L	W. H. G. Baker	31st DCOL
1909	R. E. Anstruther	BW	A. H. Williams	38th CIH
	G. B. Henderson	15th Sikh R	H. R. C. Mead	8th GR
1910	A. F. Smith	CG	C. W. Mason Macfarlane	7H
	L. A. Barrett	NF	F. de B Allfrey	9L
1911	R. St L. Fowler	17th L	G. Watson	96th BerI
	J. G. Crabbe	Grey	N. H. Edwards	7 GR
1912	M. S. H. Jones	CIH	G. T. Cartland	RB
	D. Beanland	22nd PunjR	R. H. Stable	122 RajputI
1913	D. W. Hunter-Blair	Gordon	E. C. E. Smith	9L
	A. L. W. Neave	GC	G. H. Lane	103rd MahLI
1914	A. H. Blacklock	ASH	A. A. E. Filose	39th CIH
			G. H. St P Bunbury	15th Ludhiana Sikhs
1915	D. W. Bisshopp	RB	G. S. Rawstone	Sea
			D. W. Bisshopp	RB
1916	M. A. Carthew-Yorstown	BW	M. A. Carthew-Yorstown	BW
	J. H. Growse	Nor R	W. R. N. Pole-Carew	DCLI
1917	M. V. Smelt	GC	C. W. Lovegrove	Sea
	H. W. C. Craigmile	Sea	F. G. Garrard	Gord
	H. C. Daly	BW	T. H. F. Le Mesurier	QVO GFF
			F. K. W. Rodger	RS
1918	M. C. St J. Hornby	Gren G	D. J. Clarkson	N&D
	J. S. Paterson	Gren G	J. C. S. Sampson	11th GR
	J. O. Doyle	NSR	B. Mayfield	SG
1919	R. A. I. Brooke	KOYLI	F. W. Young	Lin
	J. Y. E. Myrtle	KOSB	E. J. C. King-Salter	RB
1920	H. A. Macdonald	9th L	R. R. Proud	6 GR
	I. J. Kilgour	NF	D. J. Purdon	RB
			J. F. Walker	KOYLI
1921	W. A. H. Maxwell	KOSB	W. A. G. Douglas	Devon
	A. S. Hanning	Norf	H. L. Boultbee	RWR
1922	J. E. Fairlie	SP	J. E. Fairlic	SP
	W. N. Roper-Caldbeck	BW	W. N. Roper-Caldbeck	BW
1923	G. E. Prior Palmer	9th L	K. W. Ross-Hurst	6 GR
	N. M. H. Tighe	WY	J. H. Brown	DLI
1924	The Master of Belhaven	RSF	Sir W. de Barttelot	CG
			V. D. G. Campbell	Cam
	W. Enderby	Bay	B. McCall	RF
1925	H. R. Mackeson	Grey	H. R. Mackeson	Grey
	H. W. S. Monck	CG	A. S. Milner	RSig
1926	A. J. H. Cassels	Sea	L. H. Bean	SLI
	F. H. W. Barnett	KRRC	J. C. B. Shearer	RTC
1927	C. A. R. Nevill	RF	C. A. R. Nevill	RF
	J. A. M. Rice-Evans	RWF	G. C. Gordon-Lennox	Gren G
1928	P. F. Prideaux-Brune	BW	L. W. G. Hamilton	DR
	C. I. H. Dunbar	SG	R. H. Barry	SLI
1929	D. J. A. Stuart	RSF	W. G. Roe	RASC
	R. W. Hobson	12 L	H. J. C. Hunt	KRRC
1930	C. N. M. Blair	BW	A. D. Taylor	15/19 H
	P. J. Keen	Hamp	R. K. F. Belchem	RTC

Year	Sword of Honour		The King's Medal	
1931	S. J. L. Hill	RF	T. S. Taylor	14th PunjR
	J. A. R. Freeland	Q	E. C. Stanton	KRRC
1932	R. A. Fyffe	RB	G. R. D. Fitzpatrick	Roy
	Hon H. A. C. Howard	CG	S. R. Fox	KOYLI
1933	H. C. Lyons-Montgomery	2 GR	A. N. W. Kidston	ASH
	R. J. S. Rust	RF	I. C. S. Rose	KSLI
1934	R. V. E. Hodson	12th FFR	D. L. Darling	RB
	C. S. M. Madden	KRRC	R. M. P. Carver	RTC
1935	G. E. Pike	Gren G	N. Croyenden	Ches
	S. M. Rose	RF	B. H. Ewart	RTC
1936	H. A. Jefferies	RIF	H. A. Jefferies	RIF
	D. S. Shuttleworth	KOYLI	T. H. Acton	RB
1937	H. J. Mogg	O&BLI	A. J. C. Stanton	14/20 H
	T. R. Glancy	19th L	D. W. Jackson	RWK
1938	F. E. F. Johnston	2nd L	E. G. B. Davies-Scourfield	KRRC
	C. Blair	Sea	C. B. Joly	RTC
1939	P. N. Steptoe	HLI	R. W. Ingall	6 GR

APPENDIX H: AWARDS OF THE SWORD OF HONOUR, 1943–6
made at 161 Infantry Officer Cadet Training Unit, Aldershot (and Royal Military College)

Year	Sword of Honour		Year	Sword of Honour	
1943	W. S. Watters	RSF		W. H. Jans	Sea (of Canada)
	C. D. Stenton	RIF		W. V. Pulman	NZA
	D. W. Grigg	Ex		A. J. Kennedy	SD&GH
	G. W. Lamb	Gren G		A. J. Traplin	PPCLI
	J. J. How	SWB		L. A. Hanson	CA
1944	D. G. Aitchson	ASH	1946	J. F. G. Hayes	Q
	R. D. C. Bacon	IG		A. R. McIndoe	SG
	G. H. G. Doggart	CG		B. D. Bateman	RWR
	F. D. L. Davis	QORWKent		A. M. Cameron	ASH
	G. C. Francis	O&BLI		R. G. Lagden	QOCH
	W. L. Lyster	CH		A. R. S. Tower	CG
	N. M. Marsh	CA		J. V. Miseroy	Ex
	H. F. Hamilton-Dalrymple	CG			
1945	C. S. Eaden-Clarke	DERR			
	R. Woolman	RRR			

Information is not at present available for awards made to OCdts in the RAC OCTU.

APPENDIX I:
AWARDS OF THE SWORD OF HONOUR AND THE KING'S (LATER QUEEN'S) MEDAL, 1948–90
made at the Royal Military Academy, Sandhurst

Year		Sword of Honour		Year		King's Medal	
1948	July	N. Webb-Bowen	WG	1948	July	W. M. E. Hicks	CG
	Oct	M. H. Blakeney	RA		Oct	G. W. Daughtry	RE
	Dec	R. M. H. Vickers	RTR		Dec	R. M. H. Vickers	RTR
1949	July	J. M. Glover	RA	1949	July	M. R. Johnston	RA
	Dec	J. A. Teague	RF		Dec	H. S. L. Dalzell-Payne	QOH
1950	July	P.Burdick	Devon	1950	July	T. A. Linley	RE
1951	Feb	J. F. H. Pease-Watkin	RA	1951	Feb	J. F. H. Pease-Watkin	RA
	Aug	J. D. Bastick	RTR		Aug	J. D. C. Blake	Devon
						The Queen's Medal	
1952	Feb	A. M. Tippett	RB	1952	Feb	J. Lewins	RE
	July	M. F. T. Griffiths	RWF		July	P. C. Harvey	RE
1953	Feb	B. C. Gordon Lennox	Gren G	1953	Feb	D. R. Walters	RTR
	July	A. D Myrtle	KOSB		July	C. J. Rougier	RE
1954	Feb	Lord Patrick Beresford	RHG	1954	Feb	A. F. Heatly	RWK
	Aug	B. L. G. Kenny	QOH		July	D. H. A. Swinburn	RE
1955	Feb	P. L. Dell	RE	1955	Feb	R. J. N. Leonard	RE
	July	S. T. G. Morgan	RA		July	C. W. Beckett	RE
	Dec	A. L. Crutchley	R&NSC		Dec	N. M. Pughe	RA
1956	July	A. C. D. Lloyd	RE	1956	July	A. C. D. Lloyd	RE
	Dec	C. G. Cornock	RA		Dec	D. Kiggell	RE
1957	Aug	A. D. W. Abbot-Anderson	RB	1957	Aug	R. H. Marriott	RE
	Dec	D. F. Mallam	RTR		Dec	A. R. Brook	RE
1958	Aug	G. B. Fawcus	RE	1958	Aug	R. A. Sparrow	KSLI
	Dec	N. J. Redmayne	Gren G		Dec	A. R. P. Carden	QRIH
1959	July	H. D. H. Keatinge	RHR	1959	July	K. G. Wakely	Q
	Dec	J. L. Parkes	2GR		Dec	A. S. G. Drew	KRRC
1960	July	R. M. Gamble	KRRC	1960	July	Malik Ghulam Mohd Khan	Bal
	Dec	P. V. Hervey	15/19 H		Dec	M. J. Hammerton	REME
1961	July	R. M. Stancombe	RE	1961	July	A. R. Cattaway	RA
	Dec	C. J. P. Miers	KRRC		Dec	C. I. P. Webb	3 DG
1962	Aug	R. J. Coate	DD	1962	Aug	C. P. Hook	RE
	Dec	D. A. Williams	R&WI		Dec	C. B. Q. Wallace	KRRC
1963	July	P. G. Chamberlin	1GJ	1963	July	P. M. R. Hill	RE
	Dec	S. W. G. Pettigrew	RTR		Dec	K. A. Mitcheson	RA
1964	July	W. G. N. Ross	SG	1964	July	I. D. Zvegintzov	CG
	Dec	M. R. Farlan	RNZI		Dec	B. W. Norris	RE
1965	July	T. J. Bremridge	RA	1965	July	P. P. White	RSig
	Dec	J. F. Deverell	SCLI		Dec	N. W. F. Richards	RA
1966	July	C. H. A. Hawker	GJ	1966	July	L. D. Curran	REME
	Dec	J. T. Strong	RA		Dec	J. G. Baker	RE
1967	July	J. H. Ellicock	RA	1967	July	M. J. C. Ashmore	RE
	Dec	A. M. Mitchell	RA		Dec	P. A. Garge	REME

Year		Sword of Honour		Year		The Queen's Medal	
1968	Aug	A. G. W. Jackson	GJ	1968	Aug	A. G. W. Jackson	GJ
	Dec	P. R. P. Swanson	Q		Dec	G. F. Pearce	RNZAC
1969	July	J. R. M. Hackett	WFR	1969	July	J. T. M. Hackett	WFR
	Dec	D. A. J. Noble	BW		Dec	M. H. C. Fraser	Gord
1970	July	S. H. R. H. Monro	QOH	1970	July	A. P. Ridgway	RTR
	Dec	N. C. D. Lithgow	BW		Dec	N. C. D. Lithgow	BW
1971	July	A. H. Van Straubenzee	GJ	1971	July	C. W. M. Carter	QOH
1972	Apr	C. H. A. Burrell	RH	1972	Apr	G. M. S. Tablot	RE
	Aug	J. C. Brannam	RE		Aug	J. C. Brannam	RE
	Dec	R. C. J. Martin	GJ		Dec	P. K. Wilkinson	RA
1973	Mar	G. F. Lesinski	GrenG	1973	Mar	G. F. Lesinski	GrenG
	Mar	J. S. Lloyd	GrenG			J. S. Lloyd	GrenG
	Mar	J. W. Cornforth	RSig				
	June	Lord Balgonie	QOH		Aug	J. A. Pinel	RE
	Nov	R. E. H. Aubrey-Fletcher	GrenG		Dec	R. A. Steel	RGJ
1974	Mar	C. M. Craggs	9/12 L	1974	Apr	P. Smart	REME
	June	The Marquis of Beaumont	RHG/D		Aug	P. J. Wright	KOB
	Nov	M. B. D. Smith	RGJ		Dec	W. McDonald, BEM	RRF
1975	Mar	R. L. M. Hackett	WFR	1975	Aug	W. F. Burdett	AAC
	June	D. N. Smith	RA		Dec	R. Baxter	RSig
	Nov	M. J. Trueman	2GR				
1976	Mar	S. C. Rodwell	QOH	1976	May	M. G. Beazley	RE
	Aug	D. B. Simpson	17/21 L		Oct	I. M. Caws	RE
	Dec	T. S. Spicer	SG				
1977	Apr	M. W. Parrish	RE	1977	Mar	D. B. Simpson	17/21 L
	Aug	P. A. Duncan	RA		July	D. P. Moran	AAC
	Dec	S. M. M. Hughes	RWF		Nov	K. T. Bacon	RMP
1978	Apr	A. L. Nevill	REME	1978	Mar	P. A. Duncan	RA
	Aug	S. R. Tustin	RTR		July	S. M. M. Hughes	RWF
	Dec	N. D. Oliver	SDG		Nov	J. C. Effort	RE
1979	Apr	M. R. S. Macrae	QOH	1979	Mar	S. F. Sherry	RE
	Aug	E. F. Hobbs	GrenG		July	P. J. King	DERR
	Dec	M. W. Tovey	GH		Nov	C. A. J. Bromley Gardner	QOH
1980	Apr	S. R. C. King	RE	1980	Mar	C. J. R. Blunt	13/18 H
	Aug	M. J. C. Payne	LI		July	T. G. Tan	Sing AF
	Dec	E. C. Gordon Lennox	GrenG		Nov	C. P. Bilson	RE
1981	Apr	G. K. Bibby	GrenG	1981	Mar	T. R. P. Riall	15/19 H
	Aug	B. K. Rawat	7GR		July	A. M. Hood	RCT
	Dec	A. M. Sugden	Glos		Nov	A. C. W. Mackenzie	REME
1982	Apr	T. D. P. O'Leary	7GR	1982	Mar	C. N. Hewitt	17/21 L
	Aug	A. W. Fortescue	CG		July	A. M. Roxburgh	QDG
	Dec	A. J. Rock	RSig		Oct	T. M. Burgess	RSig
1983	Apr	C. R. Claridge	RRF	1983	Apr	D. M. Limb	Para
	Aug	M. M. Lillingston-Price	7GR		Aug	N. T. Jefferson	RA
	Dec	R. J. Mitchell	REME				
1984	Apr	A. W. M. Bridge	QDG	1984	Apr	W. N. Aldridge	RRF
	Aug	J. D. G. Merchisten	ASH		Aug	L. A. Gunn	KOSB
	Dec	D. S. Wilson	RA				
1985	Apr	D. B. Ruff	RAOC	1985	Apr	N. A. W. Pope	RSig
	Aug	S. N. Jackson, BEM	RSig		Aug	A. S. Fergusson	AAC
	Dec	C. B. Hopkinson-Woolley	4/7 DG				
1986	Apr	A. C. Mayfield	SG	1986	Apr	G. C. N. Lane-Fox	RHG/D
	Aug	P. A. E. Nanson	RRF		Aug	M. P. Grant	Para
	Dec	R. McArthur	Gord				
1987	Apr	A. E. Mallon	Q	1987	Apr	T. C. St J Warrington	10GR
	Aug	N. A. Russell	RAPC		Aug	J. P. Slay	RWF

Year		Sword of Honour		Year		The Queen's Medal	
1987	Dec	D. G. H. Hunter	RAng				
1988	Apr	No award due to course reorganization (see Graduate Sword)		1988	Apr	K. J. D. Hume	RWF
	Aug	G. W. Fletcher	RSig		Aug	P. J. Ryalls	Para
	Dec	J. R. Millard	RE		Dec	D. J. Steel	RHF
1989	Apr	A. D. MacGillivray	BW	1989	Apr	S. R. H. Dennis	RTR
	Aug	W. J. Saunders	RAng		Aug	C. J. Tupper	WRAC
	Dec	C. J. Scudds	AAC		Dec	C. R. Marks	RIR
1990	Apr	S. Gallagher	WG	1990	Apr	B. A. Duxbury	AAC
	Aug	S. T. P. Gilderson	2GR		Aug	A. A. Fyfe	LI
	Dec	T. H. Halse	Para		Dec	J. M. Cowan	RAPC

Graduate Sword of Honour Winners, 1988–90

In 1988 the sword-makers Wilkinson presented a Sword of Honour to be awarded to the Graduate student-officer considered to be the best of his course.

1988	Apr	C. K. B. Melville	RSDG
	Aug	A. J. Kasket	Gren G
1989	Apr	S. R. H. Dennis, RTR (who also received the Medal)	
	Aug	J. M. S. Wilkinson	RHG/D

1990	Apr	L. P. M. Japp	SG
	Aug	J. C. Telfer	RSDG

Editor's Note. As there are only two Standard Graduate Course intakes per year, there is no award of the Graduate Sword of Honour at the December Sovereign's Parade as no Graduates march up the steps on that occasion.

APPENDIX J:
THE OVERSEAS CANE WINNERS

Date	Cane Winner	
1973		
March	K. K. Bader	Iraq
Nov	S. A. Sohemi	Malaysia
1974		
March	K. L. Soh	Singapore
Aug	Amneck Singh	Malaysia
Dec	Halim Bin Awang	Malaysia
1975		
March	A. Akinyemi	Nigeria
Aug	B. T. Garsama	Nigeria
Dec	A. Manaf	Malaysia
1976		
March	D. M. Komo	Nigeria
Aug	L. E. Alexander	Trinidad & Tobago
Dec	P. Joseph	Trinidad & Tobago
1977		
Apr	M. El Medani	Egypt
Aug	G. H. Noori	Iraq
Dec	A. A. Young	Jamaica
1978		
Apr	J. Frempong	Ghana
Aug	C. O. Rodriquez	Jamaica
Dec	Kamaruzaman Bin Bahrin	Malaysia
1979		
Apr	L. Naivalurue	Fiji
Aug	Hamood Al Shadafat	Jordan
Dec	R. Sooroojebally	Mauritius
1980		
Apr	Mohd Tajna Bin Alwi	Malaysia
Aug	E. E. Arthuss	Belize
Dec	S. S. Mahendra	Malaysia
1981		
Apr	G. K. Ouya	Kenya
Aug	A. Asare	Ghana
Dec	P. R. Lomaboma	Fiji
1982		
Apr	G. M. Ignace	Mauritius
Aug	G. M. Clarke	Trinidad & Tobago

Date	Cane Winner	
Dec	J. M. A. Reid	Jamaica
1983		
Apr	J. M. Ikinya	Kenya
Aug	Ali Kalefa Al Rashed	Jordan
Dec	H. C. McKenzie	Jamaica
1984		
Apr	M. A. Ince	Barbados
Aug	L. Gillett	Belize
Dec	D. A. Smellie	Jamaica
1985		
Apr	R. Meade	Jamaica
Aug	Al Naamani	Oman
Dec	A. Jamal	Jordan
1986		
Apr	G. Roper	Jamaica
Aug	C. T. P. Lim	Singapore
Dec	C. B. Naresh	Nepal
1987		
Apr	J. Chekenyere	Zimbabwe
Aug	S. Manyozo	Malawi
Dec	C. F. Barham	Jamaica
1988		
Apr	K. W. C. Koh	Singapore
Aug	M. A. Al-Deam Al Anaswah	Jordan
Dec	D. A. Cummings	Jamaica
1989		
Apr	M. M. Mukokomani	Botswana
Aug	A. P. Mutta	Tanzania
Dec	M. Essien	Ghana
1990		
Apr	{ M. M. Kgwanang	Botswana
	{ HRH The Sharifa	
	G. R. Nassar	Jordan
Aug	B. Luchman	Mauritius
Dec	W. M. Mbadi	Uganda

Editor-in-Chief's Note: The Overseas Cane was instituted for the best overseas Officer Cadet on the Standard Military Course (SMC) in 1973.

282

APPENDIX K:
SASH OF HONOUR WINNERS

1984	Aug	J. Hands	WRAC	1988	Apr	E. Roberts	WRAC
1985	Apr	N. G. H. Vickers	WRAC				(REME)
	Aug	G. A. Fesemayer	WRAC		Aug	L. C. Dickenson	WRAC
1986	Apr	S. M. Kingham	WRAC	1989	Apr	I. S. Stewart	WRAC
	Aug	T. E. Bowden	WRAC		Aug	J. A. Cave	WRAC
1987	Apr	M. F. Davison	WRAC	1990	Apr	H. J. D. Vickers	WRAC
			(RAEC)		Aug	R. L. Cane	WRAC
	Aug	M. Oliver	WRAC				

Editor-in-Chief's note: the Sash of Honour is awarded to the student officer or officer cadet of the Women's Standard Course considered by the Commandant to be the best of her course.

APPENDIX L:
SELECTED RMAS SENIOR STAFF
June 1947 and December 1990

June 1947

The Commandant: Major-General F. R. G. Matthews, DSO (late South Wales Borderers)

The Chief Instructor: Brigadier M. S. K. Maunsell, DSO, OBE, (late RA)

The Director of Studies: H. H. Hardy, Esq., CBE, MBE, MA

Commander, Old College: Lieutenant-Colonel R. E. Goodwin, DSO (late Suffolks)

Commander, New College: Lieutenant-Colonel D. A. K. W. Block, DSO, MC (late RA)

Commander, Victory College: Lieutenant-Colonel G. A. E. Peyton, OBE (late 15/19 KRH)

Head of Faculty of Science and Mathematics: Dr J. W. Stevenson, MC, Bsc, PhD

Head of Department of Science: G. F. Dixon, Esq, MA

Head of Department of Mathematics: G. R. Sisson, Esq, MA

Head of Faculty of Modern Subjects and Languages: *Professor K. C. Boswell, TD, BA

Head of Department of Modern Subjects: J. W. Taylor, Esq, MBE, MA

Head of Department of Modern Languages: W. Lough, Esq, MBE, MA

December 1990

The Commandant: Major-General P. W. Graham, CBE (Gordons)

The Assistant Commandant: Brigadier J. B. Emson, CBE (late LG)

Chief of Staff: Colonel B. R. Isbell (late RE)

The Director of Studies: Dr D. E. Lever, OBE, MSc, FBIS

The Deputy Director of Studies: B. T. Jones, Esq, RD, MA

Commander, Old College: Colonel S. R. Gilbert (late RE)

Commander, New College: Colonel S. R. Daniell (late QRIH)

Commander, Victory College: Colonel D. A. Beveridge, MBE (late Queen's)

Head of Department of Defence and International Affairs: Dr J. Sweetman, MA, FRHistS

Head of Department of War Studies: D. G. Chandler, Esq., MA, FRHistS, FRGS

Head of Department of Communications: Mrs Heather Duncan, BA

*K. C. Boswell was a Professor at RMA Woolwich (as were all Heads of Academic Departments) down to 1939; on appointment to the new RMA Sandhurst post-war, he was permitted to retain his honorary title. From 1959 the post was redesignated 'Reader in Military History and English', from which evolved the Department of Military History under Brigadier (retd.) Peter Young, DSO, MC in 1961, who retained the title of Reader up to his retirement from RMAS in 1969. J. W. Taylor was also an RMA Woolwich lecturer before 1939.

SELECT BIBLIOGRAPHY
British Army Officer Schools and the Staff College

BOND, BRIAN. *The Victorian Army and the Staff College*, London, 1972. An excellent modern account and analysis by a noted historian.

BUCHANAN-DUNLOP, LIEUTENANT-COLONEL H. D. *Records of the Royal Military Academy, 1741–1892*, 2nd edition. Woolwich, 1893. Despite its age, this is still a very valuable source of basic information.

GUGGISBERG, CAPTAIN F. G. *'The Shop': the Story of the Royal Military Academy*, London, 1900. A useful short history down to the turn of the century.

MAURICE-JONES, COLONEL K. W. *The Shop Story, 1900–1939*, Woolwich, 1955. An evocative account that completes the history down to RMAW's closure at the outset of the Second World War.

MOCKLER-FERRYMAN, LIEUTENANT COLONEL A. F. *Annals of Sandhurst: A Chronicle of the Royal Military College from its Foundation to the Present Day, With a Sketch of the History of the Staff College*, London, 1900. A good source of information on RMCS to the last century's close.

SALVENSEN, FRANCIS. *Journal of a Student at Arms*, Bristol, 1989. A slightly tongue-in-cheek account of life under training at RMAS in the recent past – but no less perceptive for that.

SHEPPERD, LIEUTENANT-COLONEL ALAN. *Sandhurst, the Royal Military Academy*, London, 1980. A good, well-illustrated, modern history by the former Senior Librarian.

SMYTH, BRIGADIER SIR JOHN. *Sandhurst: the History of the Royal Military Academy, Woolwich, the Royal Military College, Sandhurst, and the Royal Military Academy, Sandhurst, 1741–1961*, London, 1961. A comprehensive and worthy analysis of all three great institutions by a very distinguished soldier, and holder of the Victoria Cross.

THOMAS, HUGH. *The Story of Sandhurst*, London, 1961. A good history aimed at a broader readership than Sir John Smyth's book by a lecturer who went on to become a celebrated historian and defence commentator.

YARDLEY, MICHAEL. *Sandhurst – A Documentary*, London, 1987. A rather controversial good hard look at RMAS and its problems in the late 1980s by a gifted author who was earlier twice under training there. It is also a valuable photographic record of all aspects of life in the modern RMAS.

INDEX

LIST OF REGIMENTAL ABBREVIATIONS

15/19H	15th/19th Hussars	L	Lancers	RH	Royal Hussars
2GR	2nd Gurkha Rifles	LF	Lancashire Fusiliers	RHG	Royal Horse Guards
AAC	Army Air Corps	LI	Light Infantry	RHG/D	The Blues and Royals
ASH	Argyll and Sutherland Highlanders	Lin	Lincolnshire Regiment	RHR	Royal Highland Regiment
Bal	Baluchi Regiment (Indian Army)	MahLI	Maharatta Light Infantry	RInF	Royal Inniskilling Fusiliers
Bay	The Bays	Man	Manchester Regiment	RIF	Royal Irish Fusiliers
Ber I	Berar Infantry	Mid	Middlesex Regiment	RIR	Royal Irish Rangers
BL	Bengal Lancers	N&D	Nottinghamshire and Derbyshire	RMP	Royal Military Police
BW	Black Watch		Regiment	RMR	Royal Munster Rifles
CA	Canadian Army	NF	Northumberland Fusiliers	RNZAC	Royal New Zealand Army Corps
Cam	Cameron Highlanders	Nor R	Northamptonshire Regiment	RNZI	Royal New Zealand Infantry
CG	Coldstream Guards	Norf	Norfolk Regiment		Regiment
CH	Calgary Highlanders	NSR	North Staffordshire Regiment	Roy	The Royals
Ches	Cheshire Regiment	NZA	New Zealand Army	Roy NF	Royal Northumberland Fusiliers
CIH	Central Indian Horse	Ox&BLI	Oxfordshire and Buckinghamshire	RR	Rajput Rifles
Cold G	Coldstream Guards		Light Infantry	RRF	Royal Regiment of Fusiliers
CR	Connaught Rangers	OxLI	Oxfordshire Light Infantry	RRR	Regina Rifle Regiment
D&D	Devon and Dorsetshire Regiment	Para	Parachute Regiment	RSF	Royal Scots Fusiliers
DCLI	Duke of Cornwall's Light Infantry	PPCLI	Princess Patricia's Canadian Light	RSDG	Royal Scots Dragoon Guards
DCOI	Duke of Cambridge's Own Infantry		Infantry	RSig	Royal Corps of Signals
DCOL	Duke of Cambridge's Own Lancers	Punj C	Punjab Cavalry	RTR	Royal Tank Regiment
DERR	Duke of Edinburgh's Royal	Punj R	Punjab Rifles	RWF	Royal Welch Fusiliers
	Regiment	Q	Queen's Regiment	RWK	Royal West Kent Regiment
Devon	The Devonshire Regiment	QDG	Queen's Dragoon Guards	RWR	Royal Warwickshire Regiment
DD	Devonshire and Dorset Regiment	QOCH	Queen's Own Cameron Highlanders	SCLI	Scottish Canadian Light Infantry
DG	Dragoon Guards	QOH	Queen's Own Highlanders	SDG	Scots Dragoon Guards
DLI	Durham Light Infantry	QORWK	Queen's Own Royal West Kent	Sea	Seaforth Highlanders
DR	Dorsetshire Regiment		Regiment	SF	Sherwood Foresters
Ex	Essex Regiment	QRIH	Queen's Royal Irish Hussars	SG	Scots Guards
FF	Fife and Forfarshire Infantry	QVOGFF	Queen Victoria's Own Guides	SHOC	Seaforth Highlanders of Canada
FFR	Frontier Force Regiment		Frontier Force	SI	Sikh Infantry
GC	Guides Cavalry	RA	Royal Artillery	SIKR	Sikh Rifles
GH	Green Howards	Raj I	Rajput Infantry	Sing AF	Singapore Armed Forces
GJ	Green Jackets	Raj R	Rajput Rifles	SLI	Somerset Light Infantry
Glos	Gloucestershire Regiment	R Ang	Royal Anglian Regiment	SP	Sikh Pioneers
Gord	Gordon Highlanders	R&NI	Rhodesian and Nyasaland Infantry	St&GH	Stormont, Dundas and Glengarry
GR	Gurkha Rifles	R&NSC	Rhodesian and Nyasaland Staff		Highlanders
Grey	The Greys		Corps	Suf	Suffolk Regiment
Gren G	Grenadier Guards	RAOC	Royal Army Ordnance Corps	SWB	South Wales Borderers
H	Hussars	RAPC	Royal Army Pay Corps	War	Warwickshire Regiment
Hamp	Hampshire Regiment	RASC	Royal Army Service Corps	W&SFR	Worcestershire and Sherwood
HLI	Highland Light Infantry	RB	Rifle Brigade		Foresters Regiment
IA	Indian Army	RCT	Royal Corps of Transport	WG	Welsh Guards
IG	Irish Guards	RDF	Royal Dublin Fusiliers	WIR	West Indian Regiment
KOB	King's Own Borderers	RE	Royal Engineers	Wor	Worcestershire Regiment
KOSB	Kings Own Scottish Borderers	REME	Royal Electrical and Mechanical	WRAC	Women's Royal Army Corps
KOYLI	King's Own Yorkshire Light Infantry		Engineers	WY	West Yorkshire Regiment
KRRC	King's Royal Rifle Corps	RF	Royal Fusiliers	Y&L	York and Lancaster Regiment
KSLI	King's Shropshire Light Infantry	RGJ	Royal Green Jackets		

ILLUSTRATION ACKNOWLEDGMENTS

4th/7th Royal Dragoon Guards, 46
British Army of the Rhine, 36
David Cobb, 163
Frank Wootton, 198–9
Imperial War Museum, 124, 125, 126 base, 127
  base, 128, 129 top, 130, 133 top, 140 top,
  142 base, 148, 149, 151 base, 152, 153, 156,
  157, 161, 164, 165, 168, 172, 173, 178, 180,
  181, 182 top, 183, 184, 185, 186 base, 187,
  193, 196, 197, 200, 201, 202, 210, 212, 213,
  214, 215 base, 216, 217, 218 base, 219, 220,
  232, 233, 234, 235, 241, 242 base, 244, 246,
  249, 250, 251, 252
Michael Burnett, 230–1
National Army Museum, 33
National Portrait Gallery, London, 3
Parachute Regiment, 191
Philip J. Haythornthwaite Collection, 35, 38
  base, 40, 44, 45, 48, 50, 51, 52 left, 57, 58
  base, 59, 76, 78, 81, 84, 85, 88, 90, 92–3, 95,
  96, 97, 100, 101, 102, 106, 110 base, 112,
  113, 121, 122, 126 top, 127 base, 129 base,
  133 base, 136, 137, 138 base, 140 base
Queen's Own Hussars, 47, 70
Rijksmuseum, Amsterdam, 30
RMA Sandhurst, 14, 255, 258, 263
Royal Academy of Arts, 38 top
Royal Artillery Charitable Institution, 257
Royal Artillery Historical Trust, 69, 82, base,
  151 top
Royal Corps of Transport, 67 top, 171
South Staffordshire Regiment, 218 top, 247
Terence Cuneo, 171, 195, 242
US Army, 225, 226, 228